The War History Battalion, the I Regiment (Royal Fusiliers), 1914-1919

F. Clive Grimwade

Alpha Editions

This edition published in 2024

ISBN 9789364734356

Design and Setting By
Alpha Editions
www.alphaedis.com
Email - info@alphaedis.com

As per information held with us this book is in Public Domain.
This book is a reproduction of an important historical work.
Alpha Editions uses the best technology to reproduce historical work
in the same manner it was first published to preserve its original nature.
Any marks or number seen are left intentionally to preserve.

Contents

FOREWORD	- 1 -
CHAPTER I	- 2 -
CHAPTER II	- 9 -
CHAPTER III	- 21 -
CHAPTER IV	- 39 -
CHAPTER V	- 54 -
CHAPTER VI	- 67 -
CHAPTER VII	- 78 -
CHAPTER VIII	- 102 -
CHAPTER IX	- 117 -
CHAPTER X	- 123 -
CHAPTER XI	- 154 -
CHAPTER XII	- 188 -
CHAPTER XIII	- 204 -
CHAPTER XIV	- 217 -
CHAPTER XV	- 235 -
CHAPTER XVI	- 252 -
CHAPTER XVII	- 262 -
CHAPTER XVIII	- 278 -
CHAPTER XIX	- 295 -
CHAPTER XX	- 306 -
CHAPTER XXI	- 334 -
CHAPTER XXII	- 349 -
CHAPTER XXIII	- 365 -

CHAPTER XXIV	- 391 -
CHAPTER XXV	- 406 -
APPENDIX I	- 430 -
APPENDIX II	- 432 -
APPENDIX III	- 454 -

FOREWORD

It was considered by the past and present members of the 4th Battalion, The London Regiment (Royal Fusiliers), that some permanent record of the part taken by the Regiment in the European War should be compiled, and a War History Committee was formed in February 1920 to consider the preparation of such a record.

At the unanimous request of the Committee Captain F. Clive Grimwade undertook to write the Regiment's War History.

The Committee desire to express their keen appreciation of the manner in which he has overcome the difficulties of compiling such a History and of his devotion in carrying out this long and arduous work.

The Committee wish to express their thanks also to Lieut.-Col. Marchment, to Captains Boutall, Garratt, Croll and Hetley, and to other officers who have given Captain Grimwade valuable assistance; to the author's mother, Mrs Grimwade, for her assistance in arranging information as to officers' personal services and in correcting the drafts of the book; and to the Regiment's Honorary Colonel, Lord Marshall, for facilitating the publication of the book.

THE WAR HISTORY COMMITTEE,
4TH BATTALION, THE LONDON
Regiment (Royal Fusiliers).

LESLIE T. BURNETT, LIEUT.-COL. (*Chairman*).
G. H. M. VINE, MAJOR (*retired*).
H. J. DUNCAN-TEAPE, MAJOR.
S. J. ELLIOTT, MAJOR.

February 1922

CHAPTER I
MOBILISATION—DEPARTURE OVERSEAS

Of the London Volunteer Corps the unit now known as the 4th (City of London) Battalion, The London Regiment (Royal Fusiliers) is one of the most ancient. Called out as a Trained Band in 1643 to share in repelling a threatened Royalist invasion of the City during the Civil Wars, it has had a practically unbroken history for nearly three hundred years. After the regular constitution of the Volunteer Forces in the middle of last century it achieved some distinction as the 1st Tower Hamlets Rifle Brigade, and despatched a machine-gun detachment to the fighting in South Africa in 1900. In 1903 it became affiliated to The Royal Fusiliers, as the 4th Volunteer Battalion of that distinguished Regiment. On the reorganisation of the auxiliary forces in 1908 by Lord Haldane, it acquired its present designation, which we will abbreviate to the more convenient title by which it became known in the Great War, namely, The 4th London Regiment.

Prior to the War the training provided for the Territorial Force was only such as to furnish the nucleus of a Second Line Army. Fourteen days in camp each summer, an easy musketry course, and a few drills at headquarters could not develop a soldier fit to meet fully trained troops. That this was recognised by Lord Haldane is evidenced by the fact that his scheme provided for a period of six months' training at home for all Territorial soldiers should war break out, prior to their despatch on active service.

But they were none the less given a definite rôle in the defence of the Motherland. Possibly this was not always realised to the full by all the officers and non-commissioned officers of the Regiment; but it was unmistakably brought home to them one evening in February 1914 when a secret meeting of officers was convened at Headquarters in Hoxton for the explanation of the scheme of mobilisation and of the task which the Regiment would be called upon to execute should war occur.

At that date the scheme of Mobilisation was already complete. Under it the 1st London Infantry Brigade, of which the 4th London formed a part, was entrusted with the supremely important task of guarding the London and South Western Railway between London and Southampton during the mobilisation and embarkation of the Expeditionary Force from the latter port. The section allotted to the 4th Battalion was the main line from Waterloo Station to Farnborough (inclusive); the Alton branch from its junction with the main line near Brookwood to Bentley Station; and the branch from the last-named station to Borden Camp. These dispositions were worked out in the greatest detail, and arrangements were made for the efficient guarding of all railway stations, signal boxes, junctions, tunnels and bridges, and for a system of constant patrolling of the line.

The Infantry of the Territorial Force not being supplied during peace time with war scale of transport, ammunition, etc., provision was made for this necessary equipment to be drawn on mobilisation, and waggons and horses in civilian employ were "earmarked" beforehand for this purpose.

The scheme having been explained, arrangements were made to detail all guards, patrols, and requisitioning parties in readiness.

When the war cloud over South-eastern Europe began to spread in July 1914 and threatened to envelop this country in the storm, the finishing touches were put to the scheme at a memorable secret meeting at Headquarters on the evening of Thursday, 31st July 1914. After that meeting few who attended it had any doubt as to what was about to take place.

The annual camp in 1914 for the 1st London Division (Major-Gen. W. Fry, C.B., C.V.O.) had been arranged for Sunday, 2nd August, and on that date, this country still not having declared its intentions as to the war, the 4th London Regiment entrained for Wareham, in Dorsetshire, where the camp was to be held, with a strength of 23 officers and about 650 other ranks under Lieut.-Col. G. P. Botterill.

Camp was reached shortly after noon, but scarcely had the Battalion marched in when an order was received recalling it to London. By 2.30 p.m. it was once again entrained, quivering with excitement and well-nourished on the journey to town with the most impossible rumours of gigantic battles, most of which apocryphal happenings it swallowed with gusto. At 2 a.m. on the 3rd August the 4th Londons marched into Headquarters, and after a few hours' rest began to put the wheels of the carefully assembled machine of mobilisation into motion. All went without a hitch. Field dressings, identity discs and small books were issued: separation allowance and next-of-kin rolls prepared. The "earmarked" horses and vehicles were collected, and with the aid of these, ammunition drawn from the Hyde Park Magazine.

Blankets, lanterns and other stores sent up the River from Woolwich were unloaded and conveyed direct to the platform at Waterloo Station, ready for issue to the Battalion on its arrival there. The machine was moving steadily. During the day the Regimental Colours were handed over to the Lord Mayor of London for safe keeping.

Shortly after midnight the 4th London Regiment entrained at Waterloo in two trains, from which at each stop the allotted platoons detrained: so that by the time the end of the sector was reached in the early hours of the 4th August 1914, the railway was already guarded. Eighteen hours before the declaration of war the Battalion was on its war station: a good lead from Territorial troops to the rest of the country!

The distribution of the Battalion was as follows:

> Battalion Headquarters, Lieut.-Col. G. P. Botterill, Surbiton.
>
> A and B Companies (forming No. 1 Double Company), Headquarters at Clapham Junction, under Capt. H. J. Duncan-Teape.
>
> C and E Companies (forming No. 2 Double Company), Headquarters at Woking, under Capt. G. H. M. Vine.
>
> D and F Companies (forming No. 3 Double Company), Headquarters at North Camp, under Capt. R. J. Jackson.
>
> G and H Companies (forming No. 4 Double Company), Headquarters at Bentley, under Capt. E. H. Stillwell.

The Transport Section returned to Headquarters at Hoxton to complete the formation of the Battalion transport on a war footing.

Brigade Headquarters were at Waterloo Station under command of Brigadier-General the Earl of Lucan. The Brigade Major was Major R. F. Legge (Leinster Regiment); and the Staff Captain, Captain Cornelius-Wheeler (3rd London Regiment, Royal Fusiliers).

On the evening of the same day Lord Grey of Falloden (then Sir Edward Grey), in the House of Commons, made his never-to-be-forgotten indictment of the duplicity of Germany's action in the pre-war negotiations and in her violation of Belgian neutrality, and the formal declaration of war followed.

The order for General Mobilisation, which was applicable to the Territorial Force equally with the Regular Army, immediately ensued, and orders to report forthwith were issued to all members of the Battalion who had not paraded for the summer training two days previously. It is to the credit of the Battalion that within twelve hours no member had failed to reply. The N.C.O.'s and men thus reporting for duty were as quickly as possible despatched from peace headquarters and reported to their respective companies on the line.

As the N.C.O.'s and men of the Battalion reported for duty they were subjected to medical examination, and a certain number were unfortunately unable to pass fit at the high standard required during the early days of the war, so that the strength of the Battalion on the 6th August was 24 officers and 785 N.C.O.'s and men.

The early days of August on the railway line afforded unmistakable proof, if such were needed, of the extraordinary power of the London soldier to adapt himself to circumstances. Men from offices, factories and docks, suddenly taken from their occupations and their homes, settled down to patrols and guards, to cooking their food and taking responsibility, as to the manner born. All were swept forward on the high flood of a great enthusiasm, and buoyed up amid minor discomforts with intense pride that their country needed them and had given them a job of work to carry out. This enthusiasm certainly bid fair at times to show signs of excess of zeal. But the zeal was tempered with an immense sense of the dignity of each and every one as a soldier in the 4th Londons: the days on railway guard thus formed the basis of the *esprit de corps* which is essential to military success and which in pre-war days it had been difficult, by the nature of things, to develop. Scattered though the Battalion was over some 50 miles of railway, disciplinary trouble of a serious nature was conspicuous by its absence.

By the middle of August the greater part of the Expeditionary Force had been embarked to France, but the Brigade remained at its war station. During the dark days which ensued, when telegram after telegram told always of withdrawal before overwhelming forces of the German Army after the glorious resistance at Mons, the Battalion continued to guard the railway, and was busily occupied in recruiting to full strength and in completing its equipment. The strength of the Battalion rose steadily and rapidly, and by the end of August 941 N.C.O.'s and men were at duty on the railway line.

The duties on the railway were extremely heavy, and no training was possible except the rudimentary instructions of the recruits who were retained at peace headquarters.

On the night of 31st August / 1st September orders were issued to the Brigade to withdraw from the line and return to peace headquarters. The move was satisfactorily completed by 12 noon on the 1st September, the duties of the Brigade on the railway being taken over two days later by the 3rd London Infantry Brigade. On return to headquarters the Commanding Officer informed the Battalion that the whole Brigade would be despatched on overseas garrison duty almost immediately, and called for volunteers, a call which met with a favourable response from all ranks.

The two following days were actively occupied with medical inspections, recruiting to fill the few remaining vacancies, etc.

On the afternoon of the 3rd September the Battalion was paraded for inspection by Major-Gen. W. Fry, C.B., C.V.O., commanding 1st London Division, who, in an address to the troops, announced that the destination of the Brigade was Malta; and conveyed to the Battalion, to the great satisfaction of all ranks, the direct assurance of Earl Kitchener that the Battalion would be retained in Malta only until it should be passed fit to take the field. This announcement was received with enthusiasm as it served to allay the disquieting rumours of the possibility of the Malta station proving to be a "sidetrack" for the period of the war.

Shortly after midnight on the 3/4th September 1914, the Battalion (strength 29 officers and 976 other ranks, fully armed and equipped) paraded and marched to Waterloo amid scenes of enthusiasm and excitement in Hoxton which will probably never be forgotten by those who witnessed them, and entrained at 3.30 a.m. on the 4th September for Southampton, embarking on arrival in H.T. *Galician* (Union Castle Line).

The following officers proceeded overseas with the Battalion:

Lieut.-Col.	G. P. Botterill,	in command.		
Major	L. T. Burnett,	second in command.		
Capt.	G. B. Scott, Adjutant	(2nd Battalion The Leinster Regiment).		
Major	R. J. J. Jackson,	commanding	F	Company.
Capt.	G. H. M. Vine,	"	E	"
"	H. J. T. Duncan-Teape,	commanding	A	Company.
"	R. N. Arthur,	"	H	"
"	H. P. L. Cart de Lafontaine,	commanding	D	Company.
"	W. Moore,	commanding	B	Company.
"	W. G. Clark,	"	C	"

Lieut.	C. R. Saunders,	" G "
"	S. Elliott	(Machine Gun Officer).
"	V. W. Edwards.	
"	F. C. Grimwade	(Signalling Officer).
"	P. B. K. Stedman	(Transport Officer).
Lieut.	H. W. Weathersbee.	
2/Lieut.	A. L. Long.	
"	J. T. Sykes.	
"	R. L. Herring.	
"	R. V. Gery.	
"	E. W. Bottomley.	
"	T. I. Walker.	
"	A. B. Lucy.	
"	A. R. Moore.	
"	T. Moody.	
"	J. R. Pyper.	
"	E. Giles.	
Hon. Lieut. and Q.M.,	E. S. Tomsett	(Quartermaster).
Major	J. F. F. Parr, R.A.M.C.T.,	Medical Officer attached.

At 4 p.m. that afternoon anchor was weighed, and the transport convoy, conveying the first Brigade of Territorial troops to leave this country, dropped down Southampton water.

CHAPTER II
THE 1/4TH BATTALION IN MALTA--
FORMATION OF THE 2/4TH BATTALION

Under escort of H.M.S. *Amphitrite*, and accompanied by four other transports conveying the remainder of the 1st London Infantry Brigade, the *Galician*, carrying, in addition to the 1/4th Londons, two companies of the 1/3rd Londons and a section of the 1/1st London Field Ambulance, made a fair passage through the Bay and reached Gibraltar without mishap. Here the convoy broke up, and the transports proceeded independently to their destination.

Nine days of the comparative peace of ship's routine formed a pleasant interlude for the 1/4th Battalion after its recent trying duties on the railway line. The passage to Malta was too short to allow the monotony of ship's inspections, watches, and roll calls to pall, and the interest of the troops was constantly quickened by the incidents of a sea voyage—all so strange to Londoners whose horizon hitherto had for the most part hardly extended beyond Hampstead Heath or Chingford. Occasional fleeting glimpses of France and Spain, the gambols of a school of whales, the brilliant hues of the African shore, and the indescribable blue of the Mediterranean all contributed to render the Battalion happy and indifferent to the discomforts of their quarters 'tween decks, where the heat was certainly trying after the Gates of the Mediterranean had been passed.

The first glimpse of Malta on the morning of the 13th September was uninspiring. From the sea no vegetation can be seen owing to the system whereby the scanty soil is walled up along the hillsides to prevent it from being washed away; and the island presents to the passing voyager an aspect of monotonous drab rock. No time was allowed for despondency, however, for, with the pilot on board, the *Galician* steamed into the Marsamuscetto Harbour at Valetta where the Battalion could feast on the riot of colour which unrolled before its eyes.

Ghain Tuffieha Camp

Melleha Camp

Selmun Palace

The responsibilities of the 1st London Brigade for the defence of the Fortress of Malta began immediately, for the day after its arrival the infantry of the regular garrison left for the front.

In the early hours of the 14th September the 1/4th Londons disembarked, and being allotted quarters under canvas in Ghain Tuffieha Camp, was introduced to the ardours of a sub-tropical summer by undertaking the longest march it is possible to make in the island—a very trying experience indeed.

Ghain Tuffieha is a summer station on the west coast of the island about eleven miles from Valetta, and is an important outpost of the main defences of the Fortress. It lies in a broad, fertile valley known as the Wied Tal Paules, which traverses the island from east to west, its eastern limit being the coast at St Paul's Bay. To the north of this valley lie the Melleha and the Marfa Ridges, two of the northernmost barriers against invasion. The coast round these two ranges of hills possesses a considerable number of sandy landing-places in well-sheltered bays, which, as they face Sicily at about three hours' passage from that island, required special guarding at this period.

The Battalion now settled down seriously to its training, and it was found necessary to deal with some 250 men as recruits. These, however, were passed through the Barrack Square stage of their training as expeditiously as possible in view of the heavy duties which fell to the Battalion in guarding the northern coast.

The guards found from the main body of the Battalion at Ghain Tuffieha were mostly night guards at the landing-places, at St Paul's Bay on the east coast, and at Ghain Tuffieha Bay, Karraba Ridge, and Gneina Bay on the west coast. In addition to these, G and H companies were immediately despatched on detachment, the former to Selmun Palace (which commands the promontory between the shores of Melleha and St Paul's Bays), the latter to Melleha (which dominates the head of Melleha Bay and the Marfa Ridge beyond it). The latter detachment was subsequently moved down the ridge to the coast near the head of Melleha Bay. The guards found by these detached companies were at Cala Mistra Fort (at the foot of Kalkara Ravine), Ir Razzet tal Blata, L'Imgiebah, and Ghain Zeituna by the Selmun force; and at Melleha Bay, Torri L'Ahmar cross roads, and Marfa Palace by the Melleha force.

The duties of the detached companies were found to be particularly onerous, and the proportion of N.C.O.'s and men employed not only on guards, but also on such necessary duties as signals, look-outs, and water-carrying fatigues, continuously totalled rather more than a third of the total strength of the detachments. Arrangements were therefore made for the relief of the detachment companies every seven or eight days, and this procedure was maintained throughout the Battalion's duty on the island.

The training of the Battalion proceeded smoothly but under conditions of some difficulty, partly owing to the number of men constantly engaged in coastal defence duties, and partly owing to the unfavourable conditions of terrain. Every square yard of the rocky hillsides which is covered with soil is devoted to some sort of cultivation by the thrifty inhabitants, and the walling up of the soil on the hillsides, which has already been alluded to, converts every hill into a series of steps, over which manœuvres are both laborious and painful. In spite of these obstacles, however, a good deal of useful work was achieved, and the Battalion rapidly began to take shape as a useful and well-disciplined unit. There can be no doubt that the experience gained by all ranks in taking their share in ordinary garrison duties at so early a stage in their embodied career proved of infinite value later when the 1/4th Londons ultimately took their place in the fighting line; and, moreover, the knowledge that they were subject to the critical—and at that period not always sympathetic—surveillance of the regular staff of the Fortress provided the strongest possible incentive to all ranks to conduct themselves with credit to their Regiment and to the Territorial Force.

Early in October a very thorough course of musketry instruction under Fortress arrangements was begun, firing taking place on the Naval ranges of Ghain Tuffieha. The companies were thus employed as follows:—2 on detachment, 2 on musketry course, 3 on company training, and 1 finding all the duties at Battalion Headquarters, the whole being worked on a roster so that each company was kept for training and detachment purposes at its greatest possible strength.

During the early days of the Battalion in Malta a few changes of distribution took place among officers as follows:

Major R. J. J. Jackson was evacuated to Cottonera Hospital sick. He unfortunately remained in hospital until early in December 1914, when he was invalided to England. Command of F Company was taken by Lieut. F. C. Grimwade, and the Machine-Gun Section was taken over by 2/Lieut. T. I. Walker, Lieut. S. Elliott transferring to E Company. The Battalion was also joined by 2/Lieut. R. C. Kelly who, however, remained with the unit for a few weeks only, at the end of which time he was appointed to the Secret Service, and with this he remained until the end of the War.

The middle of September, when the Battalion landed in Malta, found the hot season waning, and although the temperature remained high for some weeks the full intensity of the sub-tropical summer was not experienced. In the early part of October, however, the scirocco, a warm south-westerly wind which originates in the Sahara, followed, with all its usual enervating effects, which were indeed quite as trying as the intense heat of the sun had been. Towards the end of the same month the wet season set in in earnest, and from that time until the early part of December the camping ground at Ghain Tuffieha was swept by tropical rains and sand storms of considerable violence, which from time to time caused a certain amount of material damage and not a little discomfort to the troops. The memory of suddenly having to turn out and clear blocked drainage trenches and lay on to straining tent ropes in the—sometimes—vain endeavour to prevent one's temporary home from vanishing into thin air, and to rescue one's kit from a mud bath, is now sufficiently remote to be contemplated without acute distress, but the feelings which these encounters which the elements evoked at the time were by no means so calm!

During the worst phase of the Malta climate the Battalion remained under canvas, and it is of some interest—though admittedly of little consolation—to remark that no battalion had previously spent the winter in Malta in other than permanent barracks.

Thanks to the untiring efforts of the Battalion Medical Officer, Major J. F. F. Parr, the bill of health during these marked variations of climate remained extraordinarily clean, and in spite of its exposed situation the Battalion suffered less from sickness than the others of the Brigade which were accommodated in modern barracks.

The month of December, however, saw the beginning of the most delightful season in the island's year. The temperature was mild but the evenings cool; vegetation began to spring up with almost startling rapidity, and the prospect of the island, seen from the tops of the hills, when looking down on to the terraced fields set in a sea of the deepest azure, formed a most welcome and delightful contrast to the sun-baked and drab view which had greeted the Battalion on its arrival three months earlier.

At the end of November the detachments were redistributed, the defence duties on the northern coast being dealt with by one company only, half at Selmun Palace, which formed its headquarters, the other half at Melleha Bay. A fresh detachment was formed by the despatch of another company to Verdala Barracks (in the Cottonera Lines, the Southern Fortress of Valetta), for the duty of guarding prisoners of war, notably the crew of the German raider *Emden* who had just been landed on the island.

But for these changes the routine of training proceeded with little variation, and it began to be thought by some that the Battalion would be condemned to continue its duties in Malta until the end of the War; but on the 22nd December 1914 a warning order was issued that the Brigade would leave the island at an early date.

On the 23rd the Battalion (less E and F Companies on detachment), marched to Valetta to be reviewed by His Excellency the Governor on the Marsa, a sports ground near the town. The review took place on the following day and the Battalion returned the same evening, arriving in camp at 6.30 p.m.

The following Fortress Order was published on the 24th December:

> The Commander-in-Chief, after having inspected the units of Lord Lucan's Brigade this morning, desires to place on record his great satisfaction at the evident progress made by them to become efficient soldiers of the King. His Excellency, who fully appreciates the patriotic sentiments which have caused such a magnificent body of men to respond to the call of the Empire in this hour of national danger, has had much pleasure in telegraphing to Lord Kitchener reporting the high state of efficiency and fitness which the Brigade has reached. Such a result, which must have been apparent to everyone who saw them on parade this morning, could only have been obtained by the whole-hearted devotion to their Country's cause of every officer, N.C.O., and man, and the Commander-in-Chief wishes to congratulate the Earl of Lucan and the whole of his Brigade on achieving such highly satisfactory results.

No further preparations for departure were made until after the Christmas festivities, which were rendered very enjoyable by the arrival of many good things from home and by special gifts from the Corporation of the City of London and the Regimental Association, the latter organisation providing a gift of a pipe and tobacco-box for every officer, N.C.O., and man. Christmastide over, however, the Battalion concentrated on its preparations for leaving the island at short notice.

On the 28th December the detachment at Selmun was withdrawn, its place being taken by a company of the Malta Militia; that at Verdala being relieved by the 1st London Regiment, which for the time being was to remain in the island.

On the departure of the 1/4th Battalion overseas the following officers had been detailed to remain at headquarters to supervise the formation of a Reserve Battalion:

- Captain E. H. Stillwell.
- Captain W. H. Hamilton.
- Lieutenant H. G. Stanham.
- Lieutenant H. Parkhouse.

These officers were assisted by a small number of N.C.O.'s and men of the 1/4th Battalion who had been found medically unfit to proceed overseas. The intention in raising the new battalion originally was to provide a unit to supply reinforcements to the overseas battalion, but, as will be seen, this intention was subsequently modified to a large degree.

Recruiting for the new battalion, which was at first designated the 4th (1st Reserve) Battalion The London Regiment, and later was known as the 2/4th London Regiment, proceeded (as indeed for all the formations then being raised) with unprecedented rapidity, and within a fortnight over 400 men had been enrolled, while the ranks continued to be swelled daily by the advent of fresh recruits.

Colonel Vickers Dunfee, V.D., was appointed with effect from 6th September 1914 to command the new battalion with Hon. Lieut. E. V. Wellby (late Lieut.-Col. 4th V.B. The Royal Fusiliers) as Captain and Adjutant.

The available accommodation proving utterly inadequate for the growing numbers, the 2/4th Battalion moved on 23rd September, after inspection by the Lord Mayor, Sir Vansittart Bowater, to quarters under canvas at Folly Farm, New Barnet. The strength was now 6 officers and 480 other ranks, and steadily increased from this time until the establishment in all ranks was filled. Training now began in earnest—so far as the wills of every officer, N.C.O., and man were concerned—but under the most acute practical difficulties, such as were general among the newly raised formations, owing to the lack of stores of all kinds, including clothing, arms, and equipment. Gradually, however, "wooden equivalents" gave place to rifles, and mufti made its final disappearance from the parade ground. During the following month the Battalion moved into winter quarters, occupying as barracks two vacant houses at Barnet, namely, "Littlegrove" and "Beech Hill," and also some stabling and out-buildings at "Oakhill."

The Battalion owes a considerable debt of gratitude to the owners of these houses and to other local residents, notably to W. H. Vernon, Esq., and Sir Philip Sassoon, for their generosity in providing accommodation and training facilities and for extending hospitality to the Battalion in various ways, generosity which was also extended to the 4/4th (Reserve) Battalion when it was formed in the following year. Facilities for musketry training were also provided by the Enfield Rifle Club, who very generously placed their range and the services as instructors of several of their members at the disposal of the Battalion.

Training at Barnet continued until 14th December 1914, when, after inspection by Lieut.-Gen. G. H. Moncrieff, Honorary Colonel of the Regiment, the Battalion, which had now grown to a strength of 27 officers and 986 other ranks, joined the Brigade in billets at Maidstone. Here the Brigade received on the 17th a warning order to proceed on foreign service at short notice. The necessary preparation of equipment, medical inspection, inoculation, etc., was at once put in hand, and the Battalion was inspected by Major-General W. Fry, C.B., C.V.O., commanding 1st London Division, who addressed the troops.

It was fortunately possible to grant forty-eight hours' leave to all ranks before departure, destined to be the last home leave for some nineteen months, and on 23rd December the Battalion entrained at 10 a.m. for Southampton, where it embarked on H.T. *Avon* (Royal Mail Steam Packet Company), the strength on embarkation being 27 officers and 889 other ranks.

The following officers proceeded overseas with the Battalion:

Colonel   Vickers Dunfee, V.D., in command.

Major	V. H. Seyd, second in command.
Captain	W. G. Hayward, Adjutant.
"	G. H. Moore.
"	H. Morris.
"	F. C. Read.
"	H. G. Stanham.
"	H. Parkhouse.
Lieut.	L. C. Coates.
"	W. N. Towse.
"	A. H. Simpson.
2/Lieut.	R. N. Keen.
"	W. A. Stark.
"	W. R. Botterill.
"	V. S. Bowater.
"	S. N. Davies.
"	R. C. Dickins.
"	W. H. Stevens.
"	N. L. Thomas.
"	J. R. Webster.
"	L. A. Dickins.

"   L. R. Chapman.

"   H. W. Dennis.

"   E. G. Lovell.

"   H. W. Vernon.

> Hon. Lieut. and Quartermaster, J. E. W. Lambley (Quartermaster); Lieut. Casey, R.A.M.C., Medical Officer attached.

Just before departure the following telegram was received by Colonel Dunfee from General Sir Ian Hamilton, G.C.B., D.S.O.:

> Had arranged to go down and see your Battalion. Unfortunately situation renders imperative my presence at Headquarters. Can only, therefore, wish you best of good luck and hope we may meet again.

At about 5 p.m. on the 23rd December H.T. *Avon* put to sea, and the following day at daybreak the convoy assembled, consisting of:—

> H.T. *Avon*—2/4th London Regiment and two Companies 2/3rd London Regiment.

> H.T. *Euralia*—2/2nd London Regiment and 2/3rd London Regiment, less two companies, under the escort of H.M.S. *Eclipse*, which accompanied the transports as far as Gibraltar.

Melleha

Grand Harbour, Valetta

Grand Harbour, Valetta

The following appointments were made on H.T. *Avon*: Colonel Vickers Dunfee to be O.C. Ship; Captain and Adjutant W. G. Hayward to be Ship's Adjutant.

Christmas was spent at sea with as much good cheer as circumstances permitted, and after an uneventful voyage Malta was reached and H.T. *Avon* dropped anchor in the Grand Harbour at Valetta on 31st December 1914.

On the 30th December the 1/4th Battalion marched from Ghain Tuffieha to St George's Barracks and handed over its arms and equipment, as it was understood that these would be required for the relieving troops.

The strength of the 1/4th Battalion on leaving the Island was 24 officers and about 850 other ranks. Major J. F. F. Parr remained on the Island and took over the duties of Medical Officer to the 2/4th Battalion, his duties in the 1/4th Battalion being assumed by Lieutenant Casey, who had just arrived with the 2/4th Battalion. In addition Captain R. N. Arthur and Lieut. V. W. Edwards transferred to the 2/4th Battalion together with about 85 N.C.O.'s and men who were found medically unfit for active service. These officers, N.C.O.'s, and men reported on the 3rd January to the 2/4th Battalion which was thus brought to about war strength.

On the 2nd January the 2/4th Battalion disembarked and marched to quarters at St Andrew's barracks, and the same day at 6.35 a.m. the 1/4th Battalion paraded for the last time at Ghain Tuffieha, marched to Valetta and embarked on the *Avon*. That afternoon the *Avon*, conveying in addition to the 1/4th Battalion the 1/3rd Londons, put to sea under sealed orders, which were subsequently found to be for Marseilles.

CHAPTER III
THE 1/4TH BATTALION IN FRANCE--
OPERATIONS AT NEUVE CHAPELLE

The Gulf of Lyons has an evil reputation and in January 1915 its achievement did not belie its notoriety. The *Avon* was a fine ship of some 12,000 tons but being in ballast rolled unmercifully for three days; and the smooth waters of Marseilles harbour, which were reached early on the morning of the 5th January, were never more heartily welcome than to the 1/4th Londons.

Disembarkation took place the following afternoon at about 4 p.m. and the Battalion, after forming up on the quay, marched straight to the railway siding, where a train stood in readiness to carry it into the war area. To British soldiers who have served in the French theatre of war there is, we imagine, no recollection more vivid than that conveyed by the words "40 Hommes—Chevaux en long!" The fourth class French railway carriage, which is employed with fine impartiality for the conveyance of men or horses as occasion demands, is now too well known to call for lengthy comment; it is a subject over which we prefer to pass hurriedly! Into these abominations on wheels the Battalion was inserted at the standard rate of 40 men to each truck and rations for two days were issued. After a delay, which seemed to the troops as interminable as it was certainly inexplicable to them, the train at about 9.30 p.m. rumbled sedately out of Marseilles in the leisurely manner of all troop trains.

Dawn next morning found the train at Avignon where a five minutes' halt was made. The enthusiastic reception accorded to the Battalion all along the line by the French civilians and also by the military was most impressive; and the obvious satisfaction with which the arrival of fresh British troops was hailed by one and all in the Rhone Valley could not fail to impress the dullest sense with the strength of the common cause which bound us to our gallant allies.

A "Halte Repas," that is a halt just not long enough to enable the troops to detrain and cook dinners, was made at Macon, after which the journey, which resolved itself practically into a triumphal progress, was resumed. At one wayside station, the name of which has, unfortunately, passed from our recollection, a military guard of honour saluted the arrival of the Battalion, while the ladies of the district appeared with offerings of milk, coffee, and bouquets. So great, in fact, was the enthusiasm that M. le Maire sent for a cask of wine in which to assert his faith in the Entente Cordiale! Unhappily the French railway authorities were not stirred by such intense emotion and the train moved on before the wine arrived.

By the morning of the 8th the train was skirting Paris, and that day the first signs of war were reached. Near Chantilly (the famous French racecourse) reserve lines of trenches forming the outer ring of the Paris Defences were passed, while at Creil some buildings severely damaged by shell fire stood as stern remembrances of the great retreat three months earlier.

This amusing though very tedious railway journey terminated at 9 p.m. on the 7th January, when the Battalion detrained some ten miles south of Boulogne at Etaples, at that date a small, muddy, and evil-smelling fishing village. Etaples, which at a later stage of the war became such an important base camp, with accommodation for some thirty thousand men and many hospitals, was, in January 1915, not used as a British military station, and the 1st London Brigade were the first troops to be quartered there. Accommodation was provided under canvas in an exposed situation, and the severity of the weather, which was intensely cold and windy with occasional falls of snow, formed a contrast to the sub-tropical climate in which the Battalion had been basking ten days previously, which can only evoke surprise at the comparatively small amount of sickness which ensued.

The Battalion had, it will be remembered, left its rifles, equipment, and transport in Malta, and the refitting and equipment of the troops was taken in hand at once. The first step was the reorganisation of the Battalion in four companies, as follows:

New A Company—Old A and C Companies;

Captain H. J. Duncan-Teape in command.

Captain W. G. Clark second in command.

New B Company—Old B and F Companies;

Captain W. Moore in command.

Captain F. C. Grimwade second in command.

New C Company—Old D and E Companies;

Captain G. H. M. Vine in command.

2/Lieut. W. H. Weathersbee second in command.

New D Company—Old G and H Companies;

Captain C. R. Saunders in command.

Captain H. P. L. Cart de Lafontaine second in command.

The Company Sergeant-Majors were respectively Edwards, Elsom, Chennels, and Cornwall.

In addition to this reorganisation the Battalion was issued with new rifles of the long charger-loading type, with four Vickers guns, and with new equipment of the 1914 pattern (webbing); and a refit of clothing and necessaries was effected. Steps were also taken to dispose of the surplus baggage and personal belongings acquired by all ranks in Malta, and to reduce all to the scales of weight permissible in the field.

Command of the Regimental Transport was assumed by 2/Lieut. R. L. Herring, who proceeded with his section to Abbeville, and returned by road with the full war scale of 1st and 2nd Line Transport and the Battalion chargers.

These preparations which occupied the Battalion until the 25th January were interspersed with such training as the state of the weather permitted, the training being carried out on the sand dunes north of Etaples. A warning order was received on the 25th to proceed to billets near St Omer to join G.H.Q. Reserve.

The following day the Battalion moved by train from Etaples to St Omer, and thence by march route to the billeting area which had been allotted to it in two small straggling villages called Helfaut and Bilques, where it arrived about midnight. At this point the Battalions of the 1st London Brigade parted company until once more reassembled by the formation of the 56th Division a year later.

Billeting in the early days of the war was not the simple matter which it became at a later stage. For one thing, in most villages neither wire beds, cook-houses, nor ablutions existed for the troops, and the accommodation of barns and stables had not been tabulated by Town-Majors ready for the use of billeting officers. All negotiations for billets had therefore to be conducted by the billeting officer direct with the communal authorities, through whom also straw and fuel were drawn.

After a few days in Helfaut and Bilques the Battalion was driven from its billets by an epidemic of measles which attacked the civilian inhabitants, and it found fresh quarters slightly nearer St Omer in a more important village called Blendecques.

The 1/4th Londons now embarked on a course of very severe training under the immediate supervision of the Inspector of Infantry, Brigadier-General Oxley. This was, indeed, a strenuous three weeks, with breakfasts at 7.30 a.m. and dinners at 5 p.m., the hours between being occupied in tactical exercises. Usually a march of five miles in each direction to and from the training ground was involved and the exercise itself was almost invariably the "Attack in Open Warfare." In every conceivable formation, over every conceivable sort of ground, did the Battalion attack every one of the villages within reach of Blendecques, till at last it was entirely weary of the attack in any shape or form! But the grounding in field work thus obtained was excellent and so completely were the lessons rubbed into the mind of every member of the Battalion that this wearisome training bore excellent fruit as we shall see later.

Once or twice a slight variation of training was obtained in work on a new reserve line of trenches then being constructed east of St Omer. This work was carried out under R.E. supervision. The design of these trenches was strange. Their like was indeed never met with in any sector of the line held by the Battalion in the whole of its war service, and we can only be thankful that this reserve line never came into active use.

Throughout the training period the weather was continuously wet and cold, and these adverse conditions, added to the long hours without food, imposed a serious physical strain on all, and the news that the Battalion had been passed fit to join a brigade was therefore received by all ranks with extreme satisfaction.

At Blendecques the Battalion was joined by Lieut. A. Hurd, R.A.M.C., medical officer, vice Captain Casey to hospital. 2/Lieut. E. W. Bottomley was also evacuated to hospital.

On the 19th February the 1/4th Londons left the many good friends they had made in Blendecques and marched through Wittes, where it halted for the night, to Ham-en-Artois, arriving at 12.30 p.m. on the 20th, and joined the Ferozepore Brigade of the Lahore Division.

The Indian Corps (Lieut.-Gen. Sir James Willcocks, G.C.M.G., K.C.B., K.C.S.I., D.S.O.) had arrived in France in the preceding October and comprised the 3rd (Lahore) and 7th (Meerut) Divisions, the former including the following units:

LAHORE DIVISION

Major General H. D'U. KEARY, C.B., D.S.O.

DIVISIONAL CAVALRY

15th Lancers.

ENGINEERS

20th and 21st Sappers and Miners.

34th Sikh Pioneers.

JULLUNDUR BRIGADE—Brig.-Gen. E. P. Strickland, C.M.G., D.S.O.

1st Manchesters.

1/4th Suffolks.

40th Pathans.

47th Sikhs.

59th Scinde Rifles (F.F.).

SIRHIND BRIGADE—Brig.-Gen. W. R. Walker, V.C.

1st Highland Light Infantry.

4th King's Liverpools.

15th Ludhiana Sikhs.

1/1st Gurkha Rifles.

1/4th Gurkha Rifles.

FEROZEPORE BRIGADE—Brig.-Gen. R. G. Egerton, C.B.

1st Connaught Rangers.

1/4th Londons.

9th Bhopals.

57th Wilde's Rifles (F.F.).

129th Baluchis (Duke of Connaught's Own).

During the months of December and January the Indian Corps had been heavily engaged in a local operation which had raged with terrific intensity between the small village of Givenchy and the extreme right of our line; but our struggles to press forward along the canal to La Bassée had been checked by a particularly vigorous defence on the part of the enemy. The casualties suffered by the Brigades of the Indian Corps in the fighting had been so severe that it was necessary to withdraw some of them for a time from the line for the purpose of rest and reorganisation.

On joining its Brigade the strength of the 1/4th Londons was 25 officers and 828 other ranks. The Battalion was fortunate in being posted to the Division at this juncture as it had an opportunity before going into action of becoming acquainted with its neighbouring battalions with whom it was destined to share the fortunes of war during the ensuing eleven months, and of gaining some insight into the ancient, but at that date recently revived, sciences of bombing and trench mortar work. And here let us remark for the benefit of those members of the Battalion who joined the Service at a later stage and found Mills Bombs and the Stokes Mortar ready for their use, that in February 1915 the only bombs in use were those of the "jam-tin" variety, that is to say, were roughly constructed out of old tins by the troops who were to use them, filled with explosives, plugged with clay, and fused with ordinary time fuse which had to be ignited before the bomb was thrown; while the trench mortar of the day is perhaps best described as a glorified rainwater pipe bound with copper wire, and which threw a "jam-tin" bomb and was quite as dangerous to the team which manned it as to the Germans.

With their unfailing adaptability to circumstances the men of the Battalion rapidly became friends with the Indian troops whom they held in the greatest admiration. The Gurkhas in particular seemed to exercise an irresistible attraction for the men of London, who were especially impressed with the Gurkhas' playful way of throwing their murderous Kukri knives. Indeed, to such lengths did this admiration—which took the form of imitation—lead them that a Battalion order was very quickly necessary to the effect that "the game known as 'Gurkhas' played with unsheathed bayonets must cease forthwith!"

Throughout this period the weather was intensely cold and several falls of snow occurred. The billets were passably good, however, and the Battalion's bill of health remained clean.

The Battalion was unfortunate at this period in losing Sergeant-Major Dudley, who had done excellent work since mobilisation and now left for a commission in the Royal Fusiliers. He was killed a fortnight after joining his regiment. His duties were taken by Col.-Sergt. Instr. M. Harris, who filled this important position with success for nearly three years.

On the 22nd February the undermentioned officers, being the first reinforcement received by the Battalion, joined as follows:

    Lieuts. F. A. Coffin, H. M. Lorden, D. J. Leonard, and A. D. Coates.

It is now necessary for a moment to look at the course which events were taking on the wide field of the Western Theatre.

At the period with which we are dealing, the Front held by the British troops extended from the Béthune-La Bassée Road, on the right to just north of the Ypres Salient on the left, and General Headquarters (Field-Marshal Sir John French in command) were at St Omer. The British troops were divided into two Armies, of which the First Army under Sir Douglas Haig, consisting of the I Corps (Gough), IV Corps (Rawlinson), and Indian Corps (Willcocks), held the right or southern end of the line; the left being entrusted to the Second Army (Sir H. Smith-Dorrien), which comprised the II Corps (Fergusson), the III Corps (Pulteney), and the V Corps (Plumer).

The moving warfare of the autumn of 1914, which had ended by the opposing armies gradually extending their flanks until the sea was reached and had culminated in the First Battle of Ypres in October—November 1914, had given way to a siege warfare in which the belligerents were confined in continuous lines of trenches which were gradually being more heavily fortified. After the force of the German drive toward Ypres had exhausted itself, a lull in active operations ensued, hostilities flaring up here and there along the line in the shape of minor operations of terrible intensity, in which the possession of a few yards of ground was contested with ferocity by both sides. In the intervals between these small struggles, however, the battle line had been comparatively quiet during the winter months, and not materially changed, the nett result being perhaps a slight gain of ground to the British at the southern end of the line, which was balanced by a tendency to lose ground in the north.

Since the bitter struggle at Ypres in November 1914, the enemy had, in the opinion of Sir John French, shown certain signs of weakening on the Western Front, and this was attributed by him to the success which was attending the Russian offensive in East Prussia, and to the consequent withdrawal of German troops from the West. In order to assist our Russian Allies as far as possible it was necessary to have resort to active operations with the main object of holding as many of the German reserves as possible in the West, and efforts to this end were already being made by the French at Arras and in Champagne.

The ravages caused during the winter trench warfare by sickness and "trench-foot," which had had especially disastrous effects on those regular divisions composed of troops withdrawn from tropical garrisons, rendered necessary the early cultivation of a vigorous offensive spirit, and these combined considerations led Sir John French to the decision to take the offensive as soon as the condition of the ground in Flanders should afford such an undertaking a reasonable prospect of success. By the beginning of March the conditions were considered sufficiently favourable, and the terrain selected for the proposed offensive was the German positions opposed to the First Army and defending the lower slopes of the Aubers Ridge.

The objective of the First Army's attack was the advancement of our line to the high ground about Illies and Hermies as a prelude to the occupation of La Bassée, and this involved as a first local objective the capture of the village of Neuve Chapelle. The Aubers Ridge is a strongly marked hill feature, which runs in a south-westerly direction from Lille until it loses itself in the marshlands in the neighbourhood of La Bassée. Neuve

Chapelle, which had already changed hands several times in the fighting of the previous autumn, is a small village, the immediate surroundings of which are much intersected with orchards and fences, about 1000 yards from the lowest slopes of the Ridge, which, immediately opposite to it, are covered by a considerable wood called the Bois du Biez.

The German defensive position skirted in front (or to the north-west) of Neuve Chapelle and then making a sharp turn southwards, followed the line of the Estaires-La Bassée Road, for some 600 yards, from its junction with Foresters Lane (Rue des Berceaux) to its junction with the Rue du Bois, where once more turning slightly to the west it left the hamlet of Richebourg L'Avoué in the British lines, and finally made a wide sweep once more to the south in the direction of Festubert (see Map No. 1). The front of attack allotted to the Indian Corps was that part which followed the alignment of the La Bassée road between Rue du Bois and Foresters Lane, the actual capture of the greater part of Neuve Chapelle being entrusted to the 8th Division.

The attack was to be preceded by a heavy artillery bombardment, which on the Corps front would be conducted by the divisional artillery of both the Lahore and Meerut Divisions and the Corps heavy artillery, and this was to be directed towards destroying the enemy's front trenches and entanglements and certain strong posts, the searching of the Bois du Biez, in order to disperse the concentration of the enemy's counter-attack troops, and finally the building up of a "curtain of fire" (subsequently though less descriptively termed a "barrage") east of the captured positions, with the object of assisting the work of consolidating them.

The direction of the Indian Corps' attack being almost easterly converged towards that of the IV Corps on their left (this being south-easterly), and it was, therefore, necessary after the first German positions had been carried and touch with the IV Corps secured, to swing the direction of attack round more to the south, and to establish a fire position facing south in order to guard against the danger of a German flanking counter-attack from that quarter. The position selected for this was a German sap, which had been thrown out from the enemy lines towards the British strong point, Port Arthur, at the corner of La Bassée Road and Rue du Bois.

The troops holding the line of the Rue du Bois front, outside the limit of the general attack, would thus be responsible for the defence of the Indian right flank. It was hoped that the first bound would carry our line forward to the old II Corps line first occupied by Smith-Dorrien's troops in October 1914, east of Neuve Chapelle village.

The assaulting troops detailed for this task were the Gharwal and Dehra Dun Brigades of the Meerut Division, the Bareilly Brigade being in close support; while the Lahore Division (less artillery) was placed in Corps reserve, the Ferozepore Brigade being allotted to Army Reserve.

In accordance with these orders the Ferozepore Brigade moved forward from Ham-en-Artois to the Zelobes area on the 7th March, the 4th Londons marching to Calonne-sur-Lys about eight miles north-west of Neuve Chapelle, where it remained in billets in a constant state of readiness to move. On the eve of the outbreak of our offensive the order was relaxed to one of readiness to move at twelve hours' notice.

On the 10th March Lieut.-Col. Botterill was granted seven days' leave of absence on urgent private affairs, and command of the Battalion devolved temporarily on Major L. T. Burnett, who remained in command until after the termination of the Neuve Chapelle operations.

In addition to the Brigades of the Meerut Division already mentioned, on the right of the line, the troops detailed for the assault comprised the 25th Brigade of the 8th Division opposite Neuve Chapelle village, with the 23rd Brigade of the same Division on the extreme left.

An enormous concentration of artillery had been quietly effected on this front, including many of our newly arrived heavy batteries, and at 7.30 a.m. on the 10th March, some 300 guns opened a devastating bombardment on the German trenches along the frontage of attack. The severity of this bombardment was unprecedented. Trenches were obliterated, machine-guns and Germans were literally blown into the air, and so dazed were the enemy by the appalling ordeal that our men were able to stand on their parapets to watch the inferno in front of them. At 8.5 a.m. the range of the guns was lengthened on to the enemy's support trenches and our assaulting columns dashed forward. The Indians and the 25th Brigade met with little resistance, but the 23rd Brigade on the left found itself faced with a practically unbroken wire entanglement, from beyond which a deadly fire was poured into it by the enemy machine-guns. By 8.35 a.m. the right and centre brigades had effected a lodgment in the village, but the 23rd, being still held up and suffering terrible losses, the 25th Brigade swung to its left and turned the flank of the German troops who were opposing the 23rd. By this means our left was able to advance and by 11 a.m. the village of Neuve Chapelle was completely in our hands, and consolidation of the ground won was begun under cover of our artillery barrage, which effectually carried out its task of preventing the enemy bringing forward reinforcements for a counter-attack.

The street fighting, however, had resulted in considerable disorganisation of units, so that valuable hours were lost in the necessary reorganisation, and it was not until 3.30 p.m. that the advance could be resumed. The attack so far had proved—as was intended—a complete surprise, and the enemy's resistance seems to have been paralysed except on the extreme left where our troops were still under heavy fire.

The only local counter-attack which developed during the morning of the 10th was on the extreme right of the attack, where the enemy succeeded along the Rue du Bois in temporarily ejecting the Indian troops from the captured trenches, and in effecting a strong lodgment in the Orchard Trench in front of Richebourg L'Avoué. During the morning the Jullundur and Sirhind Brigades moved forward to Richebourg St Vaast and Vieille Chapelle respectively.

The afternoon advance was made on the right by the Dehra Dun Brigade, supported by the Jullundur Brigade of the Lahore Division, and the objective assigned to it was the Bois du Biez. Between Neuve Chapelle and the wood runs the little Rivière des Layes, and at a point where this stream is spanned by a road bridge the enemy had established a strong machine-gun post. The Indians made a gallant advance over 1000 yards of open country, and succeeded in penetrating the wood, but their line was enfiladed by the machine-guns on the bridge and they were unable to hold the line of their furthest advance. On the left the attack was renewed by the 25th and 24th Brigades, the hard-hit 23rd being held back, their objective being the cluster of houses at Moulin de Pietre, about a mile east of Neuve Chapelle; but their efforts also were frustrated by the machine-guns on the bridge, which our artillery was unable to dislodge. Further left still the front of attack had been extended and the 21st Brigade (Watts) of the 7th Division was also directed on Pietre; but in its advance encountered a line of undamaged German trenches which effectually barred its efforts to progress.

The position, therefore, when darkness intervened was that an average advance of over a thousand yards had been gained and held, while practically no effort had been made by the enemy to regain possession of the lost ground.

Preparations were made for a renewal of the advance on the following day, but the 11th dawned misty and the day proved to be one of equilibrium. A further advance was, attempted but the mist rendered aircraft observation impossible and artillery co-operation with the infantry extremely difficult owing to the constant breaking of our forward lines of communication by the enemy shell fire. Our troops, therefore, clung to their positions opposite the Bois du Biez and Pietre under a murderous shell fire which caused many casualties; while the enemy, by a stroke of ill fortune, was accorded a for him lucky respite, in which he was able to prepare his counter-attack.

On the evening of the 11th the exhaustion of the troops after two days' fighting rendered a relief desirable, as it was hoped that weather conditions would favour a prosecution of the offensive on the next day. The Meerut Division consequently handed over its newly won positions to the Lahore Division, the Dehra Dun Brigade being replaced by the Sirhind Brigade, while arrangements were completed for relieving the Gharwal Brigade on the night of the 12th/13th by the Ferozepore Brigade.

The same evening the 4th London moved at 6 p.m. from Calonne to Lestrem where it arrived at midnight and went into billets. Its stay there, however, was short as within two hours it was turned out in order to move further forward to Lacouture, about four miles west of Neuve Chapelle, reaching there about 7.30 a.m. on the 12th March. Similar forward moves were made by the remainder of the Brigade in view of its impending occupation of the line.

When the 4th Londons reached Lacouture the village was under shell fire from the enemy's heavy guns and the behaviour of all ranks under fire for the first time was highly commendable. But here also the hopes of rest on which the thoughts of all had been centred far more than on the German shells, were dashed, for almost immediately on arrival the Battalion received fresh orders to move forward to Richebourg St Vaast, in which village Brigade headquarters were then operating. The exhaustion of all ranks on arrival was considerable as the Battalion had been almost continuously on the move in full marching order for about eighteen hours. Richebourg was a village of some importance and a considerable number of our heavy batteries supporting the Neuve Chapelle attack were stationed in its vicinity, with the result that it received a generous share of the enemy's counter-battery bombardment and also a good deal of attention due, apparently, to the prominence of its church tower, to the existence of which the Germans objected.

Here at last the Battalion was allotted billets in which it remained until about 7 p.m., being under heavy shell fire the whole time and sustaining its first battle casualties of seven men wounded.

The mist continued during the 12th and our main operation could not be pursued. The hostile shell fire increased in intensity, but the Germans were equally with ourselves embarrassed by the difficulties of accurate observation and their bombardments were not very disastrous to us. Local advances were attempted by our troops in various parts of the line and the houses at Pietre were actually reached by the Guards of the 20th Brigade, but the ground gained was heavily swept by hostile fire and could not be retained. All day counter-attacks in mass formation were attempted by the Germans, and costly as the day was to us, our casualties must have been far exceeded by theirs, their ranks being literally mown down by our rifle, machine-gun and shrapnel fire. By dusk the enemy's attempts had exhausted themselves and for the first time in the war the Germans gave up attempts to recapture ground they had lost.

As it had been hoped that the 12th would witness the continuance of our successes it had been impossible to arrange beforehand the details of the relief of the Gharwal Brigade by the Ferozepore Brigade until the result of the intended operations should be known, and it was not, therefore, until late in the afternoon that the Brigade received orders to move forward at once in order to take part in an attack that evening on the Bois du Biez, which position it was proposed to carry at all costs. For this operation the 41st Dogras of the Bareilly Brigade, then in the trenches, were to be lent to the Brigade and relieved in their position in line by the 4th Londons. This relief, however, could not be effected in time to enable the 41st Dogras to join the Ferozepore Brigade, which consequently advanced short of one battalion.

The Brigade was not assembled in front of Neuve Chapelle until darkness had fallen, and in order to allow time for the necessary dispositions to be made, General Egerton, who for this operation commanded not only the Ferozepore, but also the Jullundur and Sirhind Brigades, arranged for the attack to commence at 10.30 p.m. At 9.30 p.m., however, orders were received cancelling the attack and indicating that the offensive had closed, and the Brigade returned to billets in Vieille Chapelle and Lacouture.

Meanwhile the 4th Londons proceeded with the relief of the 41st Dogras, and although they occupied the line only for a few hours, perhaps we may be pardoned for a rather more detailed record of the night's work than the importance of the operation warrants in view of the fact that this was the first tour of duty done by the Battalion in trenches. The sector to be occupied lay at an interval of about 300 yards from the right limit of the Neuve Chapelle attack as already described, and consisted of a frontage of some 400 yards, in front of the Rue du Bois. The line in this part did not consist of a continuous line of trenches. In the first place, the ground here, as for miles in each direction, was too waterlogged to admit of a trench being dug, and the defences, therefore, consisted of a breastwork built up above ground level, and in most parts of this sector the breastwork did not exceed three feet in height and was entirely without parados. As a result, moreover, of the recent fighting the defensive line consisted rather of a series of short breastworks with gaps between them which could only be crossed under cover of darkness. Communication trenches to the rear were non-existent and the breastwork had to be approached from the Rue du Bois, to which it ran parallel at a distance of about fifty yards, "overland." It may be of interest to those who served in this area with the regiment in the winter of 1916/17 to state that this feeble breastwork was almost in the position of the support line subsequently known as Guards' Trench.

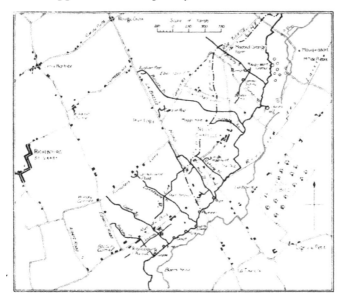

NEUVE CHAPELLE—RICHEBOURG L'AVOUÉ

This position perhaps was not an ideal one for the first introduction of a raw Battalion to trench warfare, and the situation was not improved by the exhaustion of the men or the fact that the Rue du Bois was subject to a great deal of heavy shelling which had not died down since the German counter-attacks of the day, but which continued through the night. The Battalion moved forward by platoons past Windy Corner, where it came under a heavy burst of shrapnel, and Edward Road, skirting behind the ruined factory at the corner of the Rue du Bois, and led by Indian guides, whose vague acquaintance with the language of London did not assist matters to any appreciable extent. Be it remembered also that no maps had been issued and no reconnaissance of the line had been possible to any company officer. However, the Battalion succeeded in occupying its breastwork and remained there during the night, somewhat isolated as touch with the units on its flanks was difficult to maintain owing to the breaks in the line, and all ranks acquitted themselves in an exemplary manner. The shrapnel and machine-gun fire maintained by the Germans during the night cost a few casualties, amounting to 14 N.C.O.'s and men wounded. In addition to these was 2/Lieut. A. R. Moore, who was hit in the leg on the way up to the line. This officer, however, stuck to his duty and remained with his platoon until after relief of the Battalion the next morning. He was awarded the Military Cross for his gallant conduct.

The Ferozepore Brigade attack not having materialised, the 41st Dogras returned to the trenches, and before daybreak the 4th Londons were relieved and withdrew to billets in Vieille Chapelle.

With these incidents ended the battle of Neuve Chapelle in which, although the gain of ground was much less than had been hoped for, yet some solid success had been achieved. Our line had been carried forward for about 1000 yards on a front of about two miles, and the prisoners captured amounted to 1650 all ranks. The British casualties had reached the serious total of 12,811, but the enemy's far exceeded this number. The outstanding result of the action, however, was an immense accession of moral strength to the British troops, for it had been clearly established that where we could meet the Germans on terms of equality in men and material, we were able to beat them, and the confirmation of this, supplied by the battle of Neuve Chapelle, sent a thrill of triumph in the hearts of our men all along the line.

On the night 13/14 March, the Ferozepore Brigade relieved the Bareilly Brigade on the Rue du Bois, the front line being occupied by the 57th Rifles, 129th Baluchis and 1st Connaught Rangers, the 4th Londons moving to Richebourg St Vaast in Brigade reserve.

The sector now taken over extended from Chocolat Menier Corner on the right to Port Arthur on the left, and during the tour proved to be fairly quiet, except in the left subsection held by the Connaughts, where two strong points, Port Arthur and the Orchard Redoubt, and also the Crescent Trench, a circular trench connecting them, were daily subjected to heavy bombardments.

The 4th Londons in reserve provided garrisons for the forward area as follows:

- D Company (Cart de Lafontaine) to the Orchard Redoubt, which it held in company with a party of the Connaughts.
- One Platoon of each of A, B and C Companies to the left subsection, under instruction in trench warfare by the Connaughts.
- Two Platoons each of B and C Companies (Moore and Vine) to Redoubts D5 and D6 respectively. These redoubts were close to Windy Corner on Forresters Lane, and were subsequently known as Dogs and Edward Posts.
- Machine-Gun Detachment to Port Arthur Keep, and Trench Mortar Section to the left subsection.

The platoons under instruction were relieved every forty-eight hours in order to ensure that during the tour of duty the companies were all given a certain amount of trench experience. The remaining platoons, not for the moment employed in garrison duty, were billeted with Battalion Headquarters in Richebourg, and provided working and carrying parties each night for the line.

The line was still not fully organised after the battle, and the Crescent Trench was not properly connected either to the Orchard on its right or to Port Arthur on the farther side of the La Bassée Road on its left; and as the construction of communication trenches in this area had not yet been seriously undertaken, the various companies holding those works were isolated during the hours of daylight, as were also the detached listening posts pushed forward in front of them into No Man's Land. There was thus a very considerable amount of trench work required to bring the defences to a proper state of organisation and also in the completion of the wire entanglements in front of the new advanced line, and the 4th Londons were called upon for heavy duties in this direction in conjunction with the Sappers and Miners.

The tower of Richebourg church still proved a great attraction to the enemy's heavy guns, and the village was daily subjected to severe shell fire during daytime. On 21st March it became evident that the Germans were determined to destroy the church tower, and a steady bombardment with heavy shells began, which caused infinite damage to the church itself and the surrounding houses. During this bombardment a direct hit was obtained on a billet occupied by a platoon of Highland Light Infantry, causing casualties of 12 killed and 30 wounded. Later three direct hits were registered on the church tower, which fell about noon, and this achievement was followed by a complete cessation of hostile fire, which indicated sufficiently clearly what the intention of the bombardment had been.

All ranks of the Battalion were now settling down to their duties in the trenches, showing great keenness to increase their value as fighting troops and exhibiting the greatest steadiness under the numerous heavy bombardments to which they had been exposed, and it was, therefore, gratifying to receive a word of appreciation as to their behaviour from the Divisional Commander during a visit which he paid to Battalion Headquarters on the 17th.

The Battalion was now again under command of Lieut.-Col. G. P. Botterill, and Major L. T. Burnett resumed his duties as second in command.

On the 17th also a further reinforcement of officers was received as follows:

Major E. H. Stillwell and 2/Lieuts. E. P. M. Mosely and F. F. Hunt.

The Machine-Gun and Trench Mortar Sections were now carrying out their full duties in the front trenches, and did exceedingly good work during this tour, which, for the latter section, was their first experience of working their mortars in action. During the bombardment of the 19th, 2/Lieut. J. T. Sykes, in charge of the trench mortars, was wounded by shrapnel while "spotting" for a mortar shoot, and evacuated to hospital.

On the night of the 23/24 March the relief of the Ferozepore Brigade by the 2nd Brigade began, and the forward garrisons of the 4th London being withdrawn, the Battalion on the following evening marched back to billets at Paradis, a small village near Merville. The Connaughts were relieved in the line on the following night, and the Brigade being concentrated in the Paradis area came into Army Reserve at two hours' notice to move.

The total casualties sustained by the Battalion during this tour of trench duty were 17, a very small number having regard to the severity of the bombardments to which it had been subjected.

From the 26th March until the 2nd April, Lieut.-Col. Botterill was in temporary command of the Brigade during the absence on leave of the Brigadier; and command of the Battalion for this period was assumed by Major G. H. M. Vine.

The rest billets at Paradis were retained until the 30th March, the six days being occupied in company training and route marches, and viewing of arms by the Brigade Armourer-Sergeant. On the 28th a parade service was held by Captain Cart de Lafontaine, this being the first Church Service which the Battalion had had the opportunity of attending since the middle of February.

The Battalion was now firm friends with its Indian comrades whose soldierly qualities it was learning to appreciate from actual experience. Difficulties of language formed a barrier to close intercourse, but a sort of war-cry was evolved which, being exchanged between Indian and Cockney, formed a guarantee of friendship. A shout of "Anglais-bon! Indian-bon! Allemand-NO BON!!" exchanged in passing became a frequent form of greeting.

On the night of the 31st March the Brigade returned to the trenches, relieving the Sirhind Brigade in a sector north of Neuve Chapelle village, the right boundary of which was Sign Post Lane, a road running through the lines in the direction of the Bois du Biez.

The 4th London was again in Brigade Reserve, and moved from Paradis at 7 a.m. to Les Huit Maisons, where it remained in temporary billets until dusk when it advanced to Croix Barbée, Battalion Headquarters occupying a house at the corner of Loretto and Edward Roads. This house will be in the recollection of those who served in this area in 1917 as the site of St Vaast R.E. dump. Here the Battalion was again under instruction in trench duties with the Connaughts, who were in the right subsection of the new Brigade sector, but on this occasion companies went into the line in turn as a whole, the companies not actually in trenches occupying reserve posts at Loretto, Green Barn, and St Vaast.

The right subsection was defended by breastworks and was immediately facing Pietre, the hamlet which had stood between our troops and success on the afternoon of the 10th March. It included the peculiar feature of the Duck's Bill, in regard to which a word of description may not be out of place. The name Duck's Bill brings to the minds of most 4th London men the picture of a large defended mine crater quite close to the German line, and approached by a defended sap which was generally full of water. Such it was in the winter of 1916/17, but in the spring of 1915 the Duck's Bill was a ruined farmhouse standing on a knoll just in front of the cross-road connecting Sign Post Lane with Sunken Road. This ruin was surrounded by a horseshoe trench, the points of the horseshoe resting on the cross-road, which was barricaded and connected with the front line by a rough breastwork. The defences here were still in an unfinished condition as the farmhouse was the extreme point of our advance in this sector in the battle, and the road barricades were under the continual watch of German snipers in Pietre. On the night of our entry into this sector the farmhouse had just been demolished by German incendiary shells and the ruins were still smouldering.

"A Bosche had been buried," writes Captain Moore, "in the hastily constructed parapet, face downward, and with his booted feet sticking into our trench. They were Bosche boots, so presumably were on Bosche feet, and every time one passed in the dark one knocked them—a truly gruesome spot."

The Duck's Bill farmhouse was finally disposed of when the mine crater was blown in 1916.

The reserve posts to which the companies in reserve were detailed were defended keeps forming with others the Croix Barbée line of defence. The aftermath of the battle, which had taken the form of such vigorous shelling by the enemy, now exhausted itself and this tour proved particularly quiet. The enemy's attention was paid principally to the roads and communications in rear of our trenches, but his shelling was sporadic and harmless.

On the 11th April the Battalion moved out of Croix Barbée, marching at 5 p.m. for Paradis, where it was joined the following day by the remaining units of the Brigade, now in Divisional reserve.

Of the rest in Paradis little need be said. The twelve days were spent in training under company arrangements and in bathing, completing issues of deficiencies in clothing, etc. On the 16th and 17th April, however, practice attacks on trenches were carried out as a brigade exercise, and although no definite information was, at the time, conveyed to the units as regards the purpose of the practice, the exercise was in preparation for the rôle which the Brigade would be called upon to play during its next tour in the line. It was, therefore, with the greater satisfaction that the 4th Londons carried out the exercises in leading the assaulting columns beside the Connaught Rangers.

The novitiate of the Battalion was now over, and it was accepted as being in every way able to do its full duty as a unit of the Ferozepore Brigade, and the knowledge that it had "found itself" was in itself the best possible incentive to all ranks to uphold worthily the honour of their regiment. The weather was of the most perfect spring type, and the ground and dykes were once more in their normal condition for the time of year. Speculation was rife, therefore, as to the task which was destined to be set the Brigade on its return to the line.

A warning order was received that the Brigade would relieve the Dehra Dun Brigade on Saturday, the 26th April, in a sector in front of Neuve Chapelle village, extending from the La Bassée Road on the right to Sign Post Lane on the left. The 4th Londons were to take over the left centre subsection, the other front line battalions being the Connaughts, the 9th Bhopals and the 57th Rifles, with the 129th Baluchis in Brigade reserve. But this relief was destined not to take place.

During the day disquieting rumours went round—started as inexplicably as such rumours always are—that things were not well in the north near Ypres: rumours of heavy fighting, of defeat, and of dastardly crimes on the part of the enemy. That the incredible brutality of the Germans was indeed an accomplished fact all the world now knows, and we must now review the tremendous happenings in the Ypres salient which caused the outbreak of a storm destined to rage with ever-increasing fury for the next three weeks.

CHAPTER IV
THE 1/4TH BATTALION IN THE SECOND BATTLE OF YPRES, 1915

Since the exhaustion of the enemy's drive towards Ypres in November 1914, the Ypres area had not been the scene of any important operations, although from time to time fierce struggles had raged here and there for the possession of points of minor tactical importance. Early in April 1915 the British lines had been extended slightly northward, and a sector had been taken over from the French troops on the left. On the 22nd of that month the line from Steenstraate (near the Yser Canal) as far as the Poelcapelle Road east of Langemarck was held by a Moroccan Division of the French Army. Thence the line took a south-easterly turn towards the Passchendaele-Becelaere Road and was occupied by the Canadian Division. On the right of the Canadians, British divisions held the trenches which ran east of Zonnebeeke in the direction of Hooge.

On the afternoon of the 22nd the French lines were subjected to a heavy bombardment, following which at about 5 p.m. our aeroplanes reported that they had seen thick clouds of yellow smoke issuing from the German trenches between Langemarck and Bixschoote. These arose, as is now well known, from poison gas, of which the effect was so terrible as to render the troops exposed to it practically incapable of action. The smoke and fumes at first hid everything from sight, and hundreds of men were immediately incapacitated. Within an hour the whole position had to be abandoned with the loss of fifty guns. This horrible and unlooked-for attack was so overpowering in its moral effect that our gallant allies were unable to combat it, and being totally unprovided with means of defence against so diabolical a contrivance, were forced—as indeed any troops would probably have been under the like conditions—to abandon their position without offering resistance. The confusion and moral effect were doubtless increased by the fact that the trenches thus attacked were occupied by Africans whose firm belief in the supernatural rendered it so much the more difficult for them to withstand this assault.

The immediate result of this gas attack was that the left flank of the Canadian Division was in the air and was in imminent danger of being entirely cut off. But the Canadians stuck to their positions with magnificent tenacity and during the night repulsed numerous German attacks. In the disorganisation following the gas attack the Germans had succeeded in establishing themselves on the west side of the Yser Canal at Lizerne, thus threatening to drive a wedge between the Canadians on the right and the French and Belgian troops on the left.

By 10 o'clock the next morning the position, though by no means re-established, was slightly easier, touch being definitely ensured between the Canadians' left and the French right, about 800 yards east of the Canal; but in order to effect this junction so great an extension of the British lines had been necessary that no reserves were available for counter-attack. The enemy's artillery fire was severe all day and the situation was rendered exceptionally difficult by the loss of so many allied guns in the gas attack.

It was arranged between Sir John French and General Foch, who was in command of the French Army on our left, that the latter should make immediate arrangements for the recapture of the original French Line, and for this purpose it was necessary for the British to maintain their present position without further retirement; but it was clear that the British troops could not be allowed to remain in the precarious position held by them during the last twenty-four hours unless the French attack were delivered within a reasonable time. In the meantime such reinforcements as were immediately available from neighbouring Corps were being rushed up into Ypres to strengthen the temporary line between ourselves and the French.

On the 24th a heavy German attack breached our lines at St Julien. This might have initiated an extremely critical situation but for a powerful counter-attack organised and launched by Brig.-Gen. Hull (afterwards G.O.C. 56th Division), who, with his own Brigade and parts of battalions belonging to six different divisions all new to the ground, was successful in stemming the tide of the enemy's advance, although attempts to recapture St Julien were repulsed.

Early in the morning of the 25th the left flank of the Canadian division was driven back after two days' magnificent fighting, and by the evening the allied line north of Ypres ran practically east and west from the neighbourhood of Boesinghe on the Canal to the south outskirts of St Julien. The general tendency of this line was to bow inwards towards Ypres. The seriousness of the threat to the whole British position east of Ypres is obvious. It was now possible for the enemy to shell any point in our lines from both sides of the salient, while his positions being about two miles farther to the south than they had been prior to the gas attack of the 22nd, he was able to keep the arterial road from Ypres to Zonnebeeke under continuous and heavy shell fire from guns of all calibres.

During the whole time considerable confusion was created by the alteration of areas caused by the sudden relinquishment of the forward positions; and by the fact that fresh troops on arrival in the Ypres area had at once to be absorbed into the firing line to prevent the enemy from exploiting his initial success. This confusion was heightened by our lack of artillery, which was inadequate to keep down the heavy German fire, and our casualties were in consequence continuously heavy. Ypres was itself kept under very heavy shell fire which vastly increased the difficulty of maintaining supplies of munitions and food.

The Lahore Division was ordered on the 23rd April to move to the Ypres area, and on the morning of the 24th orders were received by the 1/4th Londons that the contemplated relief of the Dehra Dun Brigade on the La Bassée Road would not take place and that the Battalion would be ready to move—possibly by train—at 1.30 p.m. By 2 p.m. the Battalion had joined in the Ferozepore Brigade column followed by the first line transport. In ignorance of its destination, and quite unaware of the bitter struggle then going on at Ypres, the Battalion expected to entrain at Merville, and a great many packs were filled with eatables and comforts for a long train journey.

However, when Merville, Indian Corps railhead, was passed it became evident that whatever journey was before the column would be made on foot. The march was an exceedingly trying one and was made under "forced" conditions. The roads were in a bad state after the winter rains, and a good deal of opening out in the column was inevitable, so that the five-minute halts which took place each hour were mostly spent in "closing up." Hour after hour the column moved on under the burden of full marching order, now over uneven pavé, now in deep ruts and thick mud. Merville, Vieux, Berquin, Strazeele, were passed in succession. Daylight gave place to dusk and dusk to darkness but still the column struggled forward. From all battalions stragglers now began to line the sides of the road, unable after the physically weakening experience of trench life to keep up the pace. At last about 10.30 p.m. a long halt was made just outside Godewaersvelde, a small village at the foot of the Mont des Cats. Here a rest of some forty minutes was obtained on the roadside while double lines of guns, ammunition columns, and transport blocked the road.

Finally at about 10.45 p.m. the Battalion moved forward into Godewaersvelde, but the village was packed with troops, and the companies, therefore, had to content themselves with such shelter as could be found beneath the parked lorries in the streets.

But the end of the march was not yet. After a hasty breakfast the Battalion was again on parade before 6 o'clock on the morning of the 25th, and once more joining the Brigade Column struggled up the steep hill at Boescheppe, at the top of which another delay was caused by a cross-current of vehicular traffic. The distress of the troops was now so evident that orders were received to lighten packs, and garments of all sorts, principally gifts of knitted garments sent out from ladies in England, were left by the roadside.

Through Westoutre and Reninghelst the column marched on to Ouderdom, where it arrived at about 2.30 p.m. with orders to billet in huts. Most of the huts were already fully occupied and the greater part of the 1/4th Londons were compelled to bivouac in the fields adjoining. Ouderdom is about seven miles south-west of Ypres, and the object of the forced march was at last clear. Some little idea of the storm raging in the salient could be gathered from the bivouacs, as throughout the afternoon and night the air vibrated with the continuous thunder of artillery in which the rapid and sharp rafales of the French "seventy-fives" away to the north were plainly distinguishable.

Shortly after midnight orders were received that the Division would be pushed into the firing line that day, the 26th April, and at dawn the Battalion was once more formed up. Shovels and picks were issued alternately to all the troops for the purpose of digging themselves into such positions as they might be able to gain, and to each platoon was issued a yellow flag for signalling its location to the artillery. In these early days of the War no arrangements were made for the formation of a "battle surplus," and consequently the whole available strength of officers and men prepared to move forward. Packs were now stacked to relieve the troops of superfluous weight, and at 4.30 a.m. the companies began to move off at five minutes' intervals.

The exhaustion of the men made progress inevitably slow. The roads traversed were fortunately not receiving much attention from the enemy's artillery, though a steady bombardment of Ypres with shells of the heaviest calibre was proceeding. By about 9.30 a.m. the Battalion was concentrated in a field adjoining Outskirt Farm at La Brique, where it proceeded to dig itself into assembly trenches (see map No. 3).

Meanwhile the Jullundur Brigade had concentrated farther to the east, between St Jean and Wieltje, while the Sirhind Brigade in Divisional Reserve had moved round the south of Ypres to a position north-west of Potizje.

The 1/4th Londons' position[1] during the hours of waiting in the morning was behind the crest of the spur which runs westward from St Jean, past La Brique towards the Canal, and though out of view from the German trenches was undoubtedly located by the enemy's Taubes, whose reconnaissances over our lines were entirely unmolested. This, combined with the close proximity of the Battalion's position to several British and French batteries, brought it a fair share of German shrapnel during the morning, the shelling being from both the north and south sides of the salient. Happily but few casualties were sustained.

[1] It has been thought convenient in the account of this action to designate buildings and other topographical features by the names by which they afterwards became generally known, though they were not in every case so named in April 1915.

Below the hillside on which the Battalion lay concealed and distant something more than half a mile the gaunt ruins of Ypres stood out clearly in the morning sunlight, the fast-crumbling tower of its wonderful Cloth Hall still erect, a silent witness of the tragedy which was being enacted. All the morning shells were falling into the town, a steady and merciless bombardment without the least cessation or abatement. From the centre of the town dense columns of black smoke rose continuously, and the crash of explosions and the clatter of falling débris followed each other without respite. The cross-roads at which the St Jean road left the town were in particular a target for the German heavy guns. All the morning the 50th (Northumberland) Division T.F. was moving from Ypres along this road to St Julien, and as each platoon passed the fatal cross-road at the double a heavy shell fell close by thinning the ranks. It seemed to every spectator of this horrible yet fascinating sight that the German artillery fire must surely be directed from some point within the British lines.

At 12.40 p.m. the Brigade received orders to prepare to take part in a divisional attack in conjunction with the French in a due northerly direction, with the object of relieving the pressure on the left of St Julien and of endeavouring to push the enemy back. With this attack the 50th Division would co-operate on the right of the Lahore Division in an attempt to recapture St Julien itself.

The Ferozepore Brigade's frontage was on the right of Boundary Road (the Ypres-Langemarck Road) and extended as far as English Farm, beyond which the Jullundur Brigade was responsible as far as Wieltje Farm on the extreme right, and the general line of assembly was on the forward slope of the spur some 600 yards north of La Brique.

The Brigade's advance was led by the Connaught Rangers on the left, the 57th Rifles in the centre, with the 129th Baluchis on the right. The 1/4th Londons were to follow the Connaughts, while the 9th Bhopals remained in reserve in La Brique.

At 2 o'clock the attack was launched under a heavy bombardment from all available British and French batteries, but such was the shortage of ammunition that this support died down for lack of supplies in about five minutes, after which the German batteries were free to search intensively the whole area of the Brigade advance, causing a good many casualties in the assaulting columns.

From the line of assembly the ground subsided gently to a shallow depression running across the direction of advance, beyond which, at a distance of some 1000 yards from the crest on the La Brique side, the hill swelled to a second skyline which impeded further view. Just below the crest of the further spur an unfenced lane, Buffs Road, followed the contour running eastwards from Boundary Road. None of this land was intersected by trenches, the Allied trenches being several miles ahead and to the rear of the German positions.

The 1/4th Londons moved from their position of waiting at about 2.30 p.m., and shaking out into four lines of platoons in file with B Company (Moore) on the left, and A (Duncan-Teape) on the right of the front line, followed by D (Saunders) and C (Clark). The German shrapnel was now searching both slopes of the spur pretty severely and men began to drop, but the Battalion steadily breasted the rise from which it could overlook the shallow valley towards Buffs Road. The sight which met their eyes defies description. The valley was covered with a ragged crowd of agonised and nerve-racked men, both Moroccans and Indians, who, having thrown down their arms and everything which could impede them, were streaming back from the front trenches suffering the tortures of poison gas. It was a revolting sight. The attack had clearly failed and our leading troops were broken and in retirement. But the men of the 1/4th Londons were splendid. Without wavering for a single instant they trudged steadily forward, though indeed almost completely exhausted, maintaining the intervals and distances between platoons with the precision of the parade ground. Never was there a more striking example of the results of training and discipline. The "attack in open warfare" which had been so roundly cursed by one and all in the days of training at Blendecques had indeed so sunk into the minds of everyone that instinctively the troops remembering only their orders to "follow the Connaughts at all costs" carried out under the most trying ordeal the lessons which had been drilled into them.

The Battalion continued to advance as far as Buffs Road, where a halt, believed at first to be temporary, was called. No trench line existed here but the ditch on the near side of the road had been widened. This was already filled with the remains of the 2nd K.O.S.B. (who had been fighting continuously since the action at Hill 60 on the 17th April, and were now reduced to under 100 all ranks) and by the reserve company of the Connaughts. The majority of the Battalion were, therefore, unable to obtain shelter in the ditch, and the digging of a fresh line some fifteen yards in rear was at once put in hand.

Early in the advance Moore (B Coy.) was hit in the foot and his company was taken over by Grimwade. Considering the severity of the enemy's shrapnel fire the advance was made with surprisingly few casualties, and although owing to the massing of the whole Battalion on one line of narrow frontage some intermingling of platoons on halting was inevitable, this was rapidly set to rights with little difficulty. The enemy's bombardment soon died away considerably, though for a while he maintained a steady machine-gun fire sweeping the crest of the ridge ahead of Buffs Road.

The troops leading the attack had moved forward steadily at zero hour and had pushed over the crest line in front of Buffs Road descending the further slope towards Turco Farm. The front German trench north of the Farm was reached and occupied, but before the position was properly established dense yellow clouds of poison gas issued from the enemy lines and, being gently wafted by the breeze, bore down on our defenceless troops. Under the horror of this ordeal the greater part of the line broke and a general retirement ensued which affected most severely the French and Indian Battalions, as already described. About 100 of the Connaughts and the Manchesters (Sirhind Brigade), however, managed to cling gallantly to their ground under Major Deacon, though they were shortly afterwards ejected by a strong enemy counter-attack which followed the gas cloud. They eventually succeeded in consolidating a line in the immediate vicinity of Turco Farm.

Shortly after the 1/4th Londons were established on Buffs Road Lieut.-Col. Botterill became a casualty, and Major L. T. Burnett assumed command of the Battalion. It was decided by Major Burnett that the overcrowding of the Buffs Road alignment was so great and wasteful of fire power, quite half the Battalion being unable to get into position to use their rifles, that a redisposition of his forces was desirable, and accordingly C and D companies withdrew to a position in support some 300 yards in rear of Buffs Road, where they dug themselves in.

During this time the Regimental Aid Post under Lieut. Hurd, R.A.M.C., was established at Irish Farm and the Battalion stretcher-bearers under Corpl. Fulford worked with great coolness in evacuating the wounded under heavy fire.

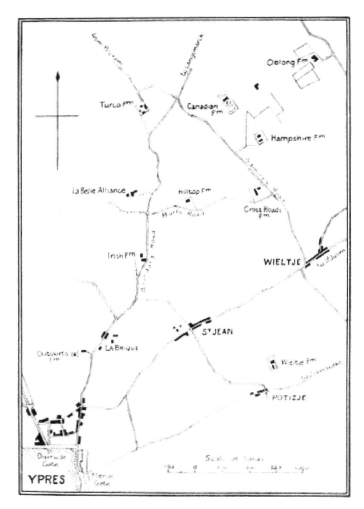

THE SECOND BATTLE OF YPRES, 1915

At about 4.30 p.m. orders were received that the reserve company of the Connaughts was to push forward and reinforce their two leading companies, supported by the 1/4th Londons. But, after consultation with Major Burnett, Major Hamilton of the Connaughts decided that the severity of the enemy's fire was so great that there was no reasonable probability of achieving a result commensurate with the inevitable loss of life, and the orders for the projected advance were cancelled. An attempt to reinforce the advanced troops was, however, actually made at about 7.30 p.m. by the 15th Sikhs and the 1/4th Gurkhas of the Sirhind Brigade, supported by the

9th Bhopals. This advance was carried out in good order, the Indians passing through the 1/4th Londons and disappearing over the ridge in front under a veritable hail of fire; but although touch was obtained with the leading companies of the Connaughts, the position of the German trenches could not be ascertained in the gathering darkness, and Lieut.-Col. Hills, who was in charge of the operation, decided to dig in on the position gained.

In conjunction with Bhopals' attempt an attack was also delivered by the Turcos of the French Brigade Moroccaine, who passed over the 1/4th Londons' trench in the gathering dusk. They were met in the crest line by a frightful machine-gun fire under which they advanced steadily, suffering heavy losses. A young French officer in charge of these Africans filled all who saw him with the deepest admiration of his coolness. Smoking a cigarette and lightly swinging a small rattan cane, he stood up on the sky line with his loose blue cloak thrown negligently over his shoulders, directing the advance of his men with all the indifference to danger of which his wonderful nation is capable. None of these gallant fellows were seen again.

During the whole of the 26th very good work was done by 2/Lieut. A. D. Coates, who was employed as *liaison* officer between Brigade Headquarters and the advanced troops. This gallant young officer succeeded several times in passing through the enemy's barrage and was the means of providing Headquarters with valuable information as to the course of events at Turco Farm.

Meanwhile the 1/4th Londons remained in readiness for action on Buffs Road, which was shelled heavily at intervals, especially at about 6 p.m., when the German shrapnel caused a great many casualties. The enemy's fire, however, died down after the evening advance by the Indians had been checked. The night was particularly quiet, and Sergt.-Major Harris at La Brique was able to get rations up to the Battalion and issue them.

The 27th April broke grey and cold and the morning was misty. During the early hours the enemy's artillery was remarkably inactive and the work of strengthening the Battalion's position was proceeded with without molestation by the Germans. The signs of battle were few indeed and it seemed almost impossible to realise the critical position of the British troops. The sense of detachment from the serious events of the preceding afternoon was enhanced by the unbroken state of the countryside in the immediate neighbourhood and the presence of several cows, which by some marvellous chance had escaped the enemy's shells and continued to graze lazily in the field in rear of the Battalion's position, as they had done during the battle on the previous afternoon.

The lull, however, was only the calm which proverbially precedes the storm, for about noon the enemy's guns opened with intense violence on the British positions and the 1/4th Londons received their full share of these hostile attentions. Fortunately, however, its position behind the crest secured it from heavy loss.

During this bombardment Major Burnett was ordered to report to Brigade Headquarters, where he received orders for an attack to take place in half an hour's time. When he got back to the Battalion under ten minutes were left in which to explain the orders to his company commanders and to make all preparations. The Battalion was to execute a further advance in a north-easterly direction on to Oblong Farm, which was given as the objective. In order to reach the assembly position, it was necessary for the Battalion to move about 200 yards to the right flank in order to come up on the right of the Sirhind Brigade, who, in the early hours of the morning, had relieved the most advanced troops of the Ferozepore Brigade.

The hurried nature of the attack precluded any possibility of reconnaissance of the ground by the officers and allowed no time for the explanation of the work on hand to the rank and file. The position of the German trenches was unknown and the difficulties and obstacles which might be met with during the advance were entirely undisclosed.

The movement of the Battalion toward its position of assembly for this unpromising enterprise was carried out steadily although with considerable loss. The British and Canadian artillery, which were co-operating in giving support to the attack, were again lamentably short of ammunition, so that an intense bombardment of some five minutes left them unable to render further assistance. Thus as the Battalion in moving to its flank came near the crest of the spur behind which it had hitherto been concealed from direct observation by the enemy, it became a very clear target for the hostile artillery, and the German guns being no longer harassed by our artillery, were able to pour a devastating fire upon the companies.

The actual "jumping-off" position was the ditch on the south side of Buffs Road which, at this point, was bordered by a hedge. The Battalion advanced in two lines of two companies in open order, each company formed in three waves, and the leading companies were C (Clark) on the left and D (Saunders) on the right, followed respectively by B (Grimwade) and A (Duncan-Teape). In order to ensure that the waves in each company should move forward together, it was necessary to collect the whole of each wave in the ditch before it moved; and this could only be effected by "feeding" the men along the ditch in single file, from the western end of the Battalion's frontage, the hedge in rear being impenetrable. The result of this slow progress was that the remainder of the Battalion waiting its turn to go into the ditch was compelled to wait on the hill, under a high explosive and shrapnel fire which was both intense and accurate. The result needs no description, but under this very trying ordeal the Battalion was perfectly steady, each platoon grouped together and waiting its order to move with the greatest nonchalance.

Before following the actual advance of the 1/4th Londons it will be convenient to explain the object and scope of the operation of which it formed part.

During the morning arrangements had been made for the Lahore Division to co-operate in an attack which was projected by the French Brigade Moroccaine. The general direction of the French attack was to be along the Ypres-Langemarck Road, as on the previous day, and the Lahore Division was to take all possible advantage of the French advance to gain ground, but without committing itself to the attack before the French troops had secured its left flank. The Lahore Division's attack was to conform to the French movement but on the east side of the Langemarck Road; the Sirhind Brigade occupying the left of the Divisional front next the French with the Ferozepore Brigade on its right.

The objective of the latter was, as already stated, Oblong Farm, a moated farmstead some 1700 yards from starting-point, the attack being led by the 1/4th Londons on the left and the 9th Bhopals on the right. The Connaughts followed in support at a distance of 400 yards, while the 57th Rifles and the 129th Baluchis, both of which regiments had been seriously weakened in the action of the 26th, were in reserve.

At 12.30 p.m. the leading waves of the two assaulting battalions moved forward under a continued heavy shell and machine-gun fire. The ground over which the advance was to be made was for the first 700 yards an unenclosed plateau which afforded the enemy good observation of our movements, and then sloping gently downwards to a somewhat more enclosed depression rose beyond it once more towards the objective. The objective itself was not visible from starting-point, and it appears probable that in consequence of the very hurried preparations for the attack, its position was not fully appreciated by all concerned and thus it was not recognised. However this may be, it is certain that the general direction of the attack after crossing Admirals Road became diverted too much towards the north and thus some encroachment was made on the frontage for which the Sirhind Brigade was responsible. This was probably accentuated by the fact that the position selected as starting-point lay at an acute angle to the direction of advance, so that a change of direction was necessary during the advance itself—always an operation of great difficulty.

As far as Admirals Road cover was non-existent. On topping the crest of the hill the Battalion came under an exceedingly severe rifle and machine-gun fire, and losses were consequently heavy. The succeeding waves, however, pushed on steadily as far as the near edge of the depression described above, in the vicinity of Hampshire Farm, when it became clearly impossible to get down the forward slope of the valley under the raking fire of the enemy, without incurring frightful losses. Half the leading companies were already hit, as were also Saunders, fatally wounded, Grimwade, Stedman, Leonard, and Coates. It was, therefore, decided by Major Burnett to hold the line gained and there to reorganise the Battalion pending the arrival of reinforcements, when it might be possible to carry the line forward.

A small part of C Company under Clark and of B Company under Giles, however, were successful in gaining the bottom of the valley, but finding himself isolated and further advance impossible without support, Clark, who assumed command of the composite party, took up a position to the right of Canadian Farm, where the men dug themselves in with their entrenching tools and hung on gallantly under a murderous fire. Splendid service was rendered by two N.C.O.'s of this party, Sergeant A. C. Ehren and Lance-Corporal C. Badham, both of B Company, who passed through the barrage three times unscathed with messages between Captain Clark and Battalion Headquarters.

Excellent work was also done by the Machine-Gun Section under 2/Lieuts. Walker and Pyper, who skilfully brought their guns into action on the left of Hampshire Farm and assisted in no small measure to keep down the hostile rifle fire from the enemy trenches on the further side of the valley. Their position, however, was shortly afterwards discovered, evidently by a Taube, which continued its reconnaissance over our lines without let or hindrance, and the section came under heavy shell fire and was forced to fall back on the main position, with Walker dangerously wounded, Sergt. Phillips killed, and several other casualties.

At about 2.30 p.m. the enemy's artillery fire abated considerably, but by that time the advance of the whole Division had been definitely checked on an alignment generally corresponding with that occupied by the 1/4th Londons, and reports were received that the French also had failed to gain their objectives.

Later in the evening the French attempted to renew their offensive, but once more were met with clouds of poison gas which definitely broke up their attack, and a report having been received from Col. Savy, the French Commander, that his losses were so heavy as to preclude all further attempts, orders were received that the Brigade would consolidate its position.

During the evening before dusk the Ferozepore Brigade was again subjected to violent shelling, which inflicted considerable loss on all battalions. During this later bombardment Lieut. Coffin was buried by a high explosive shell.

After darkness fell the 1/4th Londons were withdrawn from their advanced line to Brigade Reserve in rear of Cross Roads Farm where they set about digging fresh trenches. The Connaughts and the Bhopals withdrew to the line of Admirals Road near Cross Roads Farm, in which Brigade Headquarters were now established, while the Rifles and Baluchis took up a position to the rear.

The night passed without incident and with very little shelling, and the opportunity was taken to collect the wounded whom it had been impossible to evacuate under the heavy fire of the afternoon. 2/Lieut. E. Giles, who from many volunteers was selected for this work, set a splendid example of devotion to duty and worked hard throughout the night in endeavouring to relieve the sufferings of his men.

The day's losses had been heavy and the gain of ground nil, but the bearing of the Battalion under somewhat disheartening circumstances had been worthy of the highest traditions of regular troops. Something, however, had been achieved as, in spite of his use of poison gas, the enemy was no nearer Ypres and our line, though strained almost to breaking point, was still holding. It appears indeed that the gallant front shown by the Lahore Division was successful in deceiving the Germans as to the extent of our resources, and deterred him from pressing the advantages he had already gained.

The casualties of the afternoon of the 27th April were in officers:

> Capt. C. R. Saunders and 2/Lieut. A. D. Coates, killed; Lieut. P. B. K. Stedman, died of wounds; Capt. F. G. Grimwade, Lieuts. F. A. Coffin and D. J. Leonard, and 2/Lieut. T. I. Walker, wounded; and in N.C.O.'s and men, 32 killed (including C. S. M. Chennels), 132 wounded, and 13 missing.

During the 28th the 1/4th Londons remained in position in rear of Cross Roads Farm, and beyond a good deal of shelling in which gas shell was freely used by the enemy the day passed without important incident. Luckily the bombardment this day was not very costly to the Battalion or, indeed, to the Brigade as a whole. The Lahore Division was transferred from V Corps to a special counter-attack force then formed under command of Gen. Plumer, and it was arranged that the Sirhind and

Ferozepore Brigades should be prepared to co-operate with an attack contemplated by the French who were still on our left flank, making such advance as might be justified by the results achieved by our Allies. The French attack, however, did not materialise in consequence of the very heavy losses of the preceding two days and our Allies confined themselves to artillery action.

During the evening the enemy turned a large number of guns on to St Jean and in a few hours the work of destruction, already far advanced, was almost completed. In the darkness the church was clearly visible in flames, the windows being lit up by the conflagration within: before morning the tower had fallen, the roof had collapsed, and nothing but smouldering ruins remained.

The 29th April found the Ferozepore Brigade still holding its trenches and orders were again issued to it to be prepared to co-operate with the French. But during the morning definite orders were received that the French attack was postponed, the assault of the enemy positions being a more formidable proposition than could be tackled by the Allied troops in their then exhausted and numerically weak condition.

The German bombardment continued throughout the 29th, and the Battalion remained inactive beyond the further strengthening of its trenches. It did, however, have the satisfaction of seeing a Taube brought down close to its lines by our anti-aircraft guns.

Before daybreak on the 30th, the Ferozepore Brigade was relieved and marched out of the salient, the 1/4th Londons proceeding by way of Buffs Road and La Brique to hutments at Ouderdom. While passing through La Brique the Battalion was met by a reinforcement of about fifty N.C.O.'s and men from the 3/4th Battalion in England, conducted by Major E. H. Stillwell. Accompanying this draft were 2/Lieuts. L. G. Rix and B. Rivers Smith.

The roads out of the salient were being very heavily shelled during the relief, the cross roads at Vlamertinghe being in particular accurately bombarded with heavy shrapnel. But Major Burnett was able to save a great many casualties by varying the route of some platoons.

At about 7.30 a.m. on the same morning the Ferozepore Brigade moved from the hutments to bivouacs close by to avoid the effects of the continuous shelling to which the concentration camp was subjected, but returned to the huts at night. The day was spent in rest and reorganisation. The Battalion was undoubtedly a little shaken after its rough handling and very seriously reduced in strength. Over 600 rifles had left Ouderdom on the morning of the 26th, but at the roll call which took place on return on the 30th only 235 names were answered, apart from the newly arrived draft which had not been in action.

St Jean Village in April 1920

The following awards were made for services rendered:

Capt. W. G. Clark, D.S.O.; Sergt. A. C. Ehren, D.C.M.; de France.

In this, its first serious action, the 1/4th Battalion had firmly established its reputation by its remarkable steadiness under unprecedented circumstances, and, though the price paid was heavy, it had the satisfaction of having contributed materially to the undying glory of the British defence of Ypres.

At 7.45 p.m. on the 1st May, the concentration of the Division being now complete, the Ferozepore Brigade marched from Ouderdom *via* Reninghelst, Westoutre, to Meteren, arriving there at 12.30 a.m. on the 2nd. A rest was made here until the afternoon when the route was resumed, Doulieu being reached about 10 p.m. The march was completed the following evening, when at about 7 p.m. the Brigade returned to its former billets in the Paradis area.

CHAPTER V
OPERATIONS DURING THE SUMMER OF 1915

In spite of the severe tax placed on his resources by the ever-increasing weight of the enemy's assaults at Ypres, and the consequent difficulty of finding sufficient reserves of men and material to embark on a new attack on a large scale, Sir John French decided early in May to adopt the bold course of launching a fresh offensive at the southern extremity of the British front. He was led to this resolve partly by the hope of diverting the enemy's attention towards the south and thereby easing the pressure against Ypres, and partly by the desire to assist the French who were launching an offensive south of the La Bassée Canal.

The ultimate objective of this new undertaking was the opening of the road to Lille, and the necessary preliminary to this was the expulsion of the enemy from his defences on the Aubers Ridge and the establishment of the British troops on the La Bassée-Lille Road.

This attack was entrusted to the First Army, whose operations were divided into two separate zones. In the north the assault was to be made by the IV Corps at Rouges Bancs with the object of turning the Aubers defences from that flank; while farther south the I and Indian Corps were to secure the line Ligny-le-Grand—La Clicqueterie Farm.

The Indian Corps attack was to be carried out by the Meerut Division—the Lahore Division still being weak after its recent fighting in the salient—on a front from the right of the Corps sector near Chocolat Menier Corner to Oxford Road (on the left of La Bassée Road). The rôle of the Lahore Division, which would occupy the line in front of Neuve Chapelle with the Jullundur Brigade, was to support the Meerut Division's attack with artillery, machine-gun and rifle fire, and particularly to secure the left flank of the assaulting columns during their advance by being prepared to operate as occasion might arise against the Bois du Biez.

The attack was launched on the 9th May at 5.40 a.m. after a forty minutes' bombardment of the enemy lines by all available guns.

The assaulting columns advanced with the greatest valour, but were met by a murderous machine-gun and rifle fire, under which they were literally mown down. The survivors struggled on in spite of the frightful losses they were suffering, but practically none of the 1st or Meerut Divisions reached the enemy's front trench. Farther north the 8th Division effected a lodgment in the enemy's trenches, but after hanging on gallantly throughout the day were forced at night to return to their original positions after suffering appalling casualties. From all along the line came reports of what amounted to total failure. The surprise effect which had proved so valuable at Neuve Chapelle in March was wanting this day, and our artillery had been inadequately supplied with high explosive shells to enable them to destroy the German machine-gun emplacements.

Meanwhile reports were received from the French of some considerable degree of success. On the following day Sir John French decided not to pursue his offensive in the north, but to limit his further efforts to the area south of the La Bassée Road, and accordingly preparations were made for the resumption of operations on the 12th.

The Lahore Division had reached the Neuve Chapelle area after its march back from Ypres on the evening of the 4th May, the Ferozepore Brigade finding accommodation in its former billets at Paradis, which it left the following day for Riez Bailleul.

On the evening of the 8th the Brigade moved forward to take up its prearranged position of assembly in support to the Jullundur Brigade.

The position taken up by the 1/4th Londons and the 9th Bhopals was in shallow assembly trenches in the orchards about the junction of Sign Post Lane with Rue Tilleloy. These trenches were hastily dug and very shallow, without either traverses or any sort of shelter; and it was therefore fortunate that the weather was unusually warm and fine for the time of year. The Connaughts and the 57th Rifles occupied the old British front line (as it had been before the battle of Neuve Chapelle) astride Sign Post Lane.

During the whole of the 9th, 10th and 11th May the 1/4th London remained in these trenches under continual heavy shell fire: though owing to the lack of success with which the main operation had met it was not called upon to advance.

On the evening of the 11th it was withdrawn with the rest of the Brigade to billets at Riez Bailleul. On return to billets great discomfort was caused to all ranks by the discovery that the billet in which the packs had been deposited during the three days spent in trenches had been burnt to the ground, involving the total destruction of its contents together with a mail from home. The following day the Indian Corps Commander (Sir James Willcocks) visited the Battalion and expressed his deep appreciation of its conduct at Ypres.

The 12th May dawned dull and misty and artillery observation was exceedingly difficult; and for this and other causes the renewal of the attack was again postponed until the 15th. The Meerut Division was again responsible for the Indian Corps attack. The Lahore Division adopted a role similar to that which it had played on the 9th, and the Ferozepore Brigade moved forward once more on the evening of the 15th May to its former assembly positions about Sign Post Lane.

In order to endeavour to secure the surprise effect which had been lacking on the 9th it was decided this time to deliver the attack at night, and after a preliminary bombardment the assaulting columns dashed forward at 11.30 p.m. on the 15th. On the right of the attack in the region of Festubert and La Quinque Rue considerable success was achieved by the 7th Division, and some advance was also made by the 2nd Division which was operating on the immediate right of the Indians.

The Meerut Division, however, was again faced with a hail of lead from the enemy lines under which it was impossible to live, and though the troops did all that men could do, by 4 a.m. on the 16th, after two gallant efforts, the attempts of the Indians to advance were definitely checked and the remains of the assaulting columns were once more back in their original trenches.

From this date onwards operations were confined to the southern area in the neighbourhood of Festubert, and though the battle continued to rage until the 25th May, the Indian Corps was no longer concerned in it beyond the preparations necessary to enable it to conform to the advance on its right flank.

During the early part of the month the 1/4th Londons received further officer reinforcements as follows:

- Capt. A. A. N. Haine.
- Lieut. S. G. Monk.
- Lieut. D. C. Cooke.
- 2/Lieut. J. S. B. Gathergood.

The Battalion remained in its shallow trenches until the 18th May under less favourable conditions of weather than previously, and the exposure caused a large number of casualties through sickness, including Lieuts. Rivers, Smith and Cooke, and 2/Lieut. Gathergood, who were evacuated to hospital.

On the evening of the 18th May the Ferozepore Brigade took over the front line from the Jullundur Brigade, the 1/4th Londons relieving the 4th Suffolks on the right, between the La Bassée Road and Oxford Road, the subsection including Port Arthur Keep where Battalion Headquarters were established. This tour of duty was uneventful and the troops were occupied principally in repairing the damage done to the entanglements and defences by the enemy's shell fire during the days of the battle. A certain amount of shell fire was, however, experienced causing a few casualties, including Captain Haine, who was hit on the 22nd. The enemy also paid a good deal of attention to the back areas and the regimental transport now established at Rouge Croix was heavily shelled on the 25th, and again on the 26th, with such severity that it was compelled to change position to Riez Bailleul.

During this period also the issue of gas masks to all ranks was completed.

On the 30th the Sirhind Brigade, which had been in divisional reserve during the battle, came forward and took over the line from the Ferozepore Brigade, the 1/4th Londons handing over their trenches to the 1st Manchesters and withdrawing to billets at Riez Bailleul.

After the end of May no further attempt was made on the Indian Corps front to conduct operations on a large scale. The difficulties under which the Indian battalions were labouring in the supply of reinforcements to replace casualties were extreme. The Indian concentration camp at Marseilles was continually receiving reinforcements from India, but of these an increasing proportion was found to be unfit for despatch to the front, and as the summer wore on the native regiments of the Corps gradually ebbed in numbers until amalgamations began to be effected to maintain units at anything approaching war strength. In these circumstances offensive operations against so strongly defended a position as the Aubers Ridge were out of the question, especially having regard to the continued shortage in the supply of shells. At the same time the general situation did not permit of the Indian Corps being entirely withdrawn from the line for a prolonged rest and reorganisation. The story of the next three months is, therefore, one of unceasing hard work in and out of the line without any of those opportunities of distinction which are as necessary to the well-being of a battalion—and especially a native battalion—as a regular supply of rations.

This increasing numerical weakness of the native battalions threw a greater burden of work and responsibility on the British units, both Regular and Territorial, though even they experienced the greatest difficulty in obtaining the regular supplies from home of that fresh blood which was so earnestly desired. The 1/4th London returned from Ypres in May at a strength well under 300 all ranks, and at no period during the remainder of its attachment to the Indian Corps did its strength approach even 450; in other words, for months on end, in sentry-go, working and carrying parties, and patrols, every man was doing two men's work; and this with a very scanty proportion of rest behind the line. Out of 126 days from the end of May to the beginning of October the 1/4th Londons spent 92 days in trenches, and of the remaining 34 in billets not one was spent beyond the reach of the enemy's guns.

With the exception of one tour of duty in the Min House Farm sector the 1/4th Londons spent this summer on the right of the La Bassée Road either in the trenches in front of the Rue du Bois, which included the well-remembered positions of the Orchard Redoubt and Crescent Trench, or in reserve, usually in Lansdowne Post, a large redoubt on Forrester's Lane. The summer months saw very great improvements in the Rue du Bois trenches. The isolated listening posts, like grouse-butts, which had formed the advanced positions in March were now joined into a continuous line of breastwork, connected with the Rue du Bois by numerous communication trenches. Shelters for the trench garrisons were also constructed, but these gave protection against nothing more serious than rain—and not always that. In this waterlogged area the sinking of a deep dugout was an impossibility, and the shelters were in consequence mere "rabbit-hutches" built into the breastwork and covered with corrugated iron and a few sandbags, which imbued the occupants with an entirely unjustified sense of security. At the same time the wire entanglements in No Man's Land were constantly extended and strengthened. With all these defences steadily growing, the duties of the Battalion on working parties, both when occupying the line and when in reserve billets, were onerous and unceasing. Patrolling work by night was vigorously prosecuted as being practically the only available means of fostering the growth of the "offensive spirit." Trench routine in 1915 was marked by a feature which in subsequent years almost entirely vanished—the constant employment of rifle fire. At this period the infantryman had not succumbed to the insensate craze for bombs which later ruined his powers as a rifleman; and every night, in one part of the trenches or another, saw something in the nature of an organised shoot by the infantry, bursts of rapid fire being directed on the enemy's parapet. These practices were of great value, not only in keeping the men skilful with their rifles, but also in maintaining their moral superiority over the enemy which might otherwise have become seriously impaired through their knowledge of the inequality of our strength in artillery.

The enemy's activity during this summer was for the most part confined to artillery fire which at times attained serious proportions and inflicted severe loss; indeed throughout the period under review the toll of casualties was steady and continuous.

Out of the trenches the 1/4th Londons withdrew to reserve billets either at Pont du Hem, L'Epinette, or La Fosse, and while in reserve were invariably called upon for working parties in the forward area, so that the opportunities available for training and repairing the damage inevitably caused to parade discipline by long-continued trench life were almost entirely wanting. At this period, moreover, "back-of-the-line" organisation had not reached the high pitch attained in later years. Baths were an infrequent luxury, concert parties—of an organised type—unheard of, recreational training still without its proper recognition. Such infrequent rests as were granted to the troops were thus of comparatively small recuperative value.

But in spite of these numerous difficulties the Battalion was steadily increasing its military efficiency and its morale throughout the summer was high.

Rouge Croix, La Bassée Road

The Doll's House, La Bassée Road

One of the most unpleasant tours of duty was at Min House Farm, already alluded to, a sector on the left of Neuve Chapelle, facing Mauquissart, which the Battalion took over for a week in July as a temporary measure during a readjustment of Brigade boundaries. The breastworks here were especially weak and very much overlooked from the Aubers Ridge. Wire was embryonic and communication trenches poor. Moreover, the area appeared to be the subject of particular hatred on the part of the Bosche, who shelled it frequently and heavily. Min House (or Moated Grange) Farm, where Headquarters were established, was perched on the crest of a little knoll which afforded the Headquarters staff a good view over the sector, but, probably for this very reason, the Hun objected to it. In fact before the tour of duty came to an end the farm was totally destroyed by shell fire and Battalion Headquarters had been forced to make a hasty exit to Ebenezer Farm, which, being outside the sector and unprovided with signal communications, was not ideal for the purpose of a Headquarters.

An extraordinary incident occurred during the last week of June, which seems worth recording. One night a patrol of the 129th Baluchis left the British lines to investigate the condition of the enemy's wire. On its return one man, Ayub Khan, was missing and all endeavours to recover his body were fruitless. The following evening Ayub turned up again, and being taken before his company commander related how he had entered the German trenches and passed himself off as a deserter. As is well known the Germans were always anxious to secure the defection of the native troops, and Ayub Khan's arrival was therefore hailed with enthusiasm. He was taken to the rear and examined carefully. Having kept his eyes open and seen all he could, Ayub Khan persuaded the Germans to let him return to our trenches in order to bring more of his friends over. In a weak moment the Germans agreed to let him go; but instead of greeting Ayub and his party of fellow-deserters, they were faced a few days later with a notice board which was displayed on our parapet commenting on the incident in suitable terms. Not being a humourist, the Hun lost his temper, and it is at this point in the story that the 1/4th Londons become concerned. The luckless notice board was displayed on Crescent Trench then occupied by D Company. At 8.30 a.m. on the 27th June the enemy opened on the board with 5.9 howitzers, and almost the first shell hit Capt. Cart de Lafontaine's Headquarters, causing him a severe attack of shell-shock and killing his subaltern 2/Lieut. F. F. Hunt. All the morning the "hate" was continued with great loss to D Company, and by midday the Crescent Trench was practically obliterated. Company Sergt.-Major Risley showed great coolness in controlling his men and withdrawing them as far as was practicable out of the zone of fire, and set an excellent example of steadiness under a most trying ordeal. He was subsequently awarded the D.C.M.

On the 16th June Major L. T. Burnett, who had been in temporary command of the 1/4th Londons since the 26th April, was promoted Lieut.-Colonel and appointed to command, Major G. H. M. Vine assuming the duties of second in command.

At the beginning of September, however, the Battalion was exceedingly unfortunate in losing Major Vine, who was sent to hospital with eye trouble, and Lieut.-Col. Burnett being on leave at the time the command of the Battalion was assumed until his return by Lieut.-Col. Murray of the 89th Punjabis.

Early in August Capt. and Adjt. G. B. Scott also said farewell to the Battalion on taking up an extra-regimental employment, and the Adjutancy was given to Capt. W. G. Clark, D.S.O., and subsequently to Capt. E. Giles.

The following officers joined during August and September:

> Lieuts. R. V. Gery, D. J. Leonard, C. Gaskin.
>
> 2/Lieuts. S. E. Lyons, H. B. A. Balls, H. Jones, C. C. Spurr, A. G. Sharp, R. Johnstone, W. J. Boutall, F. C. Fanhangel, S. E. H. Walmisley, A. S. Ford, G. L. Goodes and H. J. M. Williams.

In N.C.O.'s and men the Battalion was less fortunate, and up to the end of September 3 N.C.O.'s and 14 men, all veterans of Neuve Chapelle or Ypres, were the only reinforcements from home.

The casualties in officers for the same period were:

> 2/Lieut. F. F. Hunt, killed.

Capt. H. P. L. Cart de Lafontaine, wounded (shell-shock).

Capts. H. W. Weathersbee and H. M. Lorden, and 2/Lieut. A. G. Sharp, to hospital.

Arrangements had now been completed for the launching of an offensive on the high ground south of La Bassée Canal in the direction of Loos and Hulluch. The opening day of the offensive had been fixed for the 25th September, and as the Indian Corps was not concerned with the main action it will be needless for us here to review the course of events south of the Canal.

North of the Canal, however, a subsidiary operation of some magnitude had been organised with the strategic object of increasing the pressure on the German defences north of La Bassée to such an extent that he would be compelled under the strain of our main offensive in the south to relinquish the La Bassée line altogether and retire to the east of the Aubers Ridge.

To this end an ambitious programme had been drawn up for the Indian Corps which temporarily included the newly arrived 19th Division. The preliminary attack was to be made by the Meerut Division under cover of a smoke and gas attack to the north of Neuve Chapelle, with the object of establishing a new line in the first instance along the road from the Ducks Bill to Mauquissart. The experience of previous actions having clearly shown that initial success had frequently been converted into subsequent failure by a delay in following up the first advance, it was arranged that the Jullundur and Ferozepore Brigades and the 19th Division should be prepared immediately to exploit whatever success should be gained by the Meerut Division by pushing forward at once to the line Moulin d'Eau—La Tourelle—east edge of Bois du Biez, while the Sirhind Brigade "leap-frogged" through them to Lorgies. It was hoped that considerable moral effect might be obtained by the use of poison gas against the Germans, and to magnify this as much as possible arrangements were made for the building up of smoke screens, one by the Meerut Division to cover the left flank of its attack and one by the Jullundur Brigade on the right of the attack; for the projection of a heavy smoke cloud by the Ferozepore Brigade on the Rue du Bois and by the 19th Division (holding the extreme Southern Section, south of the Boar's Head salient); and for an attempt simultaneously to set fire to the Bois du Biez by means of incendiary bombs.

Systematic wire cutting on either side of the La Bassée Road was begun on the 21st September, and a feint attack was conducted by the Ferozepore Brigade late in the afternoon of the 22nd in conjunction with the divisional artillery. This feint attack took the form of a heavy bombardment of the enemy's front line by all available guns, starting at about 5 p.m. After five minutes the guns lifted on to the enemy's support line and the infantry in the line (Connaughts and 57th Rifles) by means of rifle fire, lifting dummies on to the parapet and flashing their bayonets, endeavoured to produce an impression among the Germans that an attack was imminent. In the midst of the confusion caused to the Germans by this demonstration our artillery once more shortened its range, firing shrapnel on the enemy's front line. It was believed that this feint attack had the desired effect: the fire of our guns was certainly accurate and well distributed, and elicited but little reply from the enemy. The hostile machine-gun fire, moreover, betrayed some perturbation inasmuch as it was extremely erratic, the bullets passing high over the Rue du Bois and doing no damage. The 1/4th Londons were at this period in Lansdowne Post.

On the 23rd the weather changed, and the favourable dry season which had given such promise of success for our schemes gave way to heavy rains. The wind, too, veered round to the south-east so that it blew towards our lines instead of towards the enemy's. This was particularly disastrous as it would nullify the effect of the smoke screens and render the use of gas impossible. It was determined, however, to do all possible to carry the offensive through to success, and the Lahore Division was ordered to be completely ready to move forward by 6 a.m. on the 25th September.

Once more, however, the attempt to advance on this front was foiled. Possibly the feint attack on the 22nd had been somewhat too theatrical to impress the enemy and had merely indicated our intentions to him. Certain it was, however, that on the 25th he was holding his trenches in particular strength and there remained stolidly throughout the day in spite of our smoke screens and demonstrations, to which he replied with vigorous machine-gun and shell fire. The attempt of the Meerut Division to push forward proved abortive, and the Lahore Division was unable to get forward, there being not the least sign of weakening on the enemy's front opposite to them. There is no doubt that this failure was in part at least due to the treachery of the elements. The smoke screen was utterly ineffective; gas could not be used at all.

The 26th saw the general situation unchanged and the enemy still sitting in his front line and showing not the least disposition to leave it.

On the evening of the 26th the 1/4th Londons relieved the 57th Rifles in a line of reserve posts on the Rue du Bois in the vicinity of Chocolat Menier Corner (Dog, Cat, Pall Mall and "Z" Orchard Posts).

The weather had now definitely broken and heavy rains fell, reducing the trenches to veritable seas of mud. The Battalion continued to occupy the Keeps until the evening of the 30th, the duty having passed quietly with the exception of a small amount of enemy shell fire; but a large proportion of the shells being "blind" no casualties were caused. On relief on the 30th the 1/4th Londons once more withdrew to Lansdowne Post. On the 2nd October the Ferozepore Brigade was relieved by the 19th Division and moved out to billets in the La Gorgue-Riez Bailleul area. Here it remained resting and training for a week, throughout which the weather remained vile in the extreme.

On the 11th October the Ferozepore Brigade once more took over the Neuve Chapelle sector from the Jullundur, the 1/4th Londons occupying the right subsector with a detachment of the 89th Punjabis[2] in Hills Redoubt and Battalion Headquarters in Sandbag Alley. On the left of the 1/4th Londons the Brigade sector was taken up as far as Château Road by the 57th Rifles while the Connaughts were on the extreme left as far as Sunken Road.

[2] The 89th Punjabis reached France in June and replaced the 9th Bhopals in the Ferozepore Brigade.

Two days later the Ferozepore Brigade conducted a second feint attack in conjunction with other operations which it is not necessary to detail. On this occasion the feint was timed to take place shortly after midday, the morning being occupied by our guns in a systematic wire-cutting shoot, which was followed by a heavy bombardment of the enemy trenches during the projection of the smoke screen. Following the smoke screen, smoke barrages were formed on the flanks of the feint attack at 1.45 p.m., and simultaneously with them the infantry in the line operated with rifle fire and demonstrations similar to those employed on the former occasion to give the illusion of a pending attack. The wind again was unfavourable, this time blowing the smoke along No Man's Land between the lines instead of over the enemy's trenches; and owing to the strength of the wind the smoke screen never became dense enough to conceal the bomb guns by which it was delivered. During the whole period of the operation our front and rear lines were subjected to a heavy fire from the enemy's artillery, which caused very great damage to our breastworks and wire, guns as heavy as 8-inch being employed with great intensity between 12.45 and 1.30 p.m. This bombardment caused large numbers of casualties in the 1/4th Londons, it being impossible to clear, even temporarily, the bombarded trenches owing to the necessity of maintaining as intensely as possible the bursts of rifle fire in accordance with the scheme. It is a matter of grave doubt as to whether these demonstrations were worth the casualties they cost; and it seems abundantly evident that no useful purpose can have been served by carrying through a prearranged scheme essentially dependent on the weather when the conditions on the appointed day were unfavourable. Perhaps the best comment on the undertaking is to be found in the orders for the operation, which included a warning to the effect that "dummies must not be raised too high so as to show the sticks, as they were before"!

After the disturbance caused by this operation the sector relaxed to a condition of remarkable calmness, which was maintained during the remainder of the tour of duty. This came to an end on the night of the 27th October when the Ferozepore Brigade was relieved for the last time in France by the Jullundur. The 1/4th Londons were relieved by the 4th Suffolks and withdrew to billets on the Merville Road at Estaires, the remainder of the Brigade concentrating in the same area.

The casualties for the month of October included Lieuts. C. Gaskin and D. J. Leonard, both wounded, the latter accidentally. During this rest a reinforcement of about fifty N.C.O.'s and men joined the Battalion.

Rumour had been active for some time as to the possible transference of the Indian Corps to another theatre of operations, and on the 31st notification was received that the Lahore Division would embark at Marseilles early in November, but that the Territorial units would not accompany it. The gradual withdrawal of the Division from the line had in fact begun, and when the 1/4th Londons returned to the reserve trenches in Loretto Road on the 4th November it had said good-bye to its good friends of the Ferozepore Brigade and was temporarily attached to the Jullundur. The following day its attachment was transferred to the Sirhind Brigade, the Jullundur having also made its final withdrawal from the line.

On the 7th the Battalion relieved the 27th Punjabis (Sirhind) at Ludhiana Lodge, and provided detachments to hold Church and Hills Redoubts and Curzon Post, the front line being held by the 4th King's. The three Territorial battalions of the Division, the 4th Londons, 4th King's, and 4th Suffolks were all now unattached and were handed over to XI Corps, who were taking over the line from the Indians with the Guards and 46th Divisions, and a few days of constant change of positions ensued during the progress of the relief.

On the 8th the 1/4th Londons withdrew to Loretto Road. This day the long connection of the Battalion with the Indian Corps, with which it had passed through pleasant and rough times alike on terms of the closest friendship, was finally severed. Lieut.-Col. Burnett, Capt. W. G. Clark, D.S.O., and a detachment of the Battalion marched to Croix Barbée to bid good-bye to the divisional commander, Major-Gen. Keary. In the course of an address to the detachment the General said that on the occasion of the departure of the Indian Corps from France and the consequent severance of the Battalion from the Division, he wished to express his thanks to the regiment for the good work they had done. Their loyalty and devotion to duty had been worthy of all praise, their bearing in action left nothing to be desired, and their discipline had been excellent throughout. On conclusion of this address the General handed Lieut.-Col. Burnett a written Order of the Day.

On the 10th the Battalion moved forward into Brigade reserve at Pont Logy, and this day was attached to the 137th Brigade of the 46th Division. The weather was still exceedingly wet, the trenches full of water, and the conditions in the line owing to the lack of dugouts were unusually uncomfortable. On the evening of the 14th the Battalion finally left the Neuve Chapelle area, billeting at Croix Barbée for the night and continuing its journey the following day by motor-bus to Lillers, where it became attached to the 140th Brigade of the 47th (London) Division.

This concludes the first phase of the 4th London Regiment's service in France. The year 1915 all along the line had been one of equilibrium after the defensive battles of 1914.

We have said enough of the Battalion's life in the Indian Corps to indicate that the year 1915 was one of very hard work and continued strain on all ranks. Out of 255 days spent in the Lahore Division the Battalion was actually in trenches for 142 days, in reserve billets providing working parties for 76 days, and at rest only for 37 days; and although it was worn out and weak when it withdrew to Lillers in November it was a thoroughly seasoned fighting battalion, every officer and man of which was an experienced soldier.

CHAPTER VI
THE 1/4TH BATTALION IN THE 47TH DIVISION

The 47th (London) Division to which the 1/4th Londons were now attached had just withdrawn for a period of rest and reorganisation from the trenches around Loos where they had seen a good deal of heavy fighting in the battle of the 25th September. The Division had come out from England in March 1915 and had first been engaged as the extreme right Division of the British Army at Festubert in May. Although serious losses had been suffered in the attacks on Hill 70 in September, the battalions of the Division had subsequently received strong reinforcements from home, and the majority of them were far larger than the 1/4th Londons who, at the date of attachment to the Division, numbered only 24 officers and 435 other ranks.

The Division, which was under command of Major-Gen. C. St L. Barter, K.C.B., K.C.V.O., comprised the following Infantry Brigades:

140th Infantry Brigade—Brig.-Gen. G. Cuthbert, C.B.

1/4th London Regiment (Royal Fusiliers).

1/6th " " (Rifles).

1/7th " "

1/8th " " (Post Office Rifles).

1/15th " " (Civil Service Rifles).

141st Infantry Brigade

1/17th London Regiment (Poplar and Stepney Rifles).

1/18th " " (London Irish Rifles).

1/19th " " (St Pancras).

1/20th	"	"	(Blackheath and Woolwich).

142nd Infantry Brigade

1/3rd	London	Regiment	(Royal Fusiliers).
1/21st	"	"	(First Surrey Rifles).
1/22nd	"	"	(The Queen's), Kennington.
1/23rd	"	"	(East Surrey, Clapham Junction).
1/24th	"	"	(The Queen's), Bermondsey.

Pioneer Battalion

4th   Royal Welsh Fusiliers.

The Division was attached to the IV Corps (Rawlinson) of the First Army (Haig).

The first day after arrival at Lillers (16th November 1915) was devoted by the Battalion to cleaning up uniforms and equipment which had, through the prolonged duty in waterlogged trenches, become caked with weeks of mud. The general discipline of the 47th Division and of the 140th Brigade in particular was exceedingly good; and although the battle discipline of the Lahore Division had been excellent, and the training and experience which the 1/4th Londons had gained while attached to it of the highest order, yet it cannot be gainsaid that the parade discipline among the Indian Brigades had not been given that amount of attention which the long years of war showed to be necessary, even in the field, to ensure the best results in action. We have already indicated that this weakness in the Indian Brigades arose through their continual deficiency in numbers and the consequent long periods of trench duty which had been imposed on them.

The sudden change, therefore, from trench duty to a period of rest, in which ceremonial mounting of guards and drill were prominent features, created a totally new environment for the Battalion which was entirely beneficial.

The whole Battalion, from the Commanding Officer to the most recently arrived draft, was determined to maintain the reputation of the Battalion;

and by dint of hard work on and off parade the 4th Londons became rapidly second to none in the Brigade in all the duties they were called upon to carry out—and they were the more impelled to this effort by the realisation that they were the senior Battalion of the Brigade, not only in precedence, but also in point of active service experience.

At Lillers the Brigade spent about a month, passed for the most part in very cold and wet weather, in a thorough course of training, in which particular attention was paid to drill and bombing. At this period the question of the thorough organisation of bombing—or as they were then called "grenadier"—sections with the proper quota of bayonet men, throwers and carriers was attracting a great deal of thought, and the time devoted to this particular branch of the art of war was subsequently found, as will be seen later, to have been well spent.

Each Battalion mounted daily a quarter guard and an inlying piquet of one officer, two sergeants, and thirty rank and file, and the ceremonial mounting of these duties was carried out with all possible pomp on the Grande Place at Retreat.

In addition to this the peace-time system of "extra drills" as a minor punishment was re-instituted—not perhaps an altogether pleasant recollection for some—but in spite of the disadvantages such a system must always have in the eyes of those for whose particular benefit it is devised, there can be no question that this tightening of discipline had in the end a beneficial effect on all ranks, the extent of which it is impossible to overestimate.

The training period was varied by inter-battalion sports and football matches in which the 1/4th Londons achieved some success, beating the 7th Battalion 3-1, and the 6th Battalion 3-1. On the whole the month passed smoothly with very little incident worthy of mention beyond a two-day divisional route march which took place on the 1st and 2nd December.

On the 6th December the 1/4th Londons suffered a loss in the death of Sergt. Bench, who had very efficiently carried out the duties of Transport Sergeant since the Battalion's arrival in France, his death being the result of injuries caused by a fall from his horse.

During the training at Lillers a most gallant action was performed by Lieut. H. Jones. While practising throwing with live bombs one of the men dropped a bomb with the fuse burning. At great risk Lieut. Jones picked up the bomb and threw it out of the trench, where it at once exploded. His bravery undoubtedly saved several lives.

In January, the Battalion was joined by Lieut. V. C. Donaldson.

The front of attack in the Battle of Loos had extended from the La Bassée Canal on the left, where our lines were faced by the village of Auchy, to the village of Loos on the extreme right. In this attack the first objective was the line of the Lens-Hulluch-La Bassée Road, the frontage being divided more or less equally by the Vermelles-Hulluch Road, which ran directly out from our trenches towards the Germans.

North of this dividing line were three very serious obstacles, namely, Auchy itself defended by impassable wire entanglements; a work of large area and enormous strength known as the Hohenzollern Redoubt; and a group of Quarries close to the Lens-Hulluch Road.

The 9th and 7th Divisions had met with great initial success on the 25th September 1915, the former overrunning the Hohenzollern Redoubt and gaining a position beyond it on a large slag-heap known as Fosse 8, while elements of the 7th Division sweeping the enemy's defence of the Quarries before them had gained the outskirts of Cité St Elie and Hulluch beyond the Lens-Hulluch Road. The unfortunate check to the advance of the 2nd Division at Auchy, however, had exposed the left flank of the 9th Division, who were afterwards ejected from Fosse 8, while the 7th on their right had been unable to retain their advanced positions across the main road.

Desperate fighting ensued for the possession of these strongholds until the conclusion of the battle about 13th October. At that date the Germans retained possession of the whole of the Quarries and the greater part of the Hohenzollern Redoubt. Between the two the British had driven a wedge so that the part of the Hohenzollern which remained in the enemy's hands formed an abrupt salient, of which the west face was formed by a trench irreverently named by the British "Little Willie," and the south face by its obvious companion "Big Willie." Connecting the eastern extremity of Big Willie with the north-west corner of the Quarries the Germans remained in possession of Potsdam Trench, while the Quarries themselves formed another but smaller salient in the enemy's lines, well flanked on the south-east side by our positions, which caused a second abrupt turn to the east in the enemy lines.

The whole area between these confused positions was a vast maze of earthworks, for they were in the midst of what had, prior to the battle, been a strong German third system of defence and No Man's Land was traversed by innumerable short communication trenches and saps, held by the opposing garrisons by means of barricades, for the possession of which an unceasing and murderous struggle with bombs and trench mortars was still proceeding. In addition to these deadly conflicts a still more subtle warfare was being waged underground, where our Tunnelling Companies were fighting a battle of wits with the Germans by mining and counter-mining, and the blowing of mines followed by fierce local infantry fights for possession of the craters thus formed were of frequent recurrence.

A reference to a large map will render clear the extreme importance to the enemy of the possession of these two positions. Situate as they were, one on each of the two lowest spurs of the Vermelles-Hulluch Ridge, their capture by the British would have involved a very serious threat to the German defences on the line Auchy-Haisnes, and might easily have been a prelude to the outflanking of La Bassée itself. The enemy was obviously alive to these possibilities, and the daily intelligence reports gleaned from our patrols and observers made it abundantly clear that he was strengthening his trenches and wire, and was burrowing strenuously in opposition to our mining operations.

This severely contested part of the front was taken over by the 47th Division from the 9th between the 13th and the 15th December, C Section opposite the Quarries and D Section opposite the Hohenzollern Redoubt being occupied by the 141st and 142nd Brigades, the 140th Brigade remaining in reserve.

For some time after the return to the line the 1/4th Londons did not enter the trenches as a battalion, but on account of its small numbers was retained in reserve, where it performed a great deal of heavy labour in working and carrying parties for the rest of the Brigade.

On the 15th the 1/4th Londons moved from Lillers at 8.30 a.m., entraining for Nœux-les-Mines, whence it marched to billets at Labourse, training being continued while the Brigade remained in reserve.

This move was followed by a further approach to the line which took place on the 19th December, when the 140th Brigade relieved the 141st in C 1 and C 2 Sections, opposite the Quarries, the 6th and 15th Battalions occupying the front trenches with the 7th Battalion in support at Le Philosophe and the 4th and 8th Battalions in Brigade reserve at Noyelles-les-Vermelles.

Here the 1/4th Londons' duties in carrying and trench working parties in the forward areas were severe as the reserve billets were some three miles from the front line trenches.

The most active part of the Brigade's new front was C 2, the subsection now garrisoned by the 15th Londons, where on the left of the Quarries the continuous struggle already referred to in sapping, bombing and mining was proceeding with particular violence. The centre of this fighting was a work held by the British, known as the Hairpin, and two saps, Essex Trench and Shipka Pass, which pushed forward from the Hairpin towards the German lines. Essex Trench in particular was the scene of much hard fighting, for the Germans were in occupation of the further end of it and were separated from our garrison by a double barricade. This trench and Shipka Pass were coveted by the Germans, as it was through them that they hoped to obtain a lodgment in the Hairpin, the possession of which would secure the right flank of their salient at the Quarries and render their precarious tenure of that feature much more secure. With this object they had on the night of the 17th launched a determined bombing attack along Essex Trench and Shipka Pass, the enemy bombers being well supported by trench mortar and rifle grenade fire. Our garrisons, however, were ready, and none of the enemy reached our barricades, and their attack was finally dispersed by our artillery.

This attempt was renewed in the early hours of the 20th, when so vigorous an attack was delivered that the 15th London bombers in Essex Trench were forced back from their barricade for some 20 yards, and were unable for the moment to organise a counter-attack as the Germans had constructed "arrow head" trenches flanking his sap, so that he was able to bring fire to bear on our garrison from three points simultaneously.

After a personal reconnaissance the Brigadier decided on making the same evening a bid for the recovery of the lost trench. The 15th London bombers having already suffered considerable loss, they were reinforced during the day by the Battalion bombers of the 1/4th Londons, who moved up to the Hairpin. The day passed quietly but for some accurate shelling of our positions to the right of the Quarries, which was stopped by our heavy guns. At 9.45 p.m. our attack was delivered by three parties of bombers simultaneously—one in Essex Trench, one in a neighbouring sap, and one moving over the open, flanking support being given by machine-guns posted in Shipka Pass and west of the Quarries.

The first attack failed, the Essex Trench party on reaching our old barricade coming once more under a shower of bombs from three directions, while the sap party found progress impossible owing to the waterlogged condition of the sap, and the party in the open were brought to a standstill by machine-gun fire. Second and third attempts proved equally unsuccessful, and after the 23rd December attacks were discontinued though the enemy portion of Essex Trench was kept under constant trench mortar fire.

Through all these days the 1/4th London bombers remained in line, taking an active part in the unceasing battle of bombs which was pursued between the barricades, practically without intermission, and unhappily a large number of casualties was caused.

On the 22nd December a special Order of the Day was received in which Sir John French said farewell to the troops on the occasion of his relinquishment of the Commander-in-Chief; and on the same day Sir Henry Rawlinson handed over command of the IV Corps to General Wilson.

Orders were received on the 23rd that in consequence of certain signs of activity on the enemy's part, the line would be held in greater strength for the ensuing forty-eight hours, and in accordance with the prearranged defence scheme the 1/4th Londons occupied the old British front line in front of Vermelles early on the morning of the 24th. At 8 a.m. a mine near the Hohenzollern Redoubt was blown by the British, the crater being successfully occupied by troops of the 141st Brigade. The Artillery activity caused by this operation dying down shortly afterwards, the 1/4th Londons and other units in reserve returned to their billets later in the day.

During this tour of duty the Brigade Light Trench Mortar Battery, which was in line in the Hairpin sector, was joined by 2/Lieut. Goodes. The Battery did exceedingly good work during the fighting in the Hairpin. When the 1/4th Londons left the 47th Division Goodes remained with 47/1 L.T.M. Battery, and was killed at High Wood in September 1916, having been decorated, for his consistently gallant service, with the Military Cross and Bar.

Christmas Day passed in the line without particular incident beyond the daily "hates" of shells and bombs, and this year, in consequence of special orders, no attempt was permitted to indulge in the remarkable fraternisation with the enemy which had occurred during the first Christmas of the war.

On the 26th the relief of the 140th Brigade by the 142nd in C Section commenced, and the following day the 1/4th Londons withdrew to new billets at Sailly Labourse.

In Divisional reserve the Brigade devoted a few days to the usual routine of baths, cleaning, refitting and training, and on the last day of the year once more entered the trenches, but on this occasion in D Section, the left sector of the Divisional front, which it took over from the 141st Brigade, the 6th and 15th Battalions once more occupying the front system, the 8th Battalion in support to them, while the 7th who joined the 4th at Sailly Labourse were with the 4th in Brigade reserve. The new sector included the trenches opposed to the Hohenzollern Redoubt, and extended to the left to the vicinity of the Vermelles-Auchy railway. During the Brigade's short tenure of the sector the usual shelling and trench mortar activity continued but without incident of any particular interest. The 1/4th Londons continued in the wearisome and unpicturesque task of supplying working parties.

During the 2nd, 3rd and 4th of January 1916, the relief of the 47th Division by the Dismounted Division took place, the 140th being relieved on the morning of the 3rd by the 1st Dismounted Brigade, withdrawing on relief to a group of villages some seven miles behind the line in the Béthune area, the 1/4th Londons billeting at Drouvin, and the remainder of the Brigade being distributed between Verquin and Mouchin.

This relief was merely the first stage of a "side-step" which the Division was making towards the south, and on the following day the Brigade moved *via* Nœux-les-Mines to Les Brebis and made arrangements for the taking over of a sector of the line south of Loos from the French.

The 1/4th Londons' service in the Hulluch area had been arduous owing to the long marches imposed on the working parties in addition to their tasks, but it had fortunately, except among the bombers, not been a costly one, and its strength had not very much decreased since the date of its joining the Division.

During December a few officer reinforcements were received as follows: 2/Lieuts. H. G. Beal, C. W. Cragg, J. Elliott and E. W. Monk, and during January the Battalion was joined by 2/Lieut. C. F. P. de Pury (to D Company).

During December also the Quartermaster (Lieut. E. S. Tomsett) went on leave during which he fell sick, not returning to the Battalion until the 15th March 1916. In his absence his duties were carried out by 2/Lieut. S. E. H. Walmisley.

In the New Year's Honours List the names of Lieut.-Col. L. T. Burnett, Capt. W. G. Clark, D.S.O., and Capt. J. R. Pyper were mentioned in despatches and a few weeks later the award of the Military Cross to Captain Pyper was announced.

The new sector taken over by the 47th Division involved relief of the 18th French Division, and a consequent extension southwards of the British lines. This sector roughly comprised the lines in front of the villages of Maroc and Loos, and had first been taken over from the French in June 1915. The 47th Division had fought in this part of the line in the battle of Loos, and carried the British positions forward through Loos village up to the famous Double Crassier, and on to the lower slopes of Hill 70. Subsequently the French had once more taken the position over from them. This sector was divided into two subsectors known respectively as Maroc and Loos, the Maroc subsector on the right including some 1000 yards of trench extending from the vicinity of the Grenay-Lens railway to the extreme southern limit of the British advance in September 1915 and also about 1700 yards of the new positions then gained; while the Loos sector comprised entirely new positions gained in September and extended for some 1700 yards to the left completely covering Loos village and the well-known "Tower Bridge."

On the night of the 5/6 January the 140th Brigade entered the Maroc sector, the 141st occupying the Loos sector with the 142nd in Divisional reserve. The difficulties of the relief were somewhat increased owing to the fact of taking over French troops, and the difference of language was the inevitable cause of some delay, but finally, however, matters were successfully adjusted and the 140th Brigade was left in possession with the 1/4th Londons occupying the right subsection, on a frontage of some 800 yards opposite the "Fosse 16 de Lens"; the 7th Londons in the right-centre subsection, the 15th Londons in the left-centre subsection, which included the Double Crassier, and the 6th Londons on the left. The 8th Battalion were in reserve with two companies in South Maroc, and two in the old British front line just in rear of the Double Crassier, which was the danger point of the Brigade sector, not only on account of the observation of our lines which it afforded the enemy but also because it lay at the apex of an abrupt re-entrant in the British front line.

In this sector the 1/4th Londons found their own supports which were billeted in cellars in South Maroc, a mining village built on the unattractive "square" plan of American cities, and consisting of innumerable rows of artisans' dwellings, then unhappily in a state of complete ruin. The cellars of these dwellings, however, still afforded sufficient cover for the concentration unobserved by the Germans of a considerable body of troops, and the Germans were evidently somewhat disturbed at the prospect of this for their artillery, both light and heavy, paid continual attention to the village both day and night.

This sector having once more come into occupation by British troops an enormous amount of work was immediately necessary to complete the front line and company supplies of small arms ammunition, bombs, rifle grenades and trench stores of all sorts; and this support and reserve companies were kept busily engaged in this work throughout the tour of duty.

In this sector also the steel shrapnel helmet first made its appearance, so far as the 1/4th Londons were concerned. It is amusing to look back on the distrust with which its advent was first regarded by all ranks alike—although afterwards, when once its efficiency and protective qualities had been tested, it was as highly prized as it had been previously shunned. The first issue was made at the rate of one helmet per fire bay, the honour of wearing it falling to the man on sentry duty for the time being, and most remarkably disinclined the men were to assume this undesired badge of office.

On the 9th the 140th Brigade was relieved in the line by the 142nd, moving on the 13th into the Loos sector, where it took over the trenches of the 141st Brigade. The 1/4th Londons did not take part in this relief but remained in the right subsection, temporarily under the orders of the 142nd Brigade, with the 22nd Londons on their left. Here the Battalion remained until the 16th, when it was relieved by the 17th Battalion, rejoining the 140th Brigade in rest billets at Haillicourt.

On the 19th January Lieut.-Col. L. T. Burnett left the Battalion on short leave, and as it unfortunately proved, permanently, for he fell seriously ill while on leave and was unable to return to duty for nearly a year. The command was assumed during his absence by Major W. G. Clark, D.S.O., while Major S. Elliott became temporarily second in command. The loss of Lieut.-Col. Burnett was keenly felt. His nine months' command had been marked by a striking advance in the Battalion's efficiency and by the unswerving loyalty of all ranks under his command. Later he joined the Reserve Battalion in England, being subsequently transferred to employment in the War Office.

At Haillicourt the Battalion spent a few days in rest and training and returned to the trenches on the 24th January, occupying the same subsector as on the previous occasion with the 7th Londons once more on its left.

This tour of duty was marked by particularly heavy artillery activity on both sides, the Germans shelling our trenches and Maroc daily with great accuracy and using a good deal of gas shell. A certain number of casualties inevitably occurred, but, having regard to the continued intensity of the bombardment, the number was remarkably small.

On the 27th January the Kaiser's birthday was celebrated, and it was somewhat confidently anticipated that, as in 1915, the Germans would endeavour to score some success against the British. It had been known for some time that enemy mining operations in this area had been proceeding apace, and it therefore appeared not improbable that the Germans would endeavour to time the firing of their mines for the 27th. Preparations to meet this possibility were made. The Kaiser's birthday did indeed prove to be a day of considerable activity, and though the Germans delivered an abortive attack against the 15th Division on the left no infantry movement occurred opposite the 140th Brigade; and their activity was confined to shell fire, which assumed serious proportions on the 27th and again on the 28th. Our artillery, however, was ready with heavy retaliatory fire and by the evening of the 30th conditions in the Maroc sector had reverted to something approaching quietness.

During this period the newly arrived 16th (Irish) Division of the New Army was attached to the 47th Division for instruction in trench warfare, the 1/4th Londons taking over the supervision of the 8th Munsters, among whom unfortunately several casualties were caused by hostile shell fire on the 30th. The 31st January was marked principally by heavy British artillery fire, which elicited but little response from the enemy and inflicted considerable damage on his wire and defences generally.

The following day the 140th Brigade handed over its trenches to the 142nd, the 1/4th Londons being relieved by the 21st Londons and proceeding to rest billets in Haillicourt.

This tour of duty really brought to a conclusion the Battalion's service with the 47th Division, for though it did not part from the Brigade until the 9th February, the intervening days were spent in training, route-marching and cleaning.

On the 8th Brig.-Gen. Cuthbert—then in temporary command of the Division—inspected the 1/4th Londons prior to their departure, and addressed the troops; and the following day the Battalion marched to Béthune, entraining for Pont Remy (near Abbeville), and marched via Hallencourt to Citerne, where it went into billets attached to the 168th Brigade of the newly formed 56th (London) Division, an attachment which remained unbroken to the end of the War.

CHAPTER VII
THE 2/4TH BATTALION IN MALTA, GALLIPOLI PENINSULA AND SOUTHERN EGYPT

On the departure from Malta of the 1st London Infantry Brigade on the 2nd January 1915, the 2/1st Brigade became responsible in its place for the defence of the Fortress.

The 2/4th Londons settled down at St George's Barracks to a vigorous course of training. A musketry course under Fortress arrangements was begun and also special classes for the Machine-Gun and Transport sections, those for the latter being conducted by the A.S.C. at Musta Fort. The Battalion also provided a detached company to continue the duties of prisoner of war guard at Verdala Barracks, which had formerly been carried out by a company of the 1/4th Battalion.

Shortly after the relief of the garrison, Major J. F. F. Parr, R.A.M.C.T., who had been medical officer of the 1/4th Londons, was appointed to be M.O. in charge of Imtarfa Hospital.

During the 2/4th Londons' duty in Malta they were frequently called on to find the "public duties" consisting of an officer's guard at the Governor's Palace in Valetta, and guards over various government depôts, the first Palace Guard being found on the 9th February.

The 10th February was celebrated as a festival on the island, being the anniversary of St Paul's shipwreck, and the usual religious procession took place.

On the 11th February the Battalion moved from St George's Barracks to Floriana Barracks, Valetta.

The following day H.E. the Governor-General, General Sir Leslie Rundle, G.C.B., G.C.V.O., K.C.M.G., D.S.O., and staff left Malta for England, and on the 12th the new Governor-General (Field-Marshal Lord Methuen, G.C.B., G.C.V.O., C.M.G.) arrived and took up his residence at the Palace.

At this period occurred two events of paramount importance which materially affected the part which the Malta Station was destined to play in the War. The first of these was the opening on the 25th April 1915 of combined military and naval operations against the Gallipoli Peninsula; the second being the decision to throw in her lot with the Allies of Italy, who declared war on Austria on the 22nd May 1915.

The effect of the former of these events was to render British naval supremacy in the Mediterranean, and consequently the security of the Mediterranean Fleet Headquarters at Malta, of vital importance; and of the second to ensure both desiderata not only by the relief from the menace of a potential enemy at no great distance from the island, but also by the accession to the Allied strength of the powerful Italian Navy, which formed an additional protection to Malta against the possibility of a surprise raid by Austria.

From this date onwards, therefore, the function of Malta became one not so much of a fortress as of a base of operations, and a highly useful evacuating station for the casualties from Gallipoli who now began to be drafted to the island in great numbers. The accommodation on the island for hospitals being limited to the normal service requirements of peace time, the congestion rapidly became serious, and the troops of the garrison vacated their barracks, going under canvas in the barrack squares in order to provide accommodation for the sick and wounded; the 2/4th Londons moving to the parade ground at Ghain Tuffieha Camp.

On the 26th July a warning order was issued to the Battalion, which was still regarded as a draft-finding unit to the 1/4th Battalion, to prepare a draft of 400 other ranks to reinforce the 1/4th Battalion in France. The resulting deficiency in the 2/4th Battalion was to have been made up by a draft of equal size from the newly formed 4/4th Battalion in England, and although this latter draft actually embarked at Southampton, the order was cancelled; and it appears that the decision was made at this time, doubtless owing to the wastage of personnel at Gallipoli, to treat the 2/4th Londons as a service battalion and to leave the duty of provision of drafts for both the 1/4th and 2/4th Battalions to the 3/4th and 4/4th Battalions at home.

The following officers were invalided home from Malta: Major J. F. F. Parr, R.A.M.C.T., Capt. W. G. Hayward, 2/Lieuts. L. R. Chapman and N. L. Thomas. The Battalion was joined on the 13th August by: 2/Lieuts. B. F. L. Yeoman, H. G. Hicklenton, C. P. Darrington and N. W. Williams. Capt. Hayward's duties as Adjutant were taken over by Capt. L. C. Coates.

On the 12th July Lieut. Simpson was ordered to join the 2nd Royal Fusiliers, then attached to the 29th Division at the Dardanelles, and was posted to the Machine-Gun Section of that Battalion.

During this period training was proceeding to such extent as was possible in view of the congested state of the island, and detachments were supplied for fatigue duties at St Andrew's and St Patrick's Camps, Imtarfa Hospital, and for coast defence at 9th Mile Stone (between St Paul's and Salina Bays).

On the 12th August three signallers of the Battalion, the first other ranks to proceed on active service, left for the Dardanelles attached for duty to H.M.S. *Euryalus*. Two days later a warning order was issued for the Battalion to prepare for embarkation to Egypt.

Before departure from Malta the 2/4th Londons were inspected on the 14th August by H.E. the Governor, who subsequently issued a Fortress Order to the following effect:

> It is a pleasure to His Excellency to say with truth that it has been a source of satisfaction to him to have had the four Territorial battalions of the City of London Regiment under his command. Their conduct has been excellent under trying conditions lately on account of the heavy and unceasing fatigue work they have had to perform. Their appearance in Valetta, the smart way in which the men salute, the alacrity of the Main Guards in turning out, all show the efficiency of the Battalions. His Excellency wishes Officers, Non-Commissioned Officers and men "God Speed," and if from Egypt they go to the Front he looks to them with confidence to uphold the high reputation of the City of London Regiment.

On August 19th camp at Ghain Tuffieha was struck and the Battalion marched to Valetta, embarking next day on H.T. *Southlands*—which sailed for Egypt on the 21st, arriving at Alexandria on the 25th. The Battalion disembarked and marched to quarters under canvas at Sporting Club Camp on the seashore, where it remained until October 6th.

The strength on proceeding to Egypt was 30 officers and 765 other ranks, the officers, N.C.O.'s and men who were not passed fit for active service remaining under Lieut. V. W. Edwards in Malta for garrison duty, until September 1916, when they returned to the Reserve Battalion in England.

At Alexandria the Battalion provided duties, including the Main and Ras-el-tin Guards and town pickets; and also a detachment of 3 officers and 100 other ranks at Keb-el-Dick Fort, from which further guards were supplied for Chatty Cable Station, Supply Stores and other points of importance.

The Battalion was inspected by the Brigadier, the Earl of Lucan, on the 6th October, who in an address to the troops said:

> I have come here to-day to do something which is quite sad for me, and that is to say good-bye to you. I wish you all every success, good luck, and a safe return to England. I trust we shall all meet again.

I am proud that I have been in command of the 1st London Infantry Brigade and am exceedingly sorry that I am not coming with you. I had hoped that the four battalions of the London Regiment would have gone to the Front as a Brigade.

I much appreciate the hard work you all did at Malta and I send you from here with every confidence that you will acquit yourselves in the future as I know you have done in the past, and you will uphold the great reputation you have gained. I feel sure you will do great credit to yourselves and to the City of London Regiment wherever you go.

The commanding officer also received a letter from Major-Gen. Sir A. Wallace, C.B., commanding the troops at Alexandria, expressing his appreciation of the discipline and bearing of the Regiment and affirming his conviction of the exemplary manner in which it would carry out its duties on active service.

The same day embarkation commenced on to H.T. *Karroo* at Alexandria, and on the 9th, under escort of two destroyers, the *Karroo* sailed for Mudros, arriving on the evening of 12th October. The following officers did not accompany the Battalion to Mudros:

> Capts. G. H. Moore and H. Parkhouse (seconded for duty, in the Censor's Office, Cairo).
>
> Lieut. H. W. Dennis (granted leave to England) and 2/Lieut. F. R. C. Bradford (in hospital).

For two days the Battalion remained on board in Mudros Harbour, but on the 15th was transhipped to H.T. *Sarnia*, which put to sea about 3 p.m. At midnight the transport anchored off Cape Helles and the Battalion disembarked on to the Gallipoli Peninsula at W. Beach and bivouacked in dugouts in the early hours of the 16th October 1916.

The Battalion was now attached to the Royal Naval Division, the infantry of which consisted of the following units:

ROYAL NAVAL DIVISION

Major-Gen. A. PARIS, C.B.

1ST BRIGADE—Brig.-Gen. David Mercer, C.B.

"Hawke"   Battalion.

"Drake"   "

"Hood"   "

"Nelson"   "

2/3rd London Regiment.

2/4th London Regiment.

2ND BRIGADE—Brig.-Gen. C. N. Trotman, C.B.

1st Royal Marines.

2nd Royal Marines.

"Anson"   Battalion.

"Howe"   "

2/1st London Regiment.

2/2nd London Regiment.

The Division was attached with the 42nd (South Lancashire) and 52nd (Lowland) Territorial Divisions to the VIII Corps (Lieut.-Gen. Sir Francis Davies, K.C.B.).

The 2/4th Londons landed on the Peninsula at a critical period in the fortunes of the expedition, and in order to render clear the position of affairs in the middle of October, some reference is necessary to the course which events had taken since the inception of the campaign.

After witnessing the "amphibious battle" between British battleships and the land forts of the Dardanelles, which took place on the 18th March 1915, General Sir Ian Hamilton had formed the conclusion that the Navy would be unable to open the way to Constantinople without the fullest co-operation of all the military forces at his disposal.

The Gallipoli Peninsula runs in a south-westerly direction from its isthmus at Bulair, where it is spanned by fortified lines, for some fifty-two miles to its extreme point, Cape Helles, attaining in its centre a breadth of nearly twelve miles.

The northern coast of the northern portion slopes abruptly towards the Gulf of Zeros in a chain of hills extending as far as Cape Suvla, the declivitous nature of the coastline precluding serious military landings. In the southern half, which is more accessible from the sea, the main features consist of Achi Baba, dominating the extreme end of the Peninsula; Sari Bair Mountain, a succession of almost perpendicular escarpments overlooking Suvla Bay; and the Kilid Bahr plateau protecting the forts of the Narrows against attacks from the north coast.

As a result of a reconnaissance of this unpromising feature it became abundantly evident to Sir Ian Hamilton that he could achieve success and overcome the difficulties caused by the inadequacy of the landing places and the improvements made by the Turks in their defences since the 18th March, only by rapidly flinging ashore the largest possible force at several landing places simultaneously. The glorious achievement of the landings at Cape Helles and Anzac on the 25th April are now matters of history, and lack of space makes it impossible to repeat the epic here. We can only record the fact that in face of innumerable difficulties and a murderous fire from the Turkish lines and forts, landings were in fact effected. By the end of the month, by dint of furious and practically continuous fighting, the French and British were definitely though precariously established on the south-west extremity of the Peninsula on a line running from sea to sea about three miles north of Cape Helles.

It was obviously essential to exploit the initial success as quickly as possible in order to carry the Allied lines forward before the Turkish reinforcements should arrive, and in spite of the exhaustion of the troops, fighting of the most desperate character continued on both the Helles and the Anzac fronts throughout May. But so enormously strong were the Turkish entanglements and trenches, and so well placed their machine-guns, that the Allied progress was slow and achieved only at appalling cost.

On the 6th-8th June a last attempt was made on the Helles front to carry the village of Krithia and the slopes of Achi Baba, but this attack met with a similar fate to its predecessors, and the nett result after a severe struggle was an advance of some 200 yards; the line thus gained representing the most advanced position ever occupied on this front.

As a result of strong representations by the Commander-in-Chief, fresh forces were concentrated by the end of June consisting of the 10th, 11th and 13th Divisions of the New Armies, and the 52nd (Lowland), 53rd (Wessex) and 54th (East Anglian) Territorial Divisions, the two last-named being represented by infantry only.

The impossibility of attaining further success by frontal attacks at Helles now being clear, Sir Ian Hamilton determined to employ his fresh forces in endeavouring to strangle the Turkish defence by an attack across the Peninsula from Anzac, in a south-easterly direction towards Maidos; supported by a fresh landing farther up the coast at Suvla Bay.

V Beach, Cape Helles

The new operation was launched on the 6th August. The main attack from Anzac involved as a preliminary objective the occupation of the heights of Sari Bair, the possession of which would enable us to bring rifle fire to bear on the enemy communications with Helles and, moreover, bring the Narrows within field-gun range. So nearly to success did this attack attain that had it received the support which had been anticipated from the Suvla Bay landing, with its consequent diversion of Turkish reserves, there can be little doubt that the advance would have developed into one of first-rate importance. New Zealand troops did, in fact, scale the heights of the main ridge, but in subsequent counter-attacks were forced to yield to the enemy, and the few hundred yards of ground which stood between us and decisive victory were denied to us.

The actual landing at Suvla on the 8th was effected, as had been hoped, as a complete surprise to the enemy, and met with little resistance. But the exhaustion of the troops, caused by a failure in the water supply arrangements, led to the waste of many valuable hours of daylight in which no advance was possible and enabled the enemy to prepare a stubborn resistance to our further attacks, and the opportunity passed for ever.

During August and September the supply of reinforcements and munitions for the Dardanelles Army fell off seriously, and in the middle of October the position had become stabilised.

The general situation had indeed changed most unfavourably for our chances of ultimate success. The wholesale retirement of our Russian Allies during the summer had released large numbers of enemy reserves for the Gallipoli theatre, and the recrudescence of enemy submarine activity in the Ægean Sea increased the difficulties of supply and transport from the bases at Mudros and Imbros, so that whereas the Allied forces had indeed shot their bolt, the enemy's strength was still increasing.

Since the Suvla landing no further active operations had been attempted, but constant pressure was maintained on the Turkish lines by our trench garrisons in mining and bombing, while our artillery continually harassed him in his advanced and rearward positions.

The 1st Brigade was out of the trenches on the arrival of the 2/4th Londons and the first few days were therefore spent by the Battalion in the rest camp at W. Beach (Cape Helles) in providing working parties and unloading stores, while the senior officers of the Battalion visited a sector of the trenches. The fact should not be overlooked in connection with the 2/4th Battalion's record that owing to the narrowness of our foothold on the Peninsula it was impossible to withdraw troops, even when "at rest," beyond the shelled zone, and the beaches were constantly under fire of heavy batteries on the Asiatic side.

On the 19th Oct. the Adjutant, Capt. L. C. Coates, was admitted to hospital suffering from pleurisy and his duties were taken over by Capt. J. R. Webster.

The Allied lines on the Helles front stretched from sea to sea in a direction from south-east to north-west about a thousand yards short of Krithia village. The trench system was divided into two approximately equal portions by the Krithia Road, which, connecting Krithia with the village of Sedd-el-Bahr, near Cape Helles, traversed a ridge which formed the backbone of this part of the Peninsula. On the right of the road the lines were held by the French, their right flank (nearest the Narrows) being drawn back slightly on the near side of a deep gorge called Kereves Dere, the waters of which discharged into the Dardanelles. On the left of the road the lines were in the occupation of the VIII Corps, and were divided into three sections, of which at this date the right was held by the 52nd, the centre by the Royal Naval and the left, next the Ægean Sea, by the 42nd Division.

The VIII Corps front was intersected by two deep ravines respectively called Gully Ravine, near the Ægean coast, and Krithia Nullah on the immediate left of the Krithia Road, and both of these, originating in the slopes of Achi Baba, formed deep furrows through the British lines, running towards the sea in a direction roughly parallel to the Krithia Road. The high ground between the ravines formed a plateau covered with scrub and gorse, and intersected in all directions by water courses of less importance; the whole area being uncomfortably exposed to direct observation from the Turkish defences on Achi Baba. All along this front the British and Turkish lines were close together—in some places only about 30 yards apart—and a continual and deadly warfare, in which bombs played a prominent part, was being waged from sapheads pushed out from the main defensive positions and held by barricades.

The Royal Naval Division's subsector included several of such centres of activity, notably at the Northern and Southern Barricades, on the left, and at Worcester Barricade, a sap pushed forward from the Rue de Paris, in the centre.

The exposure of the whole British area to observation rendered necessary the use of very long communication trenches, to afford cover to the mule transport whereby the trench garrisons were supplied with rations and trench stores. These wide mule tracks, doubled for upward and downward traffic, were carried forward from the crest of the plateau above the beaches at Cape Helles to within a few hundred yards of the front trenches.

On the 20th October the 1st R.N. Brigade relieved the 2nd Brigade in the centre subsection, the forward system of trenches being occupied by "Drake," "Nelson," "Hood" and "Hawke," the 2/4th Londons relieving the 2/2nd Londons in the Eski line, a reserve line some 1500 yards in rear of the most advanced trenches. The Battalion occupied this line with two companies each side of the Eastern Mule Trench. The relief was carried out without difficulty, but during the move forward from bivouacs the Battalion incurred its first battle casualties, Capt. H. Morris and Privates Housden and Maunder being wounded.

At this time the Turkish Feast of Barram was proceeding, and when it drew to a close on the evening of the 22nd it was anticipated with some confidence that the enemy would attempt a demonstration against the Allied positions. The only activity, however, was on our side and our batteries both on land and sea gave the Turks a particularly hot time during the evening. During this tour the weather began to break and heavy rains fell, but apart from the wet condition of the trenches and the consequent additional work in keeping them in repair the tour of duty passed without incident of an unusual nature. On the 22nd half the company officers and non-commissioned officers were attached for instruction in the front line to the R.N. Battalions, their places being taken after forty-eight hours by the other half.

On the 27th the 2nd Brigade returned to the line relieving the 1st Brigade, which withdrew on relief to the Rest Camp, the 2/4th Londons handing over their positions in the Eski line to the 2/2nd Londons.

This day General Sir Ian Hamilton handed over command-in-chief of the Dardanelles Army to General Sir C. C. Monro, K.C.B. Sir Charles Monro's duty on assuming command was in the first instance to report as to the desirability, on purely military grounds, of evacuating the Peninsula, and alternatively as to the force required to bring the campaign to a successful issue. A reconnaissance of the position led him to the conclusion that evacuation should be taken in hand, and the adoption of this course received official approval, with results which will be recorded in their place.

In the Rest Camp the Battalion spent six days, which were occupied in work on new winter quarters and dugouts, and which passed quietly but for heavy shelling on the 29th October and the 1st November from enemy batteries on the Asiatic shore; but fortunately no casualties were suffered.

The month of November was occupied in duty in and out of the line, tours in the trenches being for seven days, followed by seven days in the Rest Camp at Cape Helles. For both the tours in line the 2/4th Londons were in reserve in the Eski lines though on each occasion companies were sent in turn to the front trenches for instruction in trench warfare. For this purpose they were attached to "Hawke," "Hood" and "Drake" Battalions.

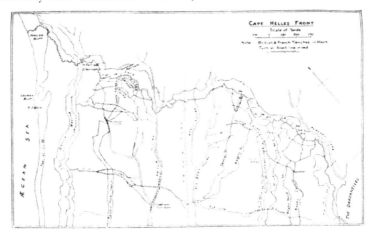

GALLIPOLI PENINSULA—CAPE HELLES TRENCHES, 1915

The Turks at this period were comparatively quiet beyond a certain amount of artillery fire, and for the companies in the Eski line the time passed by no means unpleasantly. Engaged in strengthening and improving the defences during working hours, they were allowed when off duty to go in small parties down to Gully Beach on the Ægean coast. These small excursions were the means of providing a change of diet, for the men seldom returned without a good haul of fish, caught by a stratagem in which, so rumour has it, the Mills Bomb figured prominently.

It was not long, however, before the Battalion discovered that their worst enemy on the Peninsula was the elements. The summer heat had now broken and the autumn rains were beginning with all their sub-tropical violence. The Battalion's first introduction to these deluges occurred on the 10th November, when, having just returned from the trenches to the Rest Camp, it was treated to a violent rainstorm which flooded all the dugouts and shelters.

A week later when the 2/4th Londons had returned to the line a thunderstorm burst over the lines and heavy rain fell for about two hours, flooding many trenches and rendering them almost untenable. This storm was followed by several days of rain and high wind which inflicted considerable hardship on the troops, not only while they were actually in the trenches but also by reason of the serious damage caused to the Rest Camp, so that on coming out of the line when the tour of duty was over the conditions of discomfort were unabated.

This sort of incident, which recurred during the rainy season with monotonous frequency, was far more productive of discomfort and ill effects than it would have been on the Western front; since owing to the restriction of space it was impossible to attain on the Peninsula to anything approaching the degree of "back-of-the-line" organisation which was reached in France. Wet clothes, therefore, remained wet until the sun dried them, and the inevitable result was a constantly high proportion of sickness, which during the last few months on the Peninsula accounted for vastly more casualties than the enemy's weapons. But under the most unpromising circumstances the British soldier invariably manages to make himself as comfortable as possible and to undergo severe privations with a sort of fatalistic and stoical cheerfulness, which he vainly endeavours to conceal by much "grousing." And so on the Peninsula, a locality scarcely associated as a rule with ideas of amusement, a certain amount of recreation was obtained by football matches, and by the efforts of the bands of the four London battalions who played in different battalion areas each evening when the Brigades were out of the trenches. The officers also were able to obtain some exercise through the kindness of the officers of the 2nd Royal Fusiliers (29th Division) who lent their horses, on which a few pleasant 'longshore excursions' were made.

The few days out of the trenches were occupied in supplying working parties for the construction of the new winter quarters.

On the 20th November the Battalion was issued with gas masks, and received its first instruction in defensive measures against gas attacks. It was believed at this time that steps were being taken by the Turks to employ poison gas against the Allies, but none was actually used against the 2/4th Londons.

Hitherto the Battalion had fortunately suffered but few casualties at the hands of the enemy, the total in all ranks amounting to 4 killed and 5 wounded. Sickness, however, now began to take a heavy toll of all units, and this became especially serious after the 26th November, on which day a storm of unprecedented violence burst over the Peninsula, accompanied by torrential rain, which rapidly filled the trenches and forced the occupants on both sides on to the parapets, where they crouched unable to move for fear of falling into the trenches and being swept away by the torrents which poured down them and overflowed on to the land adjoining. In the Rest Camps the dugouts were rapidly flooded out and the troops spent a night of bitter exposure. In the afternoon of the following day the wind suddenly shifted to the north, and a biting frost ensued. The cold was agonising and the water froze around the men's feet as they slept from sheer exhaustion. Greatcoats which had been drenched by the rains were so stiffened by the frost that they stood up by themselves. So severe was the cold that it was only by keeping the men constantly at work with their shovels that many were kept alive at all. On the 28th snow began to fall, and the blizzard continued throughout the day and during the 29th. In the meantime the sea had become very rough and the temporary quays and breakwaters suffered great damage, both on the Peninsula and at Mudros and Imbros, and this added seriously to the difficulties of the already over-burdened transport services.

During the first few days of December over 200 deaths occurred from exposure and over 10,000 sick were evacuated from the Peninsula; and from the statements of deserters it is probable that the Turks suffered even more severely. A famous war correspondent who was at Cape Helles at the time wrote: "Never probably since Crimean days have British forces in the field had to endure such cold as the last days of November brought to our men at the Dardanelles."

On the 29th 2/Lieut. P. C. Darrington was evacuated to hospital.[3]

[3] Darrington on recovery transferred to the 5th London Regiment (L.R.B.) with whom he served till almost the end of the War, being unhappily killed a few days before the Armistice.

On the 1st December the 1st Brigade returned to the trenches and this time the 2/4th Londons took over a sector of the front line between "Drake" on the right, and "Hood" on the left. The sector included a part of the front line known as Rue de Paris, from Sap B to Sap N, which was occupied by A and C Companies, while D Company went into support in Worcester Flats with B in reserve in Munster Terrace, the machine-guns being in front line positions. This day the enemy's artillery was more active than it had been for months, and for three hours in the afternoon the British lines generally were subjected to a violent bombardment by field guns and howitzers; but although an attack was believed to be imminent no infantry movements developed, and in the evening the situation became quieter.

Although this tour of duty was not unusually active, there were abundant signs of a considerable accession of strength behind the Turkish lines, and daily his artillery became a little more active, a good deal of shelling being caused by the registering of fresh batteries on our lines. The Turkish snipers also became particularly annoying, and their efficiency reflected itself in our casualty list which, though not large, was somewhat longer than usual. On the evenings of the 9th and the 11th the Turks employed a field searchlight from behind Achi Baba, but the experiment was not repeated and led to no incident of interest.

Col. Dunfee was granted a month's leave of absence on urgent private affairs, and left the Peninsula for England on the 5th, the command of the Battalion devolving upon Major V. H. Seyd who continued in command, with the acting rank of Lieut.-Col., until after the final evacuation of the Peninsula, the duties of second in command being assumed by Capt. R. N. Arthur.

During this tour a draft of 49 N.C.O.'s and men under 2/Lieuts. J. W. Price and S. Davis joined the 2/4th Londons from England, and was posted to companies. 2/Lieuts. N. L. Thomas and F. R. C. Bradford rejoined from hospital.

The following is an extract from Battalion orders for the 12th December:

> The Commanding Officer would like to place on record that whilst with the Grenade Section in the trenches last week No. 2827 Pte. Hedger threw back a live grenade which had fallen into the trench, thereby saving his comrades and himself from injury.

On the 9th December a relief was effected, combined with a readjustment of the boundaries of the Divisional sector on the arrival of the 29th Division from the Suvla Bay front; and practically half the centre subsection from Sap F (half-way along the 2/4th Londons' line) to the left, occupied by two companies of the 2/4th Londons, "Hood" and "Hawke," was handed over to the King's Own Scottish Borderers. On the following morning A, B and C Companies and Battalion Headquarters withdrew to the Rest Camp. D Company remained in line attached to "Drake" until the 11th, when it rejoined the Battalion.

This relief being, as already stated, carried out in the course of a readjustment of the line, the Brigade spent only four days out of the trenches, and on the 15th it took over a fresh sector facing Kereves Dere on the right of Achi Baba Nullah. Of this new sector about 750 yards were taken over from the 2nd R.N. Brigade while the French troops were relieved in about 250 yards of trench adjoining on the right. The sector was occupied with "Nelson" on the left, and "Drake" and A and B Companies, 2/4th Londons, on the right. Battalion Headquarters and C and D Companies occupied the Eski line in rear of the new sector, in this part called the Tranchée d'Amade, with one company each side of the junction with the main communication trench, the Avenue de Constantinople.

The days following the occupation of this sector were marked by considerable activity on the part of the enemy's bombers. The hostile trenches opposite the 2/4th Londons were on an overage about 70 yards from the British front line and numerous saps had been pushed out toward them, from the heads of which the struggle continued without cessation, the Grenadiers on each side plying their objectionable trade without abatement.

On the 17th B Company relieved A Company in the front trenches. Capt. F. C. J. Read this day was evacuated to hospital, being followed there next day by Lieut. R. C. Dickins.

On the 20th December the announcement was made in Corps orders of the successful evacuation of the Suvla and Anzac positions which had taken place during the night of the 19th.

The details of the scheme for this evacuation had been carefully worked out by Sir William Birdwood who had been appointed to command of the Dardanelles Army on the formation of the Salonika Army (Sir C. C. Monro assuming supreme command of the Mediterranean Forces). The scheme provided for the completion of this difficult operation in three stages, the first of which involved the embarkation of all troops, animals and supplies not required for a prolonged campaign; this was to be followed by the evacuation of troops, guns, stores, etc., not immediately required for the defence of our positions, while the third and final stage consisted of the embarkation of the rearguard troops and the destruction of all guns, animals and stores which could not be removed.

The actual evacuation had been fixed for as early a date as possible owing to the improbability of the long continuance of favourable weather; and at both Suvla and Anzac the process was completed without a hitch of any kind, only a small quantity of stores having to be destroyed, and without any interference on the part of the enemy.

Almost immediately after this operation a marked increase in the Turkish activity on the Helles front took place, probably on account of the release of large numbers of his batteries in the evacuated sectors.

In announcing the completion of this operation, the special order of the day affirmed that the Helles position was not to be abandoned, but that on the contrary the VIII Corps was entrusted with the task of holding to this theatre of operations as large as possible a force of Turkish troops in order to prevent their employment elsewhere. To this end the battalions holding the line were urged to maintain their pressure against the enemy at all points while schemes were evolved for the construction of deep dugouts, the improvement of reserve lines, and other works, which would only be necessary in the event of a long continued occupation of the Peninsula.

Information was even disseminated that large reinforcements totalling over 1600 all ranks were on the way, and were expected shortly. But behind all these precautions against the leakage of information among the Turks as to our intentions, and under cover of the various fictions above described, preparations were being pressed forward for the evacuation of the Helles front also; preparations which needed particular care not only by reason of the greater activity of the enemy than at Suvla and Anzac, but also because the enemy having been successfully hoodwinked on the former occasion it hardly appeared probable that we should be so successful a second time in masking our intentions.

Another very severe storm broke over Cape Helles on the 21st December, accompanied by heavy rain, and one of the 2/4th London machine-guns was struck by lightning in the trenches. It became evident that with the likelihood of an early complete break up in the weather the final evacuation must not be delayed; and accordingly it was fixed for the 8th January 1916, or the first fine night after that date.

On the 21st Lieut. L. A. Dickins was seriously wounded and evacuated from the Peninsula. This tour of duty indeed proved the most costly in personnel which the Battalion had carried out, and among N.C.O.'s and men 4 were killed and 13 wounded.

On the 22nd the 1st R.N. Brigade made a further "side-step" to the right in the trenches, and in the course of the readjustment A and B Companies of the 2/4th Londons were relieved in the trenches and withdrew to a fresh Rest Camp, called Cæsar's Camp. The rest of the Battalion, however, remained in the Tranchée d'Amade until after Christmas.

On the 23rd December 2/Lieut. C. S. G. Blows joined the Battalion from England.

Owing to the kindness of Mrs Dunfee and other ladies interested in the 2/4th Londons, Christmas gifts and cards had been received for every member of the Battalion, and these materially helped to infuse a little cheerfulness into a somewhat depressing and comfortless Christmastide. On Christmas Day the Battalion was practically complete in the Tranchée d'Amade, B Company and two platoons of A Company having moved forward once more from Cæsar's Camp.

The general scheme for the evacuation of the Helles front was similar to that employed at Anzac and Suvla, and in the course of the second stage of the operation, detachments of the 2/4th Londons, consisting of 63 other ranks under Lieut. S. N. Davies and 50 other ranks under 2/Lieut. S. Davis were embarked for Mudros on the night of the 31st December. These were followed the next night by 5 officers and 147 other ranks under Capt. R. N. Keen.

On the 3rd January 1916, the machine-guns of the Battalion, now increased to six, were evacuated in charge of a N.C.O. and two men, and on the following day the last battle casualties occurred, three men being slightly wounded in the Rest Camp.

The preparations for final evacuation were now practically complete. A strong embarkation staff had been formed to deal with the rapid embarkation of the last troops as they should reach the beaches; and new lines of defence guarding the beaches had been prepared for occupation in case the enemy should become aware of the operation and harass it.

On the night of the 6th/7th January, a fourth detachment of 4 officers and 118 other ranks of the Battalion under Capt. Arthur left the Peninsula, and the next night Major Seyd in command of the remainder of the Battalion (8 officers and 155 other ranks) embarked at V Beach. This completed the safe evacuation of the whole Battalion with the exception of four men who were left behind attached to the "Dumeszyl Battery" under Commander Alan Campbell, R.N.D. (since killed), for demolition work. After completion of their hazardous duties all the members of this brave unit were also safely embarked.

The total strength of the Battalion on evacuating the Peninsula (including the transport and other details who had remained at Mudros and Imbros) was 23 officers and about 560 other ranks. The total casualties sustained at the hands of the enemy had been 2 officers wounded, 16 N.C.O.'s and men killed and 38 wounded, the remaining reduction of strength having been due to sickness and exposure.

On the 7th January the enemy opened an intense bombardment, said to be the heaviest since the original landing in April 1915, on our trenches; the shelling lasting from noon till 3.30 p.m., at which time two Turkish mines were sprung near Fusilier Bluff. No attack developed except at this point, where a half-hearted advance of the enemy was easily dispersed.

The 8th January was calm and still, but at night the weather became stormy, and a steady and increasing swell did not tend to facilitate the task of rapid embarkation, and indeed rendered it very doubtful whether it would be possible to get the last troops away at all. This caused considerable anxiety to the Embarkation Staff whose task was not lightened by the knowledge of the presence of an enemy submarine which (unsuccessfully) torpedoed H.M.S. *Prince George*. Add to this the possibility that the enemy might discover the retirement in time to give trouble on the beaches; and it will be possible in at least a small measure to appreciate the great skill with which this apparently impracticable task was brought to a successful issue. By 3.30 a.m. the evacuation was completed and at 4 a.m. two of our magazines were blown up. The conflagration caused by these appears to have been the first intimation of our departure received by the Turks who promptly shelled our vacated lines heavily until 6.30 a.m.

All material was removed except a few unserviceable guns, some 500 animals and a large quantity of stores, all of which were destroyed.

It is impossible to refrain from remarking on the excellent organisation and discipline with which the evacuation was carried out, and also on the extraordinary luck which was vouchsafed both at Anzac and Suvla in the concealment of the moon.

The Gallipoli expedition must live for ever in the annals of the world's military history, as one of the most remarkable exploits ever carried out. Although failure ensued, it was indeed a glorious failure, and the wonder is rather that success was so nearly attained. The base of operations at Alexandria was 800 miles distant, and the lines of communication possessed only two inadequate and unprotected harbours at Mudros and Imbros respectively. The whole occupied zone, and also the sea in its vicinity, was all the time under hostile observation and fire; there were no roads worthy of the name, no storehouses or railways, and the activity of enemy submarines made it impossible to send to the Peninsula any storeship over 1500 tons.

Yet in the face of all these obstacles not only was the landing effected, but our position maintained for nearly nine months and the whole force safely re-embarked; and the memory of it must live for ever as one of the greatest pages of the history of the war.

After the evacuation, an appreciative order was published in R.N. Divisional Orders complimenting the troops on the discipline and devotion which had sustained them during the hardships of the campaign, and which alone had rendered the task of evacuation possible of accomplishment. General Paris, commanding the Division, wrote personally to the Commanding Officer a letter in which he said: "I must thank you and your Battalion for the good work you did when with us on the Peninsula, we all admired the cheerful spirit your men showed under very trying circumstances."

At Mudros the connection of the 2/4th Londons with the Royal Naval Division was severed, and they became temporarily attached to the 29th Division. A few days were spent on the island in rest and reorganisation, and during its stay there the Battalion was rejoined by the Transport Section and other details who had been detached from it during its duty at the Dardanelles; and a great deal of satisfaction was caused by the distribution of mails from home, the delivery of which had been delayed by the evacuation.

On the 11th January Capt. R. N. Keen was admitted to hospital, and on the 14th Sergt. F. W. Walker left the Battalion for England to take up a commission. The record of this N.C.O. will be referred to again later in connection with the 3/4th Battalion to which he was subsequently attached.

The Battalion embarked on H.T. *Ionian* for Alexandria on the 18th, arriving there three days later. Disembarkation took place on the following day, and the Battalion entrained to Wardan, a camping ground near Cairo, where it took up quarters under canvas and became attached with the other three London Battalions to the 53rd Division, Major-Gen. A. G. Dallas, C.B., in command. At Wardan company training was carried out until the 16th February, when the 2/4th Londons, with two companies of the 2/2nd Londons attached, moved by rail to Beni Mazar, where it became part of the Minia Force.

At the period of the 2/4th Londons' return to Egypt the Eastern frontier, on which the Turks had attempted to force the Suez Canal defences about a year previously, had become quiet, and the principal cause of anxiety centred in the Western Desert where the attitude of the Senussi, a warlike tribe of Arabs, had created a situation of some difficulty, which was rendered more complex by the possibility of internal disorders and religious unrest in the Nile Valley and the Delta district.

On the outbreak of war between England and Turkey the Senussi had not at first shown any disposition towards hostile action, but under the influence of a Germanised Turk named Gaafer Pasha they had become more truculent as the summer of 1915 wore on. Several breaches of the peace which occurred in the autumn left no room for doubt that military operations would be necessary to bring the Senussi to a due sense of their proper behaviour.

In November 1915 Lieut.-Gen. Sir John Maxwell, commanding in chief the forces in Egypt, concentrated the Western Force at Mersa Matruh, a town on the Mediterranean coast some 180 miles west of Alexandria. Under Maj.-Gen. Wallace, C.B., to whom command of the Mersa Matruh troops was given, several vigorous little operations were successfully carried out against the tribesmen; but the lack of camel transport and water supply arrangements restricted the scope of his activities. Preparations were therefore made to remedy these defects and thus render possible the despatch of a serious punitive expedition into the desert.

On the 11th February a newly concentrated force of the Senussi occupied the Baharia Oasis, and on the 27th of the same month they also seized the Farafra and Dakhla Oases. To combat the serious menace to the Nile Valley offered by these fresh signs of activity, Sir John Maxwell formed a new command, known as the Southern Force, under Maj.-Gen. J. Adye, C.B., with Headquarters at Beni Suef, a township on the Nile some 175 miles south of Cairo. This Southern Force was concentrated in four distinct areas for the protection of the Nile Valley and the cultivated areas, the three northern areas respectively concentrated at Wadi Natrun, Beni Salama and the Fayoum, being grouped under command of Maj.-Gen. Dallas; the fourth and southernmost being located in the Minia and Assiut provinces under Brig.-Gen. A. Stirling.

General Stirling's Minia Force was being concentrated at the period when the 2/4th Londons joined it, and comprised the following formations:

- Highland Mounted Brigade (dismounted).
- 1st Australian Light Horse Brigade.
- One squadron of Cavalry (Egyptian Army).
- Detachment of R.F.C. with two Aeroplanes.
- Nos. 1 and 2 Armoured Trains.
- 1/4th Glamorgan Battery R.F.A.
- One section Hong-Kong Mountain Battery.
- 2/1st Cheshire Field Company R.E.
- 2/4th London Regiment.

- Two Companies 2/2nd London Regiment,

and was subsequently increased by the arrival of further units as follows:

- One squadron Armoured Cars R.N. Division.
- Half section Camel Transport Corps.
- One Company Australian Camel Corps.

In spite of the great strategic importance of the Oases it was found impossible at the moment to undertake active operations, and the activities of the Minia Force were therefore confined to defensive measures. The whole Nile Valley at this time was infected by powerful religious and political influences which were at work to endeavour to induce the native population to co-operate with the enemy against the British, and although these influences had not attained the success hoped for by their instigators, they had taken a certain hold on all classes of the civilian population. It was, therefore, extremely important to counterbalance this smouldering agitation by the presence of strong military forces in provincial stations, primarily to prevent the occurrence of disturbances which might be fomented in the absence of troops, and to safeguard points of military importance, such as railway stations, bridges and canals. The natives of Egypt, though not of warlike character, are capable of violent fanatical outbursts, and the continued presence of the military, combined with frequent displays of their force, was the best means of preventing altogether disturbances which might assume very serious proportions.

Such was briefly the position of affairs at the period of the 2/4th Londons' attachment to the Minia Force, but shortly after their arrival a distinct improvement in the outlook was caused by the dispersal of the Senussi forces in the battle of Agagia on the 26th February 1916. This time it was possible to exploit the success, and the desert column pushed forward to Sollum which was occupied on the 14th March. The effect of this signal success on British prestige throughout Egypt was marked, and this effect was enhanced by the continued failure of the Turks to make any impression in the East on the Suez Canal defences. The Senussi forces were now practically disposed of, only about 3000 remaining in the field, and this remnant appeared to be disheartened, while the reputation of their commander, Sayed Ahmed, both as a temporal leader and a spiritual guide, had waned.

The danger, however, was by no means past, and the occupation by the Senussi of the Baharia Oasis, which followed soon after the battle of

Agagia, created a serious menace to the part of the Nile Valley for which the Minia Force was responsible.

The Minia District includes about 65 miles of a strip of cultivated land running north and south along the left bank of the Nile, varying in width from 7 to 14 miles. This area is intersected for irrigation purposes by numerous canals of which the largest, Bahr Yusef, runs roughly parallel to the Nile near the western edge of the cultivated strip. Beyond it sand-dunes run for some two miles into the desert. Minia itself is a town of some importance, containing about 35,000 inhabitants. The loot to be obtained from its banks and merchants, as well as the possibility of obtaining recruits from the Bedouin population, and the certainty of creating a strong anti-British influence, seemed to offer considerable inducements to raiding parties from the Baharia Oasis, and it was against this danger that the protective measures of the Minia Force were directed.

The troops at Beni Mazar, which is on the main railway line 26 miles north of Minia, comprised the following:

- 2/4th London Regiment.
- Two Companies 2/2nd London Regiment.
- One Camel Machine-Gun Section, Lovat's Scouts.
- One Troop Australian Light Horse.
- Detachment of Cheshire Field Company R.E.
- No. 2 Armoured Train.

A detached post of one company of infantry (supplied by 2/4th Londons) was furnished from Beni Mazar to guard a bridge at Saqula over the Bahr Yusef. The whole of the troops at Beni Mazar came under command of A/Lieut.-Col. V. H. Seyd.

At Beni Mazar the 2/4th Londons settled down quickly to their new surroundings and carried out company training to the extent which the circumstances permitted. The situation, however, placed a considerable restriction on the activities of the Battalion in this direction, as it was held at all times under instant readiness to move. A good deal of attention was paid, nevertheless, to long distance route marching with the deliberate intention of hardening the troops in preparation for the possibility of an advance against the Baharia Oasis.

On the 26th February a detachment of the 2/2nd Londons proceeded to Nag Hamadi to guard the Nile bridgehead there. Col. Dunfee this day returned from leave and took over once more the command of the

Battalion and of the forces at Beni Mazar, A/Lieut.-Col. Seyd reverting to his former duties as second in command with the rank of Major.

On the 28th and 29th trial runs were made on the armoured train from Beni Mazar to Maghaga with the double object of giving the troops practice in rapid entrainment and of reminding the inhabitants of the presence of British forces. A demonstration march was made through the streets of Maghaga, but the demeanour of the natives was found to be quite satisfactory. The behaviour of the inhabitants of Beni Mazar also was so peaceful at this time that it was found possible to relax somewhat the strict orders as to permitting troops to walk out in the town, and henceforth they were allowed to walk in pairs instead of parties of six as had formerly been the case, though side arms were still worn at all times.

On the 1st March Capt. H. G. Stanham was appointed to command the Saqula detachment.

The working hours of the Battalion at this period were early in the day, owing to the advance of the hot season, but in spite of the severe change from the trying conditions to which it had been subjected at Cape Helles two months earlier, the Battalion showed a remarkably good bill of health.

At the beginning of March the command in chief in Egypt was assumed by Sir Archibald Murray, and in the rearrangement of the defensive forces in the Nile Valley which ensued, the Beni Mazar troops ceased to form part of the Minia Force, which was extended farther to the south, and became attached to the Northern Force (Southern Area) under Maj.-Gen. Dallas.

On the 3rd and 5th of March practice alarms took place and the Beni Mazar Force moved tactically to Tambu, taking up a position there for the defence of the railway. The strength of the 2/4th Londons on parade at the second alarm was 16 officers and 450 other ranks.

Throughout the period of the 2/4th Londons' occupation of Beni Mazar they received the greatest possible attention and kindness from the local Egyptian residents, who overwhelmed them with presents of eggs, fowls, turkeys, sheep, cigarettes, fruit and other "consumable stores," which needless to say were gratefully received as a pleasant alternative to rations. The officers of the Battalion were constantly entertained by the local dignitaries, who extended to them all the hospitality in their power, and among whom must be mentioned Mahomed Marzouk, Mamur Markaz, Merza Mohed Ali F. Bey, Abdul Gawad, Mahomed Zubi Abd el Razech, Ahmed H. el Keesz and H. Abd el Rezik.

On the 6th April the Saqula detachment was withdrawn and on the 12th the Battalion left Beni Mazar, handing over duties to the 2/5th Devonshire Regiment. The Battalion strength, 23 officers and 586 other ranks, proceeded by train *via* Cairo and Alexandria, travelling all night, and detrained the following day at Sidi Gaber, marching to quarters under canvas at Sidi Bishr. Here the 2/1st London Infantry Brigade came together again as a Brigade for the first time since its occupation of Malta, under the command of Col. Dunfee.

On the 17th April the Brigade embarked at Alexandria on H.T. *Transylvania* which carried in addition to the Brigade, detachments of Colonial and Imperial troops, totalling together 130 officers and about 3000 other ranks. The following appointments were made on H.T. *Transylvania*:

    O.C. Ship—Col. Vickers Dunfee, V.D.

    Ship's Adjutant—Capt. J. R. Webster

    2/4th London Regiment.

On the 18th the *Transylvania* left Alexandria and during the passage all possible precautions were taken against submarine attack. No untoward incident however occurred, and on the 24th April the transport arrived at Marseilles and disembarkation at once took place.

The Battalion entrained immediately for Rouen, arriving on the 26th April, and was accommodated in the Bruyères Camp.

On arrival at Rouen the 2/1st London Infantry Brigade was finally disbanded after having been in existence for about nineteen months. Col. Dunfee, on the break-up of the Brigade, once more assumed command of the Battalion, but its remaining life as a separate unit proved to be short.

The wastage which had inevitably taken place in the ranks of the 1/4th Battalion (which had now been in France for over fifteen months) had been far beyond the capacity of the Reserve Battalion at home to replace; and with the certain prospect of being called on to fill serious deficiencies to be caused by the large numbers of additional casualties which were expected in the great battle destined to open on 1st July, it was decided by the War Office to disband finally all the units formerly comprising the 2/1st London Infantry Brigade, and to use these troops for the purpose of reinforcing their first line battalions.

The dispersal of the 2/4th Battalion at Rouen is therefore the last incident to be recorded in its separate history.

Owing to the exigencies of the campaign it was impossible to grant leave to more than a very small proportion of the Battalion in spite of its prolonged absence from the United Kingdom, and drafts were quickly sent up the line beginning on the 5th May. By the 20th June the whole strength of the Battalion in officers, N.C.O.'s and men, with a few exceptions, had been despatched to the 1/4th Londons, in the history of which the arrival of these drafts will be noted in detail in their place.

The officers sent to other units were:

Capts. W. H. S. Stevens and W. N. Towse, Lieut. R. C. Dickins, and 2/Lieuts. G. F. Bishop and H. W. Dennis to 1/21st London Regiment (47th Division).

Hon. Lieut, and Q.M. J. E. W. Lambley to XV Corps, A.C.C.

A draft of 133 other ranks was sent to the Kensingtons (13th London), but by the intervention of Lieut.-Col. Wheatley they were subsequently secured for the 1/4th Londons. Col. Vickers Dunfee was attached to 1/22nd London Regiment (The Queens) for some two months, after which he returned to England to command the 4th (Reserve) Battalion.

Thus ends the separate record of the first reserve Battalion raised by the 4th London Regiment during the war. Although the 2/4th Battalion ceased to exist as a unit, the services rendered by its personnel in the first line battalion were of a very high order, and the reinforcements composed by it were particularly welcome inasmuch as they afforded a large number of much needed non-commissioned officers, who were quickly given an opportunity to prove their value in the battles on the Somme later in the year.

CHAPTER VIII
THE 3/4TH AND 4/4TH BATTALIONS AT HOME

At home 1915 and 1916 were two years of hard work in developing the organisation of the Regiment to enable it to provide the reinforcements necessary for the maintenance in the field of its overseas battalions.

Prior to the war the 4th London Regiment—like all other Territorial formations—had no reserve cadre which was capable of being expanded into a reserve unit on mobilisation; and when therefore the 2/4th Battalion followed the 1/4th Battalion overseas in December 1914 the need of providing means of "feeding" the fighting battalions with fresh personnel became pressing. The records of the home battalions are necessarily lacking in the exciting incidents with which those of the service battalions are crowded; but they represent an enormous amount of labour carried out under conditions of great difficulty, and as a rule with very little recognition of their vital importance to the continued existence of the Regiment during the War.

Reference has already been made in Chapter II to the steps taken to raise a third line battalion under Major E. H. Stillwell on the departure of the 2/4th Battalion for Malta. This new Battalion, the 3/4th London Regiment, secured recruits rapidly, and, like its predecessor, very quickly outgrew the limits of Headquarters at Hoxton. It was therefore moved early in January to Littlegrove and Beech Hill, the two houses at Barnet which had previously been occupied by the battalion raised by Col. Dunfee. A slight stiffening of the ranks was supplied by a few members of the overseas battalions who had received a good deal of training with them but had been found medically unfit to accompany them abroad; but the vast majority of the officers, non-commissioned officers and men had but recently joined, most of them without any previous experience of soldiering. No member of the new Battalion, moreover, had seen service in the War, and the magnitude of the task imposed on the officers and warrant officers of instilling the rudiments of discipline into so unwieldy a mass of men was no light one. The enthusiasm of the early days of the War, had, however, by no means subsided, and all ranks worked with a will; and before long the Battalion, now about 600 strong, began to find its feet.

On the 8th February 1915 Capt. P. S. Cookson (late Royal Sussex Regiment) was appointed to command the Battalion with the temporary rank of Lieut.-Col. with Major W. H. Hamilton as second in command, and

Major E. V. Wellby as Adjutant. The company commanders were Capts. A. A. N. Hayne, S. W. J. Limpenny, E. D. Wilson and A. E. Wood.

The training facilities which had been extended to the 2/4th Battalion by local residents at Barnet were accorded to the 3/4th Battalion also, and the training of recruits under company arrangements proceeded as rapidly as possible and as efficiently as the circumstances permitted. No time indeed was to be lost for the 1/4th Londons were now in France, and as already described began to suffer battle casualties early in March 1915; so that it was clear that the 3/4th Battalion might at any time be called upon to make up its deficiencies. Towards the end of April it was in fact called on to supply the first reinforcement, and accordingly despatched 2 officers and 50 other ranks who, as referred to in Chapter IV, joined the 1/4th Londons in the Ypres Salient.

Third line battalions had also been formed by the other regiments of the 1st London Brigade, and hitherto these had been distributed over a wide area on the outskirts of London; but in the last week of April the four new battalions were concentrated under canvas at Tadworth (Surrey) as the 3/1st London Brigade, under the command of Col. H. C. Cholmondely, C.B. The 3/4th Battalion joined the Brigade on the 26th April.

On the 5th May the Adjutancy was taken over by Capt. E. E. Spicer with Lieut S. H. Stedman as Assistant Adjutant, Major E. V. Wellby having transferred to the 1st London Regiment.

Early in June 1915 a general reconstruction was effected in the reserve and training cadres at home; and a number of fresh battalions were formed composed largely of personnel who were not medically fit to serve overseas. To this end a composite Battalion, known as the 100th Provisional Battalion, was formed of officers, N.C.O.'s and men of the 3/1st London Brigade. On the 2nd June Capt. A. E. Wood, and 2/Lieuts. E. J. Bennet and J. S. B. Gathergood and about 100 N.C.O.'s and men left the 3/4th Battalion at Tadworth to join the 100th Provisional Battalion which was stationed at Aldeburgh. On the same day Major W. H. Hamilton was appointed to raise, equip and train a new Battalion, to be known as the 4/4th London Regiment.

Concurrently with this development the 3/1st London Brigade moved from Tadworth to billets at Bury St Edmunds. Here training was proceeded with, and the battalions of the Brigade were again opened for recruiting to make good the gaps in their ranks caused by the formation of the Provisional Battalion.

In the following month a further move took place, and the 3/1st London Brigade took over billets in Ipswich. A further step was now made in the organisation of the Home Forces and towards the end of August all personnel of the Provisional Battalion except "home-service" men were returned to their units. The 2/2nd and 2/3rd London Infantry Brigades had also been concentrated in the Ipswich area, and a new Division—the 58th—was now formed as a Service Division; and the duty of "draft-finding" for the whole Regiment henceforth devolved solely on the 4/4th Battalion under Major Hamilton.

The composition of the 58th Division was as follows:

58TH (LONDON) DIVISION

Brig.-Gen. E. J. COOPER, C.B., M.V.O., D.S.O.

DIVISIONAL CAVALRY.

Hampshire Yeomanry (Carabineers).

ARTILLERY.

290th, 291st, 292nd, 293rd Brigades, R.F.A.

58th Division Ammunition Column.

ROYAL ENGINEERS.

2/1st Wessex
2/2nd "   Field Companies.
1/5th London

58th Divisional Signal Company.

173RD INFANTRY BRIGADE.

3/1st London Regiment (Royal Fusiliers).

2nd 3/2 " "

3rd 3/3 " "

4th 3/4 " "

174TH INFANTRY BRIGADE.

5th 2/5 London Regiment (London Rifle Brigade).

6th 2/6 " " (Rifles).

7th 2/7 " "

8th 2/8 " " (Post Office Rifles).

175TH INFANTRY BRIGADE.

9th 2/9 London Regiment (Queen Victoria Rifles).

10th 2/1 " " (Hackney).

11th 2/1 " " (Finsbury Rifles).

12th 2/1 " " (Rangers).

1/1st Wessex Divisional Cyclists.

509th, 510th, 511th, 512th S. and T. Companies, A.S.C.

The duties of second in command were now taken by Major E. D. Wilson, who continued to occupy this appointment for some months till he was appointed to Brigade Staff and subsequently to Southern Command Headquarters. He was succeeded as second in command by Capt. A. A. N. Hayne.

The constant changes of station to which the 3/4th Battalion had been subjected during its short existence had, as will be readily appreciated, a somewhat deleterious effect on its training and general discipline. Prolonged life in billets is, moreover, highly unsuitable for young troops under training, and the general effect of the Division's stay in Ipswich was not altogether beneficial. All units were similarly affected. The dispatch of the Division overseas was in consequence delayed, and the troops began to become stale with "over-training." Throughout 1915 and the early months of 1916 this unsatisfactory state of affairs continued, and the routine of training, now become wearying through its monotonous repetition, was broken only by the occasional passing excitement of air raids, of which the eastern counties saw a good deal.

During February 1916, recruits called up under the "Derby" scheme to the number of 359 were posted to the Battalion and their training proceeded with all possible speed. Owing, however, to the need for bringing them into line with the remainder of the Battalion in view of the possibility of its being sent to the front during 1916, the training of these men was expedited by temporarily attaching a part of the Battalion to the 4/4th Battalion in order to ease the duties of the training staff.

In June the billets in Ipswich were vacated, and the Division removed to quarters under canvas at Blackrock Camp outside the town, where the former routine was resumed.

In these somewhat unhappy circumstances we may leave the 3/4th Battalion and return to trace the growth of the 4/4th Battalion which had sprung from it at Tadworth a year previously.

The following officers accompanied Major Hamilton to Headquarters and were posted to the 4/4th Battalion: Capt. and Adjt. W. G. Hayward, Lieut. H. E. Miller, and 2/Lieuts. W. H. Vernon and H. J. M. Williams. Hon. Lieut. J. S. Fullalove (late Devonshire Regiment) was appointed Quartermaster, and Coy. Sergt.-Major Potton (late 1/4th Londons) to be Regimental Sergt.-Major. The Commanding Officer was fortunate in enlisting into the Battalion as Warrant Officers and senior N.C.O.'s several ex-Guardsmen and members of the City Police Force, including Coy. Sergt.-Majors H. W. Dennis and J. Pearson, and C.Q.M.-Sergts. A. Reed and F. Milne. These experienced soldiers formed the nucleus of what afterwards became a very fine staff of instructors.

The new Battalion shortly after its inception became the draft-finding unit for the first and second line battalions in the field, and also the unit by which wounded and invalided officers, N.C.O.'s and men of the regiment from the front were re-equipped and passed through a "refresher" course of training, pending their return to the front as reinforcements.

The Battalion was accordingly organised in three Companies, A and B (respectively under Capts. W. Moore and F. C. Grimwade) being for the reception and training of recruits; and C (under Lieut. D. C. Cooke) being the "expeditionary" Company, the personnel being all N.C.O.'s and men returned from the B.E.F. Lieut. F. A. Coffin succeeded Capt Hayward as Adjutant, the latter taking over the duties of President of the Regimental Institutes.

Just previously to the formation of the Battalion the forces in the field had suffered immense casualties at Ypres and on the Gallipoli Peninsula; and the full weight of the German offensive on the Eastern Front where the Russians were steadily giving ground was making itself felt. Earl Kitchener had issued his second call for more men, and recruiting was proceeding rapidly for all branches of the Service; and within a month of its formation some 600 recruits had been posted to the 4/4th Battalion, while the ranks of the Expeditionary Company were rapidly swelling with returning casualties from Neuve Chapelle and Ypres.

It being obviously impossible to cope with the task of dealing with such great numbers in the cramped accommodation at Headquarters arrangements were made for taking over the billets at New Barnet, previously occupied by the 2/4th and 3/4th Battalions; and the Battalion moved to its new quarters on the 12th July, Headquarters and A Company being billeted at Littlegrove and B and C Companies at Beech Hill.

A vigorous programme of training was at once put in hand, the work being carried out at Folly Farm and, by the kindness of Sir Philip Sassoon, in Trent Park. Through the generosity of the Club Committee the full resources of the Enfield Rifle Club were again placed at the disposal of the Battalion, and it is hard to overestimate the value of the assistance rendered in the musketry training of the recruits by the many public-spirited members of the Club who volunteered their services as instructors.

Owing to the continued influx of recruits, the training companies having now each a strength of about 380, it was necessary to take over additional billets at Oakhill which were allotted to the Expeditionary Company.

Early in August, almost before the recruit training was under way, orders were received to prepare a draft of 400 other ranks to proceed, at three days' notice, to Malta to join the 2/4th Battalion. After considerable exertion the draft was equipped, fitted with khaki drill uniforms and sun-helmets, and in due course proceeded to Southampton, where it actually embarked on the transport. The orders for its departure were, however, cancelled, and the draft returned to Barnet to resume its training in the 4/4th Battalion, much to the disappointment of the N.C.O.'s and men concerned.

The supplies of webbing equipment having proved inadequate, the troops were now being provided with leather equipment of the 1915 pattern; and were armed with the long pattern charger-loading Lee-Enfield rifle. At this date the training of recruits proceeded under no efficient system such as was evolved at a later date. No set period was allowed for the preparation of the drafts, and very few facilities were provided for improving or speeding-up training beyond such as emanated from the brains of the officers and N.C.O.'s immediately concerned, with the inevitable result that a good deal of unnecessary delay and a certain lack of uniformity in the training ensued. Thanks, however, to the devoted efforts of the instructors, the recruits soon passed the initial stages and were passed as "trained" men on a syllabus which included drill, musketry, marching, physical training and bayonet fighting, entrenching, field work and the rudiments of bomb-throwing. The first draft of N.C.O.'s and men supplied by the Battalion consisting of 40 other ranks under Lieut. N. L. Thomas and 2/Lieuts. S. Davis, J. W. Price and C. S. G. Blows proceeded to the Dardanelles to join the 2/4th Battalion at the beginning of November 1915.

Recruiting had continued at a great speed during the months of July, August and September, and the training companies had assumed such unmanageable proportions that they were subdivided and a new training company, C, under Major H. J. Duncan-Teape, was formed, the Expeditionary Company being renamed D.

On the 29th August 1915 the Battalion was visited by the following ex-officers of the Regiment:

- Lieut.-Col. E. T. Rodney Wilde, V.D.
- Lieut.-Col. Harry Dade, V.D.
- Lieut.-Col. A. H. Lock, V.D.
- Major P. Lynch, and
- Major W. Stevens.

On this occasion Church Parade was held at Folly Farm, after which the Battalion marched past the ex-officers, the salute being taken by Lieut.-Col. Dade.

On the 13th November an inter-company relief took place, A Company moving to Beech Hill, and its billets at Littlegrove being occupied by B Company.

At Christmas 48 hours' leave was granted to every member of the Battalion, two leave parties being formed for the purpose.

During this period the Reserve Battalions of the 1st London Division were stationed in all parts of the Home Counties, and the supervision of training by those responsible was naturally extremely difficult; and it was consequently decided to bring together all these battalions into one Divisional camp, the site selected being near Salisbury Plain.

The move to Salisbury took place in January 1916, the 4/4th Battalion proceeding on the 11th to No. 7 Camp, Hurdcott (between Salisbury and Shaftesbury), where it found itself for the first time in company with the 4/1st, 4/2nd, and 4/3rd Battalions, the remainder of the Division being quartered at Hurdcott and Fovant.

No troops of the 4th London Regiment were after this date quartered at Barnet, but before finally saying farewell to this the first station of so many hundreds of the members of the Regiment, we must once more express the indebtedness of the Regiment not only to those gentlemen who so generously afforded the Battalion the use of such excellent training grounds, but also to Mr Kingwell and Mr W. H. Vernon, the owners respectively of Beech Hill and Littlegrove, for the pains taken by them to render these houses comfortable for the troops, and to the many local residents who extended kindness and hospitality to the Battalion, among whom Mr Eldred of Cockfosters must not be forgotten.

About this time the designation of the Battalion was changed to the 4th (Reserve) Battalion London Regiment, a corresponding alteration being made in the titles of the other 4th and 3rd line battalions of the Division.

Major H. J. Duncan-Teape assumed the duties of second in command in January 1916.

The immediate result of the move to Salisbury Plain was an immense strengthening of the *esprit-de-corps* of the Battalion which now found itself for the first time together in one camp, and a considerable increase of efficiency and improvement in discipline followed. The Hurdcott camps were arranged on suitably designed principles with well ventilated sleeping huts and roomy messing and recreation rooms which contributed in no small degree to the comfort and physical welfare of the troops. The 4th (Reserve) Battalion was, moreover, exceptionally fortunate in becoming the possessor of an excellent training and sports ground some 5 acres in extent. Work was immediately set in hand to construct a bayonet fighting assault course and a bombing ground, and considerable improvements were made in the practice trenches which had been left in a half-completed condition by the former occupants of the camp.

The 3rd line Division now came under the command of Col. Williams, C.B. (late Somerset Light Infantry), who was succeeded in the command in May by Col. S. H. Godman, D.S.O. (Scots Guards), whose kindly personality will be held in grateful remembrance by all who came into personal touch with him.

Voluntary recruiting had come almost to a standstill during the preceding December, and the training of all the N.C.O.'s and men who had joined the Battalion previously was now practically completed. Numerous drafts had been sent out to the 1/4th Battalion in France, and the activities of the training staff of the Battalion were therefore somewhat restricted. But in March the whole of the training reserve camps in England became veritable hives of activity; for in that month the first groups of men enlisted under the "Derby" scheme of recruiting were called up, and were posted to their respective home training battalions.

The recruits allotted to the Regiment under this scheme were clothed at Headquarters (though not equipped or armed) and drafted straight to Hurdcott, and within the space of a week no fewer than 650 were posted to the 4th (Reserve) Battalion. In the following week a party of 220 N.C.O.'s and men of the 3/4th Battalion were sent to the 4th (Reserve) Battalion for the completion of their training, which was found on examination to be in a variety of stages of advancement.

It will be readily appreciated that the sudden advent of so large a body of totally untrained men strained the instructional facilities of the Battalion to the utmost, and it was deemed advisable somewhat to modify the system of training which had proved sufficient hitherto. The recruits were posted to companies as usual, an extra company, E (under Lieut. Miller), being now formed, but the company staffs assumed responsibility only for clothing, equipment, messing, pay and other administrative and disciplinary duties, the whole of the training being entrusted to a specially selected staff of officers and N.C.O. instructors, who were as far as possible relieved of company and battalion duties. It is believed that the Battalions of the London Reserve Division were among the first to adopt this system of coping with the problem of draft-production which, in modified and improved forms, gradually became recognised as the most efficient and was generally adopted.

It should be understood that the brief description which follows of the work of the Reserve Battalion is somewhat anticipatory. The scheme of training which was in force in the last year of the War was obviously not evolved in a day, but was the fruit of three years' experience. But it is thought that the present is perhaps the most suitable juncture for the inclusion in this history of these notes, as the period now under review saw the inception of the great training scheme whereby the country produced its citizen soldiers who fought the great battles of 1916, 1917 and 1918.

The system as originally evolved in the 4th Battalion was intended to apply to "barrack-square" instruction in drill only, but as training proceeded, it was found desirable not only to ensure uniformity of instruction, but also for economy of instructors and the avoidance of delay in the completion of training, to apply it to all branches of training. "Specialist" officers and N.C.O.'s were therefore appointed to take charge of each different subject of instruction, such as drill, musketry, bombing, Lewis Gun, physical training and bayonet fighting, entrenching and wiring, and "anti-gas" measures; the whole training school being under the executive control of an "officer in charge of training."

This development was made the more desirable inasmuch as the War Office now was tightening up the whole system of training, in view of the continued heavy casualties at the front which rendered necessary not only the fullest and quickest possible development of the untrained man-power of the Empire, but also the regular and rapid filling up of deficiencies in the ranks of the fighting troops. Under the War Office scheme (the wisdom of which is demonstrated by the fact that in broad principle it remained unaltered until the Armistice, modification only being found desirable in matters of detail) the period allowed for the conversion of the recruit into a trained soldier was fourteen weeks. This period was subdivided with considerable skill and foresight, the first two weeks being occupied in completing the equipment of the recruit, coupled with light drill and physical training, together with lectures on a few general subjects with the object of gradually settling him into his new conditions of life, and to allow for his complete recovery from the effects of "anti-typhoid" inoculation. The serious training of the recruit therefore lasted twelve weeks, which in the 1st London (Reserve) Brigade were subdivided into two distinct periods. The first of these concerned the "individual" training of the recruit in the subjects to which reference has been made above, and which lasted for ten weeks. It was proceeded with in accordance with War Office instructions, which laid down the number of hours to be devoted weekly to each subject. During this period also the recruit was put through a special table of musketry practices on the open range, and it concluded with a series of tests of individual proficiency in each subject, the passing of which decided the recruit's claim to be classed as a trained soldier.

Throughout these three months the training proceeded by platoons, each platoon of recruits living, messing and working together, with the object of impressing on them, from the earliest days of their service, the importance of the platoon as a unit in action. The latter part of the "individual" training period saw the sub-division of each platoon into Lewis Gun and bombing sections, training being arranged for in accordance with the particular requirements of each. The "individual" training having been completed, the final fortnight was devoted to platoon "combined training" in field work as a properly organised platoon, the men working in full marching order, loaded to the weight which they would be called upon to carry in the field. The physical strain of the last fourteen days was undoubtedly considerable, but the results attained by it were amply justified, not only from the point of actual instruction imparted, but also from that of the highly important question of selection of N.C.O.'s, for each section of the platoon in "combined training" was in charge of a recruit N.C.O., the specialist instructor being attached merely for the purpose of supervision.

On completion of this final and most interesting period in the recruit's training, he proceeded on "draft-leave" for four clear days, on return from which he was reported as ready to proceed overseas, was medically inspected and finally fitted out; and as a rule his departure overseas ensued within a few days.

Such was the course of life in a Reserve Battalion, and it will not be disputed that the duties of an instructor were both multifarious and exceedingly onerous, while the degree of personal application and physical endurance which the recruit himself was called upon to display was severe to a degree. Owing to the frequent changes of personnel among the N.C.O. instructors, it is impossible to record the names of all those who were in turn employed in this manner, but it would be unjust not to acknowledge the splendid devotion of the training staffs or to recognise with gratitude the extreme importance of the rôle played by them in the War. Neither can we refrain from remarking that, however complete the scheme of training, and however efficient the instructors, it would have been nearly impossible to carry it into effect in the short period allowed but for the intense keenness and willingness to learn displayed by the vast majority of the many thousands of recruits who were trained in accordance with it.

The instructors themselves were drawn entirely from N.C.O.'s who had served with the 1st or 2nd line battalions overseas, and had either been invalided to the United Kingdom or were sent home for six months "on exchange." In order to avoid staleness no instructor who was fit for overseas service was permitted to retain his appointment for more than one year, at the end of which period he himself returned to the front as a reinforcement, his place on the training staff being taken by one more recently returned to England.

Officer instructors were selected and retained on a similar principle, the period of appointment to the establishment of a training reserve unit being (in the case of physical fitness for service overseas) a maximum of six months.

The officers of the first training staff appointed in the 4th (Reserve) Battalion were:

    Capt. F. C. Grimwade, in charge of training.

    2/Lieut. E. G. Dew, Assistant to Training Officer.

    2/Lieut. A. G. Croll;   Musketry Instructors.

    2/Lieut. G. H. Hetley

    2/Lieut. R. K. Caparn, Physical Training

    2/Lieut. L. A. Allen, Lewis Gun   Instructor.

    2/Lieut. L. C. Haycraft, Bombing and Anti-gas

Signalling instruction was provided under Brigade arrangements, the first Brigade Signalling Officer, 2/Lieut. R. C. Hunt, being supplied by the 4th (Reserve) Battalion.

Early in February 1916 the 4th (Reserve) Battalion received a very welcome reinforcement in the shape of 50 men of the Second Trinidad Contingent, and the honour done to the Regiment in selecting it for the training of this draft, representative of one of the smallest and yet most ancient and loyal outposts of the Empire, was much appreciated. About the same time four Trinidad officers, 2/Lieuts. L. Farfan, H. Dow, R. L. Fabien and J. MacDonald, were gazetted to the Battalion. It was rapidly realised that the difference of climate between the West Indies and the snow-laden winds of the "Plain" was too severe, and it became evident that this keen and efficient platoon must be transferred to a more suitable environment. After about six weeks with the 4th (Reserve) Battalion, therefore, they were sent to complete their training with the 7th Royal Fusiliers at Falmouth and later attached to the 3/4th Devonshire Regiment in India.

In April Major H. J. Duncan-Teape rejoined the 1/4th Battalion in France, the duties of second in command being assumed by Major G. H. M. Vine.

During May the Battalion was inspected by Col. S. H. Godman, D.S.O., commanding the Division, who presented C. S. M. Risley, D.C.M., with his medal. The Battalion also received a visit from Lieut.-Col. E. T. Rodney Wilde, V.D. At the end of May the Division was reviewed by Field-Marshal Earl French, commanding the Home Forces.

Although the whole of the Battalions at Hurdcott and Fovant Camps existed for the training of recruits and were in no way formations which were likely to be sent overseas as units, they were included in the scheme which had been prepared for the defence of Great Britain in the event of an attempt at landing by the Germans.

This scheme provided for the maintenance of a permanent defence force on the East Coast and at other points where it was deemed likely that any attempt at invasion would be put into effect. In addition to this, arrangements were made for the rapid concentration from other sources of a mobile force for use, in the event of active operations taking place, as a general reserve. To this general reserve the units of the 3rd line groups of the 1st London Division contributed a quota of officers, N.C.O.'s and men varying from time to time with the numbers of men who were sufficiently advanced in their course of training to render their inclusion in the force useful.

During the period at Hurdcott frequent test concentrations took place, in several instances the parade being followed by a test route march. These parades were always attended by the platoons of the 4th (Reserve) Battalion detailed for the time being to this duty and passed off satisfactorily.

On the 2nd June 1916 Major W. H. Hamilton, who had commanded the Battalion since its formation, was gazetted to the 4th Battalion Duke of Cornwall's Light Infantry and almost immediately proceeded to join his new Battalion at Meerut.[4] He was succeeded in temporary command of the Battalion by Major G. H. M. Vine. On the occasion of Major Hamilton's departure the troops testified to their appreciation of his unfailing kindness and sympathy with all ranks throughout the period of his command by lining the camp road and heartily cheering him as his car passed down it.

[4] Major Hamilton remained with the 4th D.C.L.I. until the following year when he was attached to the 4th Hants Regiment. With this Battalion he proceeded to Mesopotamia and took part in the victorious advance which culminated in the occupation of Baghdad. He was later appointed to command the detachment of the Hants Regiment which accompanied the gallant little force led by General Dunsterville to endeavour to secure the oilfield of Baku on the Caspian Sea.

In the latter part of July command of the Battalion was assumed by Col. Vickers Dunfee, Major Vine resuming the duties of second in command.

On the 1st July 1916 began the great series of battles on the Somme, the Regiment's part in which will be described, and almost immediately calls were made for drafts of all ranks to fill the very serious gaps caused by the heavy casualties sustained by the 1/4th Battalion during the battle of Gommecourt; and between this date and the middle of October when the 56th Division was finally withdrawn from the Somme battles a total of some 30 officers and 400 other ranks were despatched. These very heavy calls naturally depleted the ranks of the home Battalion very seriously and took nearly all the "Derby" recruits who had joined in the previous March.

With the object, apparently, of effecting an ultimate economy in staff, a reorganisation of considerable importance took place on the 1st September 1916 among the whole of the 3rd line units of the Division. So far as the Fusilier Brigade was concerned this took the form of amalgamation of the four existing battalions into two, the 1st and 2nd Battalions becoming the 1st (Reserve) Battalion, and the 3rd and 4th Battalions becoming the 3rd (Reserve) Battalion. Each of these new battalions for the time being retained a double establishment of officers, warrant officers and N.C.O.'s and were organised in eight companies till the despatch of personnel on draft permitted a reduction to be made. The composite battalion was made responsible for the provision of reinforcements and for the reception of ranks returned from overseas for each of the two Regiments of which it was composed.

These amalgamations of necessity involved extensive repostings of officers, in particular among those of senior rank. Command of the new 3rd (Reserve) Battalion was assumed by Lieut.-Col. T. Montgomerie Webb, formerly commanding the old 3rd (Reserve) Battalion, Major G. H. M. Vine being appointed second in command. The duties of Adjutant, Quartermaster and Training Officer respectively were also assumed by officers of the old 3rd (Reserve) Battalion (namely, Capt. McGlashan, Capt. Coombe and Major H. Moore, M.C.), the officers who had previously held the corresponding appointments in the old 4th (Reserve) Battalion being posted as follows:—

    Capt, F. A. Coffin (Adjt.) to Brigade Staff.

    Lieut. Fullalove (Q.M.) to new 6th (Reserve) Battalion.

    Capt. F. C. Grimwade (Training Officer) to command A Company new 3rd (Reserve) Battalion.

Col. Vickers Dunfee was appointed to command the new 1st (Reserve) Battalion, an appointment which he retained until his demobilisation in December 1918.

It must be confessed that the immediate result of this amalgamation, involving as it did the extinction as a separate entity of the 4th (Reserve) Battalion, was a heavy blow to the *esprit de corps* of all ranks, which was in the circumstances at least comprehensible. The rank and file at a critical stage of their training came under the command of officers and N.C.O. instructors who were unknown to them, while the instructors of the old 4th (Reserve) Battalion experienced a natural and very keen disappointment at not being permitted to complete the task to which they had applied themselves with such devotion for many weeks past.

A closer acquaintance with the new surroundings, however, resulted in a gradual disappearance of these feelings of regret, and in due course a new *esprit de corps* and a closer bond of union between the two Regiments concerned took their place. At the end of its existence in November 1918 the 3rd (Reserve) Battalion had become an extremely happy one, in which no sort of distinction existed between the 3rd and 4th London Regiments, and each worked for the welfare of all.

CHAPTER IX
THE FORMATION OF THE 56TH DIVISION

From May onwards during the remainder of 1916 the history of the Regiment in France is that of the 1/4th Battalion, into which the 2/4th Battalion was merged; and we may therefore proceed to follow its fortunes from the date of its attachment to the newly formed 56th Division.

At the date of the 1/4th Battalion's arrival in billets at Citerne on the 9th February 1916, the 56th Division was just being concentrated. The 47th Division, which comprised chiefly battalions of the 2nd London Division of pre-war days and which the Battalion had just left, had joined the British Armies in France as a Division; but the units of the old 1st London Division, which had been among the first Territorial units to leave England, had hitherto been scattered throughout the Army attached to different regular divisions. The 56th, therefore, though junior in precedence, owing to its comparatively late formation, to many other Territorial Divisions which had left England as complete organisations, consisted entirely of battalions which might fairly be described as veteran, since all had seen a good deal of stiff work up and down the lines.

The infantry battalions were brigaded as follows:

56TH (LONDON) DIVISION—Major-Gen. Sir C. P. A. Hull, K.C.B.

167TH INFANTRY BRIGADE—Brig.-Gen. F. H. Burnell-Nugent, D.S.O.

1/1st London (Royal Fusiliers).

1/3rd London (Royal Fusiliers).

1/7th Middlesex.

1/8th Middlesex.

168TH INFANTRY BRIGADE—Brig.-Gen. G. G. Loch, C.M.G., D.S.O.

1/4th London (Royal Fusiliers).

1/12th London (Rangers).

1/13th London (Kensingtons).

1/14th London (London Scottish).

169TH INFANTRY BRIGADE—Brig.-Gen. E. S. D'Ewes Coke, C.M.G., D.S.O.

1/2nd London (Royal Fusiliers).

1/5th London (London Rifle Brigade).

1/9th London (Queen Victoria Rifles).

1/16th London (Queen's Westminster Rifles).

The Division was attached to the VI Corps (Keir) of the Third Army (Allenby).

The record of the next three months may be passed over quickly as they were devoted solely to organising and training the new Division in areas well to the rear of the trenches, and it was not until the early days of May 1916 that the various units came under fire as a Division. This prolonged period of rest, which indeed was the longest ever spent in this manner by the Battalion in the whole course of its active service history, was of considerable importance in order that staffs and units might become thoroughly acquainted with each other, and that the individual battalions of each Brigade might have a sufficient opportunity of creating the divisional *esprit de corps* which experience has shown to be so necessary in action.

But the three months of routine work will provide us with a useful respite in which to make some reference to one or two developments in organisation which were carried out before the British forces plunged into the dreary and protracted struggles of the Somme, and which affected the 1/4th Londons equally with other units.

One of the developments which took place about this period, and which had an effect on the general efficiency of the Army so far-reaching that its value can hardly be overestimated, was the formation of Army and Divisional Schools, in which the lead was taken by the Third Army. These schools, as is well known, were established under selected bodies of instructors to achieve the double object of keeping the fighting troops, through the medium of the regimental officers and non-commissioned officers who attended them for short courses of instruction, in touch with the progress made from time to time in the art of war, and particularly in the more technical branches, such as gas, bombing, Lewis gunnery, etc., and also of assisting battalions to provide efficient courses of instruction and training for their own personnel while out of the trenches for short periods. The success which in general attended these efforts was great and their influence on the action of our troops in the great battles of the latter part of the War was undoubtedly far-reaching.

The 56th Divisional Schools were first established under Major D. V. Smith, D.S.O., 1/1st Londons, at Givenchy-le-Noble and Ambrines in April 1916.

Attention was also directed at this time towards training the infantry to assume greater responsibility for the general maintenance and strengthening of the forward trenches in their own occupation, and thereby releasing the Royal Engineers for works requiring more technical skill. To this end the early days of March saw the formation in the Division of trench pioneer squads in each battalion consisting of selected men under the supervision of a subaltern officer. These squads were given special training in erecting wire entanglements, constructing strong points and consolidation of newly captured positions. The first trench pioneer officer of the 1/4th Londons was 2/Lieut. V. C. Donaldson, and under him the trench pioneers began to shape well towards efficiency; but the need for the existence of such squads was subsequently modified to some extent by the attachment to each Division of a specially trained Pioneer Battalion, the 1/5th Cheshire Regiment joining the 56th Division in this capacity. The Pioneer Battalions were fighting units but, as their name implies, were employed more particularly on constructional work rather beyond the powers of the ordinary infantry officer to direct or of the troops to execute, and in active operations their usefulness in consolidating new trenches and similar duties was established beyond a doubt. The advent of such highly trained units had a tendency somewhat, perhaps not altogether rightly, to depreciate the value of battalion pioneer squads, and ultimately these were done away with. The duty of trench working parties, whether in active operations or in holding trenches, afterwards fell equally on all the personnel of the companies, while in the 56th Division if not in others, general direction was given to the Battalion's activity in trench work by a "Works" officer attached to Battalion Headquarters. This appointment established early in June 1916 was first filled in the 1/4th Londons by Capt. R. N. Arthur, and remained in existence until the end of the War. The Works officer became responsible for making arrangements between company commanders and the Royal Engineers for the supply of the material required for the trench work undertaken by the companies in the line, for detailing the working parties supplied by the Battalion while out of the line, and in general forming a link between the Commanding Officer and the company commanders in the matter of trench work.

A further development occurred in the formation of a Headquarters Company, called in the 1/4th Londons for ease of distinction K Company. The object of this change was to separate so far as was reasonably possible the fighting personnel of the Battalion from the administrative personnel, such as transport, headquarters clerks and telephone operators; and to relieve the company commander of responsibility as regards clothing, pay and accommodation, etc., of such administrative personnel by bringing them under the direct control of a Headquarters officer, usually the Assistant-Adjutant, to whom as a rule such men were more accessible than to the company officers. This left the companies more intact as fighting units and much reduced the work of company quartermaster-sergeants in looking after large numbers of men who in practice were seldom with the company. Upon the whole the system worked exceedingly well; though, as was almost inevitable, K Company showed from time to time a tendency to assume unreasonable proportions and required a little "weeding out."

At least a passing reference must be made to the 56th Division's famous concert troop, the Bow Bells. The uniform excellence of its entertainments from its inception till the end of the war was the means of providing all ranks of the Division from time to time with hours of intense pleasure and mental rest of inestimable value.

Lastly, mention must be made of an institution which made its appearance in the Battalion about this time and carried out exceedingly useful work, namely, the Regimental Canteen. Thousands of 1/4th London men have happy recollections of Sergt. Plumbley and his assistant Pte. Blight, who, like the sutlers of former wars, followed the Battalion in all its wanderings with their welcome stocks of tobacco, chocolate, notepaper, newspapers and other useful articles, and, fair times or foul, were always to be found with their little shop neatly set out in a dugout or a ruined cottage not very far in rear of the most advanced troops of the Battalion.

The Battalion occupied its comfortable quarters at Citerne for about a fortnight amid conditions which presented a total change from those amidst which it had passed the previous year, and which brought a corresponding benefit to the troops by way of mental as well as physical recuperation. The Hallencourt area, lying as it does on the broad rolling hills of Ponthieu on the west bank of the Somme, formed a complete contrast to the dreary flats and marches of Flanders not only in the pretty variation of the landscape but also because this part of the country was unscarred by the ravages of war. At Citerne, moreover, the Battalion for the first time since it joined the Ferozepore Brigade in February 1915 was stationed beyond the range of heavy gun fire. Citerne is but a small village, but its kindly and warm-hearted folk, from M. le Maire downwards, will always be held in grateful remembrance by those of the 1/4th Londons who had the good fortune to enjoy their hospitality.

The fortnight's sojourn here was devoted principally to training, but the amusement of the Battalion was not overlooked and football matches with other units and concerts in the tiny village theatre made a welcome break in the routine of parades.

At Citerne the 1/4th Londons became possessed for the first time in France of a Chaplain, the Rev. R. Palmer, C.F., Brigade Chaplain, being attached to the Battalion on the 19th February. The Battalion was also rejoined at Citerne by Capt. W. Moore, who had been hit at Ypres the previous April, and was further strengthened by the arrival of a draft of 95 N.C.O.'s and men.

On the 27th February the Division moved to a fresh training area on the opposite bank of the Somme, Divisional Headquarters opening at Domart, when the 168th Brigade Headquarters and the Battalion were billeted in Vauchelles. Here the programme of training was continued until the 12th March, on which day a second move was made, this time to the Doullens area, all the battalions of the 168th Brigade occupying billets in the town.

On the 8th March a further reinforcement of 100 N.C.O.'s and men arrived from the 4/4th Battalion and was posted to companies. At this time also the bad news was received that Lieut.-Col. L. T. Burnett, who had gone on leave in January, was unfit to return overseas, and Major W. G. Clark, D.S.O., therefore continued in command of the Battalion, with Major W. Moore as second in command.

Doullens did not provide a refuge to the Brigade for long for the 15th March saw the Division once more on the move to the Le Cauroy area (east of Frevent), the 1/4th Londons taking over billets at Beaufort. In this area the Division settled down steadily to a period of training which continued without interruption and with very little incident calling for notice for nearly seven weeks, during which the strength of the Battalion, as of all other units, gradually crept up, if not to war strength at least to such size that it became abundantly evident that the Division was not destined to remain for long in billets behind the line. Drafts joined the Battalion consisting of 2/Lieuts. G. E. Stanbridge, G. H. Davis and A. G. Blunn, and also of 87 other ranks on the 22nd March; of 12 other ranks on the 6th April; and a final reinforcement of 33 other ranks arrived on the 20th April; these additions bringing the Battalion to the respectable strength of nearly 600 all ranks.

During the same period the Battalion suffered losses among officers in Capt. J. R. Pyper, M.C., who was seconded to the 168th Brigade Machine-Gun Company; Lieut. S. E. H. Walmisley, who after carrying out the duties of Quartermaster for nearly four months during the absence on sick leave of Lieut. E. S. Tomsett, was appointed to the Central Training School, Rouen; and 2/Lieut. C. R. P. de Pury who was seconded as R.T.O.

On the 23rd March Major W. G. Clark, D.S.O., left the Battalion on short leave and he also succumbed to a severe breakdown while at home and was unable to return. Command of the Battalion was carried on temporarily by Major W. Moore until the 8th April, when Lieut.-Col. L. L. Wheatley, D.S.O., Argyll and Sutherland Highlanders, Staff Captain 168th Infantry Brigade, took command.

It would be but tiresome to follow the daily routine of the Battalion during this prolonged period of rest where one day's work so much resembles that which preceded it, and we may therefore be forgiven for passing quickly over this part of the record. Enough has been said to show how from the Battalion point of view the Division came into being and was prepared for the work allotted to it, and it remains therefore for us to pass on and endeavour to recount the manner in which the 1/4th Londons performed their task.

CHAPTER X
THE 1/4TH BATTALION IN THE BATTLES OF THE SOMME, 1916

I. *The Attack on Gommecourt*

The spring of 1916 was marked by two enemy offensives, at Verdun and on the Italian front, both of which tried the resources of our Allies severely. In order to draw off German troops to the East the Russian offensive against the Austrians had been started in May, but in spite of this the German pressure against Verdun continued to increase.

Sir Douglas Haig had for some time intended to undertake an offensive operation on a large scale during 1916 in conjunction with the French, and in view of the continual increase in the strength of the British Armies it was clearly desirable that the launching of the battle should be delayed as long as possible consistent with the advance of the summer. But in view of the great pressure at Verdun it was decided that the British attacks should begin at the latest at the end of June, with the objects of relieving our Allies and of pinning as many enemies as possible to the front opposite the British Armies, in addition to the tactical improvement of our positions.

The part of the enemy's lines selected for attack was the right of the British front, opposite which the Germans occupied high ground forming the watershed between the River Somme and the rivers flowing north-east into Belgium. The general direction of this watershed, which consists of a chalk country of broad swelling downs and deep well-wooded valleys, is roughly from east-south-east to west-north-west. The aspect of this country bears a general resemblance to parts of Wiltshire, and the gentle undulations of the higher slopes of the hills, which descend with unexpected abruptness into waterless valleys lined with banks whose declivitous sides seem to have been shaped by human agency, cause the resemblance to be one also of detail. From this watershed a series of long spurs runs south-westerly towards the Somme, and on their lower slopes the German lines ran from Curlu near the river at first north and then almost due west to Fricourt, a distance of some 10,000 yards. At Fricourt the lines took an abrupt turn northward for a further 10,000 yards when they crossed the Ancre, a tributary of the Somme, near Hamel. From this point they continued in a generally northerly direction, passing through Beaumont Hamel, west of Serre and between Hébuterne and Gommecourt. In the neighbourhood of the two last-named villages the lines crossed the summit of the main watershed, and thence descended gently in a north-easterly direction towards Arras.

On the 20,000 yards between the Somme and the Ancre the enemy had already prepared a strong second system of defence about two miles in rear of the front system; and on the whole front from Gommecourt to the Somme he had spared no effort in the nearly two years of his uninterrupted occupation to render these positions impregnable. The strengthening of woods and villages into fortresses, and the skilful use of the ground in siting trenches and gun and machine-gun emplacements, had in fact woven his successive lines of trenches into one composite system. Yet further in rear he was still at work improving existing defences and constructing new.

The front of attack on which the British armies were to operate covered the whole of the above described line from Gommecourt to Curlu—a total of about 17 miles—while the French were to co-operate on a wide front immediately south of the River Somme.

The story of the struggle which, lasting from the beginning of July until the early part of November, gave us possession, first of the forward trench systems, then of the crest of the ridge, and finally of the whole plateau and parts of the further slopes, divides itself into phases, which can be dealt with in turn to such an extent as the record of the 1/4th Battalion is concerned with them. For the present we are concerned with the enormous preparations which preceded the opening of the struggle and of the first phase of the battle which began on the 1st July 1916.

Dealing with the preparations for the battle generally, an enormous amount of work was required in improving road and rail communications; in digging assembly trenches and dugouts, for use not only as shelters but also as aid posts and stores for ammunition for small arms and trench mortars; and in constructing many additional machine-gun and gun emplacements. The water supply for the assaulting troops presented a serious problem, and Sir Douglas Haig records in his Despatches that in this connection over a hundred pumping plants were installed and over 120 miles of water mains laid.

During most of the period in which this preliminary labour proceeded the troops were working under most trying weather conditions and frequently were harassed by heavy enemy fire.

The particular tasks for which the 168th Brigade, and in particular the 1/4th Londons, were called upon will be referred to in their places at greater length.

After remaining in training in the Frevent area for the latter half of March and the whole of April the 56th Division moved forward on the 3rd and 4th of May into the VII Corps area (D'Oyly Snow) and took over from the 46th Division a sector of the line in front of the village of Hébuterne and facing Gommecourt.

The line was occupied by the 167th Brigade, the 168th moving in reserve to Souastre, a small village some three miles west of the front trenches. The Battalion moved by march route from Beaufort on the 6th and arrived at Souastre after a ten mile march at 9 p.m.

Two or three days were occupied in training, and on the 11th May the Battalion began to supply working parties of considerable size. Of these, one of 200 all ranks was despatched to Pas and employed in felling and sawing trees to form props for gun pits and dugouts; and another of 250 all ranks went to the chalk quarries of Hénu, where they were given a task in digging road material. These working parties, the first of many weary tasks, constituted so far as the Battalion was concerned the first direct active preparations in the area of battle for the Somme offensive.

The Battalion's duty at Souastre lasted a fortnight. Work, however, did not take up the whole of the Battalion's time, and opportunity was found for a football match with the Kensingtons, which was played on the 12th May and resulted in a draw at one all. A few days later the Battalion entered representatives at the London Scottish sports at St. Amand, securing second and third places in the "open" 200 yards.

On the 15th Major H. J. Duncan-Teape rejoined the Battalion and was appointed second in command. The works programme was now beginning to be operated by Brigade Headquarters to the fullest extent and the greatest possible working strength was daily employed, the chief tasks being the digging of cable trenches for the signal services, the construction of new dugouts and the deepening and strengthening of existing communication and fire trenches.

D Company and one platoon of B Company in fact were despatched on the 18th to Hébuterne, where they were billeted for night digging work; and every available man of the remaining companies was detailed for work of one sort or another. So insistent was the demand for more labour that on the 20th May the band and every available man of the transport section had to be put to work on digging parties.

On the 20th and 21st May a series of Brigade reliefs took place, the trenches being occupied by the 169th Brigade, who replaced the 167th; while the 168th withdrew in Divisional reserve to Grenas, a hamlet near the Doullens-Arras Road, where Brigade Headquarters opened on the 21st.

The Rangers and Scottish were billeted close by at Halloy; but the 1/4th Londons and the Kensingtons remained in the forward area attached to the 169th Brigade, the latter battalion occupying W sector, on the right of the Divisional front. The 1/4th Londons moved on the 21st in Brigade reserve to Bayencourt, about a mile and a half south of Souastre and slightly nearer the trenches.

On the 22nd the detachments in Hébuterne were relieved by C Company, who took over their tasks. Each night of the period of duty in Bayencourt the Battalion continued to supply large numbers of men for fatigues of various sorts, the parties being small and divided amongst a large number of tasks. These working parties were equipped as lightly as possible, the men carrying water-bottles and respirators over the left shoulder; a bandolier of fifty rounds over the right shoulder; and their rifles with bayonet in scabbard fixed. But although the troops moved "light" the duties were onerous, partly from the long hours of work and the strain induced by the short available time in which to complete apparently impossible tasks; and not least by the bad weather, the season from the middle of May onwards being for the most part wet. Hitherto practically no casualties had been sustained, the first recorded casualties at the enemy's hands during the Battalion's attachment to the 56th Division occurring on the 24th May, when two men were wounded at work in Hébuterne.

On the afternoon of the 28th May the 1/4th Londons relieved the Kensingtons in W subsector of the Divisional front, the Battalion still being under the orders of the 169th Brigade. The Kensingtons took over on relief the billets at Bayencourt.

The Divisional sector as taken over from the 46th Division early in May had consisted of the original line taken up by the French troops in October 1914 during the extension of the battle line from the Aisne to the sea. This line the French had continued to hold until they were finally relieved of responsibility for it in June 1915, when the British extended their lines southward to the Somme. The frontage of the sector extended as shown on Map No. 4 from the Bucquoy Road on the right to a point opposite the most westerly point of Gommecourt Wood on the left, being divided into two subsectors, W and Y, by an imaginary line running roughly parallel to, and 200 yards north of, the Hébuterne-Bucquoy Road. Opposite the British lines the Germans held a position of enormous strength bastioned by the enclosure of Gommecourt Wood which marked an abrupt salient in their line. As was only too frequently the case the enemy possessed considerable advantages of observation over the British lines, the ground rising steadily in rear of his front trenches to the Gommecourt-Bucquoy ridge, which, although not a hill of outstanding pre-eminence, formed the summit of the Somme watershed described earlier in this chapter.

Except in the neighbourhood of villages such as Hébuterne, which are surrounded by orchards and enclosed in a ring fence, the Somme country is, like most of Picardy and Artois, devoid of hedges, and from road to road the swell of the hillside is unbroken by fence or ditch. The roads themselves, however, are in many cases "sunken," that is, contained in a deep cutting, the cover afforded by the banks playing an important part in the actions fought in this area.

A glance at the map will help to make the position clear. The trench line shown as a reserve position on the map and marked as the WR and YR lines was at the date of the 56th Division's advent the most advanced trench, so that No Man's Land varied in width from 800 to 600 yards. This fact is most important and a full realisation of it is essential to a correct understanding of the enormous task performed by the 56th Division.

In view of the impending attack the great width of No Man's Land was clearly a great disadvantage, as the time which must necessarily be occupied by assaulting columns in advancing an average of distance of 700 yards before reaching the German front line would expose them to risk of very serious loss and possibly deprive the attack completely of the weight necessary to enable it to be driven home. Nothing daunted by this difficulty, however, the 56th Division at once proceeded to make arrangements to push the lines forward and roughly to halve the width of No Man's Land. This audacious scheme was put into operation, and before the end of May the construction of the new front line—that shown as the front line on the map—was begun.

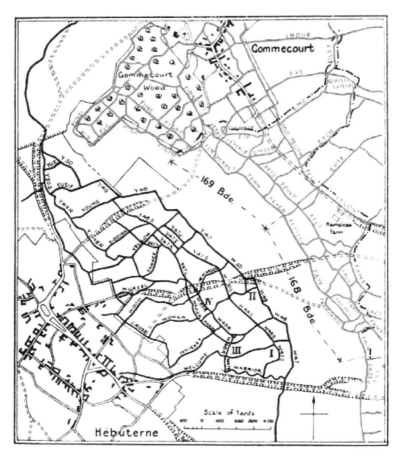

THE ATTACK ON GOMMECOURT, 1ST JULY 1916

The operation of digging a new front line at no great distance from the enemy was one of considerable difficulty. It was clearly essential to perform the work at night, and in view of the importance of the work it was equally clearly a matter of necessity to have the task set out with tapes as a mark for the troops to dig to. It was further reasonable to anticipate that as soon as the enemy became aware of the existence of the new line he would shell it violently, and therefore the new trench must be sunk deeply enough in the first night's work to enable its completion to be carried on from inside without the need for moving troops about in the open. This aim postulated a working party of great strength, for the front to be covered was nearly 2000 yards, and the noise which must inevitably arise from over a mile of shovels and picks hard at work was likely to bring down a hail of machine-gun bullets and cause very severe casualties, and even, in the presence of an enterprising enemy, the probability of a surprise attack in the middle of the work. The attempt was clearly fraught with great risk, but with characteristic boldness Gen. Hull determined to make the attempt.

On the night of the 25/26th May the setting out of the work was safely accomplished by the Royal Engineers under cover of a screen of scouts, and the following night a working party of 3000 men got to work on the digging, a line of outposts being established for their protection within 200 yards of the German line.

The Battalion responsible for W—the right or southern—sector of the new line was the 1/4th Londons, the work being under the control of Major Duncan-Teape, while the L.R.B. undertook the work in Y sector. The night luckily passed quietly, and all ranks working with a will the new trench, shown on map as W 47, W 48, W 49 and W 50, was opened and sunk to a depth sufficient to provide cover.

When the Battalion, therefore, took over W sector on the night of the 28th May, the new front line was becoming fit to occupy and had, moreover, reached the anticipated stage in which, the Bosche being alive to what had been done, it was becoming a favourite target for his shells and trench mortar bombs of all calibres. From this time onwards, in fact until the battle, the Divisional sector and in particular the new trenches were daily harassed by the enemy's fire, and constant repair work on the part of our trench garrisons was called for in addition to the continuance of new construction.

The front line of W sector was taken up by A Company (A. R. Moore) on the right with B Company (S. Elliott) on the left, supports to both front line companies being found by D Company (Giles), while C Company (Long) was in reserve at Hébuterne. Battalion Headquarters occupied dugouts beneath a roller flour mill in Hébuterne. The move forward from Bayencourt for this relief being made in daylight was carried out across country along tracks, platoons moving separately at 300 yards distance.

After relief the Kensingtons in Bayencourt remained at the disposal of the 1/4th Londons for working parties, for the construction of the new front line was but a small beginning of the task which still remained to be completed before the opening of the battle. In addition to the first line there was to be dug a control trench immediately in rear of it, and a new support line—the WS line—and all these were to be connected up by the advancement from the old WR line of Warrior, Welcome, Whisky, Woman and Wood Street communication trenches. These defensive works completed, there was also the erection of the necessary wire entanglements in front, the construction of dugouts for shelters, company headquarters, ammunition stores, and signal offices; the laying of armoured signal cable from all headquarters dugouts back to battalion and brigade, the digging of cable trenches for lines of particular importance, the collection of the necessary supplies of small arms and trench mortar ammunition and bombs in dumps; and other tasks of varying importance and interest. Enough has been said, however, to indicate that with only a month in which to do all this work it was clear that the Battalion was not likely to find time hanging heavily on its hands while in the line,—and indeed it did not.

The tour of duty proved somewhat unpleasant. The works programme was, of course, the outstanding duty, and all ranks put their shoulders to it with a will, but the heavy rains which fell each day made it hard to keep pace with the time-table set for the work, while the remarkable aggressiveness of the enemy's guns added to the digging scheme by providing much undesired practice in trench repair work.

During the night following the relief the Battalion's positions were heavily bombarded by heavy guns and trench mortars, which caused much damage and several casualties, especially in the left company front. Capt. Elliott had to be dug out of the trench which was blown in on him, and he was sent to hospital suffering from severe concussion; and 3 N.C.O.'s and men were killed and 12 wounded. Capt. Elliott was unhappily never able to return to France, and in him the Battalion lost an officer of remarkably cool and sound judgment and of wide sympathy with the welfare of his men.

The 30th May opened with a heavy bombardment of our lines at 12.15 a.m., which was repeated half an hour later. About 2.50 a.m., following further bombardment, the S.O.S. signal was received from the Queen Victoria's Rifles in Y subsector, who reported the enemy advancing. A very quick response to the call was made by our artillery, which laid down a barrage on S.O.S. lines; but no infantry movement developed on our front. At about 5 p.m. the enemy turned his attention to Battalion Headquarters in Hébuterne, which were heavily shelled and severely damaged. The sentry on duty was badly wounded, as were also four other men of the Headquarters staff and four of D Company billeted in an adjoining dugout. The total casualties for the day amounted to 31, of whom 16 in B Company were cases of severe shell shock following the previous day's bombardment.

This unpleasant degree of Bosche activity continued during the night, when our working parties were harassed and seriously delayed; and the 31st May saw no abatement of the shelling. Battalion Headquarters again received a "hate" at about 5 p.m., and the casualties for the day were Lieut. H. B. A. Balls, wounded at duty, and in N.C.O.'s and men, 1 killed and 3 wounded.

Throughout this tour of duty the promptness with which the Divisional artillery responded to calls for retaliatory fire against the enemy's activity was excellent and did a great deal to inspire all ranks with confidence in the gunners.

Further heavy bombardments occurred on the 1st June, which caused a very great deal of damage to the new trenches. On the afternoon of the next day the 1/4th Londons were relieved by the London Scottish, withdrawing on relief to Bayencourt, where tea was served and valises picked up from the stores. In the evening the Battalion was concentrated in huts at Souastre. The Kensingtons had also been relieved by the Rangers, who with the Scottish now came under the orders of the 169th Brigade.

A day was spent in Souastre by the Battalion in cleaning trench mud from uniforms and equipment, and in the evening it moved by march route *via* Hénu to Halloy, where it came once more under the orders of the 168th Brigade in Divisional reserve.

During this period of preparations for the battle the strength of the Battalion had been steadily creeping up with reinforcements from home and from the disbanded 2/4th Battalion. The drafts from the 2/4th Battalion were particularly valuable; they had all seen active service and, moreover, they were rich in potential N.C.O.'s. Throughout the hard fighting which followed the Battalion was fortunate in having so great an internal reserve of strength in this respect. As already recorded the 2/4th Battalion had been on overseas service for nearly eighteen months without the grant of any home leave. Through the special intervention of Lieut.-Col. Wheatley several large allotments of leave were made to the 1/4th Londons, and these were used chiefly for the benefit of the 2/4th Battalion reinforcements, but it was of course inevitable that large numbers of men should be unable to obtain leave before the 1st July.

The drafts received were:

>7th May—2/Lieuts. F. R. C. Bradford, C. S. G. Blows, J. W. Price and S. Davis, and 214 other ranks from the 2/4th Battalion.
>
>14th May—44 other ranks from the Reserve Battalion.
>
>24th May—130 other ranks from the 2/4th Battalion.

When the last-noted draft joined, the Battalion was treated to the annoying spectacle of watching a further 100 men of the 2/4th Battalion marching by *en route* for the Kensingtons.

The day following arrival at Halloy being Sunday, a parade service was held, the first since the 14th May; and later in the day a further reinforcement, this time composed entirely of officers, reported to the Battalion from the disbanded 2/4th Battalion, as follows:

Capts. R. N. Arthur and H. G. Stanham, Lieuts. W. R. Botterill and W. A. Stark, and 2/Lieuts. H. W. Vernon, B. F. L. Yeoman, H. G. Hicklenton and N. W. Williams.

The two first-named officers had been mobilised with the 1/4th Battalion in August 1914, and were thus particularly welcome. The officers of this draft were distributed among the companies, and Capt. Arthur took over the duties of Works Officer as Major, an appointment he continued to fill until the 27th June, when he was evacuated to hospital seriously ill.

The 5th, 6th and 7th June were spent in training, of which the principal feature was a practice attack over trenches constructed to represent those opposite the sector of line which the Battalion had just left, in preparation, of course, for the coming battle. Following the last day's practice the Battalion was inspected by the Third Army commander, Sir Edmund Allenby, who was accompanied by Major-Gen. Hull and Brig.-Gen. Loch, and expressed himself satisfied with all that he had seen and also with what he had heard of the Battalion's behaviour during its recent tour of duty. A report of this kind may read curiously at first in view of the fact that the Battalion had been in France for eighteen months and had proved its steadiness in the line on many occasions: but remember that the 56th Division was brand new, and commanders so far did not know how their troops would shape in action. Praise from Allenby at this stage was therefore praise indeed.

The same day the Battalion was once more sent adrift from its own Brigade and became attached for duty to the 169th Brigade, though it retained its billets at Halloy, and the 168th Brigade took over W and Y sectors, Headquarters moving from Grenas to Sailly.

The Battalion now became responsible for the various works duties in the back area, relieving the L.R.B. in this monotonous task; and from this date onwards remained hard at work on various tasks until almost the eve of battle. B Company was despatched to Mondicourt, an important and vast R.E. dump on the Doullens-Arras Road, for work under the R.E.'s. The remaining companies were split up to supply parties for the daily work, the total numbers found each day being 8 officers and 350 other ranks, employed on such varied tasks as digging road material in Halloy quarries; carrying logs at Pas for gun emplacements; shifting and loading timber at Mondicourt; and working in the R.E. workshop at Pas. This programme was pushed forward without a break until the 12th June, the only intermission being an inspection on Sunday the 11th, of such remnants of the Battalion as were available, by Sir Charles Wakefield, then Lord Mayor of London, who was accompanied by Major-Gen. Hull and Col. Evelyn Wood, and addressed the troops.

On the 13th a further redistribution of Brigades took place, the 168th remaining in line but retaining W sector only; Y sector was handed over to the 169th Brigade; while the 167th moved back into reserve. This move placed the Brigades in the positions they were destined to occupy on the day of battle. The same day the 1/4th Londons moved forward, leaving Halloy at 5 p.m., and marching *via* Authie, St Leger and Coigneux to Bayencourt, where it was joined in billets by B Company from detachment at Mondicourt. A Company was pushed straight on to Hébuterne, when in spite of its long march and late arrival in billets it set to work on its share of the Brigade works programme at 5 a.m. on the 14th June.

The remaining companies were also set to work on the 14th in Hébuterne on parts of the Brigade scheme, working hours being nightly from 9 p.m. to 5 a.m. The parties were much split up, 280 being detailed to the 2/2nd Field Company R.E., 140 to the 5th Cheshires and 140 to the Brigade Signal Officer for digging cable trenches. The tasks were various, but were all directed in one way or another to the completion and repair of the new trench system and the necessary dugouts for the impending offensive. Night after night, for fourteen nights in succession, did the Battalion continue these stiff working parties. Each night there was a march of nearly three miles in each direction between billets and work, each night the Bosche was unpleasantly active with machine-guns, and nearly every night it rained steadily. That the Battalion carried out this depressing duty—for there is nothing with which the average infantryman gets more quickly "fed up" than continual working parties—with such efficiency and keenness is all the more to its credit. Conditions were not comfortable and the men were beginning to be tired; but they stuck to it well for they knew the urgency of the work and how much remained to be done in an impossibly short time.

On the 21st June the 167th Brigade took over the whole Divisional sector for six days in order to give a final rest to the 168th and 169th and to keep them as fresh as possible for battle. The 168th withdrew to its old rest billets at Halloy, but again the 1/4th Londons were left behind as works battalion, remaining in Hébuterne attached to the 167th Brigade and sticking to its works programme.

On the 23rd June Lieut. W. J. Boutall rejoined the Battalion from home and was posted to D Company, but almost immediately took up the duties of Assistant Adjutant.

A draft of the 2/4th Battalion arrived on the 24th, consisting of Lieut. J. R. Webster and 40 other ranks.

Affairs in the line had now begun to "tune up." Some days previously the British 9·2 batteries in Bayencourt had begun to register, while on the 24th the preliminary bombardment of the enemy's lines began systematically, with occasional intense periods, alternating with intervals of quiet. This continued daily—and nightly—much to the discomfort of those who were lucky enough to occupy billets with more or less sound ceilings, for their nights were continually disturbed by large pieces of plaster falling on them at each concussion! The attack had been originally projected for the 29th June, and in preparation for this the 168th and 169th Brigades returned to the line in the afternoon of the 27th, the 1/4th Londons advancing from Bayencourt, taking over the whole of W sector from the 8th Middlesex.

The sector was occupied on a three-company frontage as follows:

> D Company—(Giles) with two platoons in W 47 and 48, one platoon in W 47 S and one in billets in Hébuterne.
>
> A Company—(A. R. Moore) with two platoons in W 49, one in W 49 S and one in billets in Hébuterne.
>
> C Company—(Sykes) with two platoons in W 49 and 50, one in W 50 S and one in Napier Trench.
>
> B Company—(W. Moore) with two platoons in reserve dugouts in Cross Street. The two remaining platoons of B were detailed for special duties as Brigade carrying parties respectively under the Bombing and Machine-Gun Officers.

The Somme Battle was the first important offensive in which steps were taken to reduce the number of officers actually taking part to the smallest possible limits, and a "battle surplus" of officers and also of warrant officers, N.C.O.'s and men was therefore left behind in bivouacs near Souastre when the Battalion moved into the line. This precaution, which was always afterwards adopted, was the means of avoiding unnecessary casualties and of providing an immediate reinforcement, as might be required, of fresh officers who would be acquainted with the men. The officers left in "battle surplus" were Capts. H. G. Stanham and A. L. Long, Lieuts. J. R. Webster and H. W. Vernon, and 2/Lieuts. C. S. G. Blows and N. W. Williams; and these were joined on the eve of battle by Major H. J. Duncan-Teape and Lieut. W J. Boutall, both of whom remained in the line until the last possible minute. Lieut. W. R. Botterill also left the line before the battle to proceed to Woolwich R.M. College.

During the day of relief the British bombardment of the German lines was still proceeding, occasional intensive bursts being used. At about 7.45 p.m. on the cessation of a burst the enemy put down a very heavy retaliatory barrage on the W and WR lines, causing a good deal of damage, especially to the latter. In the course of this shelling D Company's headquarters were blown in and Capt. Giles was seriously wounded, one of his company staff killed and another wounded. Poor Giles, who had done magnificent work as platoon commander, adjutant and company commander, and had never missed a day's duty since August 1914, died in hospital from his injuries a few days later. He was a gallant and unselfish officer. His place in command of D Company was taken by Stanham, who came forward from surplus.

During the evening two patrols were despatched from New Woman Street to examine and report on the condition of the enemy's wire and front line trenches. They returned at 12.30 a.m. on the 28th, bringing samples of German wire, which was reported as too thick to admit of access to the front line. About the same time a rocket signal was sent up from the Bosche line, a red light followed by two more in quick succession, and this was the prelude to a sharp bombardment of our lines for about fifteen minutes. Somewhat later, about 3.45 a.m., a second barrage came down, this time on Hébuterne, but the damage caused was not great. As the day wore on the enemy's activity became less intense though he exhibited great persistence all day in his efforts to locate our batteries near Cross Street and our trench mortar emplacements in W 47. At night working parties were set on to the almost final preparation of cutting gaps in our own wire at intervals of about 50 to 70 yards to allow egress to the assaulting columns. This work is naturally rather tricky, and the gaps, the cutting of which was left till the last minute, must be so concealed if possible as to avoid the risk of the enemy marking them down and plastering them with shell fire.

The day's casualties amounted to 2 officers, Lieut. W. A. Stark and J. W. Price wounded, and 2 men killed and 11 wounded.

During the evening patrols had again been despatched to investigate the enemy's wire and trenches, and this night greater success was achieved. The right patrol which approached the Bosche line in front of Farm-Farmyard was under 2/Lieut. W. H. Webster, who on looking over the enemy's parapet found he had selected a firebay containing a party of Bosche hard at work. Unfortunately the alarm was given and the presence of the patrol being disclosed by Véry lights it was forced to withdraw.

Late on the evening of the 29th the warning was received that the attack was postponed for forty-eight hours, until the 1st July.

Throughout the 29th our preliminary bombardment continued with gradually increasing intensity; but it was noticeable that in spite of the damage it was clearly doing to the enemy's defences it was not by any means successful in silencing his batteries. The German artillery was in fact unpleasantly lively, and from 6.30 a.m. until about 4.30 p.m. W sector was subjected to intermittent harassing fire from field and machine-guns. This more or less desultory fire was followed at 6 p.m. by a sharp enemy barrage. All the evening the enemy's activity continued, and the remarkable number of Véry lights which he put up indicated his growing nervousness. There was indeed now every reason to believe that the Bosche expected our attack. The long-continued British bombardment of trenches, dumps, cross roads and battery positions, the systematic wire-cutting, and the activity of our air forces, could have left no room for doubt in the enemy's mind that an important offensive was being launched. In some parts of the battle front, indeed, the Germans had displayed notice boards inviting the British to start their attack; and though probably these emanated from individual bravado they formed some indication that surprise effect was not to be expected, and that there was good reason to believe that the Germans would with their usual thoroughness have made preparations to offer the most stubborn possible resistance to our projected advance.

The 29th also demanded its toll of casualties from the Battalion, and this day 28 N.C.O.'s and men were wounded.

The 30th June opened with a heavy barrage on W sector and Hébuterne at about midnight, but this subsided after a few minutes and little further activity was displayed by the enemy during the early morning hours. As dawn approached the enemy's nervousness evidently increased, and he maintained an almost continuous discharge of Véry lights. From 7 a.m. onwards, however, the enemy artillery once more began to show signs of liveliness which increased as the day passed. The WR line in the vicinity of Woman and Cross Streets was in particular heavily shelled, and altogether a great amount of damage was done to our trench system. This action of the enemy did not call for any particular retaliatory measures from our artillery, which proceeded with the preliminary bombardment according to its programme. The losses sustained by the Battalion on this day amounted to 2 N.C.O.'s and men killed and 21 wounded, making a total of 69 casualties during the three days the Battalion had held the line.

Little has been said of the actual occupation of the Battalion during these three days; there is so much to relate of the battle day itself that space does not permit us to dwell overmuch on the preceding period. But be it understood that all the time the works programme was being pushed on with feverish haste, though progress was slow owing to the continued rain and the great delay caused in the projected new work by having to divert from it a large proportion of the available strength to repair the damage caused by the daily German bombardments.

During the evening the Battalion formed up in its prearranged assembly areas in readiness for the attack on the following morning.

The part which the 56th Division was called on to play in the offensive was that of a combined operation on a comparatively small front in conjunction with the 46th Division, which was in line opposite the northern flank of the Gommecourt Salient and adjoining the 56th. These Divisions which, with the 37th (not engaged), formed the VII Corps and were the right flank of Allenby's Third Army, were the two most northern divisions operating in the Somme offensive.

Adjoining the 56th on the right lay Hunter-Weston's VIII Corps, comprising from left to right the 31st, 4th and 29th Divisions in line, with the 48th in support. One Brigade of this last-named Division—the 143rd—was in line between the 56th and the 31st, and its sector formed a gap on which no forward move was attempted. The Gommecourt operation was therefore entirely isolated, though forming an inherent part of the one great offensive plan.

South of the VIII Corps the British battle front was taken up by the X Corps (Morland), III Corps (Pulteney), XV Corps (Horne) and XIII Corps (Congreve), these forming with the VIII, Rawlinson's Fourth Army.

The 56th Division's objectives, which will be easily followed from the map, were to capture and consolidate a line running almost due north from a strong point at the south end of Farm-Farmyard, through Fame, Felon, Fell, Fellow, and the Quadrilateral to the junction of Fillet and Indus. From this point the line was to be continued to the "little Z" (a point about 2000 yards north of the apex of the Gommecourt Salient) by the 46th Division, who were to clear Gommecourt village and park.

The 168th Brigade on the right of the Divisional sector attacked on a two-battalion front from the strong point on the right to the junction of Felon and Epte on the left. Strong points were to be consolidated on the extreme right and also at the junctions of Felon with Elbe and Epte. From this point the 169th Brigade was to continue the line to the junction of Fir and Firm and also to the point of union with the 46th Division.

The 167th Brigade was in Divisional reserve, and one battalion, the 1st Londons, was detailed to supply 600 men to dig communication trenches across No Man's Land after the attack.

The 168th Brigade group was disposed as follows:

HEADQUARTERS IN MARDI TRENCH

ASSAULTING BATTALIONS—

Right—London Scottish.

Left—Rangers.

SUPPORTING BATTALIONS—

Right—Kensingtons, with a special task of digging a fire trench to form a defensive flank across No Man's Land from the head of Welcome Street.

Left—1/4th Londons.

168th M.G. Company—In tunnelled emplacements in the WR line for overhead covering fire.

3-inch L.T.M. Battery (Stokes), (with half the 167th Brigade Battery)—In emplacements in the front line control trench.

In addition the following troops were at the disposal of the Brigadier for the operation:

- One Company 5th Cheshires (Pioneers).
- One Section 2/2nd London Field Company, R.E.
- Y 56—2-inch Mortar Battery.

The artillery affiliated to the Brigade consisted of four 18-pr. batteries and one 4·5-inch howitzer battery, comprising the southern group.

Similar attachments were made to the 167th Brigade, and over and above these there remained at the disposal of the Divisional artillery, a counter-battery group consisting of two 18-pr. and one 4·5-inch howitzer batteries; and two 18-pr. batteries in reserve; while of trench mortars there were one 2-inch battery (X 56) and two heavy (9½-inch) mortars.

During the evening of the 30th June the other battalions of the Brigade began to move into W sector to take up their assembly positions. The assembly areas are marked on the map in Roman numerals as follows:

I. London Scottish (right front).
II. Rangers (left front).
III. Kensingtons (right support).
IV. 1/4th Londons (left support).

As each battalion arrived and took over its area the various companies of the 1/4th Londons withdrew to No. IV area in rear of the Rangers. In order to avoid congestion and cross traffic in the communication trenches several platoons of the 1/4th Londons had to withdraw to assembly position over the open, and by 10 p.m. this operation was completed.

The 1st July was a glorious summer day, and the light haze which tells of great heat hung over the rolling hills of this great plain which was destined to become the scene of so great a struggle. With the earliest grey of dawn the Germans opened an intense bombardment on all our trenches, to which no reply was made by our artillery. This severe shelling started at about 2.45 a.m. and lasted for nearly an hour: in the course of it part of the Rangers were blown out of their assembly trenches and compelled to make a temporary withdrawal to our area, causing a good deal of congestion and confusion.

At 6.25 a.m. our week old bombardment increased to "hurricane" intensity and every gun, trench mortar and machine-gun on the British front from Gommecourt to the Somme came into action, pouring a hail of shot and shell into the enemy lines with merciless precision and rapidity. Under such a colossal weight of metal it seemed that nothing could live, and it was confidently hoped that the bombardment would go far towards breaking down the enemy's morale and power of resistance to our attack.

At 7.25 a.m. a smoke barrage was raised along the whole front of the attack by firing smoke bombs from the front trenches, and under this at 7.30 a.m. the British battalions moved to the assault under cover of a creeping barrage, a moving curtain of fire.

On the 168th Brigade front the attack was made by each assaulting battalion on a four-company front, each company in column of platoons in extended order. The attack as a whole, therefore, moved in four "waves," and following as a fifth wave moved a trench-clearing party consisting of two platoons of B Company of the 1/4th Londons.

These platoons under 2/Lieuts. L. R. Chapman and H. G. Hicklenton had the duty of completing the capture of each trench line by killing the remaining garrison, clearing the dugouts, and collecting and sending back the prisoners; thereby saving delay to the assaulting waves, who would otherwise have had to perform these duties themselves to avoid the risk of an attack from the rear after they had passed the first objective. These platoons were made up to a strength of 1 officer, 3 N.C.O.'s and 36 men organised in four sections (clearing, bombing, blocking and communicating), but during the hours of waiting after assembly had already lost 26 men hit.

At the same time as the assaulting waves moved forward the Battalion, less the two platoons of B Company above, advanced and occupied battle positions in the area vacated by the Rangers, as follows:

> A Company—(A. R. Moore) two platoons in front line trench and two platoons in Boyau de Service, Sector W 49, between Whisky Street and Woman Street.
>
> C Company—(J. T. Sykes) two platoons in W 50 and two platoons in the Boyau de Service, north and south of Bucquoy Road.
>
> D Company—(H. G. Stanham) formed up in line in trench W 49 S and W 50 S.

The WS line occupied by D Company had been very severely damaged by the German bombardment and communication was therefore extremely difficult. The company was inevitably much split up under the two platoon commanders, G. H. Davis and B. F. L. Yeoman, while Stanham took up a central position where he hoped to keep in touch with both flanks.

The two remaining platoons of B Company were employed as follows:

> 1 Platoon—Carrying party under Brigade Bombing Officer.
>
> > 1 Platoon—1 Section—Carrying party to 168th M.G. Company.

3 Sections—In reserve in Napier Trench.

> Battalion Headquarters (K Company) were disposed as follows:

Clerks, signallers, pioneers, snipers, etc. (34 other ranks)	In dugout and control trench of Woman Street.
Company runners (16 other ranks)	In a sap adjoining.
Battalion Bombers	In a "crump" hole near the Woman Street Battalion H.Q. dugout.
Battalion Trench Pioneers	W 50 R.
M.O. and Staff	Aid Post (Junction of Wood Street and Cross Street).

Band	Ditto.
Reserve Lewis Gunners	Divided between A and B Companies.
Regimental Police	In control posts, chiefly at intersection of fire trenches with communication trenches throughout the sector.

A runner from the right company (A) reporting it in position arrived at Headquarters at 8.15 a.m., but no report was received from any other company, and from this time onwards throughout the day communication was exceedingly difficult on account of the very heavy German barrage which fell on all lines in W sector immediately after zero. It was reported, however, by observers that all had successfully formed up on their battle positions.

We must now turn for a moment to the leading battalions.

On the right the London Scottish advanced under the effective cover of the smoke barrage, which was in fact so thick as to render the maintenance of the correct direction a matter of difficulty, and occupied Farm, Fell and Fate as far north as the Bucquoy Road, and also the greater part of the strong point at the southern extremity of attack. The blocking of the adjoining trenches and consolidation of the captured lines was at once put in hand. The left companies appear to have been drawn off somewhat towards Nameless Farm but seem to have kept in touch with the Rangers on their left.

Shortly after 8 o'clock the Scottish were joined by a company of Kensingtons, who did good work in the consolidation of Farm-Farmyard.

On the left four companies of the Rangers also crossed No Man's Land, and although the position is obscure there can be no doubt that parties of all companies succeeded in reaching the final objectives in Felon, Elbe and Epte, and gained touch on Nameless Farm Road with the 169th Brigade on the left.

At these advanced points bomb fighting in the communication trenches began and the struggle was pursued along the line with varying success. Realising the pressure that was being brought to bear on his now dangerously weak companies the O.C. Rangers asked for two companies of the 1/4th Londons to lend the weight necessary to carry forward his attack again.

This order was received by Lieut.-Col. Wheatley at 8.45 a.m. and at once he ordered A and C Companies to reinforce the Rangers in Fetter, and D

Company to move up to the W front line in their place. Telephone communication having been cut by the enemy shell fire this order was despatched by runner to the front companies; but of six runners despatched by different routes, and two additional runners sent after fifteen minutes' interval, only one returned after an unsuccessful attempt to find the left company. The others were all killed. We must pause here to offer a tribute to the bravery of runners, a class of soldier whose gallantry was only too seldom adequately rewarded; their duties compelled them to attempt to pass through impossible barrages without the moral support of comradeship, and to face almost certain death in the forlorn hope of getting through with a vital order. But never once did they flinch from their duty.

At 9.5 a.m. a report was received through the Rangers that Rangers and 1/4th Londons were together in the German front line, and this was followed at intervals by other reports indicating their further progress, till at 10.25 a.m. a message from the Rangers reported parties of both battalions in the second German trench. Following the receipt of this information at 10.45 a.m. Lieut-Col. Wheatley despatched the Battalion Trench Pioneers to help consolidate the trenches gained.

The above messages probably convey a substantially correct idea of what occurred, but owing to the failure of all means of communication on account of the intensity of the German shell fire, the movements of A and C Companies will probably never be known in detail. At 11.50 a.m. an untimed message was received from Capt. A. R. Moore (A Company) reporting that he was still in W 49, his battle position, though at 9.5 a.m., as we have seen, he was reported to have crossed to the German line; and probably this latter report is correct. The situation, however, evidently required clearing up, and a patrol consisting of L.-Corpl. Hyde and Pte. Lear despatched from Battalion Headquarters succeeded in returning with the information that A Company had gone forward. L.-Corpl. Hyde was awarded the Military Medal for his good work, and subsequently recommended for a commission by Lieut.-Col. Wheatley; he was unfortunately killed in action later in the Somme Battle whilst completing his training with C Company.

At 1 p.m. a message was received from Stanham (in reserve) that his Company had suffered about fifty per cent. casualties and that his position had become untenable. He was ordered to maintain his position.

By this time the situation on the other side of No Man's Land was becoming desperate. The work of consolidation was almost impossible owing to the German barrage, and the sustained bomb fighting was rapidly becoming an unequal struggle owing to the impossibility of replenishing the dwindling supplies of bombs. Again and again with unsurpassed devotion the carrying party endeavoured to pass through the barrier of German shells with the coveted supplies of bombs to our harassed troops—but passage was impossible and the gallant carriers only added to the roll of casualties.

At 1.30 p.m. a patrol returned from the German lines to Battalion Headquarters. This had been despatched at 11 o'clock on a demand from the Brigadier for information as to the left of the Brigade in the German line, and Ptes. Whitehead and Buckingham had volunteered for the duty. According to this patrol a party of the Rangers under Lieut. Harper were holding on to the junction of Et and Felt, but was urgently in need of bombs. Further, none of the 168th Brigade were then in the German third line. This report was passed on to Brigade and to the Rangers, and a special bomb carrying party from the Battalion was ordered across to relieve Harper's need. But none reached the German line, all being killed or wounded in No Man's Land. For their bravery and devotion to duty Ptes. Whitehead and Buckingham were rewarded with the Military Medal, and the former was subsequently granted a commission.

At 2.30 p.m. the front of the Battalion Headquarters dugout was blown in by a shell, which killed seven and wounded seven men. At the time the dugout was occupied by a large number of Headquarters staff, including the Colonel, the Adjutant, the Signalling Officer and Major Moore, but of these luckily none was hit.

All this time the German shell fire continued without abatement, and at 3.30 p.m. further heavy casualties were reported by D Company. At 3.45 p.m. Brigade Headquarters ordered D Company to withdraw to the WR line, and a report was received from Stanham at 4.45 p.m. that his withdrawal with 1 officer and 20 men was complete.

Meanwhile the Brigade was gradually being compelled to give ground and, owing to its lack of bombs, to loose its slender hold on the enemy's positions. At about 2 p.m. the remnants of the Rangers, together with a few 1/4th Londons and some Queen Victorias from the 169th Brigade on the left, were driven into Fate, where they made a last determined stand; but at 3.10 p.m. they were finally ejected from the German lines and withdrew to the British trenches.

On the right the Scottish and Kensingtons met with a similar fate. A gallant fight was put up by the remains of the Battalion under Capt. H. C. Sparks in Farm-Farmyard, but by 4 p.m., both his flanks being in the air and his whole force being in imminent danger of extinction, Sparks decided to withdraw, this operation being stubbornly and successfully carried out after the removal of as many wounded as possible.

At 6.30 p.m. the 1/4th Londons reformed in the WR line between Wood Street and Woman Street, and later in the evening moved into the trenches west of Hébuterne.

The other battalions of the 168th were also withdrawn and the sector was taken over by the 167th Brigade.

The story of the 169th Brigade attack is, like that of the 168th, one of initial success which could not be maintained. The line Fell-Feud was carried in the early hours of the morning by the Queen Victorias and London Rifle Brigade, but the intensity of the German shell fire and the enfilading of the captured positions by machine-guns in Gommecourt Park prevented the Queen's Westminsters from carrying the Quadrilateral. Later in the day lack of bombs, as in the case of the 168th Brigade, proved the deciding factor, and resulted in a gradual loss of the Brigade's grip on the enemy trenches, and after desperate struggles the late afternoon hours found them also beaten back to their original lines.

So ended the first day on which the 56th Division had been in battle, a day on which after the most stubborn fighting and unsurpassed devotion the gain of ground was nil, and which dealt London the severest blow in loss of personnel that it ever suffered on any single day throughout the War.

The losses in the Division during the period 24th June to 3rd July amounted to 4749 all ranks, of whom 35 officers and 412 other ranks were killed, 107 officers and 2632 other ranks wounded, and 40 officers and 1532 other ranks missing. In the 1/4th Londons the losses for the same period totalled the appalling number of 16 officers and 534 other ranks. These dreadful losses were borne fairly equally by all companies, for all had been exposed to the same deadly and unrelenting shell fire throughout the day.

Of A Company, gallantly led to the second German line by Capt. A. R. Moore, M.C., but 18 returned. Moore himself and one of his subalterns, F. C. Fanhangel, were killed, the other subaltern, A. G. Blunn, being captured with 7 others. The rest of the company were killed. Moore's end, like his life, was one of courageous devotion, and has been simply told by one of his own sergeants: "Capt. Moore was wounded in the wrist about thirty minutes before we went over. Nevertheless he led the company, revolver in hand, and on the sunken road at the rear of Nameless Farm I saw blood flowing from his back. He still pushed on, and then I was shot through the leg and took shelter in a shell hole. The last I saw of Capt. Moore he was still going ahead...."

The two platoons of B Company which went forward as clearing party were severely handled. Both the subalterns, Chapman and Hicklenton, were hit and only 10 men got back from the German line. 2/Lieut. A. S. Ford on carrying party duty was also hit.

Of C Company only two platoons got forward as the order to advance failed to reach Sykes, the company commander. But its casualties under the terrific German barrage were as heavy as in any company, and after Sykes had been wounded and both his subalterns, T. Moody and F. R. C. Bradford, killed, the remnants of the company were brought steadily out of action by Company Sergt.-Major Davis, who was rewarded with the D.C.M.

D Company, which remained in reserve all day, had perhaps the most trying time of all. From 2.30 a.m. until withdrawn at 3.30 p.m. it sat still under the most intense artillery bombardment, but was kept splendidly in hand and ready to move by Stanham and his only remaining subaltern, G. H. Davis. B. F. L. Yeoman became a casualty early in the day.

Of the Headquarters officers Major W. Moore and 2/Lieut. V. C. Donaldson were wounded.

Magnificent work was done throughout the day by the Medical Officer, Capt. Hurd, and his staff, who, though the number of casualties far outmeasured the facilities for dealing with them, continued their work without a break throughout the day and the night following. In this work splendid help was rendered by the Padre, Rev. R. Palmer, who organised and led search and carrying parties in No Man's Land and brought in many wounded who were unable to move.

The morning of the 2nd July was spent in the dreary duty of ascertaining the casualties and reorganising the companies, and in the afternoon the Battalion marched to billets at St Amand.

With the results of the day's fighting on other parts of the front we are hardly concerned here. From Fricourt to the Somme the day was successful and the bulk of the objectives were captured and held. But from Fricourt northward the tale throughout was one of complete check. Everywhere our troops met with initial success which everywhere was later changed into disaster with appalling losses.

There is no doubt that in the northern half of attack the British offensive was fully anticipated by the Germans. It would indeed have been difficult to carry out such immense preparations over a period of several weeks prior to the battle without permitting indications of the impending attempt to become visible to hostile aerial scouts. But it had been hoped that the weight and long continuance of the preliminary bombardment, even though it disclosed its own purpose, would prove so intense as to nullify all the German efforts to resist.

We must here make some reference to the battle of the 46th Division on the northern face of the Gommecourt salient. Against this ill-fated Division the German fire was terrific. On the right the South Staffords were completely shattered by the enemy's machine-guns before they could cross No Man's Land; on the left the Sherwood Foresters succeeded in gaining the German front line, and isolated parties appear even to have struggled forward as far as the second trench, but were rapidly ejected. Soon after zero the whole of the 46th Division's assaulting troops were back in their own line after suffering appalling losses: their attack was a complete failure. At the time, therefore, that the 56th Division was making headway into the German positions, instead of the enemy feeling, as had been hoped, the pincers closing on him from both sides of his salient, he was relieved from all menace on his right flank facing the 46th Division, and free to throw the whole weight of his artillery and infantry against the 56th Division.

But the causes of the 56th Division's failure must be looked for deeper than this.

Primarily it may be said to have been due to the shortage of bombs. The great distance which carrying parties had to traverse over No Man's Land with fresh supplies and the intensity of the German barrage through which they had to pass were both such that the facilities for getting bombs forward were inadequate. It should be remembered that the 168th and 169th Brigades captured three lines of German trenches and held them against all attacks in spite of the gruelling enemy fire for many hours. It was only when bomb supplies failed that they were ejected.

There are three other factors in this battle to which we may refer as having contributed to the failure.

First, the enormously strong deep dugouts in the German lines, which were large enough to give shelter to the whole trench garrison except the few necessary sentries, had proved too strong for all except the heaviest guns; and those of the heaviest calibre had not been directed against them. The German garrisons were therefore able to remain in safety until the last moment when our barrage lifted off their front lines and they were able to man their parapets. The strength of the German defences was increased by the density and depth of their wire entanglements, which had been most skilfully sited with the support of machine-guns firing in enfilade.

Secondly, the insufficient attention paid on our side to counter-battery work. The batteries told off for counter-battery fire were too few and of too light calibre. Throughout the day the cry arose from all Headquarters to silence the German guns, but the few batteries available, though served magnificently by splendid gunners, could not cope with so gigantic a task.

The third and most important cause lay in the cunning skill with which the German barrage was used. We have referred above to the manning of the German parapets by their garrisons after our barrage had passed over; but not in every case did this happen. In many instances a greater refinement of skill was exhibited. As the British barrage lifted off the first objective and the leading waves of the assault poured over it, down came the enemy barrage like a dense curtain, cutting them off for ever from their supports and their supplies. The barrage having thus trapped them, the front trench filled with Germans swarming up from their subterranean shelters, and these poured a hail of machine-gun fire into the backs of our waves which were pushing forward to the next line.

After the experience of two more years of organised trench to trench attacks, it may be that failure for the reasons detailed above seems a little obvious; but it would not be fair to pass them over without pointing out that this was the first trench to trench attack of the whole War which had been organised on so vast a scale, and it was clearly impossible to provide against all eventualities when there was no previous experience to act as a guide. It should be remembered that in the south, where a greater degree of surprise was attained, the arrangements for attack—which were substantially the same as in the north—worked splendidly and resulted in marked success. And in subsequent attacks attention was paid to the experience gained on this great opening day of the First Somme Battle in increasing the strength of counter-battery artillery and in making more efficient arrangements for "mopping-up" captured lines.

As regards the 168th Brigade attack, in addition to the above general criticisms, it may be remarked that the event showed that on the left of the Brigade at least there was insufficient weight in the attack. The Scottish on the right had to advance 250 yards and were able to carry their objectives; but on the left the depth to be penetrated was about 450 yards, and this proved too great for the available strength of the Rangers, who were organised in five waves, even when strengthened by two additional waves supplied by the companies of the 1/4th Londons.

A deal of congestion in the trenches and a great many casualties were caused by the lack of those deep dugouts with which the Germans were so well supplied, and in the case of the 1/4th Londons at any rate it seems likely that they might have been of more use when called upon had they been able to obtain efficient shelter during the hours of waiting.

We have sufficiently elaborated the causes of failure. It must not be forgotten that a very real and important result was achieved by the Londoners this day. The strategic object of their attack was not primarily the capture of ground but the holding of German troops and guns from the area of our main attack. This was an unpleasant rôle, but a highly important one, and there can be no manner of doubt that it was to a very large degree fulfilled. The Division's achievement is summarised concisely in the message of congratulation issued by Lieut.-Gen. D'Oyly Snow on the 4th July:

> The Corps Commander wishes to congratulate all ranks of the 56th Division on the way in which they took the German trenches and held them by pure grit and pluck for so long in very adverse circumstances. Although Gommecourt has not fallen into our hands, the purpose of the attack, which was mainly to contain and kill Germans, was accomplished, thanks to a great extent to the tenacity of the 56th Division.

A remarkable incident occurred on the Divisional front on the 2nd July. At about 2.30 p.m. that day a number of German stretcher-bearers were seen to issue from their trenches and begin collecting the many British wounded who were still lying round about their first three lines of trenches. Prompt measures of precaution were taken by the Division, and all guns were made ready to open fire on barrage lines should any intention be shown by the Germans to take advantage of the temporary truce. As, however, the enemy stretcher-bearers continued their humane work quietly, our own stretcher-bearers followed their example and began collecting casualties from No Man's Land. During this extraordinary armistice no attempt was made by the Germans to come outside or by our men to go beyond the line which had formerly been the German wire entanglements. After about two hours of this work, which was the means of saving many lives, the stretcher-bearers returned by mutual and tacit consent to their own lines and the War was resumed!

The casualties suffered by the 46th Division were exceedingly heavy, and the treatment it had received was so severe that it was deemed necessary to withdraw it from the line temporarily, and arrangements were made for the 56th Division to assume responsibility at once for the 46th sector as well as its own.

This arrangement unfortunately deprived the 168th Brigade of its well-earned rest. But though tired and in need of reorganisation after the heavy losses it had sustained the Brigade's morale was good, for it felt justifiably proud of its effort of the previous day. The relief of the 46th Division began on the evening of the 2nd July when the Scottish and the Kensingtons took over the line from the left of the 56th sector of the Fonquevillers-Gommecourt Road.

The 1/4th Londons remained at St Amand during the 3rd July, busily engaged in reorganising its platoons and making up as far as possible deficiencies in equipment and ammunition. In the evening the 1/4th Londons and Rangers took over from the 138th Brigade the remainder of the 46th Divisional sector, the Battalion relieving the 5th Lincolns on a front adjoining that occupied by the Kensingtons the previous night.

The condition of the trenches was found to be shocking and the material damage caused by shell and trench mortar fire was severe, but the number of dead whose bodies had not yet been removed, and of wounded who still were lying out in No Man's Land provided a great deal of work of the utmost urgency. Fortunately the enemy did not interfere with this work of clearing up the battlefield, and his lack of activity was doubtless due to his being similarly employed. Reports were received at night that enemy patrols were active in No Man's Land, but no encounters took place and the Germans seen were probably covering patrols for stretcher-bearing parties.

The following day passed without unusual incident except for a certain amount of enemy shelling during the afternoon, which did considerable further damage to the Battalion's trenches. During the night a storm of terrific intensity burst over Fonquevillers, adding to the general discomfort by filling the trenches with water.

The two remaining days spent by the Battalion in this sector were occupied in continuing the work of removing the dead, baling out and clearing blocked trenches, and generally attempting to reorganise the broken-down defences as well as possible.

On the evening of the 6th July the 168th Brigade was relieved in Z sector, as the 46th Divisional line was called, by the 169th, and the Battalion, handing over its trenches to the Queen's Westminsters, moved by platoons into billets at St Amand, a welcome issue of dry underclothing being issued to the troops on arrival.

At this point the Battalion may be said finally to have finished its share in the battle of the 1st July. Although not detailed as one of the assaulting battalions in the attack, the strain to which it was subjected both in actual hard work prior to the battle and by reason of the enemy fire during the action, was as heavy as that borne by any unit of the Division, while its casualties were among the most severe. Starting at Bayencourt on the 13th June the Battalion had supplied heavy working parties with long hours of work and with a three-mile march in each direction to and from work for fourteen nights in succession, always harassed by the enemy fire and frequently wet through. For three nights of unusual enemy activity they had held the line prior to the battle, and this duty was followed without respite by the day of battle itself. After a brief interlude of two days in billets it had once more returned to the trenches on the additional and unexpected duty at Fonquevillers, and had there passed a further four days in extreme discomfort—a record of which we think any battalion might justly be proud.

The extended front now held by the Division rendered a prolonged rest for the Brigade out of the question, and the Battalion's sojourn at St Amand was of only three days' duration. Of these days the first two were occupied in refitting the troops as far as possible, and in cleaning up and drying clothing after the days spent in the line. The last day, Sunday 9th July, was occupied with Church Parade and, in the afternoon, a Brigade Parade at Souastre for inspections by the Corps and Army Commanders, both of whom addressed the Brigade in congratulatory terms.

On the afternoon of the 10th the 168th Brigade returned to the trenches at Hébuterne, there relieving the 167th. An adjustment of sectors was now effected as a result of which the 168th Brigade held the right sector of the Divisional front, comprising the old W sector and the part of Y sector south of the Hébuterne-Gommecourt Road; in the centre was the 167th Brigade between the Hébuterne-Gommecourt and the Fonquevillers-Gommecourt Roads; while the 169th Brigade held the left of the Divisional front.

The 168th front was occupied by the London Scottish in the right subsector and the Kensingtons on the left. The 1/4th Londons took over billets at Bayencourt, while the Rangers moved to Sailly.

On the 17th the Battalion relieved the London Scottish in the right subsector of the Brigade front, the relief being complete by 6 p.m. The same day the Rangers took over the left subsector from the Kensingtons.

The principal operation carried out by the Battalion during this tour of duty was the filling in of the advanced front line. This had been so seriously damaged during the battle as to become almost untenable, and the labour which would be involved in its repair and maintenance did not appear to be justifiable. Accordingly the task of filling it and the communication trenches as far back as the WS line was carried out on the night 18/19th July. The portion from Whisky Street southwards was dealt with by 2 officers and 140 men of C Company, while the part north of Whisky Street was filled in by 120 men of the Kensingtons. A covering party in No Man's Land of 2 platoons' strength secured the safety of the working party.

This step clearly indicated that all ideas of an advance on this front were—for the moment at any rate—given up, but the rôle played by the Division during the remainder of its duty at Hébuterne was such as to foster an offensive spirit in the troops by means of constant patrolling activity and a general policy of aggression against the enemy's defences and working parties. This rôle was the more important on account of the striking developments which were occurring in the British offensive operations nearer the Somme, where the pressure which was being brought to bear on the Germans was severe and continually increasing. Gradually the enemy was being compelled to push his reserves into the fight and limit as far as possible his activities on other parts of the front. Any action at Hébuterne, therefore, which could prevent the withdrawal of the opposing garrison to the battle area further south had a direct and important bearing on the fortunes of the British arms.

On the nights of the 20th, 21st and 22nd July strong patrols were sent out from the Battalion under 2/Lieuts. W. E. Osborne, H. W. Vernon and J. C. Graddon respectively, with the object of securing a live prisoner captured from a German patrol. No success, however, was achieved.

On the 23rd July an inter-battalion relief again took place and the Battalion was relieved by the London Scottish withdrawing on relief to Brigade support billets at Sailly, but leaving B Company in the Keep in Hébuterne to furnish working parties.

The Battalion remained in Sailly supplying working parties in the forward area until the end of July. Advantage was taken of this period out of the line to straighten out some "cross-postings" which had occurred among drafts of N.C.O.'s and men recently sent up from the Base, and drafts of Queen's Westminsters and 3rd London men were despatched from the Battalion to rejoin their own units. At the same time the Battalion received drafts of 4th London men from the Queen Victorias and the Kensingtons, to whom they had been sent in error.

On the last day of July the Battalion once more took over from the London Scottish the right subsector of W sector, B and C Companies occupying the WR line as the most advanced position with A Company in support and D in reserve.

During the ensuing tour of duty the work of trench repairing, wiring and patrolling was actively prosecuted, but no incident worthy of record occurred. The enemy's activity, both in artillery and trench mortar fire, became rather more marked, and Hébuterne itself attracted more attention than had been the case prior to the battle. The enemy's shell fire produced, however, an ample measure of retaliation from our guns, which bombarded his trenches with good results.

On the 4th August the Battalion withdrew again to Brigade reserve at Bayencourt, handing over its trenches to the London Scottish, and was employed in furnishing working parties and in training.

Since the 1st July the Battalion had received some very valuable reinforcements of officers which repaired the deficiencies caused by the battle, as follows:

> 13th July—Capt. F. C. J. Read from the 2/4th Battalion, Lieut. A. G. Sharp, 2/Lieuts. P. F. Smalley, J. C. Graddon, Y. R. Oldrey, W. H. Calnan, C. E. Lewis, W. E. Osborne, J. W. Chapman, F. J. Foden, C. F. English and J. T. Middleton from the Reserve Battalion.
>
> 16th July—2/Lieut. G. E. Stanbridge from the Reserve Battalion.
>
> 6th August—2/Lieut. F. R. R. Burford from the 3/4th Battalion, 2/Lieuts. C. J. Brodie, O. D. Garratt, C. H. T. Heaver, A. Potton, W. Quennell and C. M. Taylor from the Reserve Battalion.
>
> 7th August—2/Lieuts. C. W. Denning, M.M., S. J. Barkworth, M.M., E. McD. McCormick, T. B. Cooper, M.M., W. H. Davey, D.C.M., C. F. Mortleman commissioned direct from the 1/20th Londons.
>
> 9th August—2/Lieuts. N. A. Ormiston, R. E. Grimsdell and W. Richards from the Reserve Battalion.
>
> 10th August—2/Lieut. J. W. Price from Hospital and 2/Lieut. L. W. Archer, commissioned from the ranks of the Battalion.

On the 5th July a draft of 60, of whom 58 were N.C.O.'s, arrived from the 2/4th Battalion, a particularly welcome addition to the strength in view of the losses which had been sustained. Early in July Lieut. L. G. Rix, the Transport Officer, had been appointed Brigade Transport Officer, and his place in the Battalion was filled by Lieut. G. V. Lawrie, attached from the Scottish Rifles.

2/Lieut. N. W. Williams was wounded at Fonquevillers on the 6th July, and on the 18th the Battalion suffered a further great loss in the Quartermaster, Lieut. E. S. Tomsett, who completely broke down in health and was invalided to England. Tomsett had filled the appointment of Quartermaster with great credit since November 1913, and had served over thirteen years with the Battalion, his previous service having been with the Rifle Brigade. On recovery from his illness Tomsett was granted a combatant commission in recognition of his services and appointed to command the depôt at Hoxton. His duties as Quartermaster in the 1/4th Battalion were taken over by Lieut. H. B. A. Balls.

The 10th August found the Battalion once more—and for the last time—resuming possession of W sector, the relief of the London Scottish being completed by 4.45 p.m. During the progress of the relief Hébuterne was intermittently shelled and a direct hit was scored on Battalion Headquarters, though fortunately without inflicting casualties. A six-day tour of duty produced but little of interest beyond the usual trench routine. Patrolling in No Man's Land was actively pursued, and resulted in establishing definitely the energy being displayed by the Germans in repairing their defences, and also their acquiescence in our possession of No Man's Land, which seemed to be undisputed. The German artillery continued to shell Hébuterne and the Orchard, near Cross Street, a good deal, while his constant machine-gun fire at night interfered seriously with our work of wiring in front of W 48.

On the 12th Major-Gen. Hull presented ribands to those who had been decorated for their work on the 1st July, the presentation being made on the football field at Bayencourt.

A warning order had now been received that the Division was to be relieved by the 17th Division and to withdraw for training in rear of the line, in the St Riquier area near Abbeville.

The 168th Brigade was to concentrate at Halloy before proceeding to the new area, and the first step in this concentration was the relief on the 16th August of the 1/4th Londons and Rangers by the London Scottish and Kensingtons respectively. On relief the 1/4th Londons moved to billets in Sailly, leaving C Company at the Keep in Hébuterne for working parties until the 18th, when the whole Battalion marched at 7 p.m. to Halloy, arriving in huts there at 11 p.m. By the 21st the whole Brigade group was completely out of the line and the following day moved to the new area, the Battalion entraining at Doullens at 11.40 a.m. and, detraining at St Riquier shortly before 6 p.m., marched thence to billets at Le Plessiel.

CHAPTER XI
THE 1/4TH BATTALION IN THE BATTLES OF THE SOMME, 1916

II. *The Battles of September and October*

As we have pointed out in the preceding chapter, the 1st July was a day of almost complete check to the British attack from Fricourt northwards. Between Fricourt and the Somme, however, a certain measure of success had been attained, while south of the river the French had made a considerable advance.

This limited success was exploited to the fullest extent during the first half of July, and by the 14th, after very fierce fighting, in which eleven British Divisions were engaged, our lines were pressed forward through the series of fortresses forming the first German system of defence.

The Main Ridge of the Somme watershed runs east-south-east from Thiepval, above the Ancre, across the Albert-Bapaume Road, towards the Péronne-Bapaume Road. About a mile and a half west of the latter road it is completely severed by a narrow and deep ravine in which lies the small township of Combles; and about half way between Combles and Thiepval it is deeply indented by a valley which separates the villages of Bazentin-le-Grand and Bazentin-le-Petit, the head of this valley being dominated by the high ground on which stands High Wood. The ridge, therefore, divides itself into three sections, all on the same general alignment, as follows: In the west, from Thiepval, astride the Albert-Bapaume Road to High Wood; in the centre, from High Wood to the Combles Valley; in the east, the high ground about Sailly Saillisel on the Péronne-Albert Road.

The German second system of defences followed roughly the near side of the crest of this Main Ridge, including the villages (from east to west) of Maurepas, Guillemont, Longueval (with Delville Wood), the Bazentins and Pozières. The third system lay on the further slope of the ridge and included the villages of Morval, Lesbœufs, Flers and Gueudecourt.

On the 14th July the British attacked the second system on a front from Bazentin-le-Petit to Longueval. This attack, which was successful, was pressed forward to High Wood, of which practically the whole was captured, and thus secured for us a footing on the Main Ridge, dividing the German forces on the west and centre portions of it. The advance was consolidated and rounded off locally in the direction of Guillemont; but the new positions formed an abrupt and narrow salient in our line, and before a further advance to the German third system could be contemplated it was necessary for the British hold on the Main Ridge to be widened. It was considered by G.H.Q. that the Pozières-Thiepval series of fortresses at the western extremity of the ridge was too powerful to yield to frontal attack, and it was therefore decided to extend the hold on the centre portion of the ridge. This postulated the capture of Guillemont, Ginchy and Combles, and a swinging-up of the British right flank which rested on the Combles valley. The French were to co-operate on the right of the Combles valley by the capture of Frégicourt and Rancourt. Combles itself, immensely fortified and strongly garrisoned, was too formidable an obstacle to be likely to fall into our hands by direct attack, except at an appalling cost of life; and it was therefore to be enveloped, the British advancing on the heights west of it and the French to its east.

It is with this great outflanking movement for the capture of Combles and the securing of the Main Ridge immediately west of it that the 56th Division and the Guillemont was first attacked on the 23rd July, but it was not until after repeated attempts that it finally fell into our hands on the 3rd September. On that day the line was advanced to the outskirts of Ginchy and to the Wedge Wood-Ginchy Road, Falfemont Farm falling to us on the 5th.

Meanwhile local improvements had been made in our positions in various parts of the line, and the bitter fighting of August, though productive of no very deep advance was of the greatest value. It not only widened our hold on the ridge, but also by a series of unrelenting sledgehammer blows had a cumulative effect on the German morale and thus paved the way for the greater successes of September.

The 168th Brigade continued training in the St Riquier area until the end of August, the 1/4th Londons retaining their billets at Le Plessiel. The training was rendered peculiarly interesting by reason of the first appearance of the "Heavy Section Machine-Gun Corps," better known as Tanks. These engines of war, which were regarded at first by the troops with a good deal of wonderment and not a little misgiving, only arrived in France on the 25th August. No time was lost in testing them and giving infantry troops an opportunity to co-operate with them in practice prior to their employment in action.

The 56th Division received the compliment of being one of the units selected by G.H.Q. to co-operate with Tanks on the occasion of their first appearance in battle, and accordingly a series of practice schemes was begun on the 26th August, the Brigades of the 56th Division being employed in turn. Needless to say the interest aroused by the strange appearance of these iron monsters was intense and speculation was rife as to their potential value in action, not only among the troops, but also among the many staff officers who were present at the demonstrations. Unfortunately the time allowed for "tuning up" the engines was inadequate, the result being that during the first practices the Tanks showed a most undesirable predilection for breaking down—a habit not calculated to inspire with confidence the infantry who were expected to follow them. However, these difficulties were largely overcome, and by the 2nd September, when the 168th Brigade's turn for practising with them arrived, the Tanks were working well.

In spite of the misgivings as to the tactical value of the Tanks which presented themselves to the minds of those inclined to pessimism, their arrival undoubtedly gave enormous encouragement to the troops who were enabled at last to realise that the enemy were not always to be first in the field with new inventions; and the anticipation of a great surprise effect when the Tanks should first appear before the enemy trenches brought all ranks to the tip-toe of expectation. The strict injunction which was issued to avoid mention of the Tanks in correspondence was most loyally obeyed.

On the 2nd September a warning order was received that the Division would move forward to the battle area, and the following day the 168th and 169th Brigades moved to the Corbie area. The Battalion left Le Plessiel in the afternoon of the 3rd, marching to St Riquier, where it entrained for Corbie, a town of some size at the confluence of the Ancre and the Somme. Here the Battalion detrained at 11.15 p.m., marching, with the Rangers, to billets at Vaux-sur-Somme. The remainder of the Brigade was accommodated a mile further forward at Sailly-le-Sec.

The Division now came under the orders of the XIV Corps (Cavan), the extreme right of the British Army, consisting of the 5th, 16th and 20th Divisions, which had this day been operating on the Guillemont front in the action already alluded to.

On the morning of the 4th orders were received, without any previous intimation that they might be coming, for the Battalion to move forward at once. The whole Battalion, less personnel of the transport and vehicles, marched out of Vaux-sur-Somme within one hour of the receipt of these orders—a credit to the high state of organisation to which the Battalion had been trained since leaving the Hébuterne area. Boutall writes: "The march was a long and tedious one and I think I am right in asserting that not a single man fell out on the way. I distinctly remember Lieut.-Col. Wheatley congratulating himself on the fact."

This march terminated at a large concentration camp known as the Citadel about two miles north of Bray. At the Citadel the Battalion was able to form a vague idea for the first time of the enormous effort being put forth by the British in this already long drawn-out struggle. The concentration camp covered an enormous area on the rolling hillsides above the Somme and presented an astounding spectacle of numbers of units from every arm of the Service—gunners, infantry, engineers—besides vast stores of materials of all kinds. The roar of the guns in the inferno of the battle line seemed to speak to the troops of the great and yet increasing power of the British Armies, and filled every heart with hope and confidence. To many of those who remembered the lean days of 1915 when the British battle line was starved for men and shells, this first contact with the reality of the Empire's strength was almost overpowering.

On the 5th September the Division took the place in Corps Reserve of the 20th Division, which had been withdrawn from the fighting line, and in the evening of the same day the relief of the 5th Division in the line began.

The front taken over from the 5th Division was the extreme right of the line from its junction with the French, overlooking the Combles valley to the left of Leuze Wood. The 169th Brigade (relieving the 15th) took over the right sector and the 168th Brigade (relieving the 95th) assumed responsibility in the left sector.

September had set in with steady rain which had already converted all the roads, tracks and camping grounds into seas of liquid mud. The Battalion, which since arrival at the Citadel had been held at short notice to move, advanced during the afternoon of the 5th, in full battle kit in the direction of the line. The state of the ground made marching an impossibility, and after sliding along for some time uncomfortably in the mud, orders were received for the Battalion to return to the Citadel. The change of plan was, as usual, received with philosophical resignation, and the men turned in to take advantage of the short respite only to be roused again a few hours later the same evening when the advance to the line began at 11.15 p.m.

At this hour the Battalion, which with the Rangers was in Brigade support, left the Citadel, arriving in its allotted position in Casement Trench at 5.30 a.m. on the 6th September. This trench was now reduced to a series of shell holes which the bad weather had rendered most uncomfortable, and was a part of the original German system opposite Maricourt.

The departure from the Citadel was marked by a most unfortunate accident. As the column began to move the explosion of a bomb which had been left buried in the mud occurred at the head of D Company, and this very seriously wounded Capt. A. L. Long, the company commander, and 2/Lieut. A. G. Sharp, and caused casualties to 19 N.C.O.'s and men.

With the advent of daylight the Battalion first came face to face with the ghastly desolation of the Somme battlefield. In all directions every sort of landmark seemed to be obliterated. A few torn stumps marked what had been Bernafay and Trones Woods, the village of Guillemont was practically effaced, and the only signs of life in the neighbourhood of the Battalion were numerous batteries of artillery in action. Here the nucleus personnel left the Battalion and returned to the Citadel, where the Q.M. stores were established. At 2 p.m. the Battalion changed its position to Chimpanzee Trench in the neighbourhood of the Brickfield, south of Bernafay Wood, and here it received a foretaste of the German barrage. After dark the forward move was resumed, and the Battalion entered the support trenches in rear of Leuze Wood, on the Wedge Wood-Ginchy Road, relieving the 4th Gloucesters. This trench formed a "switch" in the second German system which had fallen into our hands on the 3rd September.

The Battle of Ginchy, 5th-10th September

The disposition of the Brigade was now as follows:

- In front line, Leuze Wood:—London Scottish.
- In support, Wedge Wood-Ginchy Road:—1/4th Londons.
- In reserve, Maltzhorn Farm:—Rangers.

> The Kensingtons were attached to the 169th Brigade, and were in line to the south of Leuze Wood.

During the night the enemy's bombardment of the front line and Wedge Wood Valley increased in intensity and two platoons of the 1/4th Londons, under Lieuts. Oldrey and Garratt, were ordered forward to reinforce the Scottish in Leuze Wood. This advance was successfully accomplished, the platoons managing to get through an unpleasantly heavy barrage with only one casualty. No enemy attack materialised, and towards dawn, the hostile bombardment having subsided, the two platoons rejoined the Battalion.

Throughout the 7th September and far into the night the enemy shelled Wedge Wood Valley and the support line heavily, and the Battalion suffered a good many casualties, chiefly among ration and water-carrying parties, while communication with Battalion Headquarters was exceedingly difficult. The Wedge Wood-Ginchy Road which ran immediately in front of the trench was sunken at this point, and the bank was honeycombed with German dugouts, among them one which had been used as an aid-post, and which produced an ample supply of bandages, lint and field-dressings, and also cigars and tobacco—trench stores which were promptly taken on charge by the Battalion.

The road itself was littered with German dead, the remnants of the battle of the 3rd, who had apparently been caught by our barrage, of the destructive nature of which evidences were everywhere to be seen. "Unfortunately," writes an eyewitness, "the sunken road was an attraction to countless flies in the daytime. So numerous were they that from the road arose a continuous hum which was audible at a considerable distance. They swarmed over into the trench and settled on our food in such numbers that they often found their way into our mouths at mealtimes."

During the afternoon of the 7th orders were issued for the 56th Division to extend its front to the left by taking over the sector held by the right Brigade of the 16th Division. This consisted of a trench following the Leuze Wood-Guillemont Road, from near the north corner of Leuze Wood, for about 500 yards to the left. This relief was to be effected by "side-stepping" the 168th Brigade to the left, its trenches in Leuze Wood being handed over to the 169th Brigade. In pursuance of this scheme the Battalion took over with A and D Companies the advanced front line— about 200 yards' frontage on the immediate left of Leuze Wood—from the 7th Inniskilling Fusiliers. Immediately after relief these companies began to dig assembly trenches for the impending continuance of the offensive, and this task was completed before dawn on the 8th September. The Rangers meanwhile had come up in line on the left of the 1/4th Londons, while the Scottish on relief in Leuze Wood by the 169th Brigade had withdrawn into Brigade support, where they were joined by the Kensingtons.

The 8th September was occupied in improving the assembly trenches, and in establishing an advanced report centre in a German dugout at the south-west corner of Leuze Wood—by now corrupted by the ever-ready wit of the Cockney into "Lousy" Wood—while under cover of darkness the Cheshire Pioneers connected the Wood with Wedge Wood by a communication trench. In addition a great deal of work was carried out in collecting advanced dumps of tools, bombs, ammunition and water, in the west edge of Leuze Wood. All this work was effected under very heavy shell fire under which the Battalion sustained some loss.

Orders had now been received for the resumption of the offensive on the 9th, and during the night the 1/4th Londons and Rangers occupied their newly dug assembly trenches, while the Kensingtons advanced to the Wedge Wood support trench, the Scottish remaining at Maltzhorn Farm. The advanced report centre in Leuze Wood was taken over by the 1/4th Londons and placed under charge of Capt. Houlder (17th Londons attached). Capt. Houlder, who could speak German fluently, was instrumental during the action in gaining from prisoners much useful first-hand information which he was able to pass back to Battalion and Brigade Headquarters. The terrifying aspect of this huge British officer, coupled with the fact that he always had a loaded revolver conspicuously displayed during his investigations, no doubt increased the desire of his victims to respond to his enquiries!

The battle of the 9th September was an attack on the whole front of the Fourth Army, the French co-operating on our right. The object of the XIV Corps, of which the 56th and 16th Divisions were in line, was to advance the British positions from the Combles valley on the extreme right well to the east of Leuze Wood on a line running from south-east to north-west as far as the Ginchy-Morval Road, which formed the left of the 56th Division front. From this point the 16th Division was to reach a line which ran due west for some 800 yards along the road towards Ginchy and then bent northwards to include the whole of the village.

Map No. 5 shows the objectives of the 56th Division, the 169th Brigade on the right being responsible for forcing our lines forward of Leuze Wood on its north and east sides; and the 168th Brigade continuing the line as far as Point 141·7 on the Ginchy-Morval Road. The map also indicates that nearly every battalion taking part in the assault would have to make a change of direction from its starting point in order to advance to its objective.

So far as the 168th Brigade was concerned the advance was to be made in two stages, the first objective being a line of German trenches, running from the north corner of Leuze Wood towards Ginchy, and the final objective being as above described. For this purpose the dispositions of the Brigade remained as they had been on the eve of the battle, that is:

Right	Assaulting Battalion	—1/4th Londons.
Left	do.	—Rangers.
Support	Battalion	—Kensingtons.
Reserve	do.	—London Scottish.

The 1/4th Londons were disposed for attack as follows:
- Right—B Company (Lieut. H. W. Vernon).
- Centre—D Company (Lieut. G. H. Davis).
- Left—A Company (Capt. J. R. Webster).
- Support—C Company (2/Lieut. W. E. Osborne).

Each company occupied a two-platoon frontage, so that the whole Battalion was on a front of six platoons and in a depth of four waves.

The morning of the 9th September dawned mistily, but by 10 o'clock the sun's rays had dispersed the haze and disclosed to the enemy the new earth thrown up in front of our hastily dug assembly trenches. A heavy bombardment of the assembly areas on the whole Divisional front followed, lasting all the morning and causing a good many casualties. The assaulting companies having already formed up over night, the trenches were crowded with troops waiting for the hour of attack, and the experience of having quietly to endure this remarkably accurate and heavy shoot was one of the most trying of the whole engagement.

At 4 o'clock the enemy put down a heavy barrage on our lines. A quarter of an hour later our preparatory bombardment, which had opened at 10 a.m., increased to "hurricane" intensity, and for half an hour the German positions were subjected to a frightful ordeal under which it seemed that nothing could live. At 4.45 p.m. the British columns, on a front of several miles, moved to the assault.

The 1/4th Londons on getting out of their assembly trenches had to make a change of direction, pivoting on their right flank, and this accomplished, they moved forward steadily, keeping well up to their barrage and suffering comparatively little loss.

In consequence of the conflicting reports which were received during the action, the heavy toll of casualties in all ranks, and the resultant intermingling of companies in the positions gained, it has been a matter of considerable difficulty to elucidate the position and to extract from the mass of evidence a fair and impartial account of what really occurred.

It seems evident, however, that the position marked as the 1/4th Londons' first objective was innocent of the trench which it was expected to find there. At all events if a trench had ever existed on the line of the Leuze Wood-Ginchy track it had been so battered by shell fire as to be no longer recognisable as such; and it appears that the greater part of the assaulting companies overshot the mark and moved straight on to what was really the second objective, which they occupied under the impression that it was the first objective. It had been arranged that A Company on the left should consolidate a strong point on the left of the real first objective at its point of junction with the sector to be captured by the Rangers. Evidently 2/Lieut. Brodie, to whom was allotted this task, in making his change of direction to the right took a somewhat wide sweep and struck the east end of the Rangers' first objective, where a trench did actually exist, and here he formed his block practically in the position where it was intended to be. Subsequently Brodie, finding himself, no doubt, out of touch with the remainder of the Battalion, who had gone too far, came forward in the attempt to clear up the situation, but unhappily was killed, together with all his men.

The too rapid advance of the Battalion naturally brought them under the fire of our own barrage, and during the forty minutes' pause which was ordered after the capture of the first objective before the resumption of the advance on to the second, a good many casualties did in fact occur from our own shells which were dropping in and uncomfortably close to the trench which was occupied. This trench—the real second objective—was subsequently known as Bully Trench. We will therefore so refer to it in order to avoid confusion.

At 5.25 p.m. the Battalion, now including elements of all companies, once more advanced in a commendably steady manner on to a trench just topping the rise of the Main Ridge. This it occupied with very little opposition. This advanced position—Beef Trench—was an isolated trench about 150 yards ahead of Bully (the real second objective) with both flanks in the air. It was shallow and evidently only in course of construction. It afforded magnificent observation over the rearward slopes of the Main Ridge on to the German third line system in front of Morval, and in this position the work of consolidation was begun, two Lewis gun posts being pushed forward overlooking the Morval-Lesbœufs Road. Middle Copse, a small spinney about 200 yards to the front, was seen to be teeming with Bosche who were effectively dealt with by our Lewis guns.

In the meantime the right platoon of B Company under 2/Lieut. Garratt, which, in keeping touch with the Queen Victorias, had got ahead of the rest of the Battalion, had evidently become deflected slightly to the right during its advance and had dropped into the communication trench connecting Leuze Wood with Bully Trench. Apparently somewhat confusing his direction in the total absence of landmarks, Garratt moved along this trench and turned the corner to the left along Bully Trench. Here he came in contact with a Bosche bombing party, and attacking them vigorously pushed them back for some considerable distance, and eventually constructed a temporary block in the trench, probably about the centre of the Battalion's sector, *i.e.* about 200 yards short of the Quadrilateral. In this bomb fighting the men of B Company displayed great courage and dash, and their accurate throwing contributed largely to their success. Among these gallant men Corpl. Udall was conspicuous, and for his devotion to duty he was awarded the Military Medal.

During the advance of the assaulting companies of the Battalion from Bully Trench to the advanced position in Beef, a somewhat determined attack was delivered against B Company's block by a large party of the enemy led by an officer. Fortunately the shallowness of the trench exposed the enemy's advance and after a brisk exchange of bombs, in the course of which some loss was inflicted on the attacking party, including the officer who was shot by Garratt, the survivors surrendered with the exception of a few who fled pursued by the fire of our men and the Rangers. Garratt was subsequently awarded the Military Cross for his good work.

On the Battalion's left the Rangers, whose line of advance was dominated by the Quadrilateral and a small spur running from it in a south-westerly direction, had been faced with a withering machine-gun fire under which advance was utterly impossible. Their left company was unable to make progress, and by 8.30 p.m. was compelled to withdraw to its assembly positions in conjunction with the right Brigade of the 16th Division who had also been unable to overcome the German resistance. The right company of the Rangers pushed gallantly forward losing heavily, but was finally brought to a stand in the vicinity of the temporary block which was being held in Bully by Garratt. Here they were forced to take such cover as shell craters afforded them, and to reply to the Bosche fire, in which they were assisted by the party of B Company at the block. Under the gathering darkness a good many of the Rangers were able to make their way into Bully trench.

While all this was taking place two companies of the Kensingtons had occupied the assembly trenches vacated by the 1/4th Londons, and the commanders of these, appreciating the situation of the Rangers, at once made a gallant attempt to fill the gap on the left. Their gallantry, however, cost them dear, and the German barrage took a heavy toll of casualties before they reached Bully Trench. The bravery of Major Dickens was in particular remarkable. Mortally wounded some time before he reached his objective, he continued to advance at the head of his men, cheering and encouraging them until he collapsed into the trench. Later in the evening the two remaining companies of the Kensingtons were also thrown into the fight and became absorbed into the 1/4th Londons' position in Bully Trench.

Darkness had now fallen, and the position of the companies in the advanced trench was far from happy. Both flanks were in the air and heavy losses had been suffered; of the officers who had started with these companies, only four—Cooper, McCormick, Quennell and Burford—were still standing. News from Garratt showed that he was doubtful as to whether he could hold out against another attack.

Fearing to lose the advantage already gained, Cooper, who had assumed command of the force in Beef Trench, decided to reoccupy Bully temporarily, and finally clear it of the enemy. The withdrawal was successfully accomplished in the dark, but the enemy was found to be firmly established with an apparently ample supply of bombs on his side of the block, which had now been completed with the help of the Kensington and Ranger reinforcements; and further attempts to extend our gains northward in Bully were abandoned. Communication being now re-established with Battalion Headquarters, orders were received in Bully for the reoccupation of the advanced positions in Beef; and the Bully position being now much strengthened by Rangers and Kensingtons, the 1/4th Londons moved forward alone to Beef Trench.

During the remainder of the night a good deal of work was necessary in reorganising the somewhat mixed force by which the forward position was now occupied. One or two enemy patrols approached the position but were fired on and dispersed, and apart from continued shell fire and sniping the night passed comparatively peacefully.

Captain Cooper gives the following account of a remarkable incident which occurred during the night:—

> A glow was seen in a shell hole some distance to the front and on investigation this proved to be from the cigarette of a battalion N.C.O., a corporal (Fergusson), who had formed part of one of the forward posts. He had become separated from his men and wounded in the back so that he was unable to walk. He stated that he had been uncertain of his position and so had crawled into a shell hole. A Bosche patrol had found him and removed his shoulder badges and taken the contents of his pockets, but had propped him up in a comfortable position and had left him his water-bottle, cigarettes and matches. He was calmly and coolly enjoying a cigarette when found. He was sent on a stretcher to the Aid Post.

While these events were taking place on the Battalion's front, the Queen Victorias, the left of the 169th Brigade, had occupied their objective, and were in touch on the right of Bully. The enemy, however, had hitherto successfully resisted all efforts of the London Rifle Brigade to emerge from the east side of Leuze Wood. At about 7 p.m. the Bosche at this part of the line had launched a vigorous bomb attack along the sunken road leading from Combles, and the L.R.B. had been forced back after a most stubborn resistance which cost them heavily. During the night the Queen's Westminsters took over the extreme right of the Division.

The 16th Division on the left had also met with varied fortunes. The 47th Brigade on its left had successfully advanced through Ginchy and established itself on its objective; but the right brigade, the 48th, whose objective lay along the Ginchy-Morval Road, met with most stubborn resistance from the spur already referred to. In spite of the most gallant efforts the Brigade was unable to make progress, and eventually fell back with the left wing of the Rangers at about 8.30 p.m. and reoccupied their original position on the Wedge Wood-Ginchy Road. About this time the London Scottish were ordered into the fight in order to endeavour to clear up the situation in this part of the field. After the march forward from Maltzhorn their preparations were completed at about midnight, and shortly after they attacked from a position to the left of the Rangers' assembly trenches towards the Quadrilateral. The enemy was still vigorous in his defence, and after losing their direction in the intense darkness, the Scottish were ultimately withdrawn, having first rendered a good account of themselves in a lively little hand-to-hand fight with a party of the Bosche. During the night the 16th Division was relieved by the 3rd Guards Brigade.

Shortly after dawn on the 10th 2/Lieut. McCormick, who had come back to Battalion Headquarters with a report of the situation, returned to Beef Trench with orders for the immediate evacuation of the advanced position. Accordingly, after establishing two Lewis gun positions in Beef Trench, the withdrawal was proceeded with as rapidly as possible, the activity of the German snipers in the growing daylight making movement difficult except in the smallest parties. The return of the 1/4th Londons to Bully Trench caused congestion which was subsequently intensified by the arrival of a large reinforcement of London Scottish. This Battalion made efforts during the day to prolong the line in the direction of the Quadrilateral, while the Guards, working eastward along the Ginchy-Morval Road, sought to join hands with them, but the Germans were well supplied with bombs and put up a very gallant resistance. The continued occupation of the spur—which on the previous day had stopped the 16th Division—moreover forced an unpleasantly deep re-entrant in the British line, leaving the left flank of the 1/4th Londons dangerously exposed. An effort to rout out the pertinacious defenders of this spur was made during the afternoon by the 168th Stokes mortars, who fired 35 rounds with good effect into the enemy trenches.

The position on the right flank of the Battalion was still less satisfactory than had been hoped for. At 7 a.m. and again at 3 p.m. the Queen's Westminsters had made local attempts to gain the previous day's objective, but each time without success.

Throughout the day the Battalion's position was kept under heavy German shell fire which caused the already heavy casualty roll to mount higher and higher, and it was found necessary to relieve the congestion in Bully by withdrawing the Rangers and Kensingtons to the rear. Communication with Headquarters was rendered exceedingly difficult, though, as always, there was no lack of brave volunteers to try to pass through the German barrage, and these in some cases succeeded in reaching the report centre in Leuze Wood. Moreover the trench, only a shallow and half-finished work to start with, was becoming badly shattered and was filled with wounded men, whom there was no means of evacuating, for all the stretcher-bearers with companies had themselves become casualties. Throughout this trying day all ranks displayed magnificent spirit and clung to their hardly won gains with grim determination. That night the 168th Brigade was relieved, the 1/4th Londons handing over their objective to the 8th Middlesex of the 167th Brigade. Following the relief, which was complete by midnight, the Battalion moved by companies—by now sadly reduced in numbers—to Casement Trench, whence the Battalion moved as a unit to Billon Farm, near Carnoy, arriving in bivouacs there at 5.30 a.m. on the 11th September.

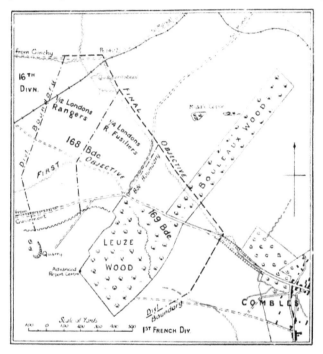

THE BATTLE OF GINCHY, SEPTEMBER 1916

The five days' duty just completed were perhaps the most strenuous the Battalion had yet experienced. Almost all the time exposed to bad weather conditions and to very heavy and accurate artillery fire, the spirit of the men was magnificent; and their steadiness, after the loss of 15 out of the 20 officers who led the companies into action, as well as a large proportion of N.C.O.'s, was unsurpassed. Their fighting qualities too were firmly established, for they had taken their objectives up to time-table and handed them over intact twenty-four hours later. The total casualties during the five days amounted to 22 officers and about 250 other ranks.

The officer casualties were as follows:

> 7th and 8th September—Capts. F. O. J. Read and H. G. Stanham, 2/Lieuts. W. Richards, A. Potton, J. T. Middleton, C. H. T. Heaver and L. W. Archer, wounded.
>
> 9th and 10th September—Capt. J. R. Webster, 2/Lieuts. C. J. Brodie, F. J. Foden, W. E. Osborne, C. E. Lewis, C. S. G. Blows and C. F. Mortleman, killed; Lieuts. H. W. Vernon and G. H. Davis, 2/Lieuts. J. W. Price, V. R. Oldrey, C. F. English, N. A. Ormiston and J. C. Graddon, wounded; and 2/Lieut. W. H. Davey, D.C.M., missing, presumed killed.

Throughout the 11th and 12th heavy fighting continued in which the 167th Brigade co-operated with the Guards on the left in numerous efforts to clear out the re-entrant and reach the Ginchy Quadrilateral. This magnificently defended position, however, held out against the most gallant attempts of the attackers. During the night of the 11/12th September the 167th Brigade was also relieved, the line being taken over by the 16th Brigade of the 6th Division.

The Battalion remained at Billon Farm for three most welcome days of rest and reorganisation during which the weather, which now once more became fine and warm, was of inestimable value in cheering the troops after their somewhat trying experience. The relief to the men's spirits on emerging even for a short spell from the ghastly featureless waste of the battle area to surroundings where trees still bore their leaves, roads still crossed the hillsides, and houses were not completely effaced, was immense; and by the time the period of rest was over the Battalion was once more braced up to continue the struggle.

One or two changes occurred during this period among the officers of the Battalion, of which the most important was the assumption of the Adjutancy by Lieut. W. J. Boutall on the evacuation to hospital of Capt. R. L. Herring, who had occupied this trying position practically since the Battalion joined the 56th Division. 2/Lieut. Garratt assumed the duties of Assistant Adjutant almost immediately afterwards. Capt. J. T. Sykes left the Battalion for attachment to the Indian Army, and the signalling officer, Lieut. E. W. Monk, to join the R.A.F. The latter's duties were taken over by 2/Lieut. S. J. Barkworth, M.M. In addition to these 2/Lieut. A. C. Knight was evacuated to hospital.

The Battle of Flers-Courcelette 15th-18th September

The renewal of the offensive was not long to be delayed. The object of the High Command was to follow up the blows delivered against the German positions as rapidly as possible, and to leave the enemy little respite for reorganisation and rest. The constant hammering on his defences had already had an appreciable effect on his morale, and it was hoped that before long the strain on his resources would prove so great that the situation would develop rapidly in favour of the Allies.

The next general attack was arranged for the 15th September, the assault being launched on the whole battle front from Morval to Le Sars on the Albert-Bapaume Road. The great pivoting movement by which the British right flank was to be swung forward in line with the left on the Main Ridge had now reached an important stage, and the operations of the XIV Corps were now more than ever bound up with the fortunes of the French south of Combles. The French were aiming at establishing themselves astride the Bapaume-Péronne Road at the village of Sailly Saillisel, about two miles north-east of Combles; but the task presented unusual difficulties owing to the restriction of the lines of possible advance between the deep Combles ravine on the one flank, and the extensive wood of St Pierre Vaast on the other. The evils of this confinement were aggravated by the fact that the enemy position about Morval at the extreme east end of the Main Ridge dominated the whole of our Allies' line of advance. It was therefore essential to the success, not only of the French in their ultimate object but also of the combined "squeezing-out" process which was being applied to Combles itself, that the British should at once possess themselves of such portions of the Main Ridge as remained in the enemy's hands. This entailed the breaking of the Third German system on the line Morval-Lesbœufs-Flers, and this was the task of the XIV and XV Corps on the 15th September.

The positions held by the Division at the opening of the battle were as follows:

> 167th Brigade—On the line north of Leuze Wood and intersecting the south end of Bouleaux Wood which had been captured on the 9th by the Queen Victorias, and thence along the south-east edge of Leuze Wood for about half its length.
>
> 169th Brigade—On the right of Leuze Wood, in a line running due north and south, between the 167th and the French.
>
> 168th Brigade—In reserve bivouacs in Angle Wood Valley, the Battalion being at the head of the Valley near Wedge Wood.

The position which the Battalion had captured on the 9th September was now held by the 6th Division, who formed the centre of the Corps while the Guards were on the extreme left.

The general idea of the attack was that the Guards and 6th Divisions should attack positions in the German third line facing Lesbœufs, while the 56th Division was to form a defensive flank facing the Combles ravine.

To establish this defensive flank the 169th Brigade on the right was to push forward of Leuze Wood and occupy a position roughly north and south with its left flank astride the sunken road from Combles, about 300 yards east of the edge of Leuze Wood. The 167th was to clear Bouleaux Wood in two stages and establish a line parallel to and about 100 yards in front of its east edge. The 1/4th Londons were to follow up the advance of the 167th Brigade and then "leapfrog" through it on to the German third line immediately in front of Morval whence they would connect up between the left of the 167th Brigade and the right of the 6th Division.

The 15th September was on the greater part of the battle front a day of big successes. At an early hour Flers fell before our assault, and by the afternoon the British line had been pushed far beyond it; the whole of High Wood was taken, and before nightfall Martinpuich and Courcelette on the left had been added to the gains of the day.

On the extreme right, however, the advance suffered a rather severe check. The Guards, who occupied the left of the Corps front, were able to make solid advances between Flers and Lesbœufs, but the 6th Division adjoining them were held up by the Quadrilateral at Ginchy, whose brave defenders still maintained their position most stubbornly; and this failure naturally reacted on the 56th Division who occupied a narrow wedge between the Quadrilateral and the Combles ravine.

At 5.50 a.m. the three tanks which were to make their début with the Division left their departure points for the first objective, and at 6.20 a.m. the infantry assault was launched. Almost three hours later, at 9 a.m., the 1/4th Londons left their bivouacs in Angle Wood Valley and moved forward in artillery formation towards the battle position on the crest between the north edge of Leuze Wood and the west face of Bouleaux Wood. Progress was not rapid owing to the heavy state of the ground, and under the German shell fire a good many casualties were sustained. The advance was made, however, in good order, and with admirable steadiness.

The 169th Brigade made very slight advances on the south of Leuze Wood; while the 167th managed to secure the part of its first objective which lay outside Bouleaux Wood. The 8th Middlesex of the latter Brigade even made a heroic attempt to reach the second objective, but had to be brought back. The enemy barrage was heavy and fell, as it so often had in the Somme battles, between the assaulting columns and their starting-point, thus cutting them off from supplies and reinforcement, while the accurate intensity of their machine-gun fire from their positions in the Quadrilateral made advance an utter impossibility. After ten hours' fighting, during which the assaulting Brigades did all that men could do, the Corps Commander telephoned to Gen. Hull that the Division would make no further attempt against Bouleaux Wood that day.

The 1/4th Londons luckily avoided the slaughter of the battle line this day, for a few minutes prior to its advance from Angle Wood Valley an order had been despatched to Brigade Headquarters to the effect that in consequence of the check of the 6th Division in front of the Quadrilateral the 168th Brigade would not occupy its battle position. This order was transmitted by Brigade and reached the Battalion during its advance. Upon receipt of it the Battalion was at once brought back to its assembly area at Angle Wood Valley where, in common with the remainder of the Brigade, it remained in bivouacs till the early hours of the 18th September. This operation cost the Battalion a large number of casualties among N.C.O.'s and men from the German shell fire, and one officer, 2/Lieut. J. W. Chapman, wounded.

During these days Angle Wood Valley was a distinctly unhealthy locality. The German artillery maintained a searching fire over the whole area, and exacted a fair toll of casualties. The weather, which a few days previously had shown signs of mending, had once more turned wet and the shell holes, which formed the only available cover, became not the most desirable resting-place for the troops. The strain was great, but the situation was as usual not only borne by all in the Battalion with an almost stoical resignation, but enlivened occasionally with those rare flashes of humour which have made the London soldiers famous during the War in three continents.

The story of the tanks on the 15th September is too well-known to need elaboration here, and is, moreover, too much outside the actual experience of the Battalion to allow of more than a passing reference. The moral effect on the Germans was immense, and considering that their employment had scarcely passed the experimental stage, the success gained by them was conspicuous. As was anticipated, however, the tanks promptly became a mark for a tremendous concentration of enemy fire which made their room far more desirable than their company. Of the three attached to the 56th Division one did useful work in the vicinity of the Quadrilateral, and after trampling down a good deal of wire and putting an enemy machine-gun team out of action returned to make a personal report of its adventures. The careers of the other two were sadly abbreviated, and the end of the day found them derelict—one west of Bouleaux Wood, and one south-east of Leuze Wood—though not before they had dealt out a certain amount of destruction to the German defences.

Orders were received while the Battalion remained in Angle Wood Valley for the resumption of the offensive on the 18th September. The objectives on the XIV Corps front were on this occasion very much more modest than they had been three days earlier, and so far as the 56th Division was concerned were as follows:

> 169th Brigade—The sunken road from Leuze Wood to Combles, between the east edge of the wood and the orchard west of Combles.

> 67th Brigade—The east edge of Bouleaux Wood for a distance of 600 yards from its southern extremity, and thence a line through the wood to Middle Copse. From Middle Copse the objective was continued in a northerly direction by the 6th Division.

> The 168th Brigade remained in reserve in Angle Wood Valley, but the 1/4th Londons and the London Scottish were attached to the 167th.

For this operation the Battalion was detailed as the left assaulting battalion of the 167th Brigade, its objective being the portion between Middle Copse (which was held by an advanced post of the 7th Middlesex) and the east edge of Bouleaux Wood. For this purpose its assembly position was the old German communication trench connecting Bully Trench with the north corner of Leuze Wood. The right of the Brigade frontage was taken up by the 3rd Londons.

The hour of assault was fixed for 6.15 a.m. on the 18th, and to enable it to reach its assembly position by 5.15 a.m. as ordered, the 1/4th Londons moved from Angle Wood Valley at 3.30 a.m. But the ground was impossible. All vestige of tracks had long since disappeared, and the countryside in every direction was a vast slippery quagmire in which so far from keeping any sort of march formation it was next to impossible for the men, laden as they were with battle equipment, to stand upright at all.

Zero hour arrived, but the Battalion as well as the 3rd Londons was still slipping and struggling a long way short of its assembly area. The British barrage opened and was at once replied to by a withering machine-gun fire by the enemy. Seldom has the Battalion been exposed to so accurate and devastating a fire. The only alternative to complete destruction was to take cover in the waterlogged shell holes, which movement was carried out with alacrity by all ranks: in this unexpected position an order reached the Battalion abandoning the attack and recalling it to Angle Wood.

On the right the much suffering 169th Brigade was able to achieve a series of local bombing successes which carried their line appreciably nearer Combles. From the 6th Division on the left, shortly after midday came the cheering news that the Quadrilateral had at last fallen, together with the trench to the north of it.

This important success, which had so long eluded the grasp of the successive Divisions who had sought it, paved the way for the magnificent achievements of the 25th September, which will be recounted later, its especial importance being that it was practically the last heavily fortified stronghold on the central portion of the Main Ridge to resist the British attacks.

The abortive operation of the 18th cost the Battalion a good many casualties in N.C.O.'s and men, and one officer, 2/Lieut. W. H. Calnan, wounded.

The same evening the 168th Brigade relieved the 167th in the Leuze Wood trenches, the London Scottish occupying the front system, which comprised Beef and Bully Trenches. The 1/4th Londons took over from the 3rd Londons the support line, which ran diagonally through Leuze Wood in a north and south direction. Leuze Wood was at all times an unhealthy locality and formed an unfailing source of attraction for every conceivable sort of German projectile. The 3rd Londons had already suffered heavily here, and the night of the relief proved to be no exception to the rule. Throughout the evening the wood was plastered with high explosive shell, and even the inadequate shelter of the trenches hastily dug, damaged and waterlogged as they were, was exceedingly welcome. The position was, without exception, the muddiest that had yet fallen to the lot of the Battalion. "To stand still," writes a company commander, "was to sink gradually until the whole of the legs to well above the knees were immersed and movement was correspondingly difficult." Lewis guns and rifles had become choked with mud so as to render the Battalion practically defenceless, but with much labour they were cleaned, and some rations which were found in the trench distributed. Dawn broke on a chilled but yet remarkably cheerful Battalion. The continued strain of heavy shell fire and conditions of physical misery were, however, beginning to have their effect, and several men who in earlier actions had given ample proof of their courage, collapsed. "One man of D Company who had previously shown himself one of the stoutest-hearted, lost his mental balance and suddenly became possessed of the idea of killing all the Germans in the German Army, and had to be forcibly restrained from mounting the parapet. 2/Lieut. Barkworth, who came up from Battalion Headquarters, succeeded by sheer strength of personality in restraining him and getting him back to H.Q."

The 19th September was a day of comparative quiet on the battle front, though shelling and sniping continued in a desultory fashion. Rain fell steadily and the condition of the trenches, appallingly bad to start with, became so wretched as to defy description.

During the night of the 19th a large working party of the 5th Cheshire Pioneers, under the supervision of the Brigade Major (Capt. R. E. Neame, V.C., D.S.O., R.E.), and covered by a screen of one and a half companies of the Scottish, dug a new trench 800 yards long. This new work, Gropi Trench, ran forward from Beef Trench towards the German line, parallel to the west edge of Bouleaux Wood, as far as the Morval tram-line. The task was successfully completed before dawn, but with the advent of daylight and the consequent exposure of the newly turned-up earth, the whole brigade area was again subjected to a heavy bombardment by the enemy's artillery. The German snipers again became particularly active, and every rash movement was promptly punished. Under this gruelling there was nothing for the Battalion to do but to keep quietly in its trenches and make the best of an unpleasant state of affairs. That night the Kensingtons came forward from Angle Wood Valley and took over the support line from the Battalion, and also Bully Trench in front of it. The relief was completed by 9.30 p.m., and never was relief more welcome. The Rangers at the same time took over the Beef and Gropi system from the London Scottish. On withdrawal from the trenches the Battalion moved by companies to bivouacs at Falfemont Farm, arriving there at 10.45 p.m.

No further movement was made during the 21st and 22nd September, and these two days were fairly quiet as the principal target for the German guns was provided by the numerous British batteries in Angle Wood Valley, which received heavy punishment.

Between the 20th September and the 2nd October the following reinforcements joined:

> Capt. R. N. Keen, Lieuts. W. H. Vernon and A. Bath, 2/Lieuts. C. A. Speyer, C. Potter, W. R. Gifford, H. W. Spiers, L. C. Haycraft, L. J. R. Atterbury, C. P. Russell, T. R. Fletcher and S. A. G. Richardson.
>
> 2/Lieut. T. Siddall (25th Londons).
>
> 100 N.C.O.'s and men.

> A few days after joining Lieut. A. Bath and 2/Lieut. C. P. Russell were evacuated, the former with a broken ankle, the latter sick.

The men of this draft represented so far as the 1/4th Battalion was concerned the firstfruits of the "Derby" scheme, and it must always be a matter for regret that the dreadful losses already incurred by the Battalion made it inevitable to pitchfork this fine material straight into the inferno of the Somme without any opportunity for it to become previously assimilated into the ranks of the Battalion. The Somme battles were a severe ordeal even to the most veteran soldiers; and the bearing of these young and inexperienced troops in the trials of the latter half of the Battalion's Somme fighting stands to their lasting credit.

As we have already remarked, the Cockney soldier, however wretched his conditions, is never so depressed by his surroundings as to be unable to find humour in the situation of the hour. The Battalion had now spent seven consecutive days in the desolation of the battle area practically without shelter from the pitiless torrents of rain which combined with the German shells to churn the whole surface of the ground into a disgusting glutinous mass; the troops were soaked to the skin and plastered with mud from head to foot; but the unconquerable spirit of cheerfulness held them together, dirty and dishevelled as they were, a well-knit and disciplined fighting unit. The condition of the ground, which added so vastly to the labours of the troops, is illustrated by a story told by an officer who was present:

> A man attempted to cross the valley and started to plough his way through the mud, but rashly omitted to lace up his boots, which he had previously removed. His negligence was quickly visited upon him, for scarcely had he begun his journey when the mud claimed one of his boots, which became stuck fast. His powers of balance were unequal to the task of putting his foot back in the boot, and he toppled over, both his hands becoming firmly embedded. His efforts to regain a standing position were prolonged and violent, but after a time successful, and finally, boots in hand, he proceeded on his way amid the cheers of the onlookers, who accepted his performance as being arranged for their especial amusement, and were particularly interested in the man's lurid observations on the subject of boots, mud and war generally.

There were a few occasions, however, when circumstances seemed too strong even for the 1/4th Londons, and one of them occurred that night when the rum jars which arrived with the rations were found, alas, to contain—lime juice!

On the evening of the 22nd September the 168th Brigade was relieved in the left subsector by the 167th and the Battalion moved back to the comparative peace of Casement Trench, where it occupied bivouacs until the afternoon of the 24th, making preparations for the next bout in the battle line.

The Battle of Morval, 25th September

The continuance of the offensive had been arranged for the 21st, but the weather conditions placed such a handicap on the chances of success that it was postponed, first until the 23rd and again till the 25th September, when once more the battle broke out on a front from the British right at Combles to a point half-way between Flers and Martinpuich. The French were to co-operate in this attack on the right of Combles ravine. The objectives of the XIV Corps included the villages of Lesbœufs and Morval, and, as on the occasion of their earlier attempt on the 15th, the 56th Division was to form a defensive flank facing south-east over Combles.

A series of local bombing operations was conducted on the 24th by the 169th Brigade on the extreme right in conjunction with the French, which gave them an increased hold on Combles Trench immediately in front of the village, and appreciably improved their jumping-off positions for the following day. During the night also the two tanks allotted to the Division moved forward to their rendezvous in the quarry west of Leuze Wood.

For the battle of the 25th the three Brigades of the Division were all in line, the 169th on the right, with the 167th in the centre and the 168th on the left. The 1/4th Londons were the right assaulting Battalion of the 168th, their duty being to clear the northern end of Bouleaux Wood and to establish a line of posts overlooking the ravine, while the London Scottish on the left continued the defensive flank in the direction of Morval (see Map No. 6).

At 4.30 p.m. on the 24th the Battalion marched from Casement Trench to occupy positions of assembly, relieving the 7th Middlesex in the Gropi-Ranger system as follows:

    C Company—Left front, in Ranger Trench.

    B Company—Right front, in Gropi Trench, and the small communication trench leading forward to Ranger Trench.

    D Company—Support, in Gropi Trench.

> A Company—Reserve, in the southern part of Gropi Trench and Middle Copse.
>
> Battalion Headquarters were established in a dugout west of the north part of Gropi Trench and the Aid Post in the quarry west of Leuze Wood.

The evening of relief was fortunately fairly quiet, but owing to the complete obliteration of all landmarks some difficulty was experienced by the guides provided for the companies in locating the positions to be occupied. However, Middle Copse was eventually reached, and this point being gained a little prospecting discovered Gropi Trench, after which the relief proceeded smoothly and was completed without unusual incident. Gropi Trench, which had been dug by the Cheshires, was found to be very well constructed, and the excellent cover it afforded was the means of sparing the Battalion a good many casualties from the enemy snipers, who were active from the direction of Bouleaux Wood during the morning of the 25th.

After a preliminary bombardment by all available batteries the British attack opened at 12.35 p.m. on the 25th, but the 168th Brigade's positions being well in advance of those occupied by the 5th Division on its left, its attack was deferred until seven minutes later in order to allow the 5th Division to come up into line. The creeping barrage, under which the Brigade's advance was made, was supplied by batteries firing from Angle Wood Valley, and being thus in enfilade was particularly efficient and accurate; and under its excellent protection the 1/4th Londons and the London Scottish advanced steadily at 12.42 p.m.

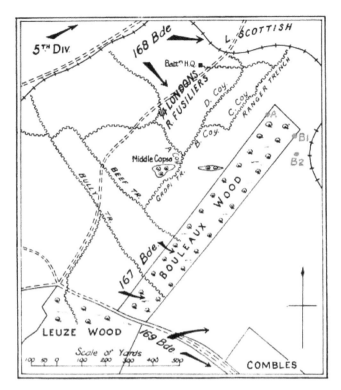

THE BATTLE OF MORVAL, SEPTEMBER 1916

The advance of the Battalion was led by C Company (Grimsdell) in two waves at 50 paces distance, followed by D Company (Cooper) in similar formation. B Company's rôle was to conform to the advance and protect the Brigade's right flank against any possible hostile action from the southern half of Bouleaux Wood, while A Company in reserve moved forward to occupy the positions vacated by the assaulting companies.

The Battalion reached its objectives in the northern fringe of the Wood with little opposition, and with slight loss, killing a large number of Germans in the western edge of the Wood. A great many of the enemy were also put to flight, and these were caught on the open hillside on their way to Combles by the Lewis gunners of the Scottish advancing on our left, who did great execution among them. The consolidation of the strong posts allotted to the Battalion at once began, but was considerably interfered with by German snipers, who were still clinging to their posts farther south in the Wood. Under their fire Grimsdell (in charge of C Company) fell, shot through the head. This harassing fire rendered communication with Battalion Headquarters a matter of some difficulty, and continued through the night, as the 167th Brigade on the right had not been successful in pushing through the southern extremity of Bouleaux Wood. By nightfall the new posts were completed and occupied as follows:

- Post A—By 30 men and Lewis gun of C Company.
- Post B1—By 25 men of D Company.
- Post B2—By 30 men and 1 Lewis gun of D Company.

These posts were improved and wired by parties from the Royal Engineers and the Cheshire Pioneers, while A Company subsequently constructed an additional post in the tram-line embankment north of the Wood.

Meanwhile the London Scottish had been equally successful on our left, and had taken possession of the German trench running north-east from Bouleaux Wood in the direction of Morval; and farther still to the north the Guards Division had captured Lesbœufs, while the 5th Division were hammering at the western outskirts of Morval.

The positions now occupied by the Brigade were of immense importance, as they secured excellent observation over the northern exits of Combles; and information received through the French from a German officer prisoner being to the effect that the Combles garrison was making preparations to fight its way out north-eastwards, the further operations of the Brigade were directed towards working round the north side of Combles and cutting off its communication with Morval. This scheme naturally affected the left flank of the Brigade more than the right flank, on which the Battalion was posted.

Shortly after midnight the 167th Brigade gained a foothold in Bouleaux Wood on the right of the Battalion, and a reconnaissance made by Lieut.-Col. Wheatley soon after dawn on the 26th showed that the Wood was finally cleared of the enemy. Touch was rapidly gained with the 1st Londons and the line established in front of the east edge of the Wood.

A few hours later definite information was received that the enemy had evacuated Combles and that troops of the 56th Division had entered it and had met in its deserted streets patrols of the 56th French Division.

The remainder of the day passed quietly for the Battalion, and a distinct lull occurred in the enemy's shell fire, while owing to the clearance of Bouleaux Wood the ground west of it, which had been on the previous afternoon so much swept by snipers, was now quite peaceful.

Combles having fallen into our hands the most immediate need was to improve touch with the French and carry the united line forward east of the village. Early on the morning of the 26th Sept. the French captured Frégicourt and succeeded in establishing themselves in touch with the 169th Brigade south of Combles, thus securing the whole of Combles Trench; while on the north of the village they managed to push patrols forward towards the sunken road leading to Morval. The road was occupied by the Rangers who had orders to occupy if possible the main German third line between Morval and Frégicourt. This was found still to be strongly held and the assistance of the Division's two tanks were requisitioned. Unfortunately both these machines became badly "ditched" before reaching their objective, and the Rangers' attack was therefore abandoned.

That evening the Battalion was relieved in Bouleaux Wood by the Kensingtons, and withdrew to Bully and Beef Trenches with feelings of immense elation at having contributed materially to this striking and solid success.

During the 27th September the trenches held by the Battalion were heavily shelled, but no attempt was made by the enemy to launch a counter-attack on the Brigade's front, and the Germans were evidently content to accept the loss of Combles as irretrievable. In the evening the 168th Brigade handed over its positions to the 2nd French Division, and the Battalion, without relief in Bully and Beef Trenches, withdrew to Casement Trench.

The casualties sustained by the Battalion during this highly successful operation were remarkably few, amounting to 2 officers (2/Lieuts. R. E. Grimsdell, killed, and E. McD. McCormick, wounded), and about 30 N.C.O.'s and men killed and wounded.

During the evening of relief reports of the full success of the battle of the 25th September reached the Battalion, including the splendid news of the fall of the famous series of German redoubts on the Thiepval Ridge. This welcome intelligence, combined with the knowledge of the Combles success, put all ranks into the highest spirits, and created the pardonable expectation that a "break-through" on a large scale was imminent. How premature these high hopes were the Battalion was to learn to its cost on the 7th October.

Mention should be made here of the tasks performed by R. S. M. Harris during the period the Battalion was operating in the Leuze Wood and Bouleaux Wood area. He was responsible for organising all carrying parties up to advanced Battalion Headquarters with water, rations and munitions. These duties he carried out in a highly praiseworthy manner, both he and his small band of carriers being continually called upon day and night to tramp up the long Angle Wood Valley, often in the rain, on practically impassable tracks and more often than not under shell fire. "As Adjutant," writes Boutall, "I highly appreciated the assistance he gave me in thus relieving me of a considerable amount of additional work and anxiety. I do not remember a single instance during this whole period when he failed us, in spite of the difficult and heavy tasks we were obliged to impose on him."

The Battle of the Le Transloy Ridges 1st-18th October

Owing to the shortening of the line consequent upon the fall of Combles, and the extension to their left of the French, the 56th Division was now withdrawn and moved out of the battle area, the Battalion marching at 2 p.m. on the 28th Sept. from Casement to Ville-sur-Ancre, where rough but welcome billets were occupied. The Division's rest was destined to be short-lived, for the following day a warning order was received that it would take the place in the line of the 6th and Guards Divisions, which had suffered considerably during a prolonged period in action.

The Battalion at this stage was unfortunate in losing Lieut.-Col. Wheatley. The prolonged exposure had already undermined his health, and at this period he was recommended a rest by the Medical Authorities. He refused to go to hospital, and compromised by going to the Divisional Rest Station, Major H. J. Duncan-Teape taking command, but so keen was the Colonel to be with his unit, that without having sufficiently recovered he returned on October 2nd.

The sector to be occupied was about 2000 yards in frontage, running in a north-west to south-east direction through the eastern outskirts of Lesbœufs, and was taken over on the evening of the 30th September with the 169th Brigade on the right, and the 167th on the left, the dividing line being the Lesbœufs-Le Transloy Road. The left subsector (or northern half of the line) lay just below the crest of the ridge above Lesbœufs, and orders were issued for the advancement of this part of the line to positions from which direct observation could be obtained over the German positions in front of Le Transloy, in preparation for an early renewal of the offensive.

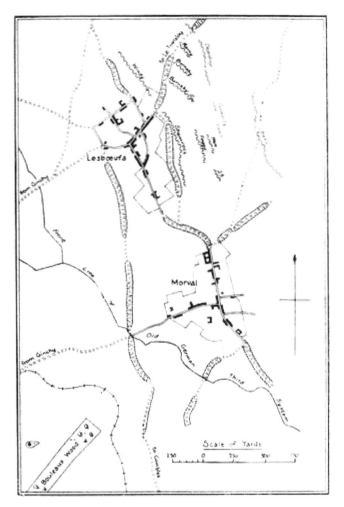

THE BATTLE OF THE LE TRANSLOY RIDGE, OCTOBER 1916

The 168th Brigade remained in Divisional reserve, and on the morning of the 30th the Battalion, together with the London Scottish, moved forward to their former bivouac area between Trones and Bernafay Woods, the Kensingtons and Rangers remaining at the Citadel.

The Battalion remained in the Trones Wood area during the 1st and 2nd October, and a Brigade relief having been ordered for the following day, moved forward at 4.30 p.m. to Lesbœufs, relieving the 2nd Londons. The positions taken over by the Battalion formed the left subsector of the Brigade front and extended from the Lesbœufs-Le Transloy Road, which formed the left boundary, for some 800 yards southwards to the junction with the London Scottish, who were in line on the right, the latter battalion being the right flank of the British Army. The Kensingtons moved into Brigade support in the old Morval-Flers line, and the Rangers occupied bivouacs at Ginchy.

The main position taken over by the Battalion was a roughly constructed trench known as Shamrock, about 50 yards east of the sunken road leading from Lesbœufs to Morval. In advance of this main position, which was allotted to A and B Companies, were a number of embryo trenches in varying stages of construction and quite isolated from the main line. Of these isolated trenches the chief was Rainy, which adjoined the Lesbœufs-Le Transloy Road, about 300 yards ahead of Shamrock, and Foggy, some distance farther south and separated from Rainy by a gap of probably 300 yards. C and D Companies and Battalion Headquarters took up positions in the old Lesbœufs-Gueudecourt line west of the village.

The resumption of the offensive was imminent; and it was indeed first fixed for the 5th October, though subsequently postponed till the 7th owing to the continuance of adverse weather conditions.

A great deal of constructional work was immediately necessary in assembly and communication trenches, as well as in the completion of the necessary advanced dumps of munitions and stores of all kinds. Working parties from the Battalion, of the greatest available strength, began work on part of these tasks on the night of the 4th, the new trenches to be dug comprising communications to join Rainy with Shamrock and with a small advanced position on the crest of the ridge overlooking Le Transloy. In addition the road at Rainy was barricaded. Large working parties were also provided by the Kensingtons to provide an advanced assembly position for the attack by connecting Rainy and Foggy, and by the Cheshire Pioneers and the R.E.'s on other tasks. This latter task, however, could not be completed in one night and was continued the following evening. The shocking state of the ground prevented it from ever being finished, and on the day of the attack only about 150 yards of trench had been added to Foggy. On the night of the 6/7th also a fresh assembly trench for the use of the centre battalion was taped out by the Brigade Major, and dug by the Kensingtons. This work was called New Trench.

Although the weather once again had embarked on a dry spell the long continued rains had rendered working tasks immensely difficult of accomplishment, and the tenacious character of the mud added incalculably to the labour of digging and of reaching the site of the work. The isolation of the various tasks in this appalling swamp, from which every landmark had been swept out of existence, and the constant harassing fire of the enemy's machine-gunners, caused great delays to working parties in even locating their work, and all these factors together tended to reduce the work actually carried out far below expectations.

The Battalion, not being originally detailed for the assault, was relieved in the trenches on the evening of the 5th by the Rangers and moved by companies on relief to bivouacs between Ginchy and Guillemont, leaving A and C Companies in line for the completion of their tasks begun the previous night. The following day, however, intimation was received of a change of orders, and the Battalion returned to the trenches that night as the centre assaulting battalion of the Brigade, its place in brigade support being taken by the Kensingtons.

So far as the 56th Division was concerned the attack of the 7th October was for the purpose of advancing the line some 1400 yards farther down the reverse slope of the Main Ridge, in order to provide a suitable "jumping-off" line for a further offensive to be launched later against the fourth German line in front of Le Transloy, which guarded the Bapaume-Péronne Road. The advance was to be made under a creeping barrage, in two stages, to objectives which were not marked by enemy trenches, but on the farther of which the Division would dig itself in. On the Division's right the French line would also be advanced by the 56th French Division, with whom touch was to be gained on the Frégicourt-Le Transloy Road.

The 168th Brigade's assault was entrusted to the London Scottish (right), 1/4th Londons (centre) and Rangers (left), the dispositions for attack of the Battalion being as follows:

> D Company—(W. H. Vernon) two platoons in New Trench and two platoons in 25 Trench; in touch with London Scottish.
>
> C Company—(Speyer) in Foggy Extension; in touch with Rangers.
>
> B Company—(Gifford) in Shamrock.
>
> A Company—(Keen) in support in the sunken road.
>
> Battalion Headquarters (Col. Wheatley) were in dugouts south-west of Lesbœufs, and an advanced report centre (Major Duncan-Teape) was established in the southern outskirts of the village.

The plan of attack was for D, C and B Companies to advance at two minutes after zero to the first objective, the two platoons of D in New Trench being especially detailed to the task of "mopping up" some German gun pits some 150 yards to the front which were believed to be held by a few enemy snipers. At the same time A Company was to occupy Foggy

Extension. After about fifteen minutes' pause on the first objective, the assault on the second objective would be pursued by C and B Companies only.

Reference has already been made to the difficulty experienced prior to the attack by working parties in locating their tasks, and similar difficulty was met with by all troops throughout the operations. The consistently bad atmospheric conditions had rendered aerial photography almost impossible, and all through the action the doubt which existed in the minds of commanders as to the exact position of trenches, our own as well as the enemy's, was a fruitful source of confusion and loss. The assembly of the companies for attack was indeed only accomplished after serious delay owing to the extraordinary but largely justifiable bewilderment of the guides detailed to the Battalion. C Company only reached its position just before dawn after having been led several hundred yards out of its way, to find on arrival that its assembly trench was only knee deep and already filled with wounded. Add to these obstacles to success, the fact that, owing to the previous terrible losses in commissioned ranks, it was impossible to avoid sending into the battle as many as nine officers who had not been previously in action with the Battalion at all, having only a few days earlier arrived from England, and it will be appreciated that the probabilities of success were not great. Zero was fixed for 1.45 p.m., and at that hour the barrage dropped. Two minutes later the Battalion rose out of its trenches and made a gallant attempt to advance. The story of the remainder of the day is a pitiful tragedy.

The gun pits which had been allotted to the two platoons of D Company in New Trench were found to be alive with bravely-manned machine-guns, and under their withering fire D Company simply melted out of existence. C Company, following slightly to its right, was able to avoid total extinction by taking cover in shell holes in dead ground close by, but 2/Lieut. C. M. Taylor fell under this fire at the head of the leading wave of the Company. B Company, following on from Shamrock, met the full blast of the enemy counter-barrage, and suffered heavy losses, but pushed bravely on and eventually filtered into the same general line as was already held by C Company and the remains of D. Under the devastating fire from the gun pits further advance was impossible, and the troops continued to suffer loss where they lay. The afternoon wore on and the Battalion remained clinging to its position, about 50 yards from its starting-point, until after dark. Sergt. H. F. Page of D Company displayed magnificent coolness, and from his shell hole passed a busy afternoon picking off the German gunners in the pits with great deliberation. He was subsequently commissioned to the King's Own Regiment (Royal Lancaster). All ranks alike were exposed to the fire and all suffered proportionately. L. C. Haycraft, a promising young subaltern of D Company who had already proved his worth with the bombers of the Civil Service Rifles in the Hairpin at Hulluch, made an attempt after dark to ascertain the enemy's position, but he never returned from his reconnaissance.

Gifford, in charge of B Company, also fell, as did his platoon commanders, Fletcher and Richardson, the two last wounded; and C.S.M. James, who received the Military Medal for his good work, took charge of the Company and brought it out of action at the end of the day.

On the left the Rangers had met with a similar fate at the hands of the machine-gunners in Dewdrop Trench, before whose fire they had been stopped dead with ghastly loss immediately they rose from the assembly trench.

The London Scottish, on the right, gained a little success, their right flank achieving a maximum advance of about 400 yards, but their left felt the blast of the deadly guns in the pits, and they were kept out of all except the southern extremity of Hazy.

At about 8.30 p.m. the enemy delivered a counter-attack from Hazy and Dewdrop under heavy artillery support, which had the effect of forcing the Brigade definitely back to its starting trenches.

In the meantime a company of the Kensingtons had been brought up to Burnaby with the idea of forcing the Dewdrop position by outflanking it from the north, but the Germans being found still strongly in possession of Spectrum, north of the road, the attack was cancelled.

It having become obvious that the assaulting battalions were dangerously weakened, immediate reliefs were arranged, and the Battalion that night handed over its position to the Queen Victorias, who were attached to the Brigade, and withdrew to the bivouacs at Trones Wood. Here it was joined by the London Rifle Brigade. The withdrawal of the Battalion was supervised by Major Duncan-Teape, who managed by great efforts to get the whole of the remnants of the companies back over the Ridge just before daylight broke. The roll call at Trones Wood was a gloomy spectacle, for neither the 1/4th Londons nor the London Scottish could muster more than the strength of about one company.

The total losses in all ranks sustained by the Battalion on this unfortunate day amounted to about 300 all ranks, the casualties among officers being:

> Killed—Lieut. W. H. Vernon, 2/Lieuts. C. M. Taylor, W. H. Gilford, L. J. R. Atterbury and L. C. Haycraft.

> Wounded—Capt. R. N. Keen and 2/Lieuts. T. R. Fletcher, H. W. Spiers and S. A. G. Richardson.

Of this, the last of the Battalion's actions in the great Somme battles, but little more need be said. The position which it had been proposed to carry with three weak battalions was attempted again the following day with equal lack of success; and subsequently other Divisions suffered heavy casualties in the unsuccessful endeavour. Indeed the position never did fall into our possession until the enemy deliberately gave it up in his retirement of the succeeding February on to the Hindenburg line.

Lieut.-Col. L. L. Wheatley, D.S.O., had led the Battalion through many trying ordeals with the unfailing confidence of all ranks who had the honour to be under his command; but as already indicated, the strain of the long-protracted struggle, especially of the last few days, combined with continually wet clothes, had proved too much for him, and he now contracted an acute attack of dysentery and was evacuated to hospital on the 10th. He never returned to the Battalion which his compelling personality had made essentially his own.

On the 11th October the Battalion moved to the Citadel Camp, the gateway through which thirty-five days earlier it had entered the inferno of the battle; and the Division being concentrated here after relief by the 4th Division, it marched the following morning to Ville-sur-Ancre, moving thence by motor-buses to a rest area north-west of Amiens, billets being provided for it at St Vaast-en-Chaussée.

Of all the great series of actions of the War the battles of the Somme in 1916 stand out perhaps in the public memory as the most heroic, and at the same time the most appalling, and we cannot leave the subject finally without a few remarks generally reviewing the Battalion's experiences. Of the thirty-five days spent in XIV Corps area only four had been spent in rest bivouacs, and during the remaining thirty-one the Battalion had taken part in active operations five times. The losses incurred amounted to the enormous total of nearly 700 in all ranks, of whom 40 were officers.

It would be unfitting to close our account of the Somme battles without paying some tribute to the magnificent work performed throughout by Rear Headquarters under Major H. J. Duncan-Teape. The administrative ranks of a battalion in action are invariably worked to the limits of human endurance, but usually with inadequate recognition of their importance; for it is no exaggeration to say that on the efficiency with which they maintain the stream of supplies, whether of rations or munitions, to the fighting ranks, depends not merely the success, but the very existence of the troops in advanced positions. On the Somme the consistently atrocious weather increased tenfold the fatigue and strain of the administrative portion of the Battalion: the mud swamps which had to be traversed, the severe shell fire which plastered all back areas, the wretched misery of the whole struggle, and above all the vast responsibility which rested on them, all combined to make the work of Rear Headquarters an enormous strain both mental and physical. But throughout the battles Major Duncan-Teape was constantly alert and constantly at advanced Headquarters, ascertaining exactly what was wanted, and getting it done. In Lieut. H. B. A. Balls, the Acting Quartermaster, and in R.S.M. Harris he found able and devoted lieutenants whose cool handling of all difficulties was invaluable.

The transport sections of all battalions were brigaded under Capt. L. G. Rix at the Citadel, and the 1/4th Londons' transport section under Lieut. G. V. Lawrie worked throughout magnificently and never once failed to deliver the day's supplies. Those who were present will fully appreciate what this means. The work for horses and men was exhausting and incessant; and oftentimes the limbers returned from the forward area to the transport lines only just in time to load up once more for the upward journey. The results that were obtained could only have been achieved by the whole-hearted devotion of all ranks.

Of the men in the companies on whom day after day fell the burden of physical discomfort and mental strain it is impossible to speak adequately. The record of their achievements speaks, and can be left to speak, for itself.

The decorations awarded for services rendered between the 1st July and the 7th October were:

>M.C.—Lieut. W. J. Boutall, 2/Lieuts. O. D. Garratt, S. J. Barkworth, M.M., E. McD. McCormick and Rev. R. Palmer, C.F.
>
>D.C.M.—C.S.M. R. Davis, Sergt. T. Clark, Ptes. J. O'Brien and H. S. Payne.
>
>M.M.—C.Q.M.-Sergt. R. Forbes, Sergts. H. C. Gearle, H. H. Merrell, R. Hebberd, R. R. L. Hyde, C. James and T. Lock, Corpl. J. Castle, L.-Corpls. H. Whitehead, A. Sergeant, A. J. Moger and L. R. Webb, Ptes. H. E. Hyde, W. Buckingham, A. E. Colvin, F. Hedger, W. Lawrence and C. F. Collins.

CHAPTER XII
THE 1/4 BATTALION DURING THE WINTER 1916/17

On arrival at St Vaast-en-Chaussée the 1/4th Londons were reduced in strength to about 275 all ranks, and although the morale of the troops was not impaired by their recent experiences, the Battalion was seriously in need of rest, reorganisation and reinforcement. A few days of light training, which occupied the mornings only, with games in the afternoon, went far towards recreating the troops physically; but the reorganisation of the Battalion was necessarily a more lengthy and difficult matter. No company had more than two officers, and N.C.O.'s were very few. Lewis gun teams and bombers were newly detailed to their respective duties and untrained, and the building up once more of the fine fighting battalion which had entered the trenches at Hébuterne three and a half months earlier, added to the proper assimilating of the reinforcements which were expected from England, presented a task the completion of which was likely to occupy the greater part of the winter months.

After Lieut.-Col. Wheatley had succumbed to sickness the command of the Battalion devolved on Major H. J. T. Duncan-Teape, who was appointed acting Lieut.-Colonel.

The few days' rest at St Vaast were enlivened by an entertainment given by the Bow Bells, which had an excellent effect in cheering up the men.

On the 20th October the Division moved to the Hallencourt area, where it had originally been formed, the Battalion arriving in billets at Citerne at about 5.30 p.m. after a march which, in the reduced physical condition of the troops, proved to be exceedingly trying. Probably never has the Battalion been accorded a kindlier welcome in billets than from the good people of Citerne, who, having received it in February and sent it out to battle, took a quite proprietary interest in the laurels which it brought back to them.

At St Vaast and Citerne the Battalion was joined by Capt. F. C. Grimwade, who assumed the duties of second in command with the acting rank of Major, 2/Lieuts. C. E. V. Richardson and P. Pyne. Capt. L. G. Rix also returned to the Battalion from Brigade Transport Officer, and 2/Lieut. O. D. Garratt was appointed Assistant Adjutant.

A course of light training was continued for a few days at Citerne under weather conditions which continued bright and frosty until the evening of the 24th October, when the Battalion marched at 8 p.m. in a veritable deluge to Longpré Station to entrain for a fresh area. The pitiless rain drenched all to the skin, but the men's spirits remained completely undamped, for the rumour had gone forth that the new area was far from the Somme, among the marshes of Flanders. The move from Longpré was made by tactical train shortly after midnight, and about midday on the 25th the Battalion detrained at Merville, whence it marched straight to billets between Neuf Berquin and Estaires, being now attached to the XI Corps (Haking) of the First Army (Horne).

No prolonged rest was, however, in store, for although the Battalions of the 56th Division were momentarily not prepared for active operations, they were perfectly capable of holding trenches. No surprise, therefore, was caused by the receipt the day following arrival at Neuf Berquin of orders to relieve the 61st Division in the Neuve Chapelle-Fauquissart area.

A preliminary reconnaissance of the trenches by officers of Battalion Headquarters and company commanders took place on the 26th, and on the 27th the 1/4th Londons and London Scottish moved forward and took over reserve billets in Laventie from the 2/7th and 2/8th Royal Warwickshires.

On the 28th October the 168th Brigade completed the relief of the 182nd Brigade, the 1/4th Londons and Scottish moving into the right and left subsections respectively of the Fauquissart sector, there relieving the 2/6th and 2/5th Royal Warwickshires, while the reserve billets in Laventie were taken over by the Kensingtons and Rangers.

The new Divisional frontage covered some 7000 yards from the neighbourhood of Richebourg l'Avoué on the right to a point opposite Rouges Bancs on the left, all the Brigades being in line and each finding its own supports and local reserves. The 168th Brigade held the extreme left of the Divisional front, the 169th being on its right, while the New Zealand Division was on its left. This extreme deployment of a numerically weak Division was justified by the quiet character of this area, and the fact that the German divisions opposed to it were equally with ourselves somewhat exhausted by recent efforts in the Somme battles and not anxious to venture on active operations. To such an extent indeed had our continued pressure in the south drained the enemy's resources that his lines opposite the 56th Division were but feebly held, and at the moment not capable of being strongly reinforced; and this area was therefore eminently suited to the recuperation of a battle-worn Division and to the training in active service conditions of the young troops from home who were shortly to join it.

The Fauquissart breastworks were in every way similar to those in the Neuve Chapelle area already described in connection with the Battalion's service in the Indian Corps, though being opposite the village of Aubers, which is on the highest part of the Ridge, were even more seriously subject to observation from the enemy lines than the Richebourg breastworks.

The village of Fauquissart, at this period in a condition of total ruin, consisted of a scattered collection of houses extending for about half a mile along each side of the Rue Tilleloy, which ran parallel with the British front breastworks and about 200 yards in rear of them. A thousand yards in rear of the Rue Tilleloy, and parallel to it, was the Rue Bacquerot, these two roads forming good lateral communication within the sector, though the former could only be used under cover of darkness. The sector was also served by three communication trenches starting from the Bacquerot, Elgin Street, Masselot Street and the Strand, the last named during the winter months usually consisting of a chain of unfordable lakes.

This sector was held by the Battalion with three companies in line and one in reserve, the reserve company holding three keeps on the line of the Rue Bacquerot, called Road Bend, Wangerie and Masselot Posts. Battalion Headquarters was accommodated in shelters near Temple Bar on the Rue Bacquerot.

The German lines opposite were heavily wired, and included two strongly marked salients, the Devil's Jump and the Wick. But although the enemy had the advantage in observation owing to his possession of the Ridge, his front trenches were far from comfortable owing to the presence behind his lines of the Rivière des Laies which, as the winter wore on, became more and more swollen, finally bursting its banks and rendering his forward defences completely untenable.

Our wire entanglements were exceedingly poor, and immediate attention was directed to the improvement of this important part of our defences; the parapets also were thin, firebays sadly in need of revetment, and the whole sector seriously lacking in shelter for the men. No time was lost in evolving an extensive works programme, which was promptly put into execution, the more important work being carried out under Royal Engineer supervision. The urgency of the Brigade works programme rendered the supply of large working parties necessary, and it was therefore arranged that of the two battalions for the time being in Laventie one would act as "Works Battalion" finding all working parties, while the other would devote itself to training.

The most peculiar feature of this sector lay in the immunity from shell fire of Laventie behind the British lines and of Aubers in the German territory. Each village layabout 2000 yards in rear of the respective front trenches, and both were used as reserve billets for the troops holding the line. By mutual and tacit consent the artillery on each side refrained from bombarding the other's billets; any infringement of this unwritten law on one side being met with immediate and severe retaliation by the other. During the period therefore spent in the Laventie area, the Battalion on coming out of the line had the enjoyment of occupying tolerably wind-and water-tight billets without molestation, although they were distant little more than a mile from the enemy lines. A considerable number of civilians still clung to their battered homes in Laventie, and it was strange to see French soldiers, whose divisions were serving in Alsace or the Argonne, come to Laventie "on leave from the front"!

The 1/4th Londons now settled down to a regular routine of four days in the right subsection breastworks followed by four days in billets in Laventie, tours being later extended to six days, and as this routine continued until the middle of December we need not follow it in detail.

The sector had been particularly quiet prior to the 56th Division's arrival, but almost from the day of its taking over the line conditions began to change. Possibly a certain undesirable aggressiveness on the part of the Londoners began to annoy an enemy who, but for interference, was content to conduct a perfectly peaceful war; possibly the change was due to the recovery of both sides from the fatigue and over-strain of the Somme. Whatever the reason, certain it is that as the winter wore on the whole Neuve Chapelle-Fauquissart area began to become much more lively than it had been. On our side the most vigorous system of patrolling, of daily organised shoots by guns of all calibres, trench mortars and machine-guns, and of an intensive course of sniping, quickly gave us the ascendancy and caused the Germans a pardonable irritation under which they showed themselves less and less disposed to take their punishment quietly.

In the line the Battalion was busily occupied with its share of the works programme and in patrolling in which the infrequency of encounters with the enemy in No Man's Land gradually led to the belief that his front breastwork was not occupied. This was probed further on the last evening of November when a fighting patrol of twenty men under 2/Lieut. W. H. Webster (Intelligence Officer) entered the enemy lines at the Wick Salient and found it untenanted, in a shocking condition of flood and affording ample evidence that no attempt was being made to repair the serious damage caused by our artillery fire.

During the third week in November the Battalion's frontage was extended to the right, involving the occupation by the right company of an extra 400 yards of breastwork and an additional supporting post, Erith, and by the reserve company of a fourth keep on the Bacquerot line called Lonely Post.

This new piece of breastwork was usually subjected to a good deal of enemy trench mortar fire, especially about the point at which Erith Street communication trench joined the front line. This was an unpleasant spot. Erith Street sunk into a slight depression so that all traffic using it was plainly visible to the Germans; and as it came to an abrupt end some fifteen yards short of the front line an undesirable gap occurred which had to be traversed with more than ordinary agility by those whose duty took them that way. A good deal of extra trench repairing work was imposed on us in consequence of the enemy's attentions at this point, and unfortunately some casualties occurred.

The enemy's activity was rather marked on the 26th November, during the morning of which day over seventy 5·9-inch shells fell near the Convent observation post but without a direct hit being obtained. The Convent, together with two or three other posts along the line of the Rue Tilleloy, used by the forward observation officers of our supporting artillery, consisted of a substantial brick tower some 25 feet in height, like an attenuated Martello Tower. These had been erected behind the cover of the houses of Fauquissart before the village had been destroyed. But the subsequent demolition of the houses had exposed the towers, which consequently stood up naked and unashamed within 200 yards of our front line, and their presence, possibly combined with his evident inability to hit them, seemed to be a constant source of annoyance to the enemy.

All this time the Battalion strength was steadily increasing with reinforcements from home and with the return of many who had been wounded on the Somme, till by Christmas it mustered some 700 all ranks. Officer reinforcements followed on each other's heels with surprising rapidity, and the following joined during November:

> Captains V. S. Bowater and H. M. Lorden, Lieuts. H. Jones (appointed Brigade Bombing Officer) and H. J. M. Williams, 2/Lieuts. E. G. Dew, L. W. Wreford, S. P. Stotter, H. W. Spiers, R. W. Chamberlain and W. A. Froy; 2/Lieuts. H. N. Williams, L. W. N. Jones, H. D. Rees, Bradley (to 168th L.T.M. Battery) and A. L. Harper (attached from 4th Royal Welsh Fusiliers); 2/Lieuts. F. H. Hutchins, A. G. Davis and L. E. Ballance (attached from 11th Londons); Captain H. Pentelow and Lieuts. T. Coleman (Works Officer) and H. D. Beeby (attached from Hunts Cyclist Battalion).

Captain Pentelow was unluckily hit and sent to hospital two days after his arrival.

At the end of November the Rev. R. Palmer, M.C., left the Battalion to take up the duties of Divisional Chaplain in the 24th Division, his place being taken a few days later by Rev. S. F. Leighton Green, who remained with the Battalion until after the Armistice.

About this period a Divisional Musketry Camp was formed at Le Sart, near Merville, and 2/Lieuts. Wreford and Pyne were appointed to it as instructors. 2/Lieut. E. G. Dew was also appointed Battalion Bombing Officer.

On the 21st December a readjustment of the Battalion sector was effected, and in the afternoon the sector as originally taken over from the 182nd Brigade was handed over to the 1/3rd Londons, and the Battalion marched to billets at Bout Deville.

After three days occupied in cleaning up and training, Christmas Day was celebrated as a holiday, and, the billets being beyond the range of any but heavy guns, with which the Germans were not well supplied on this front, the rest of the Battalion was quite undisturbed. But every effort was made to render the Germans' Christmas as uncomfortable as possible. At 6.30 p.m. on Christmas Eve a continuous steady bombardment of his defences by all available batteries up to 6-inch guns began, and lasted for forty-eight hours. This action was evidently much resented by the enemy, and after Christmas the trench warfare in this area was conducted with greater fierceness than it had been previously.

The Bow Bells were now established in the theatre at La Gorgue, and it was found possible to provide a free visit for every man in the Battalion to its splendid Christmas pantomime "Aladdin," which was most heartily appreciated.

During the temporary absence of 2/Lieut. O. D. Garratt, the duties of Intelligence Officer were taken by 2/Lieut. J. R. K. Paterson (Argyll and Sutherland Highlanders, attached), who remained with the Battalion for about a month.

On New Year's Day 1917 the 168th Brigade relieved the 169th Brigade in Moated Grange sector, the Rangers and Kensingtons occupying the trenches, with the London Scottish in support, about Rouge Croix and Pont du Hem on the La Bassée Road, while the 1/4th Londons remained in Divisional reserve billets at Riez Bailleul.

A week here was spent in supplying working parties, of which the labour was considerable owing to the long distance—about four miles—which had to be covered each night in each direction by parties going up the line for work. The weather, moreover, had taken a marked change, and a very severe frost had set in which increased tenfold the labour of digging. Towards the end of the week snow fell adding further to the fatigue of the long night marches.

On the evening of the 9th January 1917 the Battalion took over from the Kensingtons the right subsection of the Moated Grange sector. This sector had seen a good many changes both as regards defences and boundaries since the Battalion's previous occupation of it in the summer of 1915, and the lines now taken over extended from Sign Post Lane on the right for a frontage of some 1400 yards to a point opposite the village of Mauquissart which lay just within the German lines.

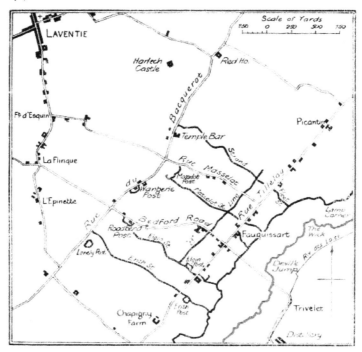

LAVENTIE, WINTER 1916-1917

The sector was held with three companies in the front breastworks and supporting posts and one in reserve on Cardiff Road. Battalion Headquarters occupied shelters at Ebenezer Farm. These positions were far from ideal. The strength of the Battalion was much scattered and difficult of control in emergency, owing to the exceedingly bad communications within the area. The supporting platoons of the front line companies, at Bristol House, Cornwall Siding and Pump House, occupied the only remaining tenable portions of what had originally been the German second line prior to the Battle of Neuve Chapelle, and were separated from each other by about 100 yards of broken down and almost impassably wet breastworks. For communication from front to rear only one trench,

Tilleloy South, was passable with any degree of safety in daylight. Between Pump House and the front line, a distance of about 250 yards, it was seriously overlooked from the German positions in the Bois du Biez, with the result that traffic up and down it was frequently sniped with trench mortar and 5·9 shells.

Always an area of considerable activity, the Moated Grange possessed several unpleasant features as a result of the active mining operations which had begun in 1915, and were still proceeding with unabated energy. The Duck's Bill Farm had given place to an enormous crater of the same name, linked with the British lines by a defended sap which left the front line at Sunken Road. The defence of this crater and sap took a platoon, whose arduous duties of continual listening and constant preparedness for an enemy raid were carried out under exceedingly rough conditions, as both the crater and the sap were full of water and shelters were conspicuous by their absence.

On the front occupied by the left company the German lines were invisible from the British breastworks owing to the lips thrown up round the Colvin craters, a series of some thirty or more of immense size which covered half the area of No Man's Land at this point. The largest of this series, the Mauquissart crater, occupied the site of what had once been our front line, and the breastwork now ran round its nearer lip. This mined area was the most uncomfortable part of the line, since the Germans were continually searching with trench mortar fire for the heads of our mine shafts while the cover afforded to enemy patrols by the crater lips themselves necessitated constant vigilance and counter-patrolling activity on the part of our trench garrison. Add to this the extreme hardship which the troops in this part of the line inevitably had to undergo owing to the total lack of dugouts and the perishing cold. The blowing of so many craters had, moreover, cut off the ditches between fields which had formerly been used for draining the trenches, with the result that there was no means of getting rid of the water which in a large number of firebays rose higher than the firestep. Under these conditions cooking in the neighbourhood of the front line was out of the question, and all cooked food had to be carried by permanent headquarter carrying parties from the Battalion cook-house near Ebenezer Farm; in the case of rations destined for the flank platoons this meant a trudge for the food carriers of over a mile in each direction at each meal.

The defences generally had suffered severely both from the enemy's shell fire and the effects of the alternation of sharp frost and heavy rain, and an immense amount of labour was called for in working and carrying parties for the breastworks as well as for the wire entanglements, which were in a very weak condition. The single communication trench, therefore, became frequently congested with long lines of troops "humping" material and food to the front line, and altogether the Moated Grange was a hard sector to run efficiently and a remarkably unpleasant one to live in.

Two tours of six days each were spent in this sector, broken by six days—not of rest, but of most exhausting working parties—in Riez Bailleul. The days in line saw a good deal of shelling and the Battalion suffered some loss, but in spite of this and of exposure to intense cold the men were probably more happy in the line than in billets. Further heavy falls of snow had occurred. The working parties supplied from Riez Bailleul were largely engaged in drawing trench stores and material at a dump on the La Bassée Road between Pont du Hem and Rouge Croix, itself nearly two miles from billets; and thence pushing it up to the front trenches on the tram-line dignified with the title of Great Eastern Railway, a further distance of upwards of 3000 yards. From railhead this material, consisting of trench boards, rolls of barbed wire, revetting frames, hurdles and other heavy stuff had to be distributed to companies in the line. These fatigues were obviously exhausting, and seldom did a party leaving billets at 5.30 p.m. return before midnight.

The most difficult task of all, however, which may not yet have quite faded from the memories of many, was connected with an ingenious scheme for draining the craters with heavy cast-iron water mains each about 16 feet long. With infinite labour these were brought to tram railhead, but at this point the difficulty of carrying pipes, each weighing some 200 pounds, along 500 yards of quagmire proved too much even for the stout hearts of Cockneys; and the high hopes which the author of the scheme had entertained of draining the craters vanished as his pipes sank in the mud. A change from this routine to the comparative peace of trench mortaring in the line was not unwelcome.

An act of gallantry occurred during the first tour which must be recorded. During one of the enemy's midday bombardments a time-fuzed medium trench mortar shell fell on the parapet of our breastwork on the lip of Mauquissart crater, and lodged in the revetting hurdle at the side of the trench. The firebay happened to be crowded with men working on the defences, and heavy casualties must inevitably have been caused but for the bravery of 2/Lieut. W. H. Webster, who rushed forward and, seizing the shell, flung it over the parapet into the crater, where it immediately exploded. For this gallant action 2/Lieut. Webster was awarded the D.S.O.

The enemy's artillery and trench mortars showed a marked increase of activity during the second occupation of Moated Grange, the craters, the Duck's Bill and Pump House, coming in for most of the punishment. The 23rd January was perhaps the most trying to the troops. During the morning "hate" a well-placed minenwerfer completely cut off the left platoon in the craters, the only approach to them being by way of an exposed and little used trench, Min Street, which involved a detour of about 3200 yards from Headquarters. Shortly after midday a second lucky German shell lighted on a dump of medium trench mortar shells which were lying within a few yards of a shelter occupied by several men of the right company. A terrific explosion took place and caused a large crater which cut off the Battalion's right flank also, but, strange to say, without inflicting so much as a scratch on any of the men in the vicinity. These incidents are recounted merely as instances of the constant annoyance caused to the troops in line by the enemy's harassing tactics, as every bit of damage caused in this way involved extra work to the already over-burdened troops in repairing it.

On the last evening in the line, the 25th, an attempt was made by a fighting patrol of the reserve company (C) under 2/Lieut. Ballance to obtain an identification from the enemy. Wire-cutting shoots had taken place for two days previously in preparation for this, and arrangements were made to support the patrol with artillery fire as occasion should arise. The enemy were found, however, to have made efficient counter-preparations, and the surprise effect of the patrol having failed, the project had to be abandoned with the loss of 1 man killed and 2 wounded.

During this tour the Battalion sustained 1 officer casualty, 2/Lieut. W. Quennell, wounded.

On the 26th January the Battalion was relieved by the 1/8th Middlesex at 10.5 p.m. and withdrew to rest billets at La Gorgue, the 168th Brigade having passed into Divisional reserve with Brigade Headquarters at Merville.

The 168th Brigade in rest in the Merville area settled down to such training as was possible, the ground being covered with snow. One or two useful instructional schemes with contact aeroplanes were carried out, but the weather conditions prevented serious outdoor work, and the training hours were, for the most part, devoted to repolishing the parade discipline of the Brigade. According to the usual custom of the Battalion when opportunity offered itself, the drums beat Retreat daily and the Regimental Quarter Guard and inlying picket mounted in the Grande Place at La Gorgue.

Two further drafts of about 70 N.C.O.'s and men joined the Battalion in January.

It had been the intention that the 168th Brigade should pass fourteen days in rest, but this idea had to be unexpectedly abandoned owing to a concentration of troops near the frozen inundations of the Yser, where it was feared that a sudden German advance over the ice might have somewhat disturbing effects on the Allies' positions. This caused the services of the 168th Brigade to be requisitioned once more, and on the 1st and 2nd February it relieved the 111th Brigade of the 37th Division in the Neuve Chapelle sector, the Rangers and Kensingtons occupying the line, while the Scottish moved as Works Battalion to billets at Croix Barbée and the 1/4th Londons as Training Battalion to Fosse.

On the 1st February 2/Lieut. C. E. V. Richardson was admitted to hospital.

After training at Fosse for six days the 1/4th Londons took over from the Kensingtons the right subsector of Neuve Chapelle sector on the 8th February.

The Battalion now found itself after a lapse of over a year once more in the area in which it had passed so many months with the Ferozepore Brigade. The sector taken over comprised the old Rue du Bois (right, centre and left) sections, and extended from a point opposite the German Boar's Head Salient on the right to some 250 yards north of the La Bassée Road on the left. Considerable changes had now taken place in the method of holding the line; old well-known trenches had fallen into disuse and fresh ones had taken their places. Those who looked for the Crescent, Orchard Redoubt, and other well-remembered spots found them broken down and no longer occupied. The front line breastwork was now occupied in isolated posts at intervals of about 150 yards, each garrisoned by a platoon. Each post was protected on its flanks as well as in front by wire entanglements, while the intervening firebays had been either filled in or choked with barbed wire.

The communications within the sector were tolerably good, but the breastwork was thin and in many places low, a natural result of leaving long portions of it unoccupied for several months.

The main line of resistance was now in the reserve or "B" line which, on the right of the sector, was represented by Guards Trench in front of the Rue du Bois, and on the left by the old British front line (as it had been before the Battle of March 1915) in Edgware Road. Battalion Headquarters in 1915 had occupied dugouts on the Rue du Bois, but were now at Lansdowne Post, which formerly had housed a whole battalion. The defence scheme provided for holding the "B" line at all costs in the event of serious attack, so that the front line became virtually a line of outposts. This method of holding the line in great depth was not only far sounder than the former method of crowding the whole strength into the front trench, but was also more economical, as the sector which formerly had demanded a garrison of a whole brigade was held by one battalion.

The line was held with two companies in the front line posts and two in support in the "B" line.

On the right of the La Bassée Road the German trenches were about 100 yards distant, and it was soon found that the enemy snipers had been allowed to gain the ascendancy over the British, a state of affairs which all battalions of the Brigade promptly set to work to correct.

The first day's occupation of this sector passed without incident, but on the evening of the 9th February, at about 7 p.m., the enemy opened a heavy trench mortar and machine-gun bombardment on the front line from Pioneer to Pope Posts, astride the La Bassée Road. The trench mortar fire was well directed, and the breastwork on the right of Pope Post was badly breached. At about 7.30 p.m. this preparatory shelling was followed by a heavy "box" barrage, and an enemy raiding party entered our lines between Pioneer and Pope Posts. An S.O.S. signal was sent up from the left company Headquarters, and our artillery responded promptly with a heavy barrage on the German front line and communication trenches.

The raiders, about twelve in number, divided into two groups, of which one attacked Pope Post and the other Pioneer Post. The attack on Pope Post was driven off by the garrison, three of the raiding party being bayoneted by Sergt. Gardiner, whereupon the others turned and fled, being followed back to the German lines by the second group.

Capt. Rix, commanding B Company, accompanied by his Sergt.-Major (Shelton) and his runner, gallantly endeavoured to pass through the barrage on Hun Street in order to take control of affairs in the front line; but all were unfortunately hit by the same shell, Shelton and the runner being killed outright while Rix died in hospital a few days later. The raiders were successful in capturing 2/Lieut. Webster, D.S.O., who was with the Lewis gun post at Pioneer Post; he is believed to have been mortally hit prior to his capture, and died in the enemy's hands the following day. In addition to these regrettable casualties about a dozen men were slightly wounded, the bulk of the loss on our side being sustained by a carrying party from the Rangers who were caught by the German barrage at Edgware Road tram railhead. 2/Lieut. Stotter (B Company) was also slightly wounded. He remained at duty for some days, but was admitted to hospital about ten days later. The reorganisation of the line was promptly taken in hand by Capt. Stanbridge (A Company) in support, who temporarily reinforced the front line with one of his platoons under 2/Lieut. Harper, and subsequently took over B Company vice Rix. The raiding party belonged, as was found from the three enemy dead left in our hands, to the 2nd Battalion, 13th Bavarian Regiment. For his coolness and good work during the raid Sergt. Gardiner was awarded the Military Medal.

The remainder of the night passed without incident, and the bright moonlight during the later hours enabled our working parties to make considerable headway in repairing the breaches in our breastwork.

On the morning of the following day an observed shoot—which caused very great material damage—was carried out by our trench mortar batteries on the enemy first and second lines. This shoot produced a certain amount of trench mortar retaliation on Guards Trench, in the course of which an unlucky shell destroyed a Stokes mortar section under 2/Lieut. Bradley, and the whole of its team, causing a block in our line at Mole Post.

No further incident of importance occurred during the remainder of this tour, though our lines were daily subjected to heavy bombardments by the enemy medium trench mortars, especially in the neighbourhood of Pioneer Post, where very considerable damage was caused to our breastworks and wire. On the evenings of the 12th and 13th, however, when this activity of the enemy began to assume somewhat serious proportions, they were effectively silenced by prearranged retaliatory shoots by our supporting artillery on the German front and support lines.

The following afternoon the Battalion handed over the right subsection to the Kensingtons, and withdrew as Works Battalion to billets at Croix Barbée. Here the Battalion supplied large working parties nightly, the principal tasks being the raising and thickening of the weak portions of the breastwork and the wiring of the new parts of the "B" line.

Throughout this winter the prosecution of the works programme placed a heavy strain on all ranks and totally deprived the periods spent out of the line of any semblance of rest. Even on the night of relief the working parties were carried out, and many times during these months companies which had held front line trenches for six days marched back to reserve billets and within an hour were paraded again for a working party from which they were not dismissed till after midnight. The necessity for this extreme pressure of work was doubtless real, but the unceasing drudgery of it could not be conducive to good work while the efficient recreation of the men by games out of the line received so little attention.

However, on this occasion it was found possible to make progress with the Brigade boxing competition, a good ring being available at the Brigade Lewis Gun School at Croix Barbée, and in this competition the Battalion gained several successes.

On the 20th February the Battalion returned to the trenches, taking over the right subsection from the Kensingtons.

Sign Post Lane, Neuve Chapelle

Ruined Farmhouse near Neuve Chapelle

This tour of duty was marked by an all round increase of activity both in trench mortar and artillery fire on both sides, the points which received the majority of the shelling being the front line about the much battered Pope and Pioneer Posts, Port Arthur and the "B" line in the neighbourhood of the Rue du Bois. The enemy was also active by day with rifle grenades, and at night with machine-gun fire.

Owing to the particular discomfort of living in Pope and Pioneer Posts an inter-company relief between the two left companies was effected on the 23rd February, A Company withdrawing into support in favour of C Company, which took over Port Arthur sector.

An attempt was made on the evening of the 26th by the 5th Division on the right to raid in force the enemy's lines to the south of the Boar's Head Salient. The enemy had exhibited numerous signs of nervousness, and it was not altogether surprising to find him quite prepared for the attempt by the 5th Division. The exact point against which the raiding party was directed, however, did not coincide with his anticipations, for the bulk of his rather sharp counter-barrage came down on the sector held by this Battalion. This barrage lasted with intensity for twenty minutes, and, trench mortars being freely employed, caused a good deal of further damage to our already weak breastworks, but inflicted practically no loss of personnel.

The following morning the Kensingtons once more relieved the 1/4th Londons, taking over the right subsection and extending it to the left as far as the outskirts of Neuve Chapelle village, the adjusted line being known as the left subsection of Ferme du Bois sector.

On relief the Battalion occupied billets as training battalion at Fosse, C Company being detached in hutments at Les Huit Maisons. Training was proceeded with uninterruptedly though the weather remained intensely cold and further falls of snow occurred. The opportunity was taken to hold a Battalion cross-country run, which passed off as satisfactorily as the arctic conditions permitted. The frost, which had lasted for several weeks, was indeed now becoming a little serious as it was utterly impossible, owing to the hardness of the soil, to carry out repairs to the trenches which were daily being more knocked about by the enemy's fire. The appalling destruction which must later be caused by the inevitable thaw filled the hearts of those who would form part of the subsequent working parties with feelings of misgiving, mingled with resentment.

On the 5th March the Battalion relieved the Kensingtons in the left subsection of Ferme du Bois, the order of battle in the front line being from the right, B, D and A Companies, with C in support in the "B" line. The additional frontage between La Bassée Road and Neuve Chapelle was also held in isolated posts.

As before the "B" line was the main line of resistance; but the great length of the "B" line sector—some 2300 yards—which had to be held in eight separate posts, with three additional posts at night, presented a difficult problem in defence to one weak company of about 120 fighting ranks. The solution of the problem was not, however, actually called for as the enemy remained unusually quiet for the whole of this tour of duty, during which the snow fell thicker every day. After an occupation of four uninteresting days the Battalion was relieved in the left subsection on the afternoon of the 9th March by 1/6th Duke of Wellington's Regiment (49th Division). On relief it withdrew to billets at Bout Deville, marching the following morning at 8 a.m. to Merville, where the Brigade entrained for the Le Cauroy area. Detrainment took place at Doullens, and the Battalion marched some six miles to billets at Le Souich, arriving shortly before midnight.

The Battalion, which had left the Somme battlefields in an exhausted condition in the previous October, had undergone a good schooling in the Flanders breastworks. The strength had been increased to some 850 all ranks, and all new drafts had become not only well assimilated, but also well trained in a rather trying trench warfare. The physical strain on the troops throughout the winter had been exceptionally severe, owing to the terrible intensity of the winter weather, and the very great amount of trench work for which the Battalion had been called upon; and of this side of the incidents of the winter sufficient has already been said for it to be realised without difficulty that, although the Battalion still had a clean bill of health, the prospect of a rest before embarking on active operations was welcomed by all.

The great retirement of the Germans was now in progress, and as the 1/4th Battalion was not actively concerned in this we may turn for the moment to follow the fortunes of the 2/4th Battalion, who had recently arrived in France with the 58th Division and were now in action in the Arras sector.

CHAPTER XIII
THE 2/4TH BATTALION IN FRANCE--GERMAN RETIREMENT FROM THE SOMME

The 58th Division, of which the 2/4th Londons formed a part, after remaining at Ipswich for about a month, was transferred to the Southern Command in hutted camps at Sutton Veny, near Warminster, on the 10th July 1916.

Here the Division, being concentrated in an area which provided excellent training facilities, had a chance to become thoroughly welded together and to show the material of which it was made in a manner which had hitherto been impossible, for the influence of scattered billets is invariably and inevitably unfavourable to strict discipline. The fullest advantage was taken of this golden opportunity, and the resultant tightening of discipline and advancement of all ranks in technical efficiency rapidly justified the change of station. A very great amount of work still lay before the whole Division before it would be fit to take its place in the line overseas, and much reorganisation in various directions was effected with entirely beneficial results soon after its arrival at Warminster.

Amidst all this work, which was carried out at fever-heat, the amusement of the men was not overlooked. An excellent Divisional band was formed, and their good services were added to early in December by the creation of a Divisional concert troop "The Goods." Not to be left behind in these achievements the 2/4th Londons formed their own concert party, called for some not too obvious reason "The Tanks," which afforded excellent entertainments under the able direction of 2/Lieuts. T. J. Bell and C. J. Graham, who were assisted by Pipe-Major Ling, Corpl. Wilkinson, L./Corpls. Smith, Ringrose and Hardy, and Pte. Rosenbloom.

The 2/4th Londons had already attained a position which is believed to be unique in the annals of the British Army inasmuch as they, a Battalion affiliated to an English line regiment, had become the possessors of a pipe band. This band had originally been formed for recruiting purposes, but with the initiation of the "Derby Scheme" its services were no longer necessary for the enticement of recruits, and it had been secured for the Battalion. The pipers wore the Glengarry cap and the Royal Stuart tartan. They were without doubt an exceedingly good band and lightened many a weary mile of road both in England and France with their stirring music.

An attempt, which originated in the 2/4th Londons, was also made to produce a Divisional magazine, and this appeared in September under the title of *The Direct Hit*. It was well received and attained the age of three months, but was then discontinued.

Shortly after arrival at Sutton Veny the Division came under the command of Major-Gen. H. D. Fanshawe, C.B., who ultimately took it to France where he remained in command for some months.

Various changes took place in the 2/4th Londons, and in November 1916 command of the Battalion was assumed by Lieut.-Col. W. R. H. Dann (Bedfordshire Regiment), Capt. W. A. Nunneley becoming second in command with the temporary rank of Major. The personnel was also strengthened by the arrival of a large officer reinforcement from the 4th (Reserve) Battalion, the majority of whom had already seen service in France in the ranks of various London Battalions.

In the latter part of January 1917 the long awaited order arrived for the 58th Division to proceed overseas. On the 23rd of that month the 2/4th Battalion left Sutton Veny with a strength of 32 officers and 976 other ranks and proceeded to Southampton, where it embarked on the *Viper*, and crossed to Havre, arriving the following morning at daybreak. Disembarkation took place at once and the Battalion, preceded by its pipe band, marched to the Reinforcement Camp at Sanvic. The following officers accompanied the Battalion overseas:

Lieut.-Col.	W. R. H. Dann,	in command.		
Major	W. A. Nunneley,	second in command.		
Capt.	E. E. Spicer,	Adjutant.		
"	E. N. Cotton,	cmdg.	A	Co.
"	E. W. Bottomley,	"	B	"
"	G. E. A. Leake,	"	C	"
"	S. H. Stedman,	"	D	"
"	H. A. T. Hewlett.			
"	H. C. Long.			

	"	W. H. Parker.	
Lieut.	B. Rivers Smith	(Bde. L.G.O.).
2/Lieut.	R. K. Caparn.	
	"	E. A. Monkman.	
	"	L. J. Bassett	(attd. L.T.M. Battery).
	"	T. Stoaling.	
	"	A. M. Duthie	(Bombing Officer).
	"	S. G. Askham.	
	"	A. R. Muddell	(attd. L.T.M. Battery).
	"	W. J. Stickney.	
	"	A. G. Croll	(Intelligence Officer).
	"	F. Stickney.	
	"	H. W. Hallett	(Signalling Officer).
	"	G. G. Hunt.	
	"	T. J. Bell.	
	"	R. McDowell.	
	"	H. E. English.	
	"	D. S. Boorman.	
	"	H. S. Daw	(Transport Officer).
	"	C. J. Graham.	

"	E. C. Pratt.	
"	S. P. Ferdinando.	
Hon. Lt. & Qm.	C. W. Cragg,	(Quartermaster).
Capt.	P. H. Burton, R.A.M.C.,	Medical Officer.
"	Rev. O'Brien,	Chaplain attached.

The next day the Battalion entrained for Abbeville, but on arrival found its orders to stay there countermanded and the journey was therefore continued to Fortel, a small village about six miles south-west of Frevent.

The unusually hard frost which was general throughout northern France in the winter of 1916/17 still held the country in its grip, and the conditions for a raw battalion even in billets were far from comfortable, but a ten days' stay at Fortel, which was devoted to training and generally acclimatising the Battalion to its new surroundings, prepared it at least in a small degree for the rigours of a winter campaign.

By the 5th February the concentration of the 58th Division was complete, and the 173rd Brigade under Brig.-Gen. Hurst began to move by easy stages to the line, the 2/4th Londons lying at Le Souich on the 6th, and at Sus-St Leger on the 7th and 8th.

The following day the Brigade moved forward and became attached to the 146th Brigade of the West Riding (Territorial) Division, for instruction in trench warfare, the 2/4th Londons being divided up between the battalions of the 146th Brigade for this purpose, with two companies in reserve at Bailleulmont and Humbercamp. The 146th Brigade was at this time holding a sector south-west of Arras facing Ransart. Ransart lies at the base of a small spur between two watercourses, both of which are usually dry, and the German trenches in front of the village were dominated at an average distance of about 600 yards by our own on the western side of the valley.

This part of the front had the reputation of being exceedingly quiet (and therefore suitable for the first tour of duty of inexperienced troops), and was the defensive position taken up by the French in October 1914 when, after the Battle of the Aisne, the battle front had become stabilised by the continued extension of the flanks of the opposing forces until they reached the sea. The British Army had taken over the area from the French in July 1915.

After five uneventful days in this sector the Battalion was relieved on the 14th by the 2/12th Londons, and having rendezvoused at La Cauchie, about three miles in rear of the line, embussed to Sus-St Leger where it went into billets for a week's rest.

The important changes which were to take place in this area during the next six weeks are so material to the development of the Campaign of 1917 that it is necessary to review briefly the operations which were being conducted further south. The termination of the battles of the Somme in November 1916 had left the enemy in possession of the whole of the Ancre Valley from Le Transloy to Grandcourt and of excellent positions on the high ground immediately north of Beaumont-Hamel; while in rear of this position he had made great progress in the construction of two more lines of defence running in a direction from north-west to south-east about Bapaume.

The advance of our troops over the Thiepval-Morval Ridge had, however, left him confined in a marked salient, of which the apex was Gommecourt Wood, between the Ancre on the south and the Scarpe where it passes Arras on the north; and conditions appeared very favourable for improving our situation in the neighbourhood of Beaumont-Hamel before the conditions of winter should render active operations on a large scale impossible. Accordingly operations which met with immediate success were reopened on the 18th November on the left bank of the Ancre between Grandcourt and Pys. These were renewed in January in the Beaucourt valley on the opposite side of the river with such marked success that the enemy was compelled to relinquish his hold on the high ground north of Beaumont-Hamel while his position in Grandcourt became precarious in the extreme.

On the night of the 5th/6th February 1917 Grandcourt was evacuated and the enemy fell back to the line Serre-Miraumont-Pys. Attacks with which these initial successes were followed up on the 17th and 18th February secured to the British complete command over the enemy's defences of the upper Ancre and Miraumont village, while they accentuated his salient west of Serre. The loss of this would lay open for us a further advance on Puisieux-au-Mont and render the defence of the Gommecourt Salient exceedingly hazardous. It was therefore to be expected that any further withdrawal on the part of the enemy from in front of Miraumont would entail a withdrawal on a large scale, and this actually occurred.

By the 24th February British troops had occupied Serre and all the enemy's defences on a line from that village to Gueudecourt, a frontage of some nine miles. On the 27th February patrols entered Gommecourt park and village, the prize so desperately fought for and withheld from the 1/4th Battalion six months earlier, and the following morning the whole of Puisieux fell into our hands. On the right the enemy's resistance was more stubborn, but an assault on Irles on the 10th March, which proved entirely successful, brought us face to face with the first of the two lines of defence about Bapaume to which reference has already been made. But even here the enemy made no determined stand, and by the 13th our pursuing columns were making preparations to assault the rear line.

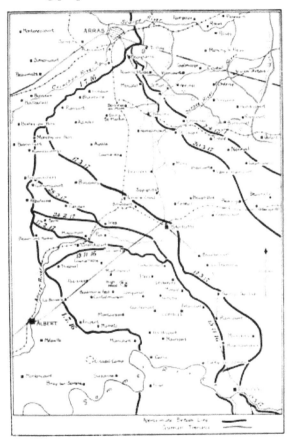

THE GERMAN RETIREMENT, FEBRUARY-MARCH, 1917

The situation, therefore, when the 2/4th Battalion returned to the line after its rest, the last two days of which were spent at Gaudiempré, was that Corps and Divisional staffs were eagerly seeking information as to any indication of the enemy's expected retirement between Arras and Monchy-au-Bois, this being the only sector between Arras and the Somme now left in his possession, which he had held at the end of the Somme operations. This entailed a heavily increased burden of night patrolling duties on all troops in the line.

On the 24th February the 2/4th Battalion moved into Bellacourt, relieving the 1/5th K.O.Y.L.I. in Brigade reserve, taking over the front line from the 1/4th K.O.Y.L.I. on the following day. The sector lay between Ransart and Blairville to the left of that previously occupied, and was held with three companies in front trenches and one in support. Battalion Headquarters were in Grosville.

The German lines opposite this sector possessed two features of particular interest in the Blockhouse, a strongly defended salient, and the Talus, a machine-gun post pushed some 200 yards forward of their main line in a hillside embankment. Two sunken roads and a watercourse in No Man's Land added to the interest of life and provided our patrols with some useful work.

The advancing British troops in the south this day were beginning to threaten Puisieux, the possession of which would lay open to attack the Bucquoy Ridge to its north. It was clear that with British forces on the Bucquoy Ridge the German reserve lines of defence and gun positions about Adinfer Wood (which supported the lines now opposite the 173rd Brigade) must either retreat precipitately or run a serious risk of being cut off. Requests for information from Brigade consequently became more and more insistent, and information was passed to the Battalion that the lines opposite had actually been evacuated. Officers' patrols under 2/Lieuts. A. G. Croll, A. M. Duthie, T. J. Bell and D. S. Boorman, which covered No Man's Land, especially in the vicinity of the Blockhouse and the Talus on the nights of the 24th and 28th, however, elicited unmistakable signs of occupation of the German defences. But the desultory nature of the enemy's machine-gun fire, and of his shell fire from the direction of Adinfer Wood, the marked decrease in the number of Véry lights put up by him at night and the constant sounds of transport moving on the roads in rear of his lines all provided indications that his retirement could not long be delayed. The patrols frequently heard working parties hard at work in rear of the enemy's lines, and it afterwards transpired that these were busily engaged in mining the roads over which our advancing troops must pursue the German retreat.

It had long been known that the enemy was hard at work on a highly fortified defensive line which left his front defences at Arras and ran in a south-easterly direction in front of Cambrai to near St Quentin. This line, the famous "Hindenburg" line, was roughly parallel to that now occupied by our advancing troops in the south and some eight miles distant from it.

Reports from British airmen showed that the Hindenburg line was now the scene of feverish activity on the part of the enemy, and this information seemed to confirm the probability indicated by the results of our patrolling that the relinquishment of the Monchy-Arras line was imminent.

A most unfortunate incident occurred on the night of the 28th February, when a strong patrol under 2/Lieut. R. K. Caparn returning to our lines was fired upon by the sentries who apparently had failed to grasp the prearranged signal, with the regrettable result that 2/Lieut. Caparn was very seriously wounded and L./Corpl. Warren, Ptes. Anderson and Vickery were killed.

On the morning of the 2nd March the Battalion was relieved by the 2/2nd Londons and withdrew to Divisional reserve in billets at Basseux and Bailleulval. Three days' training ensued, followed by a move on the 6th to Humbercamp.

The 173rd Brigade had now "side-stepped" to the right, and on the 7th March the 2/4th Londons once more entered the front line, relieving the 1/6th North Staffords in a sector known as Z1 immediately opposite Monchy-au-Bois. Battalion Headquarters opened in Bienvillers-au-Bois.

This sector was about three miles south of that previously occupied, and similar conditions prevailed both as regards ground and the German retirement. No Man's Land, which was here about 300 yards wide, fell gently from our lines to the village of Monchy-au-Bois, which had been made a network of defences by the enemy, his first line passing immediately in front of the village. In rear of the village the ground again rose gently to the Adinfer Ridge.

Bienvillers was almost daily given an unpleasantly copious allowance of gas shells which caused numerous casualties, principally to carrying parties from Battalion Headquarters. Among these was Major Nunneley, who was gassed on the 10th; his duties of second in command were assumed by Capt. Spicer, the Adjutancy being filled by Capt. A. Grover (1st Bedfordshire Regiment), who had just been transferred to the 2/4th Battalion at the request of Lieut.-Col. Dann.

The long frost had now been succeeded by a remarkably sudden thaw which created conditions of marked discomfort in the trenches. The water pent up in the soil for so long filled all the trenches to a depth of about two feet, and the trench walls everywhere began to fall in, throwing an enormous amount of work on the occupying battalions in keeping them in a defensible condition.

By night our patrols continued their activities, but each night on approaching the enemy's lines were met with brisk machine-gun fire, which showed increasing activity each day. The Battalion observers also reported daily columns of smoke in rear of the enemy's lines, arising, as was found subsequently, from the systematic orgy of destruction in which the Germans indulged prior to their retirement. There was, moreover, during these few days a very marked increase of shelling in our back areas, the villages of Pommier, Berles, Bretencourt and Bailleulmont all receiving an unusually large amount of heavy fire.

The 11th proved to be the most disturbed day of this tour of duty, the enemy being exceedingly active in machine-gun and trench mortar fire. About 100 light shells, of which many were gas, fell in Bienvillers, fortunately without inflicting loss on the Battalion. On the 12th the 2/4th Londons were relieved by the 2/1st Londons and moved in Brigade reserve to Pommier, where they continued training. The XVIII Corps Commander inspected the Battalion on the 16th.

The Battalion Orderly Room now began to be inundated by the Brigade Intelligence Staff with plans, maps and all kinds of collated information as to the villages which would lie in the line of the Division's expected advance. All preparations were made for an immediate move. Units in reserve were held in instant readiness to advance, their first line transport wagons standing ready packed.

The night of the 16th/17th March was unusually quiet, and patrols pushed out by the 2/1st Londons about daybreak on the 17th returned with the information that the German trenches about Monchy were deserted. A patrol sent forward from the 2/4th Battalion under Capt. Bottomley was able to penetrate into Monchy itself and returned about midday with the definite assurance that the village was evacuated.

The same day the order was given for a general advance of the whole of the British forces from Arras to Roye.

That afternoon the 173rd Brigade moved forward, the 2/1st Londons occupying the German front line at Monchy and some high ground south of the village, while the 2/4th Battalion was brought forward from Brigade reserve, "leap-frogging" through the leading Battalion to the German trenches east of the village. A Company pushed ahead and reached a point about 300 yards west of Adinfer Wood. Here the Battalion was in touch with the 6th South Staffords on the right. North of Monchy village the 2/2nd Londons continued the line with the 174th Brigade on their left.

The withdrawal of the Germans from the Monchy Salient involved a continual shortening of our lines as the salient became straightened out, and in order to effect this the 2/1st Londons were withdrawn on the night of the 17th to Pommier, while the 2/4th Battalion continued its advance, "squeezing-out" the 2/2nd Londons as it pushed forward. By 5 p.m. the following day it had reached a position near Rabbit Wood, a small copse on the North side of Adinfer Wood, its left being now in touch with the 175th Brigade while the 46th Division kept pace with its advance on the right.

At midnight on the 18th/19th March the 2/4th Londons were withdrawn in Brigade reserve to Ransart, which village was now occupied by Brigade Headquarters. A few hours later, at 4.30 a.m. on the 19th, the 2/1st Londons once more took up the advance towards Boiry-Becquerelle.

The advance of the 19th March covered a depth of nearly 10,000 yards, and as it was achieved with very little fighting it seems evident that the Germans' preparations for withdrawal had been conducted with great skill. From the time when they had left their original line at Monchy they had almost entirely eluded close touch with our pursuing columns, which were never able to harass their retirement to any useful extent. Very little war material fell into our hands, and it seems possible that valuable hours were lost on the 17th before the order to follow up the retirement reached battalions in the line.

The pursuit of the Germans was rendered exceedingly slow and arduous by the unspeakable destruction which met our advancing columns at every step. Cross roads had been mined and vast craters forced all wheeled traffic to deviate on to the sodden fields adjoining. Trees had been felled across the roads and added to the impediments to the advance of our artillery. Everywhere the Germans had committed wanton destruction—young fruit trees were ringed, crops were burnt wholesale, and every sort of live stock had been driven before them in their retreat. The aspect of the villages was most peculiar. At a distance they appeared to be untouched, and the red roofs of the cottages showed nothing unusual. On a closer approach, however, they were found to be ruined and the walls knocked down so that the roofs had subsided intact to the ground. Furniture, too heavy to be moved, had shared in this destruction, and its débris was lying shattered among the heaps of brick and stone. Yet further abominations had been invented, and a series of ingenious "booby-traps" were discovered in the shape of common articles such as shovels and helmets. These were left lying about in places where they were likely to be picked up by our troops, and being connected with bombs and even large mines caused explosions when they were touched.

By noon on the 19th March the 2/1st Londons had established themselves after some opposition from machine-gun fire on the line between Boiry-Becquerelle and Boyelles, in touch with the 46th Division in Hamelincourt; but further efforts to advance from this position towards St Leger, which was the objective for the day, were effectually stopped by heavy enemy shell and machine-gun fire.

Meanwhile the 2/4th Londons were once more moved forward, leaving Ransart at about 3 p.m., and by 5.30 had advanced to the line of the Boyelles-St Leger Railway on the right of the 2/1st Londons.

The 173rd Brigade now occupied the whole of the 58th Divisional front, being in touch with the Division on its right and its left joining the 30th Division who were facing Henin-sur-Cojeul. The line occupied by the 2/4th and 2/1st Londons formed a marked re-entrant in the British line, overlooking a valley which runs in a northerly direction from St Leger to Henin-sur-Cojeul. The enemy had apparently deployed on the further side of this valley and was holding the line of the Henin-Croisilles Road. Opposite the right flank of the 2/4th Londons he had for the moment considerable advantage of ground over us, as our line was dominated by a hill which protected Croisilles from observation. The following day the Brigade consolidated itself in this position, Brigade Headquarters moving forward to Boiry-St Rictrude, which was also occupied by the 2/3rd Londons in Brigade reserve, while the 2/2nd Londons moved into close support in Boisleux-au-Mont.

The line held by the Brigade extended from Judas Farm near St Leger, where it was in close touch with the Division on the right, in front of Boyelles and Boiry-Becquerelle to the north branch of the Cojeul River. North of the river the line was continued by the 30th Division, who were endeavouring to force the villages of St Martin and Henin.

The Battalion had pushed outposts beyond its main line on the railway to the Boiry-St Leger Road, but all attempts to continue the general advance beyond this line were frustrated by the heavy machine-gun and shell fire with which the enemy sprayed the forward slopes of the ridge down which the advance was to be made. At the same time signs were not wanting that his withdrawal had not reached its limit, for fires were observed in Henin and Croisilles which indicated that the systematic destruction which hitherto had been the prelude to his retirement was proceeding with unabated vigour.

On the 21st the 2/4th Londons were relieved by the 2/3rd in the right subsector and withdrew to Boiry-St Martin in reserve. For three days the Battalion remained here under conditions of extreme discomfort. The weather was exceptionally severe and the ground was covered with snow, while the open and bare hillsides were swept by biting winds. Billets were non-existent owing to the total destruction of the village, so that the change from the front line to reserve brought very little of rest or easier conditions. Indeed throughout this period of the advance the terrible exposure proved a far more serious enemy than the Germans themselves, and the casualties caused through it were five times more numerous than those caused by wounds.

The Hindenburg line was now within measurable distance, and the salient previously held by the enemy being almost entirely flattened out it was found possible to withdraw several divisions now in action. This was the more desirable not only for the provision of as many reserve divisions as possible for the impending offensive against the Vimy Ridge, but also for the tasks of rendering the devastated region covered by the advance habitable to our forces, of repairing the ruined roads, and of bringing forward the supplies of material necessary for further operations. One of the important gains of the advance was the reopening of direct lateral communication between Arras and Albert. With their usual thoroughness the Germans had completely destroyed the railway connecting these two towns, the track being torn up and the bridges demolished; and the complete reconstruction of it presented one of the most pressing necessities in the organisation of the new defences.

The 58th Division, in accordance with this programme, was now withdrawn, and on the 25th March the 173rd Brigade handed over its sector to the 174th and withdrew to Pommier, the 2/4th Londons being billeted at Monchy and put to work on repairing the roads.

Each Brigade of the Division now became split up and battalions and companies were scattered far afield on one or other of the necessary works, of which a few have been enumerated above.

On the 28th the 2/4th Londons moved further back from the line to Grenas (on the Doullens-Arras Road) leaving behind it two companies, A and C, which were attached to VII Corps troops (C Company joining the 56th Division) for road repairing at Wailly and Arras respectively.

At the end of the month the Division, now attached to XIX Corps, was concentrated, with the exception of the detachments referred to, in the area of Frohen-le-Grand, between Doullens and Auxi-le-Château, and on the 1st April the 2/4th Battalion, less A and C Companies, marched to fresh billets in Bonnières, continuing their route the following day to Vitz Villeroy, some four miles west of Auxi-le-Château.

From the beginning of March the Battalion had experienced continual rough handling, not only from enemy machine-gun and shell fire, but also from the remarkable amount of marching and counter-marching and exposure to the elements which the pursuit of the Germans had entailed. It must also be borne in mind that they had a month previously been raw troops of whom practically none had been under fire. The writer is, therefore, with all the more pleasure able to testify to the excellent bearing and strict march discipline of the Battalion as it swung through Auxi-le-Château on the 2nd April. But if the 2/4th Battalion expected rest after its labours it was soon to learn how illusive rest can be in modern war, for the next day it returned to Auxi and embussed to Beaumetz-les-Loges in the Arras area, when it once more took the road and marched to Boiry-St Martin. Accommodation here was provided for Headquarters and B Company in old German dugouts, while D Company contented itself with temporary and hastily constructed shelters in the village.

A week of hard work in laying new track on the Arras-Albert Railway followed, and on the 12th the Battalion, having been rejoined by A and C Companies, moved to Pommier and thence to Achiet-le-Grand, where the remainder of the 173rd, now under command of Brig.-Gen. Freyberg, V.C., D.S.O., was concentrated.

The Division was now in the Fifth Army area (Gough) and attached to the V Corps.

The remainder of April, with the exception of short spells of training, was entirely devoted to working parties, the principal tasks entrusted to the 2/4th Londons being the formation of a large R.E. dump at Achiet-le-Grand, the construction of a light railway at Ervillers and the repair of the Ervillers-St Leger Road.

During the period under review the Battalion received one or two small reinforcements of N.C.O.'s and men, and also the following officers:

> 18th March—2/Lieuts. G. H. Hetley, C. A. Clarke, S. M. Williams and G. E. Lester, and 2/Lieut. Acason (18th Londons).

> 27th April—2/Lieut. S. A. Seys (15th Londons).

Casualties included Major W. A. Nunneley, gassed; 2/Lieut. R. K. Caparn, wounded; 2/Lieuts. A. M. Duthie and S. P. Ferdinando, accidentally wounded; 2/Lieuts. H. W. Hallett and G. G. Hunt, sick; and in N.C.O.'s and men 10 killed, 25 wounded, and about 170 sick, chiefly from exposure.

The duties of signalling officer were taken by 2/Lieut. E. C. Pratt.

In February the Battalion was unfortunate in losing 2/Lieut. C. J. Graham, who joined Brigade Headquarters as Intelligence Officer. He filled this appointment with great success until March 1918, when he was appointed Brigade Major in the 47th Division. He was decorated with the D.S.O. and the M.C. with Bar.

CHAPTER XIV
THE 1/4TH BATTALION IN THE BATTLES OF ARRAS, 1917

Reverting now to the 1/4th Battalion, we have the task of recording its part in the great battles of April and May 1917 which developed after the German retirement, some account of which has been attempted in the preceding chapter.

On transfer from the First Army area the 1/4th Battalion was billeted at Le Souich late on the evening of the 10th March 1917. The following day was Sunday and was observed as far as possible as a rest, and this day the Battalion was joined by a reinforcement of officers, 2/Lieuts. J. F. Elders, T. Caudwell, S. Minear, C. J. Reid and E. C. Hayes, all attached from the Queen's Westminsters. On the 12th the Battalion marched in drenching rain to Ivergny, the next village to Le Souich, but on arrival the billets were found to be already occupied, and orders were received to move a mile further on to Beaudricourt, which village was reached about 4.30 p.m.

At Beaudricourt the Battalion settled down to a steady course of company training in preparation for active operations. According to the Battalion custom, whenever possible, the day's work was started by Commanding Officer's parade, and the strictest attention was paid to all points of parade discipline; while the drums beat Retreat each evening in the village street. The training included a good deal of route marching to harden the troops after their long sojourn in trenches, practice attacks from trench to trench, and "specialist" training, in the course of which every man in the Battalion received the rudiments of instruction in the Lewis gun. The opportunity was also taken to reorganise the companies in accordance with the then newly-evolved scheme, which had the object of rendering the platoon a self-contained fighting unit comprising only fighting ranks. The four sections of the platoon were definitely organised as one of Lewis gunners, one of riflemen, one of rifle-grenadiers and one of bombers; and all administrative details in the company, such as cooks, stretcher-bearers and company runners, were collected into a "headquarter" section under the immediate supervision of the company second in command.

The advantages of the new platoon organisation were evidenced by practical demonstrations to the officers of the division of methods of employing the various sections in co-operation with each other in operations such as the capture of a strong point. These demonstrations were given by a selected platoon of the Rangers, and Gen. Hull took the opportunity of announcing to the assembled officers the rôle which it was expected the Division would play in the coming attack.

In the latter part of March the Battalion lost three officers, 2/Lieuts. S. P. Stotter and R. W. Chamberlain to hospital, and Capt. F. C. Grimwade seconded to VII Corps School as Instructor.

The intention of G.H.Q. for the offensive of 1917 was to deliver a heavy blow against the German positions in the Scarpe-Ancre Salient (see Map No. 9); and in conjunction with this, and in order to secure the left flank of the attack, to wrest from the enemy his commanding positions on the Vimy Ridge, whence excellent observation could be obtained over the Plains of Douai. This scheme underwent considerable modifications before it was put into operation, firstly to secure closer co-operation with the French offensive on the Aisne; and secondly by reason of the German Retirement of March 1917, which altered the rôle of the Fifth Army and compelled them to re-establish themselves in fresh positions facing the Hindenburg line.

The Hindenburg line in the vicinity of its junction with the original German trench lines south-east of Arras being the centre of the Battalion's operations in April and May, a reference to the map will be of assistance to the reader in appreciating what follows. It will be seen that the old trench systems (*i.e.* those held by the enemy until March) crossed the valley of the Scarpe running southwards through the eastern suburbs of Arras, as far as the Arras-Cambrai Road, and then swinging south-westward followed the valley of the Crinchon River. These trenches consisted of two main systems about 2000 yards apart, the village of Beaurains being incorporated into the first system and that of Tilloy-les-Mofflaines into the second, with Mercatel and Neuville-Vitasse in rear of the second system. About three-quarters of a mile south of Tilloy was Telegraph Hill, the line between being strengthened by the enormously fortified redoubt known as The Harp. From the southern extremity of The Harp the new Hindenburg line (or rather system of trenches) struck off south-eastward, including Neuville-Vitasse, crossing the valley of the Cojeul River between St Martin and Heninel and passing thence between Croisilles and Fontaine. Between the west side of the Cojeul valley and the Scarpe at Fampoux was a "switch" line known as the Wancourt line, which crossed the Cambrai Road just east of Feuchy Chapel.

The task originally allotted to the 56th Division was the capture of Beaurains and Telegraph Hill.

The 169th Brigade which had left the Neuve Chapelle area in advance of the remainder of the Division had been placed in line at Agny, opposite Beaurains, and to this point the commanding officers of the 168th Brigade proceeded on the 17th March to make the preliminary reconnaissance for the attack. But the following day it was found that Beaurains was clear of enemy and was already occupied by the 169th Brigade who were following up energetically. The reconnaissance being no longer required the party returned to billets pending further orders.

On the 18th Lieut.-Col. A. E. Maitland, M.C. (Essex Regiment), was appointed to command the Battalion, and on the 23rd the Division moved forward into a concentration area in rear of Arras, the Battalion marching from Beaudricourt at 9.30 a.m. and arriving in billets at Beaumetz-les-Loges at 4.30 p.m. At Beaumetz the Battalion resumed its training programme though the whole Brigade was held at short notice to move in view of the possible further development of the enemy's withdrawal.

It is worth while pausing for a moment to consider the extraordinary achievement of G.H.Q. in delivering the Arras-Vimy Ridge attack as it did on the 9th April. The preparations were on similar lines to those for the Somme offensive of the previous July, and were on an even vaster scale owing to the increased number of the divisions which it was proposed to employ and to the ever-growing strength and weight of the British artillery. The preliminary work of forming reinforcement and concentration camps, laying fresh and increasing the capacity of existing railway lines, arranging for water supply, dumps of munitions and *matériel*, establishment of hospitals and the hundred and one other essential tasks had been steadily proceeding since the close of the Somme offensive in November 1916.

Imagine, then, the inevitable dislocation of the scheme when, a comparatively few days before the attack was to be delivered, the enemy suddenly withdrew on part of the front from the positions it had been intended to assault and betook himself within fortified lines of enormous strength to the rear. Dumps, railheads, hospitals, water-supply, concentration areas, guns, heavy siege and light, all had to be pushed forward to fresh and rapidly selected positions in an area which had been laid waste with all the fiendish skill of which a resourceful enemy was capable, and all the consequent modifications of objectives and orders effected at the shortest possible notice. Not only was this achieved, but it was achieved with such efficiency as to produce on the 9th April the most striking single-day success which had crowned the British Armies since the outbreak of the War.

The Battalion was soon called on for its share in this "moving forward" process of the preparations for battle, and on the 28th March it marched with the remainder of the Brigade to positions in the old British trench system opposite Beaurains, where for three days it was engaged in supplying working parties. On the 1st April it was withdrawn to Brigade reserve in Achicourt where it found comfortable billets. A very large number of British heavy batteries were in action here registering and wire-cutting for the coming battle, and the continuous din of our own guns was trying. The shells of one battery of 60-pounders firing from just in rear of the Headquarters billet cleared the roof of the house by about 18 inches.

In the meantime the pursuit of the Germans had been maintained by the 56th Division, which with the 21st and 30th on its right and the 14th on its left comprised the VII Corps (D'Oyly Snow). A relief had been effected on the 1st April, the 168th and 167th Brigades taking over the Divisional sector from the 169th which was withdrawn to reserve. By the 2nd April, the Germans having reached the Hindenburg system, the line became stabilised, and no further important alteration occurred until the day of battle. When the Battalion took over the advanced trenches from the Rangers on the 3rd, therefore, the positions which they occupied formed practically the "start-line" for the 9th April.

The 56th Division occupied a salient of which the north-eastern face was on the Beaurains-Neuville-Vitasse Road, and the south-eastern face lay opposite the north-west corner of Neuville-Vitasse. On this side the British positions had been pushed forward in the direction of Neuville-Vitasse and posts were held in the old German communication trenches leading back to the village.

This sector was held by the Battalion with three companies in the front line and one in reserve in a system known as the Circular Work south-east of Beaurains. It will be readily appreciated that as the advanced British positions were outposts in different communication trenches it was necessary in order to provide a good jumping-off line for the battle to connect these up by continuous trenches to form a front line, to supply that front line with support lines and feed it with fresh communication trenches. Clearly a good deal of digging was necessary in a very short space of time, and the Battalion was heavily engaged in this work during its tour of duty, which lasted until the 7th April. The principal trenches dug were Deodar, Poplar, Lime, Elm and Skin in the front system, and Gun, How and New Battery as communication trenches.

On the 4th April the British destructive bombardment began and continued daily according to a prearranged programme until the day of battle. This met with comparatively little retaliation.

On the 7th an inter-battalion relief was effected, the Battalion vacating the line in favour of the Kensingtons and Rangers who were respectively detailed as right and left assaulting battalions. The London Scottish moved to the old British line at Agny while the 1/4th Londons returned to dugouts in the railway cutting at Achicourt. The following day battle positions were occupied, the London Scottish moving forward to close support in rear of the Kensingtons, and the 1/4th Londons to Brigade reserve in the Circular Work.

The Division's objectives for the 9th April were as follows:

The 168th (left) and 167th (right) Brigades were to advance through Neuville-Vitasse to the first objective which was an arbitrary line (the Blue line) skirting the east edge of the village and facing the Hindenburg system. (*Note.*—The Hindenburg line between Telegraph Hill and the Cojeul River was known as the Cojeul Switch.) This first phase was entrusted in the 168th to the Kensingtons and Rangers, the latter battalion on the left being prepared to adopt special measures and form a defensive flank facing north should the 14th Division be checked at Telegraph Hill.

After a pause on this objective of about four and a half hours the London Scottish (168th) and 1st Londons (167th) were to "leapfrog" through the leading troops and carry the Cojeul Switch, the Scottish objectives being Back, Card and Telegraph Hill trenches (north of the Neuville-Vitasse-Wancourt Road). Here a further pause was to be made, after which the third phase of the battle would be taken up by the 167th Brigade, who would advance, covering the whole Divisional frontage on to the Wancourt line (Brown line).

To return to the 1/4th Battalion. The day spent in Achicourt prior to manning battle positions produced the first serious German retaliation to our bombardment. As already remarked Achicourt was "stiff" with batteries and also contained a very extensive and important ammunition dump. Doubtless the Bosche decided that the quickest way to silence our guns was to destroy their supplies of shell, and from 11.30 a.m. until 5 p.m. he bombarded the village, causing a good many casualties in the Battalion and firing several houses which formed part of the dump. The village square, moreover, was packed with lorries loaded with shell waiting to move forward with the batteries, and unluckily the enemy obtained some direct hits on these. For some time the flying fragments rendered the place remarkably unhealthy. Excellent work was done in saving two lorries by Major H. Campbell of the Kensingtons. He well earned his D.S.O. by driving two of the blazing lorries out of the square into a place of safety.

The battle positions occupied that night by the Battalion were as follows:

    A Company (Lorden)—New Battery Trench.

C	"	(Bowater)—Southend and Margate Trenches.
D	"	(Spiers)—Astride the Neuville-Vitasse Road in Battery and New Battery Trenches.

Battalion Headquarters—In North End (Circular Work).

B Company	(Stanbridge)—Attached as "moppers-up" to the Kensingtons.

The role of the Battalion was laid down to provide for various eventualities that might arise according to the degree of success achieved by the assaulting battalions, and it was therefore held in readiness either to assist the Rangers in forming a defensive flank in case of failure by the division on the left, or to lend weight to the Scottish attack on the Cojeul Switch.

At 5.30 a.m. on the 9th April, after a hurricane bombardment of the German lines, the British barrage lifted and the attack began. The advance of the 56th Division was deferred until two hours later to allow the 14th Division, whose start-line was less advanced, to come into line, and accordingly at 7.30 a.m. the Rangers and Kensingtons moved to the assault, followed by B Company of the 1/4th Londons who were equipped with Stokes mortar shells for dealing with deep dugouts.

B Company's job in mopping-up proved easier than had been expected, for the German trench garrisons had been confined to their deep dugouts for some days by the intensity of our bombardment, and the resultant difficulties with which they had been faced in getting their rations and water up from the rear made them on the whole not undisposed to surrender; and in a short time the Battalion, in Brigade reserve, was cheered by the sight of bodies of German prisoners marching in fours down the road to Beaurains in a dazed and exhausted condition.

By 9.30 a.m. the Blue line on the whole of the Brigade front was in our hands, and its consolidation was at once put in hand by the assaulting troops with assistance from the 512th Company R.E. and a company of the Cheshire Pioneers. At 11.20 a.m. the Scottish moved forward on a three company front to attack the Cojeul Switch. Their advance was met with heavy machine-gun fire, and although one company succeeded in gaining Back Trench, the furthest of the three lines forming the Cojeul Switch, and in pushing patrols beyond it, the battalion was forced ultimately to fall back to Telegraph Hill Trench, the front line of the Switch System and that nearest to Neuville-Vitasse.

At 12.30 p.m. the 1/4th Londons were ordered to advance to fresh positions on the western edge of Neuville-Vitasse, where they came under the orders of the 167th Brigade. The move was completed by 4 p.m. with A Company in Tree, C in Leaf and D in Pine; B Company (still under the orders of the Kensingtons) having by now withdrawn to reorganise in Deodar Lane after their fight.

As reports of the attack on the Cojeul Switch came in it became clear that a gap existed between the London Scottish and the 7th Middlesex, who had advanced to the assistance of the 1st Londons on their right, and at 5 p.m. Brigade ordered the Battalion forward to fill this gap. The three available companies moved forward at once, but on emerging from Neuville-Vitasse it was found that touch had been regained by the Scottish and the Middlesex, and the companies therefore took up a position on the eastern edge of the village in support to the Middlesex.

In the meantime the third phase of the attack, namely, the advance of the 167th Brigade to the Wancourt line, had been definitely checked by machine-gun fire, as had also that of the 14th Division on the left; so that the day's fighting ended with the 14th Division in possession of Telegraph Hill and The Harp, and the northern end of the Cojeul Switch; the 56th occupying the Cojeul Switch astride the Neuville-Vitasse-Wancourt Road; and the 30th on the right approaching the Wancourt line in the vicinity of the Neuville-Vitasse-Henin Road—a very substantial advance for the day.

The 168th Brigade captures for the day amounted to 5 officers and 635 other ranks, all of the 163rd R. I. Regt., 9 machine-guns, 2 granatenwerfer, 1 minenwerfer, and 2 heavy trench mortars, together with large quantities of small arms and ammunition.

In the evening the Battalion was rejoined by B Company, and Battalion Headquarters advanced to a dugout in rear of the start-line for the day. The night was marked by bombing operations in the Cojeul Switch which had the wholesome effect of clearing out the few remaining pockets of Bosche, and by 7.30 a.m. on the 10th touch had been gained with the 14th Division on the left, while the 56th Division's right had been extended further south and the London Scottish had possessed themselves of the whole of the Back-Card-Telegraph Hill system.

A remarkable instance of initiative on the part of a private soldier, which occurred on the night of the 9th April, is worth recording. Pte. Turner, a runner of D Company, lost his company and strayed into the German line. Finding a dugout entrance he began to descend the stairs, when he heard voices; and as the owners of the voices were evidently Huns he announced his arrival by throwing a Mills bomb down the dugout. The occupants apparently thought they were outnumbered and promptly gave themselves up to the number of 1 officer and 16 other ranks. Turner marshalled his bag in a shell hole outside, and the next morning was found with them, all apparently quite content to be under the leadership of one British private, outside Neuville-Vitasse. Turner's coolness was rewarded with the Military Medal.

Early on the 10th the weather, which had hitherto been cold and wet, became yet worse and the landscape was soon white with snow, from which trenches and shell holes gave no protection.

Immediate arrangements were made by VII Corps to complete the previous day's objectives, and an attack on the Wancourt line was delivered at noon, the 56th Division attack being entrusted to the 167th Brigade. During this attack the 1/4th Londons remained in support and withdrew to their former position in the trenches on the western edge of Neuville-Vitasse.

The assault of the 10th April was only partly successful on the Corps front, but the pressure was maintained on the 11th. By noon on that day the 56th Division, whose advance had developed into a flank attack along the Hindenburg line, had cleared the Cojeul Switch as far south as the Cojeul River and occupied the villages of Wancourt and Heninel.

While these successes had been gained south of the Scarpe an equally striking victory had been gained north of the river where the XVII Corps (Fergusson) of the Third Army and the Canadians (Byng) and 1 Corps (Holland) of the First Army had swept the enemy from his long established positions on the Vimy Ridge to the plain east of it, and had sensibly tightened our grip on the mining area of Lens.

Preparations were at once made to follow up this very striking success, and VII Corps issued orders for the advance to be resumed on the 14th over the watershed dividing the Cojeul valley from that of the Sensée. The 13th was therefore devoted to preparations for this attack, in forming advanced dumps and moving forward batteries, and the 168th Brigade was placed under orders to advance at short notice, though no actual move occurred during the day.

On the 14th April the enemy barrage was much heavier than it had been on the 9th, and under a murderous fire the 169th Brigade, which attacked on the 56th Division's front, was forced after some initial success back to its start-line. That night the 168th Brigade was ordered forward to form a defensive flank in the Cojeul Switch facing north-east, and accordingly the 1/4th Battalion moved after dark from the Back-Card-Telegraph Hill area, which they had occupied earlier in the day, to relieve the Queen's Westminsters on the right of the advanced line, with the London Scottish on their left and the Kensingtons and Rangers respectively in support and reserve.

The relief was completed by 4 a.m. on the 15th with the exception of an advanced post pushed well down the forward slope of the valley towards Heninel. This was allotted to two platoons of B Company, but owing to the complete devastation of the area, and the absence of landmarks, the guides detailed to these platoons failed to find the post, and its relief had to be postponed until the following evening.

The Battalion now experienced another change of command, and Lieut.-Col. Maitland having fallen sick it was taken over by Major H. Campbell, D.S.O., attached from the Kensingtons to command with the acting rank of Lieut.-Col. as from the 12th April.

The 15th proved to be a day of inaction, though the enemy's artillery was continuously active over the whole Battalion area. No further advance was attempted on the 16th and no action occurred during the early hours of the day, with the exception of a local counter-attack by the enemy, directed against the 50th Division on our left, in the course of which he managed to re-establish himself on the ridge in the vicinity of Wancourt Tower.

During the afternoon the hostile shelling slackened considerably, but at about 4.30 p.m. warning was received that he was preparing a counter-attack in force, and at 7.30 a barrage of terrific intensity fell on the Battalion's trenches. The front line companies in accordance with the prearranged scheme of defence at once cleared the advanced trenches and pushed forward Lewis gun sections about 60 yards into No Man's Land in order to smash up any attack that might be delivered. By this time darkness was gathering and movement becoming hard to detect. At about 8 o'clock, however, the enemy was observed advancing in close formation to the attack. Our Lewis guns at once opened fire and were magnificently supported by the artillery. The attack was completely smashed and no German reached our lines. The enemy barrage continued without abatement for about an hour, during which the whole Battalion area was effectively searched and a great many casualties caused. By 9 p.m., however, the bombardment slackened, and after a few hours of desultory shelling died out altogether.

During the evening the sector held by the London Scottish was also subjected to severe shelling but no infantry action occurred, and it was evident that the whole weight of the attack had fallen on the 1/4th Londons' sector. The heaps of German dead which were visible in No Man's Land on the following day bore striking testimony to the accuracy of the Battalion's Lewis gun fire.

During the attack excellent work was done under heavy fire by the medical officer, Capt. Havard, R.A.M.C., and the medical orderlies. The Aid Post was merely a corrugated iron shed built in the side of a sunken road and afforded no cover from the shell splinters which were flying in all directions.

The 17th April passed without incident on the Battalion's front, though on the left the 50th Division recaptured Wancourt Tower, the possession of which gave us complete command of the high ground between the Cojeul and the Sensée. That evening an inter-battalion relief took place, the Rangers relieving the 1/4th Londons and the Kensingtons taking over from the London Scottish. The relief of A Company had, however, to be postponed until the following night owing to the approach of daylight.

On relief the Battalion withdrew to deep dugouts in the Cojeul Switch about 800 yards west of Heninel. These were large and well constructed, and accommodated the whole Battalion underground without overcrowding. The strength of the position was enormous, and it seemed a matter for congratulation that the British attack had succeeded in dislodging the former occupants with comparatively so little opposition. It pointed to the fact that no well-defined earthwork defence is in the long-run proof against an attack delivered by well-trained troops supported by tanks and a sufficient weight of heavy artillery; and indeed, as will be seen later, the capture of "pillboxes" and scattered shell hole defences proved a greater obstacle in the third Battle of Ypres later in the summer.

The 56th Division was now withdrawn to Corps reserve; and after spending a day in the dugouts the Battalion was relieved on the afternoon of the 19th by the 16th Manchesters (30th Division), withdrawing after relief to billets in Arras.

Although the opening phases of the offensive involved the Battalion in comparatively little fighting, it had been continuously engaged in the general rough-and-tumble of shell holes and subjected to fairly continuous shell fire since the opening of the battle. Its losses during this period amounted in officers to: 2/Lieut. T. Siddall, killed; 2/Lieuts. P. Pyne and L. W. N. Jones, wounded; Rev. S. F. Leighton Green, C.F., wounded at duty.

The battle had now completely achieved its object as originally conceived by G.H.Q. The enemy was dislodged from the high ground on a wide front, and the resultant change of positions afforded our troops advantages of observation and drier foothold; and had Sir Douglas Haig been a free agent he would at once have transferred his intentions to the northern area, where he was desirous of launching his Messines and Ypres offensives. In deference to the needs of our Allies, however, it was necessary to keep the Germans active without respite on the Arras front to which they had already drawn large reserves, and this was the more important in view of the ghastly collapse of the Russian Empire and the consequent liberation of enemy troops for the Western Front. Active operations were, therefore, pursued for some time longer on the Arras front, though perhaps they should not strictly be regarded as part of the Battle of Arras.

After the withdrawal of the 56th Division from the line, fighting broke out again on a wide front both sides of the Scarpe on the 23rd April, and continued with bitterness until the 26th though with comparatively little success. Some progress was made on both sides of the Cojeul River, and the village of Guémappe added to the British gains.

The 19th April was the occasion of the Battalion's first visit to Arras, with which town it became so intimately connected in the later stages of the War. At this date the town was not seriously damaged although it had lain a short two miles from the German lines for over two years, and with the exception of the railway station and its immediate vicinity was still quite healthy for reserve billets. The Battalion was accommodated in the barracks of the Citadel, which formed a welcome change from sixteen days of shell holes and dugouts. On the 21st the Battalion embussed for Bayencourt where it encamped in the Coigneux valley. Two days were occupied here in resting and reorganising, and advantage was taken by all ranks during leisure hours of the opportunity to revisit the Battalion's old haunts at Hébuterne and to cross unmolested to Gommecourt Park. On the 24th the Battalion moved at short notice to Gouy-en-Artois, arriving in billets there at 8 p.m. While at Gouy the Battalion was inspected by the Brigadier-General.

The 56th Division was now once more placed under orders for the line, this time in the VI Corps area, the sector held by the 15th Division being taken over by the 167th Brigade on the 29th April. The 168th Brigade, being once again in Divisional reserve, moved from Gouy to Simencourt on the 27th April, and on the following day into Arras, where preparations for further active operations were made in billets. The few days in Arras were much enlivened by the excellent show given by the Bow Bells in Arras Theatre.

The impending operation was to be an attempt to break through the enemy's defences on a large scale, the Fifth, Third and First Armies all being employed on a front from Fontaine-lez-Croisilles through Chérisy and St Rohart Factory to a point north of Plouvain. The VI Corps, consisting of the 3rd and 56th Divisions in line, took up the frontage from the Scarpe to the Cojeul River, the 56th Division's objective being on a line running north and south between St Rohart Factory on the Arras-Cambrai Road and the Bois du Vert.

The sector now held by the Division was about 1000 yards east of Guémappe and Monchy-le-Preux and lay sidelong on the spurs and side valleys descending to the Cojeul River. The enemy's defences were far more difficult to cope with on this occasion than on the 9th April. The Hindenburg and Wancourt lines had been passed; the Drocourt-Quéant line was still far ahead; and the intervening area which was now to be attacked was intersected in all directions by short isolated trench lines in the siting of which the enemy had displayed his usual skill in the use of ground. His defences, disposed in great depth, were strengthened by large numbers of machine-guns cunningly placed for mutual support in sunken roads and shell holes. It was known, however, that the deep dugouts of the Hindenburg line did not exist in this area, and it was hoped that a heavy and continuous bombardment beforehand would sufficiently reduce his numbers and morale to give success to the British infantry.

The 56th Division attack was to be carried out by the 167th and 169th Brigades, the 168th being relegated to reserve, though available for the assistance of either assaulting brigade as occasion might arise.

The Battalion remained in Arras until the 2nd May when, warning being received that "zero" for the attack was fixed for 3.45 a.m., the following day it moved at 4 p.m. to assembly in The Harp. In order to secure close co-operation between the Brigades, 2/Lieut. O. D. Garratt was attached to the 169th Headquarters as liaison officer.

The night of the 2nd May was fine and cold, though the early hours were misty, and at 3.40 a.m. on the 3rd when our bombardment increased to hurricane intensity it was still almost dark. At this hour the Battalion stood to, and the vivid flashes of the guns and the streams of S.O.S. signals from the enemy lines showed that inferno had broken loose, and the attack had begun. The British barrage was good, but the enemy was evidently expecting the attack as his counter-barrage was quick and his machine-gun fire devastating in volume and accuracy.

The 3rd May was a day of great disappointment all along the line, and comparatively little success was achieved. The 169th Brigade were held up by a German strong post in Cavalry Farm and, after occupying a precarious position between it and the river for some hours, were forced back by a heavy counter-attack to their original line. The 167th Brigade was also unable to progress.

It seems clear that zero hour was too early. In the darkness it was impossible for the troops to see visual signals of command, and the delay caused by having to pass messages down the line owing to the din of the bombardment resulted in the attacking waves moving off zig-zag in shape with officers at the advanced points. In such a formation they became an easy target for the enemy machine-guns. Some greater success might, moreover, have been achieved had the creeping barrage moved forward more quickly, which would have been quite possible in view of the comparatively unbroken state of the ground.

Early in the day the 1/4th Londons had moved forward to positions in shell holes at Airy Corner, near Feuchy Chapel, and at 8.30 p.m. the Battalion, now definitely at the disposal of the 169th Brigade, received orders to advance to positions in the Wancourt line just south of the Arras-Cambrai Road. This move was followed by another at 11 p.m., which brought the Battalion into close support of the front line in Tank Trench, apparently in anticipation of a further German counter-attack. The forward movement was made under a very heavy gas shell bombardment, but gas helmets were worn and practically no casualties were suffered. Shortly after arrival in the new position the enemy shelling slackened, and as no further action appeared imminent the Battalion was once more withdrawn to the Wancourt line, the move again being made in gas helmets. A move of 8000 yards in the dark with respirators is no easy matter to troops laden with battle equipment, and the men were somewhat exhausted on regaining the reserve position. A few hours' rest, however, put them to rights, and at 3 p.m. on the 4th the Battalion was again under orders to move forward. The losses of the 167th and 169th Brigades on the previous day were so severe that immediate relief was necessary for them, and the 168th Brigade therefore took over the whole Divisional front; the Battalion relieving the Queen Victorias and Queen's Westminsters in the subsector between the Arras-Cambrai Road and the Cojeul River, with the London Scottish on its left.

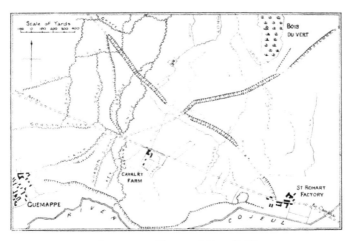

CAVALRY FARM, MAY 1917

The sector was occupied with two companies (C and D) in the front line and two (A and B) in support, Headquarters occupying a dugout on the hillside between Guémappe and Wancourt. The relief was completed without incident at 2.30 a.m. on the 5th May. The enemy evidently anticipated a renewal of our attack for throughout the day the lines were subjected to heavy shelling. Some doubt existed as to whether the enemy still remained in occupation of Cavalry Farm and of Tool Trench to the north of it, and as no movement was visible two daylight patrols were sent out in the afternoon to investigate. These patrols managed to gain the edge of Cavalry Farm, where they drew sharp rifle fire from the enemy which caused some loss; and their object being gained the patrols withdrew bringing their casualties with them. At about 10 p.m. the enemy's bombardment increased to a heavy barrage, which was especially severe on the sector held by the 14th Division on the right of the river, and it seemed likely that an enemy attack was in preparation. The 14th Division indeed called for artillery support, and this was promptly supplied by our artillery, which opened a terrific barrage on the enemy lines. After an artillery duel of about two hours the shelling on both sides slackened. The 6th and 7th May were both marked by heavy shelling, which on the part of the enemy seemed mostly to be directed towards searching for our battery positions in rear, though some loss was caused to the Battalion, and 2/Lieuts. Reid and Caudwell were killed, and 2/Lieut. Hutchins wounded, with several N.C.O.'s and men killed and wounded by stray shells.

On the night of the 7th May the Battalion handed over its sector to the Rangers and withdrew to the old German trench system north of Wancourt, Headquarters being accommodated in Marlière Caves. In this position the Battalion remained a couple of days, during which the enemy's shell fire continued at intervals but without causing serious damage.

The attack of the 3rd May was the last general attack on the Arras front, and subsequent operations were confined to local enterprises up and down the line with the object of improving and rounding off the positions gained. On the Divisional front a minor operation of this sort was immediately necessary in clearing up the situation at Cavalry Farm and Tool Trench, and the 1/4th Londons and London Scottish were detailed to capture these positions.

The Battalion moved into the line for this attack on the evening of the 10th May.

The objectives allotted to it were Cavalry Farm and the trench south-east of it, and Tool Trench for a frontage of 250 yards north of the Cambrai Road; while the London Scottish were to extend the attack on Tool Trench for a further 600 yards to the north and also capture a small copse on the extreme left. The attack was to be made in each battalion on a two company front, each company advancing in two waves on a front of two platoons. One company of the Rangers was attached to the 1/4th Londons and one of Kensingtons to the Scottish.

For two days previous to the 11th, which was fixed for the operation, the Divisional artillery had been carrying out destructive bombardments with 4·5-inch howitzers on the objectives as well as on the communication trenches leading to the rear and on the portion of Tool Trench outside the limits of attack. On the evening of the 10th a practice 18-pr. barrage was placed on the objectives, but the enemy reply was so efficient that it was decided to conduct the assault without any increase in our normal artillery activity and to endeavour to carry the operation through as a surprise.

At 8.30 p.m. on the 11th May the assaulting waves moved forward, the 1/4th Londons' attack led by D Company (H. N. Williams) on the right of the road and A Company (Lorden) on the left, with B (Beeby) and C (Rees) Companies in support. The surprise effect was excellent, and was heightened by the fact that all the objectives except the Farm itself were hidden from our trenches by a slight spur which here drops down to the Cojeul River. The enemy had thus, in the absence of a barrage, no warning of the attack, and in a few minutes the whole of the objectives were captured. Few prisoners were taken, but a party of about fifty of the enemy, fleeing from Cavalry Farm, were caught by our Lewis guns and annihilated. Lewis gun posts were at once pushed forward into No Man's Land, and the consolidation of the captured trench begun. So quickly had all this happened that the enemy artillery opening in response to an S.O.S. sent up from their lines was harmless to the leading companies, though it inflicted some loss on the support companies which were moving up to our vacated front line.

The consolidation of the captured position was aided by the Cheshire Pioneers, who completed before dawn a communication trench connecting Cavalry Trench with the new front line.

In the early hours of the 12th May the line was thinned out and only a sufficient garrison left in the captured position to hold it against counter-attack, the surplus platoons being withdrawn to the old line. After some hours the German barrage subsided and we were left in undisputed possession of our capture. This neat little operation cost but few casualties considering the advantages gained, and the completeness of the surprise is illustrated by an incident which occurred early the following morning. One of our advanced Lewis gun posts, hearing movement in front, challenged. A reply being received in German, fire was opened. Two of the team went forward to collect the bag and found a German officer shot dead and a

Sergt.-Major badly wounded. The maps which were taken from the officer's case showed some of our battery positions accurately, and it appears that this luckless pair were coming forward to Cavalry Farm to "spot" for a German artillery shoot, ignorant of the fact that it was in our hands.

The Battalion continued to occupy its new line until the evening of the 13th May, when the 168th Brigade was relieved by the 167th. The Battalion handed over its sector to the 1/3rd Londons and withdrew to a reserve position on the Cambrai Road near Tilloy, arriving there in the early hours of the 14th May. The following day a further move was made to billets in Arras.

After the Brigade's withdrawal from the line its gains were extended on the 18th and 19th by successful local operations carried out by the 167th Brigade, who completed the captures of the north end of Tool Trench and also parts of Hook and Long Trenches adjoining it.

On the 19th May the 168th Brigade moved still further back to rest billets in Berneville, and two days later the whole Division was withdrawn, with Divisional Headquarters at Warlus.

During May the Battalion received the following officer reinforcements:

>Lieuts. E. P. M. Mosely and A. S. Ford.
>
>2/Lieuts. L. W. Archer and H. T. Hannay (commissioned from the ranks of the Battalion).
>
>2/Lieut. F. Barnes (20th Londons).
>
>2/Lieuts. H. V. Coombes, N. Nunns, H. E. Jackman and W. G. Port (21st Londons).
>
>2/Lieut. S. A. Gray (23rd Londons).
>
>Capt. Maloney, R.A.M.C., vice Havard to London Field Ambulance.

During the same period 2/Lieut. Wreford was wounded and Lieut. P. F. Smalley evacuated to hospital.

The Battalion remained in rest for about three weeks, which were officially occupied in training and reorganisation. The actual training was, however, reduced to the minimum, and the Battalion's really serious duty became that of training for Battalion and Brigade sports, and the relaxation which these provided combined with the determination with which all ranks strove to gain physical fitness for the purpose of the sports was undoubtedly quite as valuable as hours spent on the parade ground. On the 23rd the Brigade was paraded for inspection by Gen. Hull, who presented ribands to those who had been decorated in the recent operations.

The following day the Battalion moved from Berneville to fresh billets in Simencourt, where the routine of training and recreation proceeded. Early in June the 56th Division returned to the line, the 168th Brigade moving to Montenescourt on the 11th and to Achicourt on the following day.

Eight days later the 168th Brigade relieved the 169th in the line, the Battalion moving into left support positions at Wancourt, where it relieved the 1/2nd Londons. Here the Battalion remained for five days supplying working parties chiefly in connection with the construction of new communication trenches to connect up the recently gained advance posts with the front line, and in connecting up the posts themselves to form a new front line. These days passed without incident beyond a certain amount of enemy shelling and trench mortar fire, and on the evening of the 26th June the Battalion moved forward to relieve the Kensingtons in the front line system, its right flank resting on the Cojeul River, where it joined the London Scottish, and its left flank about 800 yards north of the Arras-Cambrai Road in Hook Trench. This relief was completed by 1.30 a.m. on the 27th, and the sector was held with three companies in front line and one in reserve.

This tour of duty passed without important incident though the enemy's artillery exhibited some activity, principally against the back areas in the neighbourhood of Wancourt. On the 1st July hostile aircraft were especially active, making many unsuccessful attempts to pass the barrage of the British anti-aircraft batteries. This unusual anxiety of the German airmen to cross our lines was possibly due to the presence in the Arras area of H.M. the King, who was then visiting the troops in France and staying at Bavencourt Château on the Arras-Doullens Road.

That evening at 11 p.m. the 6th Queens of the 12th Division took over the portion of the Battalion's sector lying to the north of the Cambrai Road, and the following evening the remainder of the sector was handed over to the 5th Borders of the 50th Division, the Battalion withdrawing on relief to billets in Achicourt, which it reached at 5 a.m. on the 3rd July.

The part of the 56th Division in the Arras fighting was now finished, and the Division was withdrawn into Corps reserve for a welcome rest. The fighting on the Hindenburg line was practically over, though we shall have further reference to make to it in connection with the 2/4th Battalion in another chapter.

The weeks of battle had placed a great strain on the Battalion. Long marches to and from the line, shell hole bivouacs, heavy working parties, bad weather and severe shelling had all had their effect, and a period of rest and reorganisation was needed.

At 9.30 a.m. on the 4th July the 168th Brigade embussed for the Le Cauroy area, in which it had trained a year previously prior to occupying the Hébuterne trenches. The Battalion was allotted billets in Denier where it entered on a short period of rest and reorganisation in which the training was interspersed with the various rounds of the Brigade boxing competition, the finals of which were held on the 15th July.

In June Lieut. H. Jones was seconded to VI Corps School as Instructor; Capt. V. S. Bowater was evacuated to hospital; and 2/Lieut. C. W. Denning joined the Battalion, being posted to the 168th L.T.M. Battery early in July; 2/Lieuts. L. W. Wreford and A. C. Knight rejoined the Battalion in July.

The Division was now warned of an impending move to another theatre of activity, and this move occurred on the 23rd, when the Division left the VII Corps to join the Fifth Army in the Ypres Salient.

CHAPTER XV
THE 2/4TH BATTALION IN THE BATTLES FOR BULLECOURT, 1917

We must now follow the battles which had been fought during the latter part of the German retirement south of the area covered by the battles of Arras.

All along the line the German retreat had been conducted steadily and with marked success on to the Hindenburg line. Although on the whole the retreat in the south had not been accompanied by heavy fighting, the attempts of our troops to push forward and define rigidly the Hindenburg system had met with resistance which had developed here and there into fighting of the most desperate character. Nowhere had these local conflagrations been more fierce than in the line of retreat to Bullecourt. In this sector the retiring enemy was opposed by Australian troops, who together with the 7th and 62nd (and later the 58th) Divisions composed Gough's Fifth Army.

A successful advance on 2nd April in this region was followed by an attempt by the Australians on the 12th to carry the line Bullecourt-Lagnicourt, but without success owing to the inadequacy of the supporting artillery fire. Severe fighting ensued, and a counter-attack of a serious nature by the Germans on the 15th was ultimately held.

On the 3rd May the Australians' efforts met with more success, and they were able to penetrate the Hindenburg system on the immediate right of Bullecourt. The 62nd Division on their left, however, were unable to progress in the village itself, with the result that the ground held by the Australians formed a salient badly enfiladed both from the village and from the direction of Quéant.

The position of Bullecourt in the Hindenburg system was peculiar. From Heninel the line ran in a generally south-easterly direction towards Bullecourt in front of the Fontaine-lez-Croisilles-Bullecourt Road. At Bullecourt the line turned due east, passing some 500 yards in front of Riencourt. Bullecourt itself was between the front and support trenches of the first system, so that the front line formed a very pronounced salient. East of Riencourt the line once more took an abrupt turn, this time almost due south, passing in front (or to the west) of Quéant.

Bullecourt lies on a spur which falls northward into the Hendecourt valley, and its exits on all sides form a network of sunken roads. At the period under review the majority of the houses were already in ruins, and these, together with numerous fences enclosing orchards and gardens, converted the space between the front and support Hindenburg lines into a serious obstacle, of which the strength was increased by an intermediate trench half-way through the village. The Germans had, moreover, tunnelled the village in such a way that they could bring reinforcements rapidly and safely to bear on any threatened point. The small salient gained by the Australians straddling the Hindenburg trenches on the immediate east of the village, uncomfortable as it was for the occupants, was a serious menace to the enemy position; and it was reasonable to anticipate that the Germans would not easily acquiesce in this partial envelopment of their flank.

During the early days of May the Australians in the salient were subjected to numerous counter-attacks, while by dint of hand-to-hand fighting the 62nd Division had gained a firm footing in the village. On the 12th May the assault was renewed by the 7th Division, and fighting of a desperately severe character developed in the village in which our troops met with varying fortunes. In the eastern half of the village the 2nd Queen's made some progress, but at the western end no advance was possible. The situation at the sunken cross-roads at the north-east corner of the village was obscure, and north of this point no part of the enemy's support line was gained. Such was the position in "Bloody Bullecourt" when the 58th Division began to take over the line.

On the afternoon of the 12th May the Company Commanders and Intelligence Officer of the 2/4th Battalion, together with their Platoon Sergeants, were sent forward to reconnoitre the positions held by the 15th Australian Infantry Brigade with a view to taking them over. From Vaulx-Vraucourt to Noreuil the party followed the dried-up bed of the Hirondelle River, the scene of many a desperate struggle during the preceding month. The air was oppressive with the heat of a premature burst of summer weather; the stench from hundreds of unburied bodies and the ominous silence of the guns prior to the attack which was to be renewed the following day caused the whole atmosphere to be heavy with the presage of hard fighting to come. On arrival at the Australian Headquarters the party was informed of the attack organised for the following morning, so that further reconnaissance that day was useless. After the barrage had died down, however, on the 13th a fresh start was made up the communication trench, which was really the Noreuil-Riencourt Road, a bank on the east side preventing observation from Quéant.

The Australian attack was successful, although the position was not entirely cleared up, and they were now holding the first two lines of the Hindenburg system, the support line being our front line, and the former front line now forming our support. The intense artillery fire to which this ground had many times been subjected had resulted in the almost total obliteration of the trench lines as such, and the position was really held in a line of shell craters.

The arrangements for relief being completed, the 2/4th Battalion moved up on the night of the 13th/14th May to take over the left sector of the Brigade front, from the sunken cross-roads at the north-east corner of Bullecourt to a small communication trench about 500 yards to the east, C Company (Leake) and D Company (Parker) being in the front line with A (Cotton) and B (Bottomley) in support. Battalion Headquarters occupied a central position in the support line. A detached post under 2/Lieut. S. A. Seys was established in a shell hole west of the sunken cross-roads in order to secure touch with the 7th Division in the village. From the right of the 2/4th Battalion the Brigade sector as far as the Noreuil-Riencourt Road was taken up by the 2/3rd Londons.

The actual process of the relief, which was not completed until 1.30 a.m. on the 14th May, was exceedingly trying owing to the heavy shelling of the communication trench. Amongst the casualties caused by this were 2/Lieut. F. Stickney (wounded) and Capt. P. H. Burton, R.A.M.C. (killed).

The Germans, having been ejected from their trench system in this sector, were holding on in a system of unconnected shell holes on the lower slopes of the spur, and their main line of resistance appeared to be a sunken road running laterally across our front, and distant about 300 yards. A new and evidently unfinished trench line crossed the opposite hillside in front of Hendecourt.

The heavy shelling which had interfered with the relief continued throughout the night, our front and support lines being heavily bombarded, while the back areas were subjected to incessant searching with high explosive and shrapnel.

Shortly after the Battalion had taken up its position a party of some 12 Germans with a machine-gun attempted to attack C Company's line. The attack completely failed owing principally to the great gallantry of Capt. Leake. 2/Lieut. S. G. Askham, who was in the trench with Leake at the time, writes:

> We were inspecting the sentry posts and our attention was drawn to considerable movement near our front line. Without a moment's hesitation Capt. Leake leapt over the parapet and in a few seconds we heard revolver shots being fired. He had single-handed attacked a German machine-gun team who were on the point of establishing a post in a position overlooking the whole of our front line. He killed four of the team and the remainder

> were wounded by our rifle fire. Leake returned with three prisoners and their machine-gun, which he also secured.... Leake was a tower of strength to both officers and men in the Company and we all felt that he richly deserved the V.C., for which he was afterwards recommended.

The continued bombardment now began to cause difficulty in controlling the situation, for early in the morning a direct hit on the Brigade signal depôt completely wrecked all the instruments and killed the occupants of the dugout. Later, communication by power buzzer was also cut, and for the remainder of the day all communication between the Brigade and the battalions in the line had to be effected by runners.

This intermittent shelling continued until shortly after midday on the 14th, when the enemy was observed from our lines to be massing for attack in the neighbourhood of a ruined factory some 500 yards to our front. A call was made on our artillery, which immediately put down a heavy barrage under which the enemy's troops melted away. The hostile bombardment now increased in intensity and a terrific barrage came down on our lines, continuing with unabated violence all through the night. This barrage was for the greater part in enfilade from the direction of Quéant, and was therefore particularly accurate and deadly; under the rain of shells our trenches, or what little remained of them, were completely obliterated, the greater part of our front line supplies of rifle ammunition and bombs were blown up and several Lewis guns with their teams were buried. Through this appalling ordeal the Battalion stuck to their posts grimly, though suffering severe losses. Shortly before midnight the enemy launched an attack on the 7th Division in Bullecourt village, in which by dint of fierce hand-to-hand conflicts they wrested from the 7th Division some of its gains of the previous two days.

We have already pointed to the importance of the salient now occupied by the 2/4th Londons, and, fully alive to the position, the Battalion was not surprised by the attack which broke upon it at dawn the next day. The importance to the Germans of the possession of this part of the line may be gauged by the fact that the troops employed by them were the 3rd Prussian Guard.

At 4 a.m. on the 15th the enemy were seen to be massing for the attack. Our artillery once more responded magnificently to the call made on them, and their barrage caused severe disorganisation in the enemy's ranks. The attack was stubbornly pushed home by the Germans, but their barrage being lifted prematurely from our front line an opportunity was afforded to our leading companies to prepare for the shock. Advantage of this momentary respite was taken to reinforce the front line, three platoons of B

Company filling the gaps of D Company, and C Company being strengthened by a party of A Company. These precautions cost the enemy dearly, and his assaulting columns were met by a deadly rifle and Lewis gun fire from the whole of our line, which completed the work of the artillery. The German attack was broken and not a single enemy reached our line. The remnants of the assaulting battalions turned and fled down the hill, leaving an appalling number of dead and wounded.

Beyond the right of the Brigade front a small party succeeded in effecting a lodgment in a portion of the front line held by the Australians, but these were shortly afterwards ejected with the assistance of a platoon of the 2/2nd Londons.

By six o'clock the enemy counter-attack was definitely and finally broken and small parties could be seen doubling away from before Bullecourt; and a further attempt to launch an attack on the Australians about half an hour later was effectively stopped by our artillery.

After the attack had failed the enemy settled down to a slow but steady shelling of our line for the remainder of the 15th, which was spent in endeavouring to reorganise the battered remnants of the Battalion and to put the lines once more in a defensible condition. Under cover of darkness the 2/1st Londons took over the left subsector from the 2/4th Londons, which withdrew to reserve dugouts in the sunken road in front of Noreuil.

The Battalion had found itself. In its first serious action it had stood up to a frightful bombardment which had lasted without abatement for nineteen hours, and at the end of it had seen the backs of the Prussian Guard. It had paid, however, a severe price. The total casualties during the two days in the line were, in officers, in addition to the two already mentioned, 2/Lieuts. E. C. Pratt and T. Stoaling (killed); Capts. G. E. A. Leake and H. C. Long (wounded); and in N.C.O.'s and men 68 killed, 196 wounded and 2 missing.

Capt. Leake had behaved with the utmost gallantry throughout the attack. He was hit after the attack itself was over by a shell which fell on his Company Headquarters, wounding also his second in command, Capt. Long, and several of his Company staff. While being conveyed on a stretcher to the Aid Post, Leake was again severely hit by a shell which burst almost under the stretcher, killing two of the bearers. After the shelling had subsided he was evacuated, but died in hospital a fortnight later. For his magnificent behaviour he was recommended by Lieut.-Col. Dann for the Victoria Cross, and eventually was awarded the D.S.O. a few days before his death. This was conferred on him by Gen. Gough, who visited for the express purpose the C.C.S. in which Leake was lying. Lieut.-Col. Dann was awarded the D.S.O. for his excellent work in this action.

Awards of the Military Medal were made to L./Corpls. Spencer and Selby, and Ptes. Grierson, Olinski and Spence.

For three days the Battalion remained in the sunken road supplying carrying parties to the front line. The destruction caused by the hostile bombardment was such that all the necessary trench supplies in munitions and material had to be completely renewed, and, moreover, the battalion in the line was dependent on its supporting troops for their water supply. This imposed a very heavy strain on the 2/4th Battalion for the back areas were still continuously shelled, largely with gas shell, and particularly during the hours of darkness when the carrying parties were at work; and the relief of the 173rd Brigade by the 175th which ensued on the night of the 18th/19th May was welcome.

That night at 11 p.m. the Battalion handed over to the 2/12th Londons (175th Brigade) and marched to rest billets in Bihucourt, where it remained until the 29th, engaged in reorganisation and refitting and training. During this period the gaps in the Battalion were partly filled by reinforcements of two officers, 2/Lieuts. J. H. L. Wheatley and E. P. Higgs, and a large draft of N.C.O.'s and men. The 2/4th Londons were visited on the 20th May by Lieut.-Gen. Birdwood, commanding the Australians, who congratulated Lieut.-Col. Dann on the Battalion's achievement.

During the latter half of May the 58th Division extended its left flank, taking over in succession from the 7th and 62nd Divisions both of which had suffered severely. By the end of the month the Division was occupying a front of 4000 yards with two brigades in line. The 173rd Brigade took over the left subsector with the 2/1st and 2/2nd Londons in line, and the 2/3rd Londons in close support, while the 2/4th Londons moved on the 31st May in Brigade reserve to Mory, where they continued training.

Map No. 11 shows the position at this date. It will be seen that north-west of Bullecourt the Hindenburg line on the Divisional front was still not captured, though on its left the 21st Division was in possession of the front trench as far as the Croisilles-Fontaine Road. The 58th Division sector consisted for the greater part of isolated shell hole defences.

There thus remained in this area a length of about 2500 yards of Hindenburg front and about 3500 yards of Hindenburg support trench still to be captured from the enemy in order to complete the allotted task.

The first two days in the new sector passed without incident beyond the usual artillery activity. Early on the morning of the 3rd June a gas attack was carried out on the enemy's lines opposite our left by a discharge of 197 gas projectors. The gas cloud formed appeared highly satisfactory, and evidently caused the enemy some perturbation as his artillery promptly put a barrage on our forward posts. This, however, inflicted but little loss owing to the previous withdrawal of the garrisons as a precautionary measure.

Various signs of nervousness exhibited by the enemy about this time suggested that he expected the continuance of our offensive, and indeed in view of the successes already gained he might with reason anticipate that he would not be left in unmolested possession of the remaining sectors of the Hindenburg system.

On the night of the 3rd/4th June the 2/4th Londons relieved the 2/2nd Londons in the left subsector, A and B Companies (Cotton and Bottomley) occupying the forward posts with C and D Companies (Hewlett and Parker) in support. The line opposed to the Battalion was entirely in front of the Heninel-Bullecourt Road, with a support line about 200 yards in rear of it. For the greater part the line ran straight, but two small salients, the Knuckle and the Hump, had been developed into strong points of no mean order. The whole line was heavily wired, and although the entanglements had suffered from our shell fire they still presented a formidable obstacle, while the patrols sent forward nightly from our posts obtained clear evidence that the line was held in unusual strength.

The most urgent work in this sector was the linking up of our scattered shell hole posts to form a connected line, and this was pushed on with all possible speed and completed by the night of the 10th. Throughout this tour of duty the enemy continued a fairly vigorous bombardment of our trenches and back areas, which was returned with interest by our artillery.

On the night of the 11th/12th June the 2/1st Londons took over from A, B and D Companies, while C Company was relieved by the 2/7th Londons (174th Brigade). On relief the Battalion withdrew in support to St Leger, where Headquarters opened at the Château.

During the days spent in support the Battalion was reinforced by a large draft of N.C.O.'s and men, and by two officers, 2/Lieuts. C. Potter and V. R. Oldrey. The latter officer was most unfortunately hit by a stray bullet on the following day.

The principal duty of the three days following relief was the organisation and special training of A, B and D Companies to take part in an assault of the Hindenburg system opposite the Brigade front.

The front of attack extended from the sharp corner just south of the Knuckle on the right to a point about 150 yards north of the Hump on the left. As the proposed operation included the capture of two lines of trench it was decided by Corps to divide it into two days' work in order to simplify the question of the co-operation of the 21st Division on the left.

Accordingly the plan was that the first day the 173rd Brigade should capture the allotted portion of the front line, while the second day the area of operations should be extended and the 21st Division on the left should join with the 173rd Brigade in the assault of the support line.

The troops detailed for the attack were in order from right to left, 1 company 2/3rd, 1 company 2/1st, 1½ companies 2/2nd and 1 company 2/4th Londons. For the purposes of the operation the companies of the 2/3rd and 2/4th Londons were respectively under command of the officers commanding 2/1st and 2/2nd Londons. The attack was to be delivered under a heavy barrage from a strong concentration of guns of the 7th, 58th and 62nd Divisions and the Corps Heavy Artillery, together with the massed guns of the three Brigade Machine-Gun Companies. Arrangements were also made for the provision of supporting rifle, Lewis gun and machine-gun fire by the 21st Division.

The 174th Brigade was to arrange for the establishment of a line of posts along the sunken road in prolongation to the right of the 173rd Brigade's objective.

A Company (Cotton) was detailed for the first day's attack, and the special task allotted to it by Lieut.-Col. Richardson, commanding the 2/2nd Battalion, was the capture of the sunken cross-roads to the left of the Hump and of a German strong point in the front line about 100 yards north of them.

The assembly was successfully carried out during the night of 14th/15th June, and completed by about 2.15 a.m. At 2.50 a.m. our barrage opened and the assaulting waves moved forward to the attack in good order, keeping well up to the barrage and suffering very little loss.

The attack proved successful though it led to some hard fighting. The actual advance was entrusted to two platoons under 2/Lieut. Wheatley (right) and 2/Lieut. Bell (left). The objective at this point was strengthened by two "pillbox" machine-gun posts and was in line with the trench already held on our left by the 21st Division, from which it was divided by a double barricade; and Lieut.-Col. Richardson took up his Battle Headquarters in a dugout in their line, as did also Capt. Cotton. A third platoon of A Company under 2/Lieut. Boorman assembled in the 21st Division trench, and was formed as a bombing party with others to rush the double barricade at zero hour and to bomb the enemy out of their two pillboxes before our barrage had lifted off the enemy trench in order to clear it before the arrival of Bell and Wheatley with their platoons. A good many casualties were therefore inevitably caused to Boorman's platoon by our own shell fire, and he reached the traverse next to the first pillbox with only two corporals, Sherwood and Whitworth. Here the two N.C.O.'s threw bombs, which landed neatly outside the two doors of the pillbox, and directly they exploded Boorman dashed round the traverse with a bomb in each hand. Sheltering himself against the wall, he threw his bombs into each door of the pillbox before the Germans inside had recovered from the effects of Sherwood and Whitworth's attack. This neat piece of work secured the pillbox to us, but before Boorman could reorganise his party for the further advance to the second pillbox Bell's platoon had occupied the trench. A few men of Wheatley's platoon were also found to be in line. The greater number, including Wheatley himself, apparently overshot the objective, not recognising it in its battered condition, and must all have been killed or captured.

According to the prearranged scheme, Bell's platoon was withdrawn shortly before dawn, and Boorman was left in charge of the captured position with the remains of his own and Wheatley's platoons. The 2/2nd Londons were now in touch on our right, and by arrangement with them the trench was divided between the two Battalions, the 2/4th Londons being responsible from the 21st Division on the left as far as the communication trench running back from the Hump to the German support line. The shelling now resumed more moderate proportions, although it continued sporadically all day, and casualties were continually being caused in our ranks. The Battalion suffered a severe loss early in the day in Sergt. Riley, who was acting C.S.M. for the attack. He had done very good work indeed ever since the Battalion had been in France, and had throughout shown complete indifference to danger. He was shot through the chest while accompanying Boorman on a reconnaissance to endeavour to trace Wheatley's missing platoon.

In the meantime arrangements had been made for the further attack on the support Hindenburg line on the following morning, and detailed orders had been issued which provided for the assembly of the assaulting troops in the front line—the first day's objective—by 2.10 a.m. on the 16th June. This intention could not, however, be carried out, for at about 10.30 p.m. on the 15th a heavy counter-attack was launched against our new positions which caused severe fighting, in the course of which the enemy once more gained a hold on the centre of his old front line and also at two other points.

On the front held by the 2/4th Londons the counter-offensive took the form of a bombing attack, the approach of which along the communication trench opposite the right of our sector was disclosed by the enemy's own star shells, which rendered plainly visible the forms of the attackers waist high above the battered sides of the trench. A shower of Véry lights was at once put up, and with the assistance of these the attack was driven off by Lewis gun and rifle grenade fire, arrangements for which had been made most skilfully by Boorman earlier in the day. None of the enemy succeeded in penetrating our position, but many of his dead were left on the ground.

It was, however, so essential to our purpose that the enemy should not have the advantage of a day's respite before the attack on the support line, that immediate arrangements were made for a counter-attack to eject him once more from his old front line in order to leave this clear as our jumping-off point. The recapture of the line was entrusted to the 2/1st and 2/3rd Londons, who succeeded by surprise in completely recovering the whole of the front line at the point of the bayonet by 2.45 a.m. on the 16th.

At 3.10 a.m. the second day's attack opened. The order of battle was the same as for the first day, but the forces employed were larger, the 2/3rd Londons supplying three companies, the 2/1st Londons three companies, the 2/2nd Londons two companies and the 2/4th Londons two companies (B under Bottomley and D under Parker).

The attack, as for the first day, was made under a creeping barrage supplied by the Divisional artillery and the Brigade machine-gun companies, and the assault was made in one wave with a "mopping-up" wave in rear accompanied by a detachment of Royal Engineers for consolidation work.

This day again a good deal of difficulty seems to have been experienced by the advancing troops in identifying their objectives, which had become almost entirely obliterated by our long-continued bombardments, while the dust raised by the barrage rendered the recognition of surrounding physical features almost impossible. The resistance of the enemy all along the line was most stubborn, and the unusual strength in which he was holding the attacked position clearly indicated that the attack was expected. The earliest reports which were received by runner led to the belief that the objective on the two flanks had been captured. No information from the centre was forthcoming, and it gradually became evident that the direction of the flank companies was at fault, with the result that they had swung outwards leaving in the centre a gap still occupied by the Germans, who promptly began to bomb along the line against our unprotected flanks. The attack of the 21st Division on the left, moreover, failed throughout, and although a few isolated parties succeeded in reaching a line of shell holes in front of Tunnel Trench they were eventually forced to withdraw.

The orders issued to the assaulting wave were to capture the Hindenburg support line and hold on to it until supports should reach them, but all the attempts of Lieut.-Col. Richardson to push forward his supporting troops were frustrated by the intense rifle and machine-gun fire with which the ground was continuously swept, and similar efforts along the remainder of the front were stopped for the same reason.

At 11 a.m. the obscurity of the position induced the Brigadier to make a personal reconnaissance in order, if possible, to clear up the situation, but he found it impossible to get along the captured German front line, and therefore proceeded to the Battle Headquarters of the 2/2nd Londons. The information obtained there led to the belief that the 2/2nd and 2/4th Londons had carried their objectives without difficulty and at comparatively little loss, but that their flanks were in the air and in danger of being turned by the bombing attacks of the enemy. The support line was now entirely cut off as runner communication was utterly impossible under the enemy's devastating fire, and it was clear that our isolated parties who were in the objective must be suffering heavy losses.

It has been difficult to establish what happened to the two companies of the 2/4th Battalion owing to the heavy casualties sustained, but it is evident that they also mistook the objective and pushed on some 200 yards ahead of it, where they came under intense fire from front and flanks.

The most advanced party appears to have been a platoon of B Company under McDowell, who although completely out of touch with the remainder of their company held on most gallantly to the position they had gained for some two hours, at the end of which time their ammunition was exhausted and they were using a captured German machine-gun. No sign of the promised supports being visible, and the enemy evidently being about to surround his little party, now reduced to a mere half-dozen, McDowell determined to fight his way back to his comrades, and began to withdraw steadily. During his withdrawal he was hit, and on regaining consciousness found himself alone. He continued his way back to our lines, crawling from shell hole to shell hole, and managed to collect four privates, all resolved to sell their lives dearly. By this time he was completely surrounded, and his little band was destroyed by rifle grenade fire; McDowell himself was hit again and captured. To the eternal shame of the enemy let it be recorded that he lay for three days in the enemy trench before being sent to their dressing-station, and not until six days after his wounds were received were they dressed at all.

A similar fate appears to have overtaken the remainder of B and D Companies, and the probability is that having overshot their objective they were outflanked and cut off by parties of the enemy coming down the sunken road from Fontaine-lez-Croisilles. Their mistake having become evident to them, they endeavoured, like McDowell, to fight their way back, but after making a gallant stand were eventually killed or taken prisoners almost to a man. It is believed from aeroplane reports subsequently received that this gallant little body actually succeeded in maintaining themselves against all attacks for nearly two days. But all efforts to relieve them meeting with failure, they at last fell gloriously rather than surrender.

A similar lack of success attended the efforts of the other battalions, and as a result of the two days' fighting the Brigade held the front Hindenburg line and the sunken road in rear of it, from the junction with the 21st Division on the left to a point some 300 yards west of the Crucifix cross-roads at Bullecourt.

The casualties of the Brigade amounted to 48 officers and 955 other ranks, those of the 2/4th Battalion for the two days' fighting being:

> Capts. E. W. Bottomley and W. H. Parker, 2/Lieuts. S. M. Williams and J. H. L. Wheatley, killed; Capt. E. N. Cotton and 2/Lieut. T. J. Bell, wounded; 2/Lieuts. E. A. Monkman and R. McDowell, wounded and missing, and 2/Lieut. E. A. Stevenson, missing.

> In N.C.O.'s and men the losses totalled 7 killed, 53 wounded and 139 missing, the majority being in B and D Companies.

It became evident during the afternoon that the 173rd Brigade, who were weak before they went into action, would need relief that night, and arrangements were therefore made for the 174th Brigade to take over the line. In accordance with this arrangement the whole Brigade front was taken over on the night 16th/17th June by the 2/5th Londons, who pushed forward strong patrols towards the Hindenburg support line. This, however, was found to be held in strength by the enemy.

With this somewhat disastrous day the idea of immediate further offensive operations was postponed, and the 174th Brigade settled down to consolidate itself in the Hindenburg front line.

The fighting spirit displayed throughout the operation was splendid, and it is only to be regretted that the two days' work had not been arranged for a one day battle. As the event showed, the capture of the Hindenburg front line on the 15th prepared the enemy for our attempt to take the support line on the 16th, with the result that on the second day severe casualties were inflicted on our troops to no purpose.

During the second action at Bullecourt an incident occurred which is surely one of the most remarkable of the whole War. We recount it in the words of the official record, which appeared in the Battalion War Diary on the 8th August:

> No. 282496 Pte. Taylor J., of A Company, admitted to 29th C.C.S. This man had been missing since Bullecourt on the 15th June 1917, had been wounded and crawled into a shell hole. He sustained a compound fracture of the left thigh, and aided by Pte. Peters, B Company, had lived on bully beef found on the bodies of dead men.

After being in the shell hole for over six weeks Pte. Peters apparently was captured, for the following day three Germans visited the shell hole and shook Pte. Taylor's leg, but he feigned death. The following day, not being able to obtain any food, he decided to crawl back to our lines. His position was some distance behind the German line. He dragged himself to the parapet of the trench, threw himself over, crawled through the wire across No Man's Land into the sector held by the S. Staffords. Altogether he spent seven weeks and four days behind the German lines.

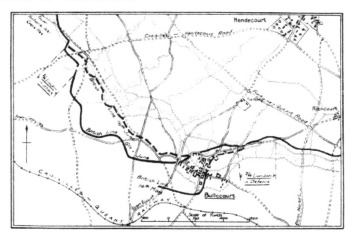

BULLECOURT, MAY-JUNE, 1917

Pte. Taylor's story was subjected to severe scrutiny by Lieut.-Col. Dann and by the Brigadier, and their opinion of its truth is witnessed by the fact that he was awarded the D.C. Medal. Pte. Peters' fate is unknown, and it is regrettable that after his devotion to his comrade it was not possible to make him a posthumous award for his gallantry.

On relief by the 2/5th Londons the 2/4th Battalion marched to Divisional reserve camp in Mory Copse, where it remained for four days in reorganising and training. The month at Bullecourt had cost the Battalion 597 casualties in all ranks, and a rest after the prolonged operations was urgently needed.

B and D Companies were for the moment practically effaced, and the few remaining details were therefore attached respectively to A and C Companies, these two composite companies being placed under command of Capts. E. N. Cotton and H. A. T. Hewlett.

On the 24th June the 58th Division was finally withdrawn from Bullecourt, its place being taken by the 7th Division, and Divisional Headquarters opened at Courcelles on that day.

The 2/4th Londons with the remainder of the 173rd Brigade had moved on the 21st to Camp at Logeast Wood, where a welcome fifteen days' rest was spent in training and reorganising, working parties being supplied daily to the R.E. dump at Achiet-le-Grand.

During this period awards were made of the Military Cross to 2/Lieut. D. S. Boorman, and of the Military Medal to L.-Corpl. Coates, for their gallant conduct on the 15th/16th June. The Battalion was joined on the 24th June by Capt. W. A. Stark and 2/Lieut. S. Davis, and by drafts of 107 other ranks on the 21st June and of 28 N.C.O.'s on the 4th July. This welcome accession of strength, especially in N.C.O.'s, who had become very few, rendered it possible once more to reorganise the Battalion in four companies under Capts. E. N. Cotton (A), G. H. Hetley (B), H. A. T. Hewlett (C), and A. G. Croll (D). The duties of Intelligence Officer were taken over from Capt. Croll by 2/Lieut. S. A. Seys, and on the 12th July, Cotton having been evacuated to hospital, command of A Company was assumed by Capt. D. S. Boorman, M.C.

The period of rest at Logeast Wood was brought to a close by a Battalion sports meeting, one of those quite informal but very keenly followed affairs which always have proved such an invaluable means of recuperation for tired troops. The following day the reorganised Battalion was inspected by the Colonel, and on the 8th July the Battalion marched through the devastated region and the ruins of Courcelles, Sapignies and Bapaume to Bancourt. Its route continued the following day to Ytres, where six days in billets were occupied in parading for inspection successively by the Divisional General (Fanshawe), the Brigadier (Freyberg) and the IV Corps Commander.

The Brigade was now in Divisional reserve, the Division having taken over a sector of line in front of Gouzeaucourt and Havrincourt Wood. The British trenches here were opposed once more to the Hindenburg system, which had not been penetrated in this region. After severe fighting in April round Epéhy our troops had established themselves on high ground on the line Villers Plouich-Beaucamp-Trescault, whence a series of spurs descend gradually in a north-easterly direction towards Ribemont, Marcoing and the Scheldt Canal—all destined to witness bitter fighting in the Cambrai battle five months later.

The Gouzeaucourt-Havrincourt Wood sector was now exceedingly quiet. This, to an extent, was of great advantage to the Battalion, since nearly 40 per cent. of its strength at the moment consisted of drafts newly arrived who had not yet been under fire. It was possible, therefore, for the new material to become properly assimilated into the Battalion before further casualties created deficiencies in the ranks.

On the night 16th/17th July the 173rd Brigade took over from the 174th Brigade the right of the Divisional front from the neighbourhood of Villers Plouich to Queens Lane, a communication trench 500 yards west of the Beaucamp-Ribemont Road.

The 2/4th Battalion remained in Brigade reserve for a few days, Battalion Headquarters and A Company being in huts in Dessart Wood, C and D Companies in Gouzeaucourt Wood, and B Company attached to the 2/1st Battalion in a support trench south of Beaucamp. Daily working parties were supplied by the Battalion for trench repair and improvement work, but very little incident worthy of record occurred. The principal excitement was provided by the intelligence that a German spy disguised as an officer of the R.F.A. was in hiding in one of the numerous woods with which the countryside is dotted, but the Battalion was not successful in tracking him down.

The only portion of the line in which there was any degree of activity was in front of the left of the Brigade sector, where an isolated spinney in the middle of No Man's Land—here some 600 to 700 yards wide—was always a target for the enemy's artillery. This spinney, known as Boar Copse, was occupied by the Battalion in the line as an advanced post, and it was decided to wire round the edge of the Copse and connect it to our front line by a communication trench. The duty of executing the work fell to the 2/4th Londons, and a working party of 4 officers and 180 N.C.O.'s and men was supplied under Capt. A. G. Croll on the night 20th/21st July. As ill luck would have it, the Germans selected this same evening to endeavour to raid the outpost line occupied by the 2/9th Londons farther to the left. The raid was carried out under an intense barrage, but our artillery answered promptly to the call made on it and the raiders were beaten off, leaving a prisoner in our hands. Unfortunately the raid caused a certain amount of shelling on the Boar Copse front resulting in a few casualties, among whom was Capt. Croll. This was exceedingly bad luck and a loss to the Battalion. Croll had done excellent work since the arrival in France of the 2/4th Battalion and had just received his company. His wound, though not dangerous, was sufficiently severe to keep him in England for almost a year. His company was taken over by Capt. C. A. Clarke.

The following night the Battalion relieved the 2/3rd Battalion in the right subsector on a front of about 1500 yards, all the companies being in line and each providing its own supports.

The trenches were well sited and well dug, being very deep and heavily traversed. Throughout this area the communication trenches were of exceptional length, Lincoln Lane in particular, which ran from Gouzeaucourt Wood to Beaucamp, being over two miles long.

Very little incident occurred during this tour of duty. No Man's Land was patrolled nightly and appeared to belong to us as no enemy were encountered.

On the evening of the 30th July the Battalion was relieved by the 11th Royal Scots and marched to the light railway at Dessart Wood, whence it entrained to Neuville-Borjonval, camping there for the night.

The following day the Battalion moved by bus from Neuville to Izel-les-Hameau, in the Arras area, the transport under Major Nunneley moving by train from Bapaume to Saulty and then by march route to Hameau.

The whole Division was now put through a regular course of re-equipment and training in preparation for the heavy work it was to be called upon to do in the offensive at Ypres. In this training particular attention was paid to musketry, the necessity for this having been clearly demonstrated in all recent actions, in which troops had shown a tendency to use bombs or rifle grenades to the exclusion of their rifles.

During this period drafts of officers were received as follows:

6th July—2/Lieut. F. A. Carlisle.

20th July—Lieut. F. S. Marsh (7th Londons); 2/Lieuts. R. Michell (6th Londons); and H. N. Bundle, W. F. Vines, E. R. Seabury and C. C. H. Clifford (13th Londons).

25th July—Lieut. D. C. Cooke; 2/Lieuts. F. B. Burd and A. J. Angel (13th Londons).

1st August—2/Lieuts. J. McDonald and F. W. Walker; 2/Lieut. C. S. Pike (7th Londons).

9th August—2/Lieut. A. S. Cook (7th Londons).

The Battalion changed its quarters on the 13th August, leaving Izel for Denier, where it proceeded with its training. Not all the time was devoted to work, but some excellent sports meetings were held—and at the Brigade Sports on the 20th the Battalion was successful in winning the Cup presented by Brig.-Gen. B. C. Freyberg, V.C., D.S.O. The importance of achievements of this nature cannot be over-rated. The longer the War continued the more obvious it became that if "rest" periods were to do any good to the men at all they must be periods of mental as well as physical rest, and games of all sorts provide the required relaxation more than anything else. On coming out of the trenches, weary, muddy, possibly hungry, and almost certainly wet through, the men's first moments of freedom were spent in a game of football.

This was an aspect of the mentality of the British soldier which we believe was never fathomed by the French villagers. Their hospitality and devotion to "les braves Tommys" was unfailing and genuine; but we feel there was a lingering notion among our kind hosts that this remarkable devotion to football was really a confirmation of the time-honoured tradition that the English are all at least a little mad.

Reinforcements of N.C.O.'s and men were also being fed into the Battalion during this period, and by the end of August the strength in N.C.O.'s and men had increased by about 240.

CHAPTER XVI
THE THIRD BATTLE OF YPRES

I. *The 1/4th Battalion on the Menin Road*

By the middle of May 1917 the British efforts on the Arras front had achieved the success which had been aimed at; and the offensive having been sufficiently prolonged to assist the French in their operations on the Chemin des Dames, the Commander-in-Chief was free to turn his attention to the northern area of the British lines.

The first phase of the operation was opened on the 7th June, when a brilliant attack by the Second Army (Plumer) carried the British line forward over the Messines and Wytschaete Ridges, from which the Germans had dominated our positions since October 1914. This operation, which was one of the most completely successful of the whole War, resulted by the 14th June in the advancement of practically the whole Second Army front from the River Warnave to Klein Zillebeeke.

One by one the points of vantage held by the enemy since the beginning of siege warfare were being wrested from his grasp. In succession the Thiepval Ridge, the Bucquoy Ridge, the Vimy Ridge and finally the Messines-Wytschaete Ridge had fallen into our hands, and there remained of this long series of heights only the series of ridges which from Zillebeeke to Passchendaele dominate Ypres on the east and north sides. It was towards these hills that the British offensive efforts were now directed.

The opening day of the offensive had originally been fixed for the 25th July 1917, but owing to the intensity of our bombardment the enemy in anticipation of attack had withdrawn his guns, and the attack was therefore postponed in order that the British guns might be correspondingly advanced. Combined with the systematic bombardment of the enemy's trenches, strong points and communications, a definite air offensive which ensured our local supremacy in this respect, and also severe gas shelling, were undertaken.

The front of attack extended for some fifteen miles from Deulemont on the right to Boesinghe on the Yser Canal—the main attack being entrusted to the Fifth Army (Gough) on a front of about seven miles from the Zillebeeke-Zandvoorde Road to Boesinghe. The Second Army on the right was to make only a limited advance with the chief objects of widening the front of attack and distributing the enemy's resistance. At the same time the

French on the extreme left (or north) would co-operate in the marshes of the Yser.

The offensive was finally launched on the 31st July 1917. The weather, which for a fortnight previously had been fine and dry and had seemed to predict success, broke on the day of the battle, and a merciless rain which changed the whole area of operations to a sea of mud fell without cessation for several days. The Corps in line on the 31st July were from left to right the XIV (Cavan), the XVIII (Maxse), the XIX (Watts), the II (Jacob) and the X (Morland). On the whole the day was one of marked success, the deepest advance being made in the northern sector of the attack. From Westhoek to St Julien the second German line was carried, while north of the latter village the assaulting troops passed the second line and gained the line of the Steenbeek as far as the junction with the French, whose attack had also met with complete success. South of Westhoek the enemy's resistance had been more stubborn, and his positions in Inverness Copse and Glencorse Wood which were strongly held by machine-gun posts proved an impassable obstacle. In this region, however, the German first line was carried, and our troops managed to maintain themselves far enough forward on the Westhoek Ridge to deny the enemy observation over the Ypres plain; the position gained running almost due south from Westhoek east of the line Clapham Junction—Stirling Castle—Bodmin Copse, and thence to Shrewsbury Forest, south of which the German second line was occupied as far as the Ypres-Comines Canal. South of the Canal also the Second Army achieved considerable success.

The rain, which began to fall in the afternoon, had a most disastrous effect on the British plan of attack. Movement over the shell-torn ground, which was transformed into a series of bogs, rapidly became impossible apart from a few well-defined tracks, and these naturally became marks for the enemy's guns. The labour of moving forward guns, relieving troops and completing the forward dumps and other preparations for the next bound was increased tenfold. The inevitable delay which ensued was of the greatest service to the enemy, who thereby gained a valuable respite in which he was able to bring up reinforcements.

The fighting of the next few days was, therefore, local in character and consisted in clearing up the situation and improving the British positions at various points in the line, in the course of which operations the capture of Westhoek was completed. Numerous counter-attacks by the enemy were successfully resisted, and the line gained on the 31st July was substantially held.

The 56th Division moved from the Third Army area on the 24th July to the St Omer area. The 1/4th Londons entrained at Petit Houvin for St Omer and marched to billets at Houlle, in the Eperlecques area, some five miles north-west of St Omer. The Division was now attached to the V Corps. Its training was continued during the opening phase of the battle, after which the Division moved on the 6th August to the II Corps area, the Battalion occupying billets at Steenvoorde, where the routine was resumed. On the 8th Major-Gen. D. Smith, C.B. (who had commanded the Division since 24th July, when Gen. Hull fell sick), left to command the 20th Division and, two days later, command was assumed by Major-Gen. F. A. Dudgeon, C.B.

The same day a warning order was received that the Division would shortly move into the line to take part in the second phase of the battle, which was to be renewed as soon as weather conditions should permit.

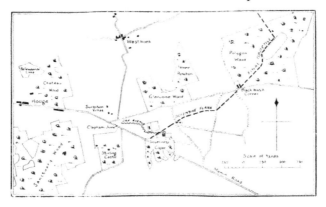

THE THIRD BATTLE OF YPRES, 1917 (1/4TH BATTALION)

On the night of the 12th/13th August the Division moved forward into the line opposite Glencorse Wood, which had been the centre of the enemy's resistance on the first day of the battle, and took over from portions of the 18th and 25th Divisions a sector between the Menin Road at Clapham Junction and the cross-roads at Westhoek, the 169th Brigade occupying the right of this front with the 167th Brigade on its left. The 53rd Brigade of the 18th Division remained in line on the right of the 169th Brigade, between Clapham Junction and Green Jacket Road, and came under the orders of Gen. Dudgeon.

On the morning of the 12th the 168th Brigade in Divisional reserve embussed at Steenvoorde for Canal Reserve Camp, Dickebusch.

The chain of machine-gun posts still held by the enemy in Inverness Copse, Glencorse Wood and Nonne Boschen was of immense importance to the Germans at this juncture; as they screened the long Spur which, running north-east from the Menin Road Ridge between the Polderhoek-Gheluvelt Ridge and the Zonnebeeke Road, formed an important *point d'appui* in the Langemarck-Gheluvelt line of defence. Their capture by the British would, therefore, drive such a wedge towards the enemy third line as to cause a serious menace to his communications along the Menin and Zonnebeeke Roads. No one was more keenly alive to the essential value of this position than the Germans, who spared no efforts to frustrate attempts to launch a further attack in this area. The continual severity of his shell and machine-gun fire against our outpost line served his purpose well, as it not only inflicted severe loss on the trench garrisons of the divisions in the line and seriously impeded the task of advancing ammunition and other stores incidental to an attack—a task already difficult enough by reason of the wet state of the ground—but also precluded efficient reconnaissance of the ground over which the attack was to be launched.

The 56th Division was the extreme right of the attack. The advance allotted to it was to be carried out by the 167th and 169th Brigades, whose objective was a line beyond the third German line of defence, and which may be roughly described as running north and south through Polygon Wood. The southernmost point of this advance was to be Black Watch Corner, and from this point it would be necessary to connect the southern extremity of the final objective with the line on the Division's right, on which no advance would be attempted. This meant the formation of a defensive flank facing nearly south.

This vital work of forming the flank was originally entrusted to the 53rd Brigade, and the importance of their rôle will be readily grasped, since on the manner in which it was carried out would hang in large measure the fortunes of the 169th and 167th and successive Brigades on the left, for the German machine-guns in Inverness Copse, if not silenced, would be free to enfilade the whole advance. The 53rd Brigade which had been in the line since the opening of the battle on the 31st July was, however, now exhausted, and so seriously reduced in strength by the tireless activity of the German machine-gunners that it was not in a condition to renew the offensive. Its task was therefore handed over to the 1/4th Londons, on whom devolved the difficult operation above described of covering the right flank of the whole attack. The only troops of the 53rd Brigade who would be actively employed would be a detachment of the 7th Bedfords, who were made responsible for capturing the machine-gun nests which, from the north-west corner of Inverness Copse, dominated the whole situation.

The 1/4th Londons were detailed for this attack on the morning of the 14th August, and it is important in view of what subsequently occurred to bear this date in mind. It must also be remembered that at this time the Battalion was some seven miles from the field of battle and that no officer, N.C.O. or man belonging to it had ever set eyes on the ground over which the battle was to be fought.

During the morning Lieut.-Col. Campbell, the Adjutant and the four company officers went forward to reconnoitre the forward area, visiting in turn 169th Brigade Headquarters at Dormy House, and Headquarters of the Battalion in line of the 53rd Brigade at Stirling Castle. It had been intended also to reconnoitre the ground over which the advance was to be made, but such was the intensity of the enemy's artillery and machine-gun fire that this was impossible, and the company commanders were compelled to return to their companies in ignorance of what lay before them. Later in the day Lieut.-Col. Campbell was ordered to report to 53rd Brigade Headquarters, but was unluckily hit on his way back, near Zillebeeke Lake. Although badly hit he made his way back to the Battalion, but being unable to carry on was succeeded in the command by Major A. F. Marchment, M.C. (1/1st Londons).

At seven that night the Battalion moved forward from Dickebusch to Château Segard, the move being completed by 11 p.m. Shortly after dawn on the 15th the forward move was continued to Railway Dugouts, in the cutting between Shrapnel Corner and Zillebeeke Lake, and here the Battalion remained during the day.

The 15th August was occupied in issuing battle equipment and rations to the companies, while Lieut.-Col. Marchment took the opportunity of conducting a reconnaissance of the forward area and communications, and of issuing his operation orders. These were explained to company commanders as adequately as time permitted, but it must be borne in mind that when the Battalion moved forward to the assault the following morning no company or platoon officer had been able to see the ground over which he was to lead his men. At 6.30 p.m. the 1/4th Londons left Railway Dugouts in battle order for the assembly area at Clapham Junction with guides supplied from the 53rd Brigade. A great deal of heavy shelling, in which four men of B Company were hit, was experienced during the advance, and in breasting a ridge near Sanctuary Wood the Battalion had to pass through a barrage put down by the Germans. Aided by the excellent discipline of the troops, however, company commanders were able to split up their companies within a few seconds, and no loss was sustained. By ten o'clock the Battalion was concentrated with A, B and C Companies in the tunnel under the Menin Road, and D Company in the trench south of the road. Battalion Headquarters and part of C Company were in the trench on the north side of the tunnel. There was no defined line of trenches in this area, the front being held by isolated shell hole posts, and the assembly was to be made on tape lines laid down under staff arrangements. The lack of shelter thus made it necessary to keep the Battalion under such cover as was obtainable till the last possible moment. During the evening an officer of each company reconnoitred the route from the concentration area to the tape lines, assistance being rendered by the 6th Royal Berkshires, and No Man's Land in front of the line of assembly was patrolled until shortly before zero hour.

The intention was to advance in a practically due east direction, while at stated points in the line of advance platoons would halt one by one, each establishing itself in a strong point, until finally, when the last platoon reached its halting point, the whole Battalion would be deployed in a line of outposts, all of which would turn to their right and face south. This advance, being made on a front of two companies, would result in a double line of posts of which the left flank would rest on Black Watch Corner in touch with the 169th Brigade, while the right flank would join hands with the 7th Bedfords in the corner of Inverness Copse.

At 3.15 a.m. on the 16th August companies began to form up on the tape lines, the assembly being completed by 4.20 a.m., when the troops were lying down in the open under a continuous and fairly heavy shell fire and a galling machine-gun fire from the direction of Inverness Copse. About 22 casualties occurred under this fire before zero hour at 5.45 a.m. The order of battle was as follows: A. Company (Spiers) on the right and B Company (Stanbridge) on the left in front; with D Company (H. N. Williams) on the right and C Company (Rees) on the left in support.

The attack was to be delivered along the whole battle front at 5.45 a.m. under cover of a creeping barrage, supported by machine-gun barrage and heavy gun fire on the enemy back areas. At zero hour the British barrage came down, well distributed and of terrific intensity. It was hoped that the danger points in Inverness Copse would be put out of action by our artillery, so that the task of the 7th Bedfords would be an easy one, but calculations in this respect were soon found to have been mistaken. The leading companies of the 1/4th Londons got away from the mark at zero, in good order and well up to the barrage, but almost immediately came under a hail of lead from Inverness Copse. The attack of the 7th Bedfords, of such vital importance to the success of the whole operation, had failed. The artillery fire had not produced the expected effect on the enormously strong enemy posts over which the barrage had passed harmlessly, and the 7th Bedfords were repulsed with loss, thereby leaving the 1/4th Londons completely exposed to the full force of the enemy's nest of machine-guns on their right flank.

Within a few minutes 5 officers and 40 N.C.O.'s and men of A and B Companies were casualties, but the survivors pushed forward steadily, though a certain amount of delay caused by the gaps so suddenly torn in their ranks was inevitable. The gallantry displayed by all ranks under this devastating machine-gun fire, to which was added enemy shell fire of great intensity, was unsurpassed, but under such a storm of bullets at close range nothing could live, and the Battalion was brought to a standstill about 200 yards from starting-point, in an old German trench which skirted a ruined farmhouse about midway between Inverness Copse and Glencorse Wood.

A party of some 60 men of all companies managed to gain shelter in Jap Avenue. Here they were organised by 2/Lieut. H. E. Jackman, under whom a strong post was consolidated and an attempt made to push forward along the trench. This proved unsuccessful owing to the continued intensity of the enemy machine-gun fire and the accuracy of his sniping. Further attempts by other companies to advance were also fruitless, and the Battalion was forced to content itself with hanging on to these small gains, from which at intervals it was able to engage with Lewis gun and rifle fire small bodies of the enemy in the open near the east end of Glencorse Wood.

An attempt was made to re-establish the situation by an attack, for which the 53rd Brigade was called upon, through Inverness Copse from south to north, but so terribly reduced in numbers were its battalions that Brigade reserve was limited to two weak platoons and further action was found to be for the moment impossible.

In the centre the leading waves of the 169th, after some resistance in Glencorse Wood which they overcame, succeeded in penetrating Polygon Wood, where they probably gained their objective. The second waves on approaching the Wood were, however, met with intense fire from front and flanks, and a few minutes later a heavy counter-attack developed which drove back the assaulting troops to the middle of Glencorse Wood. A further counter-attack in the evening forced the Brigade back to its assembly line.

On the left the 167th Brigade met with but little greater success. The advance was steadily conducted as far as a line level with the eastern edge of Nonne Boschen, where trouble was first encountered by a sea of mud— an extensive bog caused by the springs in the source of the Hanebeek— which forced the attacking battalions to edge away to their left and thus lose touch with the 169th Brigade on their right. In this position they came under heavy machine-gun fire, and the British barrage having got far ahead, were forced to fall back. By 9 a.m. this Brigade also was back in its assembly area.

Early in the afternoon enemy artillery fire over the 1/4th Battalion's front became very heavy, and retaliatory fire was directed by our artillery into Inverness Copse. No infantry action developed, and during the night the Battalion was relieved by the 12th Middlesex and withdrew, in support, to the tunnel under Crab Crawl Trench in the old British system south of Sanctuary Wood.

Here the 1/4th Londons remained during the whole of the 17th August, which passed uneventfully, and in the evening was relieved by the 8th K.R.R.C. of the 14th Division, which took over the 56th Division front. On relief, the Battalion withdrew to Mic Mac Camp, Ouderdom.

Reviewing the Battalion's work on the 16th August it must be at once admitted that it, and indeed the whole Division, failed completely to perform its allotted task. That all ranks did all that was possible to achieve it is reflected in the length of the casualty list, and it is perhaps due to those who fell to comment briefly on what appear to be the causes of failure.

In the first place the operation itself was far from easy. The sea of mud and ooze to which the line of advance had been reduced must in any case have rendered the recognition by platoon commanders of the spots at which they were in turn to halt and form their post a matter of some difficulty. But the circumstances in which the Battalion became responsible for the attack effectually precluded it from the preparations for the operation which the difficulty of the task warranted. The change of command was a further stroke of bad luck. Lieut.-Col. Marchment was already known to the Battalion, but the disadvantages under which he laboured in assuming command on the eve of battle are obvious. The issue of orders was inevitably delayed as Lieut.-Col. Campbell's reconnaissance had to be repeated by Lieut.-Col. Marchment on the morning of the 15th, and it was not till the evening of that day that the scheme could be explained to companies, and then only by officers, who themselves had not seen the ground or even the assembly position. In fact the operations of reconnaissance, issue of orders and assembly of the Battalion had all to be disposed of in twenty-two hours. In addition to these preliminary difficulties the progress of the operation itself revealed further circumstances, to which also a share of the responsibility for failure may be attributed.

The extraordinary strength of the German machine-gun posts was such that the most intense barrage which the excellent Corps and Divisional artillery was capable of producing passed harmlessly over them, and only a direct hit was sufficient to disturb the occupants.

The very serious casualties at the outset of the attack—half an hour after zero, three company commanders were the only officers left standing—

produced inevitably a certain degree of disorganisation, though the fact that despite these heavy losses the Battalion was able to establish and maintain itself throughout the day until relief, speaks wonders for the discipline of the troops and the efficiency and initiative of the N.C.O.'s. Further causes of failure lay in the previous exhaustion of the men owing to the bad state of the ground, which also made extremely difficult the preparation beforehand of forward supply dumps, and the reinforcement of the attacking troops during the battle.

Defeat is not always inglorious, and we feel that the 16th August may fairly be written down as a day on which the 1/4th Londons failed without loss of reputation in any single particular.

The casualties sustained were as follows:

> In officers—Lieut.-Col. H. Campbell, D.S.O., wounded; Lieuts. C. A. Speyer, L. B. J. Elliott, L. W. Wreford and A. G. Davis, killed; Capt. H. W. Spiers, Lieuts. A. S. Ford and E. G. Dew, and 2/Lieuts. L. W. Archer, H. T, Hannay, N. Nunns and H. E. Jackman, wounded; and in N.C.O.'s and men 182 killed and wounded.

2/Lieut. H. E. Jackman was awarded the M.C. for his excellent work and devotion to duty this day.

Throughout the Division casualties were heavy and 6 commanding officers and nearly 4000 all ranks fell on this unfortunate day.

On the remainder of the battle front varying success was obtained. In the north a considerable advance was made and the German third line was broken on a wide front. The French attack on the extreme left was crowned with complete success. In the southern area, however, the enemy resistance was everywhere more stubborn, and south of St Julien the line remained unchanged as a result of the day's fighting. The Division being concentrated in the Ouderdom area remained there training and reorganising for several days.

On the 22nd August its move to the Eperlecques area began, and on the 24th the 1/4th Londons entrained at Reninghelst siding for Watten, where it detrained and marched to Houlle.

Inverness Copse

The 56th Division had been so badly handled on the 16th August that its return to the battle area without considerable reinforcement was out of the question and it was, therefore, moved from the Ypres area to Bapaume. The Battalion accordingly entrained at Arques in the early hours of the 30th August and arrived in huts in the Beaulencourt area at 8 p.m. the same day.

CHAPTER XVII
THE THIRD BATTLE OF YPRES

II. *The 2/4th Battalion on the Northern Ridges*

After the restricted success of the 16th August, the renewal of operations on a large scale was inevitably postponed for some time through the continuance of adverse weather conditions; though in the north minor operations had the effect of widening and deepening the breach in the German defences in the neighbourhood of St Julien, combined with the capture of a good many prisoners. These local advances carried the British positions forward east of the St Julien-Poelcapelle Road and gave them a firm footing in the Gheluvelt-Langemarck line on both sides of the Ypres-Staden Railway.

The withdrawal of some of the divisions which had been engaged in the battle since the end of July being now necessary, the 58th Division was among the fresh divisions which were sent north to take part in the next large attack.

On the 24th August the 2/4th Londons marched from Izel-les-Hameau to Aubigny entraining for Hopoutre (Poperinghe), whence it marched to quarters in Dirty Bucket Camp, one of a series of camps near Vlamertinghe. The Division now became attached to the XVIII Corps (Maxse). The Battalion continued its training in the new area, paying a good deal of attention to intensive digging and musketry, and during the days spent in Dirty Bucket the company commanders and seconds in command attended a course of instruction at the XVIII Corps School at Volckeringhove.

On the night of the 28th/29th August the 58th Division entered the trenches, taking over with the 174th and 175th Brigades, the sector occupied by the 48th Division east of St Julien, the frontage extending from the Hanebeek on the right to the vicinity of Keerselare on the left. The sector was lightly held with one battalion of each brigade in the outpost line, one battalion on the Canal Bank and two in camps west of the Yser Canal.

The 173rd Brigade remained in Divisional reserve and continued training. The 2/4th Londons changed station on the last day of the month, moving to Browne Camp, about four miles north-east of Poperinghe. Here a further week's training was obtained, after which the whole of B Company spent four days at the Fifth Army Musketry Camp near St Omer. Nothing worthy of record occurred during this period except on the 1st September, when the transport lines were heavily shelled causing casualties to 26 N.C.O.'s and men, of whom 1 died of wounds, and to 13 horses, 8 being killed.

Reinforcements at this period included 2/Lieut. A. C. Knight (4th Londons) and 2/Lieut. W. D. Warren (19th Londons), and about 110 N.C.O.'s and men.

On the 9th September the 2/4th Londons moved forward to Reigersburg Camp, between Brielen and the Canal, and on the 11th-13th August the 173rd Brigade took over the whole Divisional sector.

A warning order had now been issued as to the next attack which in view of the markedly improved conditions of weather had been arranged for the 20th September. The front of attack was more extended than on the 16th August, the southern limit being the Ypres-Comines Canal near Hollebeke, and the Ypres-Staden Railway north of Langemarck marking the northern extremity.

The success which had attended the enemy's resistance to our efforts to advance in the Menin Road region had pointed to the necessity of modifying the methods of attack. The successes obtained by the British Army on the Somme, at Arras and at Messines, had caused the Germans to alter their mode of defence, and instead of a strongly held trench line they now presented to our attacks a system of concreted machine-gun posts ("pillboxes" "or Mebus") disposed in great depth in front of their main line of resistance. This system supplied their defence with the elasticity which had hitherto been lacking, and the pillboxes, being sited with remarkable skill to develop the employment of enfilade fire to the fullest extent, proved a very serious obstacle to British assaulting columns, which frequently suffered severe casualties at their hands after making a deep advance into the enemy defensive system. The pillboxes were, moreover, of such enormously strong construction that nothing short of a direct hit by a heavy shell could put them out of action. The effect of our severe artillery preparation for attacks was therefore nullified, and the occupants of the pillboxes could only be ejected as a rule by hand-to-hand fighting with bombs.

This new feature in the fighting called for prompt measures on the part of the British, and henceforward no attempt was made as a rule to penetrate the enemy's pillbox system as long as any risk existed of leaving any of these hornets' nests undisposed of in rear of the advancing troops. In other words, the attacks were arranged with objectives much more limited than formerly, while the artillery paid more attention to the pillboxes, the ultimate capture of which formed the task of special units detailed for the purpose.

The assault arranged for the 20th September was prepared on these revised lines, and all ranks were impressed beforehand with the importance, not only of locating enemy strong points quickly and rushing them before their occupants had recovered from the British barrage, but also of methodical "mopping-up" and consolidation of all ground gained.

From the 9th September onwards the work of preparation for the impending offensive was pushed forward with all possible speed, the 2/4th Londons bearing a heavy share of these necessary duties. For four of the five nights spent at Reigersburg Camp a working party of the strength of two companies was engaged in completing the advanced cable line trench, while on the last night, the 13th, the whole Battalion less B Company (still at the Musketry Camp) was detailed for carrying various sorts of R.E. material forward to advanced dumps in readiness for consolidation of the position it was hoped to gain.

On the 14th the 2/4th Londons moved to a fresh position on the east side of the Yser Canal, and for four nights following, the whole Battalion was engaged in the desperate task of laying a duckboard track of double width in front of St Julien, as far forward as possible in the direction of the enemy positions, with the object of providing a means of communication in the forward area, and of reinforcing or relieving the advanced troops after the assault should have been delivered.

This week of continual working parties was most exhausting to all concerned. The distance to be covered each night to and from the scene of the work was about three and a half miles in each direction, and the labour of the march was increased tenfold by the shocking condition of the ground, which was still waterlogged, and, away from the defined tracks, nothing but a series of lakes formed by shell craters full of water. Heavy as the cable line duties were found, the laying of the duckboard track during the latter half of the week proved still more onerous. Not only had the troops to march to St Julien from the Canal Bank, but the duckboards which were drawn from a dump at Alberta Farm had to be carried on the men's shoulders for some five hundred yards to the starting-point of the track. Progress was slow through the heavy going and the continual delays caused by German Véry lights. Although some two hundred and forty yards were laid during the four nights' work, and the track was carried forty yards beyond our most advanced positions, the task was never completed. The work was obviously fraught with considerable risk of serious casualties owing to the large numbers of men employed, and in the circumstances the losses incurred during the week were light; 11 men being hit on the 11th, while on the 15th 2/Lieut. Carlisle was killed and 2/Lieut. Pike wounded, with 2 men killed and 5 wounded.

On the night of the 18th the 2/4th Londons relieved the 2/3rd Londons in the line, which was still held by isolated posts, and the following evening assembly for the attack began at about 9 p.m.

The 58th Division front of attack was entirely north of the Hanebeek, a small stream which runs almost due east from St Julien, the attack south of the stream being undertaken by the 164th Brigade of the 55th Division. The 58th Divisional front was taken up by the 173rd Brigade on the right with the 174th on its left, the assaulting columns of the 173rd Brigade consisting of four companies, each 100 strong, of the 2/4th Londons. The 2/3rd Londons were in reserve to make a dummy attack, with one company on the waterlogged portions of the front over which no advance was possible.

The 2/4th Londons' assembly position which was defined by tape lines laid down by the adjutant, Capt. A. Grover, was on the line Janet Farm-Springfield, and covered a front of some 800 yards. Almost in the centre of this front and some 400 yards from starting-point, lay a strongly fortified area around Winnipeg cross-roads. To the right of the cross-roads the whole area as far as the Hanebeek was waterlogged and impassable, while to the left a series of enemy strong points, notably at the Cemetery and Spot Farm seemed likely to cause a good deal of trouble to the attackers. The objective of the 2/4th Londons lay on an undefined line running roughly north and south about 100 yards beyond Winnipeg cross-roads. This marked the limit of the 173rd Brigade's task, though the objective of the day lay about 500 yards further east, its principal feature being a machine-gun nest in the Schuler Galleries in the vicinity of the Hanebeek. The further advance to this final objective was entrusted to the 164th and 174th Brigades, who by a converging movement were to "squeeze out" the 2/4th Londons leaving them in occupation of what would become a line of supporting posts at the end of the day.

Before the assembly a preliminary reconnaissance of the terrain was carried out by the company commanders, and in connection with this Capt. Hetley writes:

> I think all were impressed by the wonderful sight at Admirals Road. This unsavoury road ran parallel to the front about 1500 yards or more to the rear of St Julien and when passing over it on the duckboard track, there could be seen guns in such large quantities that there seemed to be very little greater interval than 150-200 yards between them in any direction—a really wonderful contrast to April 1915, when the Lahore Division was on exactly the same spot.

On the evening of the 19th September Brigade Headquarters were established at Cheddar Villa, while the 2/4th Londons' Battle Headquarters opened in St Julien. The assembly was conducted by Capt. Grover and Lieut. Seys (Intelligence Officer) who were solely responsible for an operation which proved exceedingly difficult owing to the still heavy state of the ground. So bad was the mud that men constantly sank to their knees, and in some cases touch could only be maintained by tying the men of each section together with tapes. In spite of these difficulties the 400 men were in position by 3 a.m. on the 20th without a hitch, and with practically no casualties, although the most advanced platoons were within 150 yards of the enemy positions. The assembly completed, the 2/3rd Londons who were holding the line withdrew a short distance to the rear.

The assault was delivered at 5.40 a.m. under cover of an intense creeping barrage which proved to be excellent, and companies moved off in good order in the half light close up to the barrage. The companies were disposed as follows: on the right A Company (S. Davis) with two platoons and Headquarters of D Company (Stark) attached; in the centre B Company (Hetley); and on the left C Company (Hewlett) with two platoons of D Company attached.

The principal resistance, as had been anticipated, was encountered in the neighbourhood of Winnipeg cross-roads, and at a pillbox which lay between them and the cemetery. This was most gallantly captured single-handed by Pte. Bolton, A Company, who bayonetted three of the occupants and captured the remainder consisting of an officer and three men. A slight check at the cross-roads produced a further small bag of prisoners, sixteen in number, of whom one was an officer. On the left the chief opposition was encountered at a pillbox some 300 yards east of Springfield which was holding up the advance of C Company and of the 174th Brigade on the left. 2/Lieut. F. W. Walker, quickly grasping the situation, outflanked the position with six men, and succeeded in rushing it, capturing two machine-guns and twenty men who were sent back under escort, Walker and the rest of his party at once pushing on to the objective where touch was gained with the 174th Brigade. Within half an hour the 2/4th Londons were established on their objective, the consolidation of which was promptly put in hand, while the flank brigades after a pause of half an hour pressed forward to their final objectives in accordance with the plan of attack.

The complete success of this operation was undoubtedly due to the careful provision which had been made in advance for the capture of strong points by specially detailed units who thus ensured the efficient "mopping-up" of all ground captured, while enabling the remainder of the assaulting column to keep well up to the barrage.

Owing to the known strength of Schuler Farm in the final objective, special arrangements had been made for the attack of this point, in conjunction with the 164th Brigade, by a strong platoon of D Company 2/4th Londons with which two tanks were to co-operate in an outflanking movement from the north. The earliest reports from this region indicated that the attack had been successful, but subsequent information made it clear that the first attack failed, partly owing to the non-arrival of the tanks which stuck fast in the mud, and partly owing to unexpected resistance met with at a machine-gun post some 150 yards in advance of the farm. The capture of this post, which produced 16 prisoners and 2 guns, cost the lives of 2/Lieut. Warren and the whole platoon except Sergt. Watson and 6 men. The delay caused, moreover, was serious, and by the time the survivors of the platoon were able to continue their advance, the barrage had passed beyond Schuler Farm. Sergt. Watson, being of opinion that the strength of his party was insufficient to justify an attack on the main position, sent back his prisoners and established himself with the captured machine-guns at a point about 250 yards south-east of Winnipeg cross-roads.

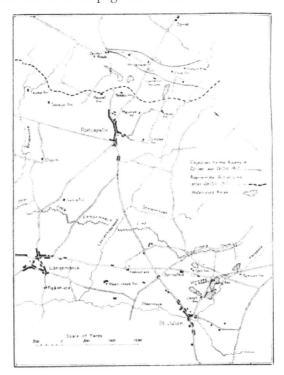

THE THIRD BATTLE OF YPRES, 1917 (2/4TH BATTALION)

The shell fire of the enemy during the advance and subsequent to the Battalion reaching its objective had been severe, and by this time not more than 100 rifles of the 2/4th Londons remained effective. Arrangements were therefore made to stiffen its line with one company of the 2/3rd Londons. A further attack on Schuler Farm, to be undertaken by the 2/3rd Londons, was organised for daybreak on the 21st.

At about three o'clock in the afternoon the enemy was observed to be advancing in fours against the brigade on our right, and the artillery was immediately called into action. In spite of heavy losses, however, the enemy continued to advance with praiseworthy courage until they deployed, when their morale appeared to break and their ranks rapidly melted under our shell fire.

During the remainder of the day a good deal of annoyance was caused by the continued sniping from Schuler Farm, of which the Germans remained in possession, but no further counter-attack developed on our front, and night fell with the 2/4th Londons' position intact. The casualties already suffered had been heavy, and three company commanders, Hewlett, Stark and Davis, had unluckily been hit, though the last was able to remain with his company until after relief the following evening, when having been wounded a second time he was evacuated.

The attack of the platoon of the 2/3rd Londons under 2/Lieut. Middlemiss on the 21st was postponed for further reconnaissance, in the course of which Middlemiss observed the garrison of Schuler Farm surrender to men of the 164th Brigade. Believing the situation to be clear he proceeded along the road, but was hit by fire from a post by the Hanebeek near that established by Sergt. Watson. Middlemiss' report, which was the first information obtained of the fall of Schuler Farm, caused the alteration of his platoon's objective to the pillbox from which he had been hit, but in the evening this was found to have been evacuated by its garrison, so that the whole position was now in our hands.

During the evening of the 21st violent counter-attacks under cover of intense bombardments were delivered against the 164th and 174th Brigade sectors, but these were dispersed, and the 2/4th Londons did not come into action though their newly-dug trenches were almost obliterated by the German shell fire and many more casualties occurred.

At 9 p.m. on the 21st, the 2/4th Londons handed over their position, intact at all points, to the 2/9th Londons, and withdrew across the Yser Canal to Dambre Camp, where they remained training and reorganising for some days.

This was the most completely successful operation in which the 2/4th Battalion had hitherto taken part, and indeed all along the line of the Fifth Army attack the new methods which have been described met with marked success.

The outstanding achievements of the day were those of 2/Lieut. Walker, Sergt. Watson and Pte. Bolton, of which some description has already been given, but reference should also be made to the excellent work of Capt. S. Davis, whose clear grasp of situations and the accurate and complete information with which he kept Headquarters constantly supplied, were of great value; of Pte. Austin, runner of A Company, who passed backwards and forwards several times with important messages through intense barrages; of Pte. Bull, the only surviving stretcher-bearer of A Company, who displayed the greatest coolness and devotion in tending wounded men under heavy fire; and Lieut. Altounyan, the medical officer, whose services were of the utmost value and carried out under exceedingly trying conditions.

Mention should also be made of Pte. Anthony of the Battalion Signallers who from an advanced point in the line established visual communication with Brigade Headquarters, his station subsequently proving of great value to the supporting artillery.

On the evening of the 19th Brig.-Gen. Freyberg, V.C., D.S.O., was seriously hit on his way to Battle Headquarters at Cheddar Villa; but he insisted on remaining at duty, and directed operations from his stretcher, though wounded in ten places, until after news of the complete capture of the objective was received the next day, when his removal was insisted upon by the A.D.M.S. who came forward to fetch him. Command of the Brigade was taken temporarily by Lieut.-Col. Dann, D.S.O.

The following decorations were awarded after this action: 2/Lieut. F. W. Walker, the D.S.O.; Capts. A. Grover and S. Davis, and Lieut. E. H. R. Altounyan, the M.C.; Sergt. Watson, Ptes. Bolton, Austin, Anthony and Bull, the D.C.M.; and Sergts. H. O. Wilderspin and F. W. Yandle, Ptes. J. W. Ling and A. Westcott, the M.M.

The casualties sustained during the action included: 2/Lieuts. H. N. Bundle, E. R. Seabury and W. D. Warren, killed; 2/Lieut. F. B. Burd, died of wounds; Capts. W. A. Stark, H. A. T. Hewlett and S. Davis, M.C., 2/Lieuts. D. S. Boorman, M. C. (at duty), A. J. Angel, W. F. Vines and A. C. Knight, wounded; and 60 N.C.O.'s and men killed, 176 wounded and 29 missing.

The 58th Division remained in line after this attack, and on the 26th September took part in the third general attack which was delivered by the Second and Fifth Armies on a front of some six miles, of which the northern limit was the Divisional sector. The attack was delivered by the 175th Brigade and a further considerable success gained, the Divisional front having been carried forward in the operations since the 19th a total distance of about 1600 yards.

On the 27th September, the 2/4th Londons moved to Brake Camp, in the Vlamertinghe area. Two days were occupied in training here, during which the area in which the Battalion was located suffered on the night of the 28th/29th September the most prolonged and serious bombing by enemy aircraft it ever experienced, the bombardment lasting without cessation from 9 p.m. to 2 a.m. Fortunately no casualties were sustained.

At Brake Camp the following joined the Battalion:

> Capt. R. C. Dickins.
>
> 2/Lieuts. C. C. Gibbs, D. G. Spring, F. J. Jones, E. G. Gardner and A. W. Dodds (21st Londons); and 2/Lieut. S. J. Richardson (7th Londons).
>
> 250 N.C.O.'s and men.

Further casualties during September included Lieut., C. Potter and 2/Lieuts. O. H. Mattison and J. McDonald, to hospital.

2/Lieut. Cook was appointed to the 173rd L.T.M. Battery.

On the 30th September the 58th Division was withdrawn from the line and concentrated as Corps reserve for rest in the Nordausques area (eight miles north-west of St Omer), and the 2/4th Londons moved by rail from Vlamertinghe to Zouafques where they went into billets on the 1st October. The train was followed and bombed during the journey by German airmen, 1 sergeant and 2 men being killed.

During the period of the 58th Division's withdrawal from the line the offensive was pressed forward under adverse conditions of weather. The season was now becoming advanced and the condition of the ground offered a far greater obstacle to our progress than the enemy's resistance. Probably no series of battles of the whole war was waged under such persistently adverse conditions, or imposed a greater physical strain on the attacking troops. In every direction the salient was by now a series of "shell hole lakes" the ground being waterlogged and the mud more glutinous than ever. An increasing number of casualties to men and beasts occurred through drowning in the shell holes of this ghastly shell-battered inferno, but though the whole forces of the elements seemed to be arrayed against us, advances of enormous importance were achieved during the early part of October, as a result of which the Allied positions were pushed forward to the outskirts of Houthulst Forest, to the east of Poelcapelle and to within 2000 yards of Passchendaele.

The prolonged continuance of active operations was obviously becoming increasingly difficult, but G.H.Q. was impelled to pursue the course of this dreary offensive partly by reason of the serious situation caused on the Italian front by the defeat of Caporetto at the end of October, and partly by the need of containing as many German divisions as possible during the preparations for the Cambrai battle, which were not yet complete.

The 2/4th Londons remained at Zouafques training and reorganising for over three weeks. Several drafts were received from the Base, which together made the considerable addition of 244 N.C.O.'s and men to the Battalion strength, thus bringing it above its numbers prior to the action of the 20th September.

On the 15th October the Battalion was joined by 2/Lieut. H. G. Langton; and by 2/Lieuts. H. A. Snell, J. R. Naylor and R. J. Richards (1st Londons). During this period also 2/Lieuts. H. E. English and C. C. H. Clifford were evacuated sick. Capt. S. H. Stedman was posted to the 173rd Brigade Labour Company at Louches.

On the 23rd October the 2/4th Londons returned by train to the Vlamertinghe area and took over quarters in Siege Camp, moving the following day to the concentration area on the canal bank, whence the battle surplus under 2/Lieut. Askham left the Battalion for the Divisional Depôt Battalion.

On the 25th October, Major W. A. Nunneley, second in command of the Battalion since July 1916, fell sick and was evacuated to hospital, his duties being taken over by the adjutant, Capt. A. Grover, M.C. Major Nunneley was subsequently appointed to command the German officers' Prisoners of War Camp at Donington Hall. Capt. Grover, M.C., was succeeded in the Adjutancy by Lieut. F. W. Walker, D.S.O. On the 22nd 2/Lieut D. G. Spring was seconded to the XX Corps School as Instructor.

The operation in which the 173rd Brigade was detailed to take part was arranged for the 26th October, and consisted of an attack on a frontage from the Ypres-Roulers Railway (south of Passchendaele) to beyond Poelcapelle. The task of the 173rd Brigade, who were flanked on the right by the 63rd (Royal Naval) Division and on the left by the 57th Division, was to carry forward the British line east of Poelcapelle for some 700 yards in a due easterly direction astride the Poelcapelle-Westroosebeeke Road. The Divisional frontage was some 1800 yards in length, and bounded on the north by the Poelcapelle-Staden Road and on the south by the Lekkerbotebeek. The assaulting troops were provided by the 2/2nd, 2/3rd and 2/4th Londons, while the 2/1st Londons were in Brigade reserve, with two battalions of the 174th Brigade concentrated in the old German trench system near St Julien, also at the disposal of the 173rd Brigade.

The first objective, which was on the line Spider Crossroads-Moray House, was to be taken by the 2/2nd and 2/3rd Battalions, while after a pause of 45 minutes, the 2/4th Londons were to "leapfrog" through them on to the second and final objective.

As in the September action, particular preparation was made for the assault of all known pillboxes by special parties, and the system of posts to be established by each company was carefully and definitely decided beforehand. The whole strength of the Battalion was necessary to cover the wide frontage allotted to it, the order of battle from the right being D Company (C. A. Clarke), C Company (Boorman), B Company (Hetley) and A Company (Dickins). In addition to the stipulated frontage the Battalion was also held responsible for some 200 yards of waterlogged ground near the Lekkerbotebeek on its right, over which touch with the 63rd Division could not be actively maintained.

The attack was to be delivered under a creeping barrage supported by heavy guns, machine-guns and smoke barrages, while look-out for enemy counter-attacks was to be maintained by aeroplanes.

On the morning of the 25th the 2/4th Londons left Siege Camp in battle order and moved forward to positions in the original front German system where they remained until the afternoon. At 3 p.m. the forward move was resumed, and the Battalion was completely assembled in its allotted area immediately east of Poelcapelle by 10.15 p.m., Battalion Headquarters being established at Gloster Farm.

The weather had for some days past shown a marked improvement, and the ground over which the advance was to be made was reported to be drying fast. But our much-tried troops could not escape their usual fate in the matter of weather, for on the night of the 25th rain fell pitilessly once more, filling up the shell holes, liquefying the mud and drenching everyone to the skin. All movement was rendered a matter of extraordinary difficulty, and when the time for the attack arrived the assaulting columns could scarcely drag themselves forward.

The British front line being composed of a line of unconnected posts, the actual "jumping-off" line was defined by tapes which made it essential to attack before daybreak. At 5.30 a.m. the British barrage came down, and the 2/2nd and 2/3rd Battalions followed by the 2/4th began their laborious advance. The barrage was disappointing, for not only was it not as well distributed as on former occasions, but, having regard to the state of the ground, it advanced far too quickly so that the assaulting troops were soon left far behind.

The 2/2nd Londons were successful in capturing four pillboxes of which three were at Cameron Houses, about half-way to the first objective, while the 2/3rd Londons on the left pushed forward to what was at the time believed to be Spider cross-roads, but was probably a less important road junction some 250 yards short of it. The line of this cross-road and Cameron Houses was, however, the limit of the advance, which was unsupported on the left owing to the adjoining division on that flank having been held up. The only post taken by the 2/4th Londons was Tracas Farm on the extreme right.

The men were now thoroughly exhausted by their efforts, and were practically defenceless as the mud had choked rifles and Lewis guns, and rendered them temporarily useless. Indeed, for over half an hour the Battalion possessed hardly a single rifle which could be fired. At this juncture the enemy counter-attacked in great force both at Cameron Houses and on the unsupported left flank, and his attack, as was to be expected in the circumstances, was successful, and our troops were driven back with severe loss to the assembly line where the enemy's advance was finally held.

After their rough handling of the morning it was clear that the attacking battalions could not pursue the offensive or remain in the line, and arrangements were accordingly made for their relief, on the south of the Poelcapelle-Westroosebeeke Road by the 2/1st Londons and on the north of it by the 2/7th Londons. The relief was completed by 10.15 p.m., and the 2/4th Londons returned to Siege Camp.

In other parts of the line greater success was achieved this day, notably in the vicinity of Passchendaele where the Canadians captured all their objectives, and on the extreme left in the area held by the French.

The 26th October must be regarded as one of the most unfortunate days ever experienced by the 2/4th Londons. The gallantry of officers, N.C.O.'s and men alike left nothing to be desired, and their defeat was at the hands of the elements far more than of the Germans. So bad indeed was the state of the ground that not a few men, becoming stuck in the mud and exhausted by their efforts to extricate themselves, met their death by drowning in the flooded shell holes.

For their good work on this day decorations were awarded to Capt. C. A. Clarke (the M.C.) and Pte C. H. W. Roberts (the D.C.M.).

The casualties sustained in this unfortunate affair were in officers: 2/Lieuts. F. J. Jones, H. G. Langton and J. R. Naylor, killed; 2/Lieut. R. J. Richards, died of wounds; Capts. R. C. Dickins and D. S. Boorman, M.C., 2/Lieuts. G. E. Lester, R. Michell, H. A. Snell and A. W. Dodds, wounded; and in N.C.O.'s and men 25 killed, 214 wounded and 109 missing—a total of 359 all ranks. This was the most costly single day in the history of the 2/4th Battalion.

The 2/4th Londons spent five days at Brake Camp cleaning up, resting and reorganising, moving on the 1st November to Roads Camp, and on the following day to St Jans-ter-biezen, about four miles west of Poperinghe. The Battalion was now reduced to an organisation of one company for fighting purposes, pending the arrival of further reinforcements to fill the gaps created on the 26th October.

On the 6th November a further move was made to P Camp near Peselhoek, north of Poperinghe, and here the Battalion remained for eight days, all of which were occupied in training except for three working parties of 100 N.C.O.'s and men under Capt. Hetley who proceeded to Gwent Farm for stretcher-bearing duties.

Passchendaele Ridge

A further attempt was made by the 175th Brigade on the 30th October to complete the unfulfilled task of the 26th, but again the state of the ground rendered the operation abortive. On the higher ground, however, Canadian troops again achieved some success, and by the 6th November had captured Passchendaele.

Thus was this stupendous offensive brought to a close. It had been maintained for three and a half months under conditions of unprecedented difficulty, and at enormous cost in personnel. Having regard to the obstacles which were encountered at every step the achievement was magnificent, and had served a definite purpose in the War, not only by securing positions on the high ground for the winter, but also by assisting our French and Italian Allies at a period when, especially in the case of the latter, any operation which could relieve the pressure on their front was of vital importance.

On the 15th November the Division was concentrated in Corps reserve, and the 2/4th Londons moved to Piccadilly Camp in the Proven area.

The 2/4th Londons now spent a prolonged period out of the battle area; occupying billets successively, after leaving Piccadilly Camp, at Coulemby on the 26th November, at Bellebrune and Cremarest (about twelve miles west of St Omer) from the 27th November to the 9th December, and at Soult Camp near Brielen, to which the Battalion moved on the last-mentioned date in anticipation of returning to the trenches.

This period of training passed with the usual routine of "back-of-the-line" training in drill, musketry, bombing, route marching and games, interspersed with highly welcome entertainments given by the Divisional concert troop "The Goods." Advantage was taken of the time spent in rest to refill the gaps in the Battalion's ranks, and an excellent opportunity was afforded of assimilating the newly-received drafts as they arrived and before they were called upon to go into action. These drafts totalled 213 N.C.O.'s and men, but even with this accession of strength the 2/4th Londons still remained considerably weaker than prior to the recent action.

Officer reinforcements were more numerous in proportion, and included:

> Lieuts. H. J. M. Williams and G. E. Lester.
>
> 2/Lieuts. R. W. Chamberlain, E. P. Higgs and L. H. Sheppard.
>
> 2/Lieut. F. B. Johnson (13th Londons).
>
> Lieut. F. J. Griffiths, 2/Lieuts. F. E. Norrish, F. G. Williams, W. H. G. Newman and W. Blair (20th Londons).
>
> 2/Lieuts. S. H. Jehu and J. R. Peryer (21st Londons).
>
> Lieut. C. A. Sampson (25th Londons).
>
> Lieuts. E. R. Howden and J. Cairns (A.S.C.).

On the 16th/17th December the 173rd Brigade took over the whole Divisional sector, which constituted the left of the II Corps front, from the Lekkerbotebeeke on the right to the Broembeek, a small stream close to the Ypres-Staden Railway on the left. The Corps line was in practically the same position as on the occasion of the Battalion's last visit to this area, and ran roughly north and south in front of Poelcapelle, and about 500 yards east of the Poelcapelle-Houthulst Road. The front line, which was occupied in a series of isolated shell hole posts, which were being strengthened and linked up to each other as opportunity offered, was held by two battalions, with support battalions in the captured German trenches around Langemarck and Pilckem.

The 2/4th Battalion took over from the 2/10th Londons the left support position in Eagle and Candle Trenches on the 16th December, thus covering a depth of about 3500 yards. The ground between the forward and rear companies was a quagmire of battered trenches, and work was immediately necessary to attempt to reduce the chaos of the defensive system to something approaching cohesion. After five quiet days in these positions the Battalion moved forward to the left front positions, relieving the 2/3rd Londons on the 20th December with three companies in line and one in support. Headquarters were at Louis Farm.

With the exception of an attack against our left company which was attempted under a severe barrage on the afternoon of the 22nd, and which was effectually dispersed, the tour passed quietly and the Battalion was relieved on the 24th December by the 2/10th Londons, and concentrated at Battle Siding (Brielen), entraining there for Elverdinghe. Casualties were 2/Lieut. Jehu and 10 N.C.O.'s and men wounded and shell-shocked.

A week at Bridge No. 1 Camp, occupied for the most part in training and bathing, was enlivened by the Christmas festivities, for which such provision as was possible had been made, the outstanding feature being the production by "The Goods" of their famous pantomime, "The Babes in the Wood," which proved an immediate and enormous success.

New Year's Day 1918 found the Battalion once more in left support positions in Whitemill, Eagle, Bear and Candle Trenches, with Headquarters in dugouts at Langemarck which rejoiced in the name of Pig and Whistle. Five days of peaceful trench work here were succeeded by an uneventful tour in the front line positions, and on the 8th January the Battalion handed over its trenches to the 17th Lancashire Fusiliers preparatory to the withdrawal of the whole Division. Concentrating on relief at Bridge No. 1 Camp the Battalion moved the following day to School Camp, Proven, where a few days' rest was obtained. The G.O.C. II Corps here presented ribands to those who had recently been decorated.

Officer reinforcements at this period were:

    27th December—2/Lieuts. P. J. Payne, N. A. Brown and V. C. Prince.

> 10th January—2/Lieuts. S. F. G. Mears, E. M. Cuthbertson, S. C. Geering and G. C. Ewing.

Early in January Lieut. D. C. Cooke went to hospital and the medical officer, Lieut. Altounyan, M.C. (wounded), was replaced by Lieut. C. E. Dunaway, U.S. Army.

On the 21st January the 2/4th Londons finally left the Ypres area after nearly five months of hard work in it, and the 58th Division was transferred to the III Corps (Pulteney) in the Fifth Army which had now removed to the extreme south of the British lines.

In recognition of their good work in these actions, all "other ranks" of the Battalion were subsequently granted permission to wear a small grenade—similar to that worn as a cap badge, but smaller—on the corners of the tunic collar.

This closes the regiment's connection with the Ypres Salient, the scene of so much hardship and suffering, but at the same time of so much gallantry and devotion to duty. Ypres occupies a position in the estimation of the Empire which is challenged by no place in which British troops served in the War; and it must be for ever a source of pride to the regiment that it was privileged to take part in the second and third battles for its liberation from the Germans.

CHAPTER XVIII
THE 1/4TH BATTALION IN THE BATTLE OF CAMBRAI, 1917

The 30th August 1917 found the 1/4th Battalion much reduced in strength moving from Arques to Bapaume, to the great satisfaction of all ranks, for all had been expecting a return to the unhealthy conditions of the Ypres Salient. On detrainment at Bapaume an evening march was made to Beaulencourt, where quarters were allotted in a concentration camp. This march was not without interest as it was the Battalion's first introduction to the "devastated area," the appalling lifeless and ruined belt of country left behind him by the Bosche in his retirement from the Ancre-Scarpe salient to the Hindenburg line. Beaulencourt lies between Bapaume and Le Transloy, and is thus on the ridge which lay beyond the old Lesbœufs lines and which had proved the final check to the Battalion's advances in the Somme battles of 1916. From the village the Lesbœufs-Morval Ridge was visible, though of those two ill-fated villages no ruins were discernible. The whole area was a vast waste of rank vegetation which was rapidly covering the scars of the previous year's battles without healing them. Shell fire had contributed comparatively little to the desolation, but villages had been completely demolished and trees felled, and the British troops themselves provided the only relief to the awful silence of this strange land from which the life of the fields had vanished.

The Battalion was now attached to the IV Corps (Woollcombe), and the first few days were spent in very necessary reorganisation of its slender resources in personnel. The casualties of the Ypres action were not replaced by drafts, and each company was reduced to two platoons. That such work as was possible was done to good purpose was shown on the 4th September, when the Corps commander inspected the Battalion and expressed himself gratified at the completeness and good order of its clothing and equipment in view of its recent withdrawal from the Flanders battlefield. This day was the third anniversary of the Battalion's departure from England.

Between the 5th and 8th September the 56th Division took over from the 3rd the left sector of the IV Corps front. The new sector was held with all three Brigades in line, each Brigade area being occupied with two battalions in front trenches, one in Brigade support and one in Divisional reserve, in positions facing the Hindenburg line from the neighbourhood of Lagnicourt on the left to south of the Bapaume-Cambrai Road in the vicinity of Demicourt on the right. Activity on the enemy's part was evidently not anticipated in this area, for by this relief the 56th Division became responsible for a front of approximately 10,500 yards.

Of this front the 168th Brigade took over the left or Lagnicourt sector, with Headquarters in dugouts about half a mile in rear of Lagnicourt, the Headquarters of the Division being in Frémicourt. This sector faced the village of Quéant, which was within the defences of the Hindenburg line. The front line of the left subsector consisted of a series of platoon posts which were not yet connected up, numbered respectively C 18/5, C 18/6, C 12/1, C 12/2, C 12/3 and C 12/4. These posts were the original battle outpost positions which had been constructed earlier in the year during the advance towards the Hindenburg line. No Man's Land here averaged 1000 yards wide, and though from most of these posts the enemy front line was invisible owing to the lie of the ground, they were all, except on the left, unapproachable from our side, except under cover of darkness. Some 500 yards in rear of this chain of defences ran a continuous trench known as the intermediate line, well constructed, with deep dugouts, moderately strong wire and a good field of fire. Battalion Headquarters were in dugouts in the sunken road on the left of Lagnicourt, and were connected with the intermediate line by a communication trench called Dunelm Avenue. Forward of the intermediate line there was but one trench leading to the advanced positions and this, Wakefield Avenue, connected with Post C 18/6.

In this area the Battalion settled down very comfortably to a period of two months' routine work in and out of the trenches, unbroken by operations of any interest, and happily almost entirely free from casualties. In order to avoid the tedium of following closely the common round of duty we propose to deal with these months by means of a few general remarks on the life of the Battalion.

During this period the Battalion was joined by the following officers:

> Capt. E. E. Spicer, Lieuts. A. Bath and A. M. Duthie, and 2/Lieut. E. L. Mills.

and by the following attached officers:

> 2/Lieuts. W. Shand, E. Petrie, C. W. Rowlands, and E. A. Ratcliffe (1st Londons).
>
> 2/Lieut. A. Franks (6th Londons).
>
> 2/Lieut. W. H. Eastoe (7th Londons).
>
> 2/Lieuts. E. L. Stuckey, C. S. Richards and A. B. Creighton (17th Londons).

2/Lieuts. F. Barnes, F. S. C. Taylor, R. S. B. Simmonds, J. L. Backhouse and E. D. Buckland (20th Londons).

Tours of duty were six-day periods as follows:

6 days in Lagnicourt left subsector	2 companies in posts.
	2 " intermediate line.

6 days in Brigade support—either side of Lagnicourt village.

6 days in Lagnicourt left subsector	Dispositions as before but companies changed over.

6 days in Divisional reserve—at Frémicourt, and so on.

The transport lines and Quartermaster's stores were at Frémicourt, where permanent horse standings, kitchens, butcher's shop and stores were erected on an elaborate scale, which appeared to suggest that all ranks were quite prepared to settle down permanently in this unusually pleasant sector.

In the line a very considerable amount of work was got through during September and October. The front line posts were linked up by a continuous traversed trench, about 7 feet deep and 3 feet wide at the bottom, and provided with "baby elephant" shelters for the garrison. Two embryo trenches in which forward company headquarters were situate— Whitley and York supports—were extended and strengthened and the intermediate line was maintained. In addition a large amount of additional wire was put out.

While in Brigade support the Battalion always occupied shelters in the sunken roads which ran parallel to the lines each side of Lagnicourt village, B and D Companies being on the north side and A and C Companies and Battalion Headquarters on the south. The dwellings here were much improved, and fresh ones were constructed, of which the best were one built under the supervision of Lieut. Bath and "Twin Villa" by Headquarters. Not all the Battalion's time, however, was devoted to the adornment of its own homes, for the support battalion was invariably called upon to supply heavy working parties, the largest of which were digging under the R.E.'s, while others were attached to tunnelling companies for the construction of additional deep dugouts at trench headquarters and in the intermediate line.

Training was not overlooked, and a great deal of valuable work was effected. In particular mention should be made of the signallers, who attained a very high pitch of proficiency under Lieut. Gray, while Sergt. Randall achieved much success with the Lewis gunners, and Sergts. Oakely and Taylor did very good work with bombers and rifle grenadiers.

In the line the enemy's activity on the Battalion's front was slight and confined to occasioned shelling and trench mortaring, of which the bulk occurred at night. The sectors right and left of the Battalion came in for a rather greater share of the enemy's hatred. The London Scottish on the right were immediately opposed to a network of trenches sapped out from the Hindenburg front line, known as the Quéant Birdcage, and in this vicinity a certain degree of bickering was always in progress, in the course of which IV Corps developed a pleasing habit of discharging gas projectors—about 600 at a time—against the Birdcage. The Bosche, however, did not retaliate. It should not, however, be supposed that the Division had settled down for a prolonged rest in this quiet sector. Day and night our excellent artillery were searching for—and finding—the enemy's "weak spots," and up and down the sector No Man's Land was every night the scene of very great patrolling activity. In this direction really useful work was effected by the Battalion Scouts under Lieut. O. D. Garratt, M.C., and Sergts. Housden and Hayes.

The great width of No Man's Land facilitated the operation of a novel method of supplying the Battalion when in trenches with rations and stores. The limbers came up nightly as usual from transport lines at Frémicourt to trench headquarters at Lagnicourt, and from this point the rations were sent up to company headquarters in half limbers and on pack mules; whereby a considerable saving of troops for work elsewhere was effected. On one of these nightly journeys a bridge over Wakefield Avenue broke and precipitated an elderly transport horse, named Tommy, on to his back in the trench. It was two hours' hard work to dig room round him to get him up and make a ramp for him to walk out of the trench! Tommy's mishap was commemorated in the new bridge which was named Horsefall Bridge.

A nasty accident in the line was averted by the coolness of Pte. Bunker, A Company. While a section was cleaning some Mills bombs one of the pins fell out and the bomb, with the fuse burning, fell among the men. Bunker picked it up and threw it out of the trench, when it at once exploded. For this action Bunker was awarded the M.S.M.

In the first week of October, while the Battalion was in line, a series of heavy explosions was heard behind the enemy line in the vicinity of Quéant and Pronville and these, combined with the sudden disappearance one night of Baralle chimney—a well-known observation point in the enemy's country—conduced to the belief, which held sway for a few days, that a further Bosche retirement was imminent. This, of course, did not materialise.

Although we are not recording the actions of the Divisional Artillery we may, perhaps, be pardoned for quoting the following crisp little record from the Divisional Intelligence Summary as illustrating how well the infantry was served by its guns. The incident occurred on the 10th October:

> Movement was seen at an O.P. or sentry post about D.7.d.4.6. An 18-pr. opened fire, but the first shot fell a few yards wide, whereupon the German observer waved a "washout" signal with a piece of white paper. The second shot, however, altered his opinion of our artillery.

His amended opinion has, unfortunately, not been recorded.

The losses of the Battalion in personnel up to the end of October were practically nil, this being accounted for by the vastness of the terrain and the fact that about 450 men were occupying some 5000 yards of firing and communication trench. On the 28th October, however, the Battalion had the misfortune to lose two promising young officers, 2/Lieuts. Elders and Barnes, both of whom were killed by shells during an enemy shoot on Posts C 12/3 and C 12/4.

During this period also the Battalion sustained a great loss in Regimental Sergt.-Major M. Harris, who took his discharge after nearly twenty-three years of soldiering in the Royal Fusiliers and the 4th Londons. Sergt.-Major Harris had served continuously with the 1/4th Battalion since mobilisation, and had filled the position of Senior Warrant Officer with conspicuous success since March 1915. The last member of the pre-war permanent staff to remain on active service with the Battalion, Harris' imperturable geniality was the means of adding enormous force to his disciplinary strictness. His share in achieving the Battalion's efficiency can hardly be over-rated, while his kindly personality was ever a factor in the social life of the Battalion. Harris was gazetted Lieutenant and Quartermaster to the Battalion in the reconstituted Territorial Army in July 1921. The duties of R.S.M. in the 1/4th Battalion were taken by C.S.M. Jacques.

At the end of October information was circulated among commanding officers that active operations were imminent. The secrets of the operations were jealously guarded, and only a vague idea was given as to what would be the opening day. On the 10th November, however, orders were issued for a feint attack to be delivered by the 56th Division, which would be on the left of the main operation. This feint was to be accompanied by a heavy bombardment by all available batteries, by a smoke screen and the display of dummy figures over the parapet. Dummy tanks were also to be erected in No Man's Land, and the illusion completed—or anyway increased—by running motor cycle engines in the front line trenches. Arrangements for this demonstration were pushed on with vigour, and it was understood that Z day would fall during the Battalion's occupancy of the line.

On the evening of the 18th, however, the 167th Brigade extended to its left, taking over the 168th sector, and thus holding a two-brigade front. The 168th Brigade was concentrated in close billets in Frémicourt and Beugny, the Battalion being in the former village.

The preparations for the offensive were conducted with the greatest possible secrecy, and in order to secure the maximum surprise effect it was arranged for the attack to be delivered without any preliminary bombardment or even registration of batteries, the road into the enemy's defences being cleared instead by a vast number of tanks.

The attack was delivered by the IV (Woollcombe) III (Pulteney) and VII (Snow) Corps, on a six-mile front, between Hermies and Gonnelieu, a subsidiary operation being conducted north of Bullecourt by the VI Corps (Haldane). The 56th Division was thus outside the actual area of advance, but was to co-operate on the opening day by means of the feint attack, for which it had already made preparations, and its further action was to depend on the success gained in the main operation. The left flank of the area of advance was intersected by the Canal du Nord, running between Bourlon and Mœuvres. The frontage in this region was taken up by the 36th (Ulster) Division, which adjoined the right flank of the 56th and was the left of the whole attack. The 36th was to attack with two brigades east of the Canal and one brigade west, the Division moving northwards along the Hindenburg system towards Mœuvres. The rôle of the 56th Division was to depend on the degree of success attained by the 36th. If the latter's attack succeeded in forcing the retirement of the enemy west of the Canal, this area would be occupied by the brigade of the 36th Division which was on the west bank; if, however, this success was not achieved the 56th Division was to attack over the open with tanks, the 169th Brigade advancing on a front between Mœuvres and Tadpole Copse, and the 167th forming a defensive flank from the Copse to our present front line.

The enormous success which attended the initial stages of the Cambrai battle needs no elaboration here. At 6.30 a.m. on 30th November the dead silence was suddenly broken by the roar of a very great concentration of batteries of all calibres up to 15-inch, and preceded by 380 tanks the assaulting divisions swept over the first and second systems of the Hindenburg line.

With the exception of a check due to the destruction of the Canal de l'Escaut Bridge at Masnières, and of another at Flesquières (where a most gallant resistance to the 51st Division was put up by a single German officer, who continued to serve his gun after all the team were killed and succeeded in knocking out several tanks), the success of the day was considerable. The villages of Havrincourt, Graincourt, Ribecourt, Marcoing and La Vacquerie were added to the British territory, and it was obvious that the surprise effect had been complete.

On the left the 36th Division established itself north of the Cambrai Road, astride the Hindenburg line, and the 169th Brigade swung its right flank northward to conform to its neighbours' movements.

The following day at an early hour the Flesquières obstacle was overcome and the British line swept forward, the villages of Masnières, Noyelles, Cantaing and Anneux being added to the bag, while on the left Fontaine-Notre-Dame was entered and the line pushed up to the southern edge of Bourlon Wood. On the left of the 36th the 169th Brigade kept pace, one of their battalions occupying the first Hindenburg trench about one of the roads forming the south-west exit of Mœuvres, and beginning to bomb northwards.

The 21st November witnessed a further deep inroad into the Hindenburg system. The 36th Division succeeded during the morning in penetrating into Mœuvres but were not able to maintain their position. On the extreme left the 169th Brigade continued their bombing attacks along the enemy trenches, and were reported in the late afternoon as having captured Tadpole Copse and the first and second Hindenburg trenches beyond it as far as the Inchy Road.

In the Battalion at Frémicourt the 20th November passed without incident, but all ranks awaited anxiously news of the battle, and for the expected orders to move forward and join in the success. No movement was made, however, and the day passed slowly, as such days of keen expectancy always do.

The hour for general action by the 56th Division was approaching, and the 1/4th Londons received orders at 3.30 p.m. on the 21st to move forward with transport and stores to Lebucquière, which was reached at 8.15 p.m., accommodation being provided in Cinema Camp. The Battalion was now prepared for action, and the nucleus personnel under Major Phillips, the second in command (attached from Montgomery Yeomanry), remained at Frémicourt.

Next morning the Battalion made all preparations for an early participation in the fight and, in order to save fatigue to the men, all battle impedimenta such as Lewis guns and magazines, bombs, tools and wire cutters were sent on limbers to an open space near Doignies.

Shortly after midday the Battalion followed, arriving at Doignies at 4 p.m., picking up its stores and bivouacking. In the meantime Lieut.-Col. Marchment, M.C., accompanied by Capt. Maloney, the doctor, rode forward to ascertain the situation from the London Scottish, who were holding the old British front line opposite Tadpole Copse.

The rain, which had started early in the day, was still falling when the Battalion arrived at Doignies. The village was a good deal knocked about, but shelter of a sort was found, and the Battalion was just well off to sleep when it was turned out again to move nearer the line for the purpose of taking over the British front line from the London Scottish early next day. About midnight the Battalion got under way in pitch darkness, and moving through Louverval reached its assembly area near Piccadilly and about 500 yards in rear of the line by 4.10 a.m. on the 23rd November. As soon as the growing daylight permitted, companies resumed their advance and took over Rook, Rabbit and Herring Trenches from the London Scottish, Headquarters occupying a sunken road north of the wood surrounding Louverval Château. On relief the assaulting companies of the London Scottish moved forward to continue the bombing attack started by the 169th Brigade.

News of the operation was slow in coming through, but by 10.17 a.m. a report reached Brigade that the attackers had been checked on endeavouring to emerge from Tadpole Copse. This check was due to a peculiar omission in the British trench maps, which had shown Tadpole Copse on the crest of a spur, and dominating all the ground in its immediate vicinity. It was found that between the Copse and the Inchy Road was a narrow and sharply marked depression bordered by the declivitous banks which abound in this undulating countryside. Beyond this unsuspected valley the Inchy Road was on an eminence just as prominent as the Tadpole Copse hill; and this position, held by the enemy in great strength, enabled them to overlook completely all the northern exits from the Copse. This valley, which played an important part in the course of the battle, was found subsequently to be correctly marked on German maps which were captured during the action.

After a stubborn fight the London Scottish overcame this obstacle and pushed home their attack in the Hindenburg front trench almost as far as Adelaide Street and in the support 100 yards beyond the Inchy Road; while a subsidiary attempt was made, without success, to capture the Factory between this point and Inchy. At these points the enemy had constructed blocks which he held strongly against all attempts to dislodge him. In the meantime the 169th Brigade had been bombing up the communications leading back to the second system of the Hindenburg lines, with the object of isolating Mœuvres, but the resistance met with here was exceedingly stubborn.

About 8 o'clock that night the enemy launched a heavy attack against the London Scottish barricades, and in the support trench they succeeded in forcing the Scottish back to the Inchy Road, though the position in the front trench was held. The Scottish had now been fighting for over twelve hours and had suffered rather serious losses, and the German counter-attack caused two companies of the 1/4th Londons to be drawn into the fight, A Company (Franks) and C (Barkworth) moving forward to reinforce the Scottish at about 8.30 p.m.

A Company, which advanced first, took up a position, acting under the orders of Lieut.-Col. Jackson of the London Scottish, in the old German outpost line outside Tadpole Copse, while No. 1 Platoon (Ballance) went forward to reinforce the Scottish company in the front Hindenburg trench. Affairs having quieted down the services of this platoon were not immediately necessary, and it shortly afterwards rejoined the company. In the meantime No. 2 Platoon (Creighton) was sent to reinforce the Scottish at the bombing block in the support trench, and while here Corpl. Johnson and Pte. Bendelow succeeded in beating off an enemy attack.

C Company, which also took up a preliminary position in the old German outpost line, was first told off to replenish the supply of bombs from the brigade dump in Houndsditch. The fresh supplies were carried to London Scottish Headquarters; and this task completed, the company occupied the rectangular work in the support trench to the east of Tadpole Copse, a portion of the second Hindenburg trench in rear of the Copse, and the communication trench connecting it with the Hindenburg third line, 2/Lieut. Mills being responsible for this communication trench and the advanced block about 250 yards along it. 2/Lieut. Stuckey occupied the main trench. These latter trenches were taken over from the 2nd Londons early on the 24th.

B and D Companies meanwhile had not been idle but had passed the night providing a covering party to a company of the Cheshire Pioneers, by whom a chain of redoubts had been dug in the line selected for the defensive flank.

At 5.30 a.m. on the 24th B Company (Beeby) moved forward, also coming under the orders of the London Scottish, and at first took up a position in support in the old outpost line outside the Hindenburg system. Almost immediately the company was ordered forward to relieve the 2nd Londons in the communication trench leading to the rear from the Quadrilateral held by C Company.

The morning passed comparatively quietly though the duty of keeping wicket behind the bombing blocks was a trying one, which entailed the constant alertness of all ranks in readiness to meet a sudden emergency. At noon, however, the enemy put down a heavy barrage on the captured portions of the Hindenburg trenches, and this was followed at 2 p.m. by a most determined attack on the advanced blocks held by the London Scottish. This met with considerable success, and though the Scottish fought with gallantry they were overcome by the weight of the enemy's onslaught, and by 2.45 p.m. the German bombers had reached the block held by Mills (C Company), who put up a stout resistance, under orders from his company commander to hold his post failing further orders. In this he was helped by the company's Lewis guns, which gave covering fire to Mills' platoon and the London Scottish, and also engaged the enemy at the Inchy Road Factory. Three of the guns were destroyed by the enemy's shell fire.

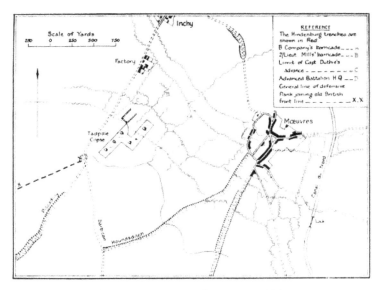

THE BATTLE OF CAMBRAI, 1917

The trench was already uncomfortably filled with casualties in addition to the men who were keeping up the fight, but in a few moments the congestion was greatly increased by the numbers of Scottish troops who began to come back and file along the trench. At about 3 p.m. about 50 of the London Scottish were seen to leave the Hindenburg support trench in the hidden valley referred to, with the object of making their way over the open towards the front trench. Realising that this vacation of the trench might enable the enemy to surge forward along it and so cut off Mills, who was still holding his own up the communication trench, Barkworth promptly ordered Stuckey to advance and form a block beyond the side trench held by Mills. Stuckey's losses, however, had been severe, and with only five men at his disposal he was unable to cope with the task in view of the great congestion of the trench. Rather than risk the sudden cutting off of his remaining slender resources in men and the laying open to the enemy of the whole Tadpole Copse position, which would inevitably result, Barkworth now decided to withdraw his advanced positions and concentrate his company, and accordingly Stuckey was ordered to block the support trench at the west entrance to the Quadrilateral, Mills gradually withdrawing and holding the enemy off till the new block was completed. In this retired position the remnants of C Company were in touch with B Company and also with the 2nd Londons, and here the enemy was finally held up.

This gallant little defence in which C Company put up a really good fight and inflicted considerable loss on the enemy, cost it about 40 per cent. of its strength in casualties and, as already stated, three of its Lewis guns.

At the same time B Company had been heavily engaged in its communication trench, of which it held a length of some 250 yards back from the second trench. Here the enemy, who had a bombing block about 50 yards from B Company's forward block, began to attack at about 2.30 p.m., but after a struggle his first attempt was thrown back. A little later the Bosche returned to the charge, and this time was successful in forcing B Company back for a short distance, but a determined counter-attack re-established the position, which, after a third and also abortive enemy assault, remained intact in the Company's hands.

While the 1/4th Londons had been thus heavily engaged the London Scottish had made a successful resistance in the front Hindenburg trench which defied all the enemy's attempts. Towards the evening the enemy's activity both in shell fire and bombing somewhat lessened, and at 8.30 p.m. D Company (Duthie) was also sent forward relieving C Company in the trenches. At the same time the Rangers took over from the Scottish in the front trench.

As the fighting on the 24th was somewhat involved, it seems desirable to restate the positions now held by the companies of the Battalion in the Hindenburg system:

> Front Line—D Company—Quadrilateral in support trench, and communication leading up to front trench.
>
> B Company—Communication trench leading from the Quadrilateral back to third trench.
>
> Support Line—A and C Companies and Headquarters—Front trench from west edge of Tadpole Copse to communication trench east of it and old German outpost line in front of the Copse.

The 25th November also witnessed very severe fighting in which the 1/4th Londons bore an important part and achieved considerable success. The fighting this day fell to D Company who had not yet been engaged, and the objective allotted to them was the recapture of the lost portion of the Hindenburg support trench as far as its junction with the communication trench, which had been defended by Mills the previous day. At the same time the Rangers were to make good the two communication trenches leading back from the front trench to the support on the east side of the Inchy Road, and also the support trench in prolongation of Duthie's attack.

We propose to narrate this gallant little action of D Company in the words of Duthie's report on the operation:

> Artillery preparation began at 12.30 p.m. It was reported to be very short on our right. Our two blocks were removed at 12.45 p.m. At Zero (1 p.m.) the attack commenced. The Company was disposed as follows:
>
> 14 Platoon, 2/Lieut. E. Petrie, Bombers, Rifle Grenadiers, Riflemen (carrying); 13 Platoon, 2/Lieut. C. W. Rowlands, with sections in same order.[5] Lewis gun sections took up a position near our blocks so as to fire along the trench and to prevent any movement in the open. Company Headquarters moved with the leading platoon. For about 50 yards very little opposition was met with but the leading bombing section was then held up by stick bombs and suffered eight casualties, which included the leading bombers. To overcome this check fire was opened for several minutes with No. 23 and No. 24 Rifle Grenades, and the trench was searched forward for about 100 yards. The shooting was very accurate and the enemy were driven back with the loss of about 5 men killed. The advance was continued by bounds of from 20 to 40 yards under cover of salvoes of rifle grenades. The first two deep dugouts were unoccupied. The third and fourth were not immediately searched but sentries were posted. It was thought that some of the C Company men who had been wounded

the previous day might still be down there. The small C.T. (about 100 yards from the Quadrilateral) was blocked about 120 yards up. At the entrance a good deal of bombing was overcome. This is a shallow trench and the far end under water. Further delay was caused by the third and fourth dugouts which were found to contain 21 of the enemy. These were finally cleared. Several were killed and the remainder badly wounded and captured. The company then pushed forward to trench junction at E 13 c. 15.75 (objective) and reached it about 2.45 p.m. The Lewis gun sections were brought up and placed in suitable positions to protect a further advance and also the blocking party in the small C.T. None of the Rangers were encountered and the trench appeared unoccupied, but bombing was thought to be heard about 300 yards further along.

[5] Companies were still organised in two platoons owing to their reduced strength, which had not been made good since the third battle of Ypres.

A small block was made in this trench about 30 yards from the junction. The enemy was now observed leaving the trench and crawling over the open towards the bank at D 18 d. 90.98 (in the unsuspected valley). Heavy rifle fire was opened and at least 30 of the enemy killed. Few, if any, got over the bank. As the trench beyond the objective appeared to be unoccupied a party of 12 including O.C. Company, 2/Lieut. Rowlands, Sergts. Norris and Arklay, moved on up the trench. No fire was opened and silence was maintained. In the next bay past the trench at E 13 c. 00.85 (50 yards beyond the objective) two men were seen firing a machine-gun which was mounted on the parapet and aimed down the bank (in the valley). This was rushed.... The gun was dismounted and brought in. Other guns were heard firing and two more were seen (at points farther along the trench in the valley described in the report by map reference). Two parties under Sergts. Norris and Arklay moved round to a point from which fire could be brought to bear. The crews of two men to each gun were killed and the guns brought in. O.C. Company and Sergt. Norris continued to advance along the trench and up to the top of the bank. Heavy bombing could be seen in Tadpole Lane and in the front line towards the Inchy Road. Further advance was prevented by the fire of our own guns firing on the trench in response to S.O.S. signal which had been sent up from the front line. The trench was very full of dead, both of the London Scottish and of the enemy. It was impossible to walk without treading on them. As our barrage continued the party moved back to our original objective and blocks were made at this trench junction. The remainder of the party carried back four wounded London Scottish, who were found in the open near the bank. Later in the evening when our barrage was discontinued an attack was made on our block. The enemy was quickly silenced. At 11 p.m. D Company were relieved by A Company.

A very successful operation, and a modest account of it by Duthie, whose personality and leadership was an important factor in the result achieved. The two men in charge of the first gun captured were shot by Duthie with his revolver. The resistance offered to the Rangers was stubborn, and but for their inability to advance it is possible a considerable success might have been achieved, since the barrage put down by our guns, in response to the Rangers' S.O.S., had the effect of shelling Duthie out of part of his gains.

The remainder of the day was inactive, no further fighting taking place till about 11.30 a.m. on the 26th, when once more the enemy attempted to force B Company's position in the communication trench. The company, however, repeated its gallantry of the former occasion, and the enemy retired later without having gained any success.

At 11.30 p.m. on the 26th the Battalion was relieved by the Kensingtons, withdrawing on relief to its former position in the Brigade support area behind the old British front line. This relief brought to a close the Battalion's active participation in the British offensive, which was now practically spent. During the very trying three days spent behind the bombing blocks in circumstances which required particular vigilance and fortitude, all ranks had behaved splendidly, and it is difficult to mention individuals when all had rendered such excellent service. A few names, however, call for outstanding mention, among these being Capt. S. J. Barkworth, M.C., M.M., and Capt. A. M. Duthie, the commanders of C and D Companies, on whom the brunt of the work had fallen, and their subalterns Rowlands and Mills. The Padre, the Rev. S. F. Leighton Green, did splendid service throughout, being always about the Hindenburg lines and going up to the advanced blocks. At night he was constantly visiting and helping with casualties and administering the last rites to those who had fallen.

The whole action as far as the Division was concerned had developed on lines completely opposed to the original plans; for whereas it had been proposed to employ the Division in the open with tanks, its fighting throughout had been hand-to-hand fighting in trenches. The regularity and sufficiency with which bomb supplies found their way to the front indicated excellent organisation. At no time did supplies fall short of the demand.

It was a surprise to a good many to find the much vaunted Hindenburg line inferior to our own defences. The outpost line which the companies first occupied was a gross delusion, for it was only six inches deep, while the main line was poor and not over well maintained, and the Bosche ideas of sanitation could only be described as a scandal.

The casualties sustained during the three days' fighting were light in view of the close contact with the enemy. Two officers, 2/Lieuts. R. S. B. Simmonds and E. Petrie, were wounded, and the total losses in other ranks amounted to about 60, including two valuable N.C.O.'s killed, viz.: Sergts. Barker and Gooch, and one, Sergt. Lintott, M.M., wounded and captured.

At midnight on the 24th November the 56th Division had passed from the IV to the VI Corps. Its position at the conclusion of the offensive operations was one of almost dangerous extension. It had captured and was holding over a mile of the Hindenburg line. Its right flank was not secure so long as Mœuvres remained in the enemy's hands; its left flank on the Tadpole Copse spur was exposed and subject to constant counter-attacks. Two of its brigades were involved in this fighting and in holding a defensive flank of 2000 yards, while the remaining brigade, the 167th, was responsible for a frontage in the old British line of 5500 yards, and had in addition to supply a battalion each night for consolidation of the captured position. It was thus unable to provide relief for the troops who had been fighting, and was without any reserve for use in case of emergency. Representations made by General Dudgeon to the Corps Commander as to the weakness of his position resulted in a battalion of the 3rd Division being at once placed at the disposal of the 167th Brigade for counter-attack purposes. This temporary relief was extended a few days later, and by the 29th the whole of the 167th Brigade had been relieved by troops of the 3rd Division and was withdrawn at Frémicourt in Divisional reserve, with two of its battalions lent temporarily to the 168th Brigade.

The three days following relief were spent by the Battalion in support in providing carrying and working parties in the front line and burying parties for the fallen. On the 29th a slight side step to the left was made so that the Battalion's right flank rested on Piccadilly and it became responsible for the defensive flank. A considerable amount of work had been done in this quarter, and the flank was now provided with a continuous belt of wire and a chain of inter-supporting posts. A communication trench had been dug from the old line across No Man's Land to the Hindenburg line parallel to Piccadilly, a distance of some 1300 yards, and from this T-head trenches had been sapped forward facing north. The defensive flank positions were only occupied at night, the trench garrison taking two companies, A and B, while C and D Companies provided patrols along the wire to prevent any attempts of the enemy to turn the position.

The 29th November passed quietly though a good deal of movement was observable in rear of the enemy's lines, so that his serious attack of the following day was not entirely unexpected.

From the Battalion's position an extensive view was obtainable over the whole terrain as far as Bourlon Wood, and early on the 30th a strong concentration of the enemy's forces was clearly visible north and east of Mœuvres.

At 10.45 a.m. the S.O.S. signal went up all along the line and the enemy attacked in dense formation under a heavy barrage. The Battalion stood to arms all day but was not required, for the gallant defence of the units in the line this day was one of the greatest achievements of the 56th Division. The enemy's attack was pressed with vigour and at one time he had driven a wedge into the Hindenburg lines and divided the London Scottish, who were still in the line, from the 2nd Londons. The position, however, was defended tenaciously and at the end of the day the whole of the Division's gains in the Hindenburg front line were maintained, while the heaps of enemy dead outside the trenches testified to the severity of the check which he had suffered.

That night the Battalion was called on for particularly active patrolling as it was anticipated that the enemy would renew his attempt on the Divisional front. The whole resources of the Division were drawn upon to meet any renewed enemy action, and Lieut.-Col. Marchment had under him for defensive purposes, in addition to the Battalion, a company of the 5th Cheshires, a company of the 7th Middlesex, the 512th Field Company, R.E., and two sections of the 416th Field Company, R.E. The Engineers were employed in digging fresh redoubts in dead ground to the rear of the defensive flank line, while the infantry companies were kept as a reserve at Battalion Headquarters. No further action occurred until the afternoon of the 1st December when a fresh concentration of enemy forces about 3.30 p.m. was crushed by our guns.

The Division had now well earned a rest, and warning was received on the 1st December that it would be relieved by the 51st Division immediately. The relief began at 7 p.m. that evening, the Battalion handing over its lines to the 6th Black Watch. It was evident that the incoming troops had been pushed forward hurriedly, for the relieving battalion arrived without Lewis guns or shrapnel helmets, and with the officers wearing slacks, just as they had risen from dinner. The relief took a long while to effect, and it was not until 4 a.m. on the 2nd that Lieut.-Col. Marchment handed over command of the sector. On relief the Battalion withdrew to billets in Beugny, but at

11 a.m. the rearward march was continued to Beaulencourt which was reached by 4 p.m., quarters being allotted in the camp that the Battalion had occupied on the 30th August.

While at Beaulencourt the Battalion received congratulatory messages which had been issued to Brigade by the Corps and Divisional commanders on the part played in the battle.

The following day the Battalion entrained at Frémicourt for the Arras area, reaching Beaumetz-les-Loges at 12.30 p.m., whence it marched to billets in Simencourt.

The honours awarded for services rendered in the Battle of Cambrai were as follows:

>D.S.O.—Capt. A. M. Duthie.
>
>M.C.—2/Lieuts. C. W. Rowlands and E. L. Mills.
>
>D.C.M.—Sergt. G. Norris and L.-Corpls. E. S. Brown and T. H. Sankey.
>
>Bar to M.M.—Pte. C. S. Ruel.
>
>M.M.—Sergts. F. Arklay, A. E. Haynes and G. J. Grant, Corpls. T. J. Court, J. W. Johnson and H. W. Wallder. L.-Corpl. T. Hodgkins and Ptes. B. M. J. Barnett, H. Evans, W. J. Hutchin, F. G. Senyard, G. Tyrell, J. Wickens and W. A. Willmott.

CHAPTER XIX
THE 1/4TH BATTALION, WINTER 1917/18--
THE RESERVE BATTALION, 1916/17

The closing days of 1917 were full of anxiety for the Allies. The operations at Cambrai had been undertaken by the British forces at the termination of the prolonged and unusually trying offensive on the northern ridges at Ypres, with the object of affording some relief to our Italian Allies. The secession of Russia from the Allied cause had had a most serious effect in all theatres of war. In the East it had afforded the tottering Austrian Empire the respite it so badly needed and had wrought the utter downfall of isolated Roumania, besides giving a severe check to the Allies' aspirations in the Balkans and Palestine. In the West it had entailed a complete reversal of the numerical position, and from the end of November onwards the German strength was being continually augmented by the arrival of divisions from the Russian front, while the Allies became subjected to an ever-increasing strain. The growing requirements of all the battlefields of the world on which the Empire's soldiers were playing their part made it impossible to maintain the British forces in France at the strength necessary to combat the threat of a very serious German offensive. Only from the Far West was any relief for the Allies to be expected. The American Army which had been about ten months in training was already being transferred to France, but it would still be some time before it would be sufficiently numerous or experienced to turn the scale against the enemy. As the winter wore on the threat of an enemy attack on a grand scale developed into a probability, which as all the world now knows, materialised on the 21st March 1918.

For some weeks, however, prior to the launching of this final effort of the Central Powers the Allies had definitely passed to the defensive in preparation for the German onslaught, and our present task is to bridge rapidly the gulf between the close of active operations at the end of 1917 and the point, which we will fix in the early days of March 1918, at which we can conveniently take up the story of the regiment in the offensive itself. We propose, therefore, to devote a few pages to bringing up to date the record of the various activities of the regiment, dealing first with the 1/4th Battalion in France, and afterwards with the Reserve Battalion at home.

I. *The 1/4th Battalion in Artois*

After three months in the devastated area around Lagnicourt, where the Battalion had been entirely removed from French civilisation, and where scarcely any had had the opportunity of sleeping under a proper roof, the billets allotted to the troops at Simencourt on the 3rd December were a great treat, and it was hoped that for at least a few days the Battalion would be permitted to enjoy its well-earned rest. On this occasion as on most others, however, the Divisional rest proved a delusion, and after two days occupied in cleaning and reorganisation the Battalion found itself once more on the road, for on the 5th it marched from Simencourt at 9.30 a.m. to Wakefield Camp, near Roclincourt (three miles north of Arras) in the First Army area.

The Division was now allotted to the XIII Corps (McCracken), which formed the right flank of Horne's First Army and comprised in addition to the 56th, the 31st and 62nd Divisions.

The following day Lieut.-Col. Marchment and the Works Officer (Lieut. Lorden) reconnoitred the sector to be taken over, and on the 7th and 8th the relief of the 94th Brigade (31st Division) by the 168th Brigade took place, the 1/4th Londons moving on the first day of relief to Brigade support and on the second day into the left subsection of the centre Brigade section facing Oppy, in trenches which it took over from the 12th York and Lancaster Regiment.

The whole area had seen a great deal of heavy fighting since the early days of the War. In May and June 1915 during Sir John French's offensive at Festubert, the French troops had attacked Notre Dame de Lorette, Ablain St Nazaire, La Targette and Neuville St Vaast. Early in 1916 the Allied positions on the Vimy Ridge, by then held by the British, had been heavily attacked by the enemy; while in the spring of 1917, in conjunction with the Third Army's operations east of Arras, the Canadian Corps had swept over the Vimy Ridge and down the slopes beyond towards the broad plains of Douai, carrying the line in front of Gavrelle and Arleux-en-Gohelle. The British front line at the end of 1917 was therefore deep in what had originally been a rear German system of defence; trenches were numerous, but poor and in bad repair, and the whole ground under numerous intense bombardments had been badly "crumped."

The Battalion's sector lay between Arleux and Gavrelle and passed through Oppy Wood, a leafless spectre of what had once been a copse, through whose shattered trunks the remains of Oppy and Neuvireuil were visible. The forward line was held in three posts, known from right to left as Beatty, Wood and Oppy. Each post took a company, with one platoon of each company in the Marquis-Earl line, a continuous trench some four hundred yards in rear. The fourth company was held in reserve in Bow Trench about 1700 yards back from the line of posts, while Battalion Headquarters occupied a dugout in South Duke Street, close to the Marquis line, which was the line of resistance.

The second defensive system consisted of the Red line, a continuous trench in front of Bailleul and Willerval, while a third system, the Green line, followed the crest of the Vimy Ridge. The observation throughout the area was excellent owing to the regular slope eastwards from the Vimy Ridge, and brigade and battalion commanders could overlook the whole of their sectors from their respective Headquarters.

The Battalion's sector was served by one main communication trench, Ouse Alley, which started from the Green line no less than 5300 yards from the front line. The administrative arrangements were distinctly good. Steam trains ran to daylight railhead in rear of the Green line, and this was connected with the Red line by a night service of petrol-electric trains. From the Red line forwards rations and stores were moved by truck. Battalion Headquarters also enjoyed the luxury of having water laid on by pipe line. Having said so much, however, we have almost exhausted the good points of the sector. The defences themselves left much to be desired. An early reconnaissance of the wire in front of the three company posts revealed an alarming weakness, for the single lines of concertina wire afforded but little obstacle to an enterprising enemy, and were placed out much too close to our parapets. The trenches, with the exception of the Red line, which was of good construction, were shallow and much knocked about.

The Battalion's first tour in this sector passed without incident, the enemy being rather surprisingly inactive, and the Battalion was able to make much progress towards remedying the defects in its defences. On the 13th December it handed over its lines to the Rangers and withdrew to Divisional reserve in Springvale Camp at Ecurie, a pleasant camp, but one of the filthiest the Battalion had ever had to occupy.

A few days were spent in training here, and on Sunday, the 16th, Major-Gen. Dudgeon attended the Battalion's Church Parade, and presented medal ribands to all available N.C.O.'s and men who had been decorated for their services at Cambrai. The Division was now expecting relief by the 31st, and, as this relief would have ensured a Christmas out of the line, considerable disappointment was caused to all ranks by the announcement on the 17th December that the relief was cancelled temporarily, and that the Battalion was to return to the trenches. The change took place the following day, and the 1/4th Londons took over the Oppy sector from the Rangers.

Five uneventful days passed in the Oppy trenches. On the whole the enemy displayed little activity beyond occasional retaliation to our continuous and systematic bombardments, which were by day and night directed against the enemy's "weak spots." At night the Bosche showed signs of considerable nervousness. A good deal of progress was made with the Brigade programme of trench and wiring work, which was carried on in intensely cold weather, and on the 23rd the Battalion once more exchanged with the Rangers and withdrew to Brigade support.

In the support area Headquarters and B Company (Spicer) were in a 30-foot railway cutting in rear of Bailleul, while A (H. N. Williams), C (Barkworth) and D (Cooper) were in the Red line. Christmas day, which was fortunately not marked by hostile activity, was spent in these positions and by means of numerous small parties in the Red line the troops were able to get as much enjoyment out of it as the circumstances permitted, but the festivity was rather damped by the death of 2/Lieut. E. L. Stuckey, a keen and promising officer, who was killed by a stray shell in the Red line.

Late on Christmas evening the enemy carried out a hurricane bombardment on the front line posts, and during the last day of the year showed some disposition to increase his harassing fire on our back areas.

On the 28th December the 167th Brigade relieved the 168th, which withdrew in Divisional reserve to the Marœuil area, the Battalion being billeted at St Aubin, where five days of training and refitting were obtained. The New Year was celebrated by carrying out the arrangements which had originally been made for Christmas, and after a quite pleasant interlude the Battalion moved on the 3rd January 1918, into the right sector of the Divisional front at Gavrelle, relieving the Queen's Westminsters. The weather was now intensely cold and the ground was covered with snow, which effectively stopped any attempts at active work. The tour of duty passed quietly and without any casualties, though the enemy's artillery and trench mortar fire continued to show an increase in volume, and on both sides aircraft activity developed.

The 62nd Division now took over the Division's sector, and on the 6th January the 56th Division passed into G.H.Q. reserve at forty-eight hours' notice to move. The Battalion handed over its trenches to the 2/4th K.O.Y.L.I. and moved to billets at Marœuil, continuing its route on the 7th to Monchy-Breton (near St Pol), where it arrived in billets at 4 p.m.

A great deal of useful training was carried out at Monchy-Breton, but the incident which probably did as much good to the Battalion as any, was the formation by Lieut. Faulkner, the quartermaster, of an orchestra which was an enormous success from its inception, and maintained its reputation until the end of the War. The orchestra included the following:

'Cellos	Ptes. Montague and Stone.
Violins	Ptes. Barton, Fairman, Perrin and Cornell.
Cornets	Sergt. Fulford and Pte. Stevens.
Trombones	Sergt. Grimston and Pte. Westerman.
Clarionets	Sergt.-Dr Ingham and Pte. Spooner.
Horn	Pte. Cuffe.
Drum	Pte. Smith.
Harmonium	L.-Corpl. Weekes.

The numerous concerts given by this excellent band, which was really well trained by the quartermaster, afforded real pleasure, not only to the Battalion and to other units of the Division, but also to the French inhabitants of the various villages in which the Battalion found temporary homes.

During December and January the Battalion was joined by 2/Lieuts. H. T. Hannay and H. O. Morris, and by 2/Lieut. A. E. Hanks (13th Londons), while Capt. G. E. Stanbridge was granted an exchange to England for six months' duty at home, after having been in France since March 1916.

By this time the possibilities of a German offensive had developed into a practical certainty, and all training was directed towards methods of defence and counter-attack. Much attention was paid to musketry and Lewis gun training. The importance of the rifle and bayonet as the infantry weapon *par excellence* was once more being realised, and the bomb and rifle grenade, which in 1916 and 1917 had to a large extent ousted the rifle from its proper function, were again recognised to be only subsidiary aids in certain circumstances, so that full advantage was eagerly taken of the chance to ensure that all ranks were "handy" with their rifles.

The defensive systems in the area lately occupied by the Division still needed a vast amount of work to bring them to a condition to resist a serious attack, and accordingly throughout the period spent in G.H.Q.

reserve each brigade of the Division supplied one battalion for work in the forward area under the Chief Engineer XIII Corps. The Battalion's turn for this duty came after seventeen days of training at Monchy-Breton, and on the 24th January it moved forward, railing from Tincques to Ecurie, and was accommodated at Stewart Camp, Roclincourt, the transport lines being stationed at Marœuil. Every available man was now put to work in one or other of the large parties which were supplied daily for the R.E.'s, the principal tasks which fell to the Battalion's lot being the wiring of the Green line and the construction of cable trenches (*i.e.* narrow deep trenches in which telegraph cables were buried to minimise the risk of their destruction by shell fire) in the forward area by night. The severity of the winter had now given place to thaw; the weather was warm for the time of year and a good deal of rain fell.

This duty continued till the end of January, when the Battalion was relieved and returned to the reserve area by train from Ecurie to Tincques, marching thence to billets at Magnicourt, which were reached on the 1st February.

An extensive reorganisation was now effected throughout the British armies in France. The ever-dwindling supply of reinforcements from home, due in part to failing resources in man-power and partly to the retention in England of large defence forces which were held in readiness against a possible German invasion, had caused the numbers in infantry battalions throughout the Army to sink dangerously below full strength. In the 1/4th Londons the casualties of Ypres and Cambrai in 1917 had never been balanced by reinforcements, and this was typical of the condition of affairs in every unit which had been heavily engaged in the preceding six months. The decision arrived at, therefore, was to reduce all Brigades to a three, instead of a four, battalion establishment, and this was carried out by disbanding one battalion per brigade and dividing out its strength among the three battalions which were retained. Inevitably such drastic action caused bitter disappointment among the battalions which had the misfortune to be selected for disbandment, and *esprit de corps* received temporarily a severe check. In the 56th Division the 3rd (Royal Fusiliers), 9th (Queen Victoria's) and 12th (Rangers) Battalions were reduced to cadre strength and transferred to the 58th Division, so that from the beginning of the month of February 1918 the infantry of the Division consisted of:

167TH
BRIGADE—   1st London Regiment (Royal Fusiliers).

1/7th Middlesex

		Regiment.	
	1/8th	do.	
168TH BRIGADE—	1/4th	London Regiment	(Royal Fusiliers).
	1/13th	do.	(Kensingtons).
	1/14th	do.	(London Scottish).
169TH BRIGADE—	1/2nd	London Regiment	(Royal Fusiliers).
	5th	do.	(London Rifle Brigade).
	1/16th	do.	(Queen's Westminster Rifles).

The Battalion received through these changes about 150 N.C.O.'s and men from the 9th Londons, 50 from the 3rd Londons and 60 from the 2/1st Londons, who had been disbanded from the 58th Division. Four subalterns also came to the Battalion as follows: Lieuts. G. G. Lewis and F. G. Athey from 2/1st Londons, H. F. Dade from 3rd Londons and W. G. Hook from 9th Londons. The new arrivals naturally felt sore at first at the disappearance of their own units, but, being all good sportsmen, accepted the inevitable, and rapidly settled down in the 1/4th Battalion. This acquisition of strength enabled the Battalion organisation of companies to be expanded to a three-platoon basis instead of the two-platoon system which had been in force since August 1917.

At Magnicourt a week's useful training was effected, in which the reorganisation necessary in consequence of the above changes figured largely. The Battalion was joined by 2/Lieuts. R. E. Campkin, C. H. Board, T. H. Mawby and G. R. Pitman.

The morale of the Battalion—as indeed of all units of the Division—was now splendid. All ranks were perfectly confident as to the outcome of the approaching offensive and the competitive spirit between companies, always strong, was fostered in every possible way. The Battalion transport under Lieut. G. V. Lawrie, M.C., also maintained high efficiency, and received special commendation from Gen. Dudgeon for the smartness of its turn-out. Amid strenuous work amusements were not overlooked and the pleasures of the lighter side of life were much added to by the extraordinarily good concert given one evening by the Quartermaster's band.

At the end of the first week of February the 56th Division's period in reserve was brought to a close and its relief of the 62nd Division began. On the 9th the Battalion left Magnicourt and marched to Marœuil, moving forward again the next day to its old trenches at Oppy, where it relieved the 2/5th West Yorkshires. In addition to its old sector the Battalion had to take over, as a temporary measure, Bird Post on the right. The front line posts were not approachable by daylight at this date as Boyne and Bedford Streets, the communication trenches leading forward from the Marquis line, had fallen in as a result of the severe weather, and had not been repaired. Other parts of the trench system also needed much repair.

This tour of duty was remarkably quiet, and with the exception of sporadic shelling the enemy was inactive. The Bosche had apparently been permitted to contract a habit of walking about in the open in rear of his lines, but B and C Companies in Bird and Beatty posts were soon able to bring home to him the unwisdom of exposing himself in daylight. The Headquarter Scouts under Sergt. Hayes also did good work in this direction from a useful fire position on a big mound near Beatty Post, whence by good marksmanship they secured six head one evening. At this period also the close liaison which the Battalion always maintained with the Divisional artillery stood it in good stead. A battery of the 281st Brigade R.F.A. had a section of 18-pr. guns in Bailleul, and the Battalion signallers having run a wire to the guns from Bird Post, the gunners settled down to a little sniping. The gunner officer in charge, Lieut. J. Powell, M.C., registered the guns on a small cart standing in Bosche ground and it was easy to switch and elevate the guns roughly on to any party of Bosche moving about. The results were most successful and the Bosche was finally cured of his desire for walking exercise outside his trenches.

On the evening of the 14th February the Battalion handed over its trenches to the London Scottish and withdrew to billets in Roclincourt in Divisional reserve. Here nine days were spent, during which the Battalion supplied working parties for the further improvement of the trenches.

From the 22nd to the 27th the Battalion was once more in the trenches for another quiet tour of duty, and on the latter date it withdrew to Roclincourt West Camp in Divisional reserve. The lack of activity at this period is evidenced by the fact that only two men were wounded during the month of February.

Attention was now fixed solely on the coming offensive, to meet which preparations were being pushed forward with thoroughness. Additional firesteps were constructed in the trenches and the already formidable wire was further strengthened.

From this date forward every tour in the trenches or in Brigade support was passed by platoons in exactly the same position, so that every man might, whenever the offensive should be launched, be well acquainted with his position.

The five days at Roclincourt West Camp were succeeded by a short period in Brigade support, in which position the Battalion relieved the Kensingtons on the 5th March. The tour of duty passed quietly with the exception of a somewhat severe enemy bombardment with gas shell on the evening of the 8th. Early on the morning of the 9th the Kensingtons carried out an excellent raid on the enemy lines north of Oppy, in the course of which about 20 Germans were killed and 4 brought back as prisoners. The raiding party was under Lieut. Lester, M.C. (since killed), commissioned from the 4th Londons. The identification obtained was normal, that is, the prisoners belonged to the German regiment which was believed to be opposed to us. These captures elicited information that the offensive was imminent, and this, combined with unmistakable signs of enemy activity, such as extensive road repairs, clearing and repairing enemy trenches formerly derelict, and so forth, left no room for doubt that the Germans' great effort could not be long delayed. Thenceforward extreme vigilance was exercised all along the line.

II. *The Reserve Battalion*

Shortly after the reconstruction of the 1st London (Reserve) Brigade, which resulted in the 3rd (Reserve) Battalion being made the draft-finding unit for both the 3rd and the 4th London Regiments, the Brigade was moved from its camps at Hurdcott and Fovant to billets in various watering places on the South Devon coast. The 3rd Battalion was fortunate enough to be allotted to Torquay, where it took up its new quarters in December 1916. As a military station Torquay was, of course, not so desirable as Hurdcott. In the first place, the scattering of untrained troops in billets greatly increased the difficulty of disciplinary control, while training grounds were farther removed and somewhat inadequate. In spite of these undoubted disadvantages, however, the change from the bitter searching winds of "The Plain" in winter time to the more genial climate of South Devon was universally welcomed, and the Battalion lived for some weeks in considerable comfort.

The Brigade was now under command of Brig.-Gen. Howell, who at the outbreak of war had commanded the Guards on the Somme.

Life in the Reserve Battalion at Torquay proceeded on very much the same routine as had obtained at Hurdcott, and an attempt at describing it in detail would only be wearisome. Once again the instructional staff had to face the "spade work" of training raw recruits, since the drain on the Battalion's resources during the Somme battles had denuded it of trained soldiers, and a fresh batch of recruits now filled its ranks.

A further modification in training organisation took place about this time, and we may refer shortly to this as it affected the functions of training battalions considerably. This modification lay in the establishment of "Command Depôts" which were formed for the reception from hospital of officers, N.C.O.'s and men returned from the Expeditionary Force who were not yet physically fit to return to their respective units. At a stage in their convalescence, in which their retention in hospital as in-patients was no longer required, such men were sent to their Command Depôt for light exercise in walking, physical training and so on, and for such local treatment as their individual cases necessitated. N.C.O.'s and men remained in the Depôt until their recovery was complete, when they were despatched to their training reserve units for a short "smartening-up" course of instruction before being once more sent overseas. The Command Depôts thus relieved training battalions of a great deal of medical and convalescent work for which they were neither equipped nor suitable, and also ensured that the staff of instructors in the training battalions were engaged for the minimum of time in "brushing-up" the trained men prior to their return to France, whereby they were enabled to devote the maximum of attention to the recruits. The Guards and the London Regiment were amalgamated for the purpose of a Command Depôt, and this was located at Shoreham-by-Sea, Sussex. Shortly after its formation, Major G. H. M. Vine was appointed from the Reserve Battalion to the Permanent Staff of the Depôt.

In January 1917, Major L. T. Burnett joined the Reserve Battalion from sick leave and was appointed second in command, a position which he continued to fill until the following July, when he was transferred to the War Office.

The South Devon station was retained for only a comparatively short period and in April the Brigade moved again, this time to Blackdown, in the Aldershot Command. Blackdown is some seven miles north of Aldershot, and is one of the many pine-and heather-covered hills in which the district abounds. Most of the barracks at this Station were hutted camps, but the 3rd Battalion was fortunate in being sent to Dettingen, a pre-war permanent barracks in which it was exceedingly comfortable.

The advantage of having the Battalion compacted in one camp became almost at once exemplified, and the desirable tightening of discipline rapidly effected a great increase of efficiency. The unsurpassed facilities for training afforded by the Aldershot Command also proved of incalculable value, and enabled the keen and efficient training staff of the Battalion to raise the unit to the position of one of the best organised battalions of a Brigade whose reputation for training was second to none.

At Blackdown, moreover, the facilities provided for the recreation of the troops were really excellent, and among these mention should be made first of the Y.M.C.A. and the Church Army, whose excellent institutions were of the greatest value. Each battalion also was provided with a sports ground, and among the pleasant memories of men trained in this Station not the least is the Blackdown Garrison Theatre, which was visited weekly by capable companies. The Sunday evening concerts in the theatre were also a very notable and valuable feature of the social life of the garrison.

Training here proceeded on the same lines, but a further modification was now introduced for the benefit of the large numbers of lads under military age who were now joining. Under the Military Service Acts no men might be sent overseas till the age of nineteen, and in order to ensure that their training should not be unnecessarily hurried a special syllabus of work was evolved for them, the original scheme being so enlarged and lengthened as to provide for such young soldiers becoming "trained" not earlier than the age at which they might be sent to the front. To ensure the smooth working of this amended scheme the young soldiers, or "A IV's" as they were called, were grouped in special companies, and in addition a number of "young soldier battalions" were added to the Coastal Defence Forces.

In January 1918 Lieut.-Col. Montgomerie Webb vacated command of the Battalion on attachment to the Royal Air Force, and the Battalion was taken over by Lieut.-Col. Hanbury Sparrow, D.S.O., M.C., Royal Berkshire Regiment, who had come to England under the six months exchange system. Under Lieut.-Col. Sparrow the Battalion continued to make great strides, and his striking personality was the means of winning every ounce of willing and devoted service from all who had the honour to be under his command. The work of the Reserve Battalion during the early part of 1918 is so much bound up with the movements of the overseas battalions under the stress of the German offensive that we may conveniently break off here and take up the story of the Second Battle of the Somme.

CHAPTER XX
THE 2/4TH BATTALION IN THE SECOND BATTLE OF THE SOMME, 1918

I. *Preparations for the German Offensive*

The southward move of Gough's Fifth Army was for the purpose of extending the British lines into an area hitherto occupied by the French. Between the 10th January and the 3rd February 1918 a considerable sector, extending from the River Omignon north of St Quentin to Barisis, in the Forêt de St Gobain south of La Fère, was taken over from the French. The responsibility for the whole of this line, some thirty miles long, in addition to about twelve miles from Gouzeaucourt to the Omignon, hitherto held by Byng's Third Army, fell upon Gough.

The 58th Division was at first in reserve and was billeted in the Amiens area, the 2/4th Londons being quartered on the evening of the 22nd January at Thézy-Glimont, a pleasant village near the confluence of the Avre with the Noye, about eight miles south-east of Amiens, where French pre-war civilisation was still almost untouched. It is needless to remark how delightful to all ranks were these peaceful surroundings after the ghastly shell-torn swamps of Poelcapelle. About a fortnight passed at Thézy-Glimont in the usual routine of training, during which one or two small drafts joined the Battalion. Lieut. B. Rivers Smith left the Battalion on the 1st February for six months' duty in England.

The most important feature of the rest period was the reorganisation of Divisions on a ten-battalion basis,[6] of which a note has been given in the preceding chapter. In the 58th Division, as in the 56th, the 4th London Battalion was selected for continued existence, and at the end of January the 2/4th Battalion was strengthened by the transference from the disbanded 2/1st Londons of 10 officers and 221 other ranks. The officers who joined from the 2/1st Londons were Capt. W. D. Ramsey; Lieuts. W. C. Morton, G. J. L. Menges, W. B. Evans; 2/Lieuts. R. H. J. Mendl, A. Woodington, C. J. C. Wildman, W. H. Parslow, S. H. E. Crane and H. W. Durlacher. After the reorganisation the infantry of the Division comprised the following units:

[6] Three Brigades of three battalions each, and one pioneer battalion.

173RD BRIGADE— 2/2nd London Regiment (Royal Fusiliers).

	3rd	"	"	"	"	
	2/4th	"	"	"	"	
174TH BRIGADE—	2/6th	London	Regiment	(Rifles).		
	7th	"	"			
	8th	"	"	(Post Office).		
175TH BRIGADE—	9th	London	Regiment	(Queen Victoria's Rifles).		
	10th	"	"	(Hackney).		
	12th	"	"	(Rangers).		

Before the Division left the Amiens area the imminence of a German offensive was a matter of common knowledge to all ranks, and so impressed with the seriousness of the situation was the High Command, that on the 5th February a most inspiring message from General Gough was conveyed in a lecture by the Brigadier, to all officers, warrant officers and sergeants of the Brigade.

The state of affairs was indeed critical and a grave crisis in the War was approaching. Some slight account of the general conditions which had brought this about has already been attempted, and there is no occasion now to recapitulate the main factors of the situation in which the Allies found themselves. We must, however, point to one or two conditions especially attaching to the British front which had a pre-eminent influence on what followed.

The gradual and ever-increasing numerical preponderance of the Germans on the British front has been referred to; translated into numbers the position may be better appreciated. During the period from the 1st November 1917 to the 21st March 1918, the number of German divisions on the Western front rose steadily from 146 to 192, an increase of 46, against which the total number of British divisions in France was but 58, and these sadly depleted in numbers. The question of the falling off in the numbers of reinforcements sent to France at this period has become the subject of an embittered controversy to which we do not propose to offer any contribution. We are, however, concerned in pointing to the result, whatever the cause, of this growing numerical disparity, which was to confront G.H.Q. with a most anxious problem. The British front was now some 125 miles long, and a glance at any war map will show that the general trend of the front was in a north-westerly direction, *i.e.* near its northern extremity the line ran comparatively close to the sea. In other words, the space available for manœuvre in the event of a considerable break-through by enemy forces was dangerously small in the vital neighbourhood of the Channel Ports; and a successful German offensive in this region might have the effect of rolling up our forces against the sea. In the south the space between the lines and the sea was greater, but a large enemy success in the southern area also had serious possibilities as it might entail the complete isolation of the British Armies from the French.

These were very briefly the two alternative possibilities which G.H.Q. had to face, and the problem awaiting solution was how to provide with the inadequate force at its disposal for the efficient defence of its lines no matter where the blow might fall. The matter was further complicated. The French were equally nervous of a sudden blow against their weak spots in Champagne and at Rheims, which might lay open the German road to Paris, and this fear rendered it impossible for them to place at the disposal of British G.H.Q. sufficient forces to make up the very grave inequality of strength which existed on the British front. The grouping of forces was, moreover, rendered more difficult by the fact that, so great were the available German reserves, it might well prove that the first enemy blow, although serious and energetic, might in reality not be the main effort. This doubt would inevitably, whatever the Allies' dispositions might be, have the effect of sterilising the British and French reserves for some days until it was quite certain that the first blow was not a feint, to be succeeded later by a still greater effort elsewhere.

Such was the problem, and surely never has a military commander been faced by a more difficult situation; for on the wisdom of G.H.Q.'s dispositions would probably rest the fortunes of the whole British Empire.

Before stating the solution adopted by G.H.Q. in especial relation to the doings of the 2/4th Battalion, we may perhaps be pardoned for glancing at one or two aspects of Ludendorff's problem which, as is now known from his own book, was by no means free from difficulty.

The vital necessity of a stern British defence of the Channel Ports was appreciated by Ludendorff as fully as by the British G.H.Q., and he was therefore alive to the possibility—knowing the British inferiority in numbers—that the overwhelming importance of the north might lead to a concentration of British divisions in the north at the expense of the southern area. But could he be certain that this course would be adopted? He might, after staking his all in the south, find that British G.H.Q. had outwitted him and anticipated his intention to attack at St Quentin. It was clearly essential that, to achieve the sweeping victory which alone could save Germany, Ludendorff must endeavour to encompass the temporary sterilisation of the Allied reserves which has been alluded to. To ensure this his plans must be shrouded in secrecy till the last moment; and the organisation of so vast an attack as was ultimately launched without disclosing its location to a vigilant enemy must have caused Ludendorff acute anxiety. That it was in fact accomplished can only beget admiration on our side for a most skilful opponent. And failure to Ludendorff, moreover, was fraught with consequences quite as awful from his point of view as his success would be to the British. Austria had gained a temporary respite in its victory over the Italians, but its army was becoming disintegrated and lacking in supplies; and no one realised more keenly than Ludendorff that the Dual Monarchy itself could not outlive a collapse of its army. In Germany the revolutionary ideas from Russia were beginning to have a weakening effect on the loyalty and steadfastness of an increasing section of the population; hunger was becoming intensified, for the comparative failure of the U-boat campaign resulted in an ever-tightening Allied blockade. And ever in front of Ludendorff loomed the spectre of gigantic American forces on their way to France, which the U-boats were powerless to stop. How many Americans had landed? How soon could they be thrown into the battle line to turn the scale against the Central Powers? These were questions to which Ludendorff must earnestly have sought an answer, and which must have brought home to him the realisation that this gigantic bid for victory he was preparing would for good or evil be the last effort which Germany could make.

The decision of G.H.Q. on these questions was that the Channel Ports must be adequately defended at all costs, and that if any sector of the line must be left weakly defended, that sector must be in the southern area, which the Fifth Army had now taken over. The depth of the space available for retirement in rear of the lines in this area no doubt had its influence in this decision; and in addition, the fact that, in the event of a considerable withdrawal of our forces under the pressure of the German attack, a natural line of defence in rear of the forward positions seemed to be offered in the line of the Somme, which at Péronne makes a wide sweep southwards, thus forming a natural barrier more or less parallel with the British front in the St Quentin district. Possibly a further factor was the apparent natural strength of the extreme south of the front between Moy and La Fère, where the Oise Canal and marshes formed a wide and difficult obstacle between the Germans and our own troops. In the southern area, moreover, it would in case of need be more easy to make use quickly of such reserves as the French might be able to place at G.H.Q.'s disposal.

II. *The Retreat from La Fère*

The Fifth Army was allotted a front of 42 miles, which was held by 17 divisions in line and 3 infantry and 3 cavalry divisions in reserve. The sector was held by four Corps, from left to right the VII (Congreve), the XIX (Watts), the XVIII (Maxse), and the III (Butler).

The III Corps, with which alone we are concerned, comprised at the date of battle the 14th, 18th and 58th Divisions on a front of 30,000 yards, a gigantic sector for 27 battalions, not one of which was at war strength. In reserve were the 2nd and 3rd Cavalry Divisions. The sector allotted to the 58th Division, in which it relieved the 30th between the 7th and 9th February 1918, was the extreme right of the British Armies and extended from north of Travécy, where it touched the 18th Division on the left, to south of Barisis, where it linked up with the French on its right. This enormous front of nearly 9½ miles was held by two brigades, the two subsectors finding their natural division in the Oise marshes and the Canal de St Quentin, which at La Fère take a sudden turn westward, thus running at right angles into the British positions. North of the Canal the country is comparatively open and gently undulating, while south of it the lines plunge through the hilly and densely wooded district of the Forêt de St Gobain.

The marsh area at La Fère is about a mile and a half wide, so that the frontage which needed active defence by each Brigade was roughly four miles. On so vast a frontage a defence by continuous trench lines was clearly out of the question, and the British defence was designed to be in great depth. It was divided into three zones of defence. The Forward Zone, about 1000 yards in depth, relied for its defence on small company redoubts with the space between taken up by hidden machine-guns. This zone was intended to act as a "shock-absorber" in which the first intensity of the enemy's onslaught might be met and checked. The main defence was to be offered in the Battle Zone, about 1500 yards in rear of the Forward Zone. The Battle Zone occupied a depth of about 2000 yards and was to consist of isolated and wired forts, again strengthened by inter-supporting machine-guns. It was hoped that a final check might be administered to the enemy's attempts in this zone, but in rear of it a further defensive system, in this case a continuous line, was to be created as a Rear Zone. Beyond this again the Somme line was to be put into a state of defence.

At the date of taking over this area from the French the defensive organisation on the lines above indicated was practically non-existent. Very little depth was provided for in the defence and in rear of the Forward Zone practically all was yet to be done. The Battle Zone redoubts were inadequate and insufficiently wired, while the Rear Zone line was merely spit-locked.

For weeks, therefore, the whole energies of every available formation, infantry holding the line, engineers, pioneers and labour corps units from all parts of the world, were concentrated on the enormous task of converting the G.H.Q. scheme into a reality. Valuable time which could have been well spent in training the infantry in defensive measures and counter-attack, and in assimilating the new personnel which had been brought into battalions by the reorganisation of January, was inevitably devoted to entrenching and wiring work, wearying in itself and trying as only work done against time can become. All ranks, however, were sufficiently impressed by the need, and all were working with the zeal born of a grim determination to prove themselves equal to the demands which would be made upon them.

The 173rd Brigade moved forward to take over the left or north brigade sector on the 7th February. The 2/4th Battalion railed from Villers-Bretonneux to Appilly, whence it marched to billets at Quierzy on the south bank of the Oise. Here it was joined the following day by the transport which had moved by road. On the evening of the 8th the Battalion was attached temporarily to the 174th Brigade south of the Canal, and on the 9th moved to the Forward Zone, where it relieved the 7th Londons. As was to be expected from the conditions under which the line was held, the Battalion was now rather scattered, Headquarters and C and D Companies being stationed at Amigny-Rouy, while A and B Companies were at Sinceny and the stores and transport at Autreville. Enemy activity in this area was almost non-existent and the whole energies of the Battalion were devoted to entrenching work, which was carried out under Royal Engineer supervision. Large working parties, totalling on some occasions 12 officers and 400 other ranks, were called for daily for a variety of tasks to which the only relief was a periodical exchange of companies for bathing at Sinceny. On the 24th February the Battalion completed the Divisional relief and moved to the extremity of the British lines, where it relieved the 8th East Surreys, Headquarters, C and D Companies occupying Bernagousse Quarries, while A and B Companies were billeted in Pierremande. In this area the Battalion spent a few quiet days, occupied in strengthening the battle positions under the Royal Engineers. On the 27th it was relieved by the 7th Londons, and returned to the 173rd Brigade, going into Divisional reserve in rear of the northern brigade subsector. In this area the Battalion was again much split up, Headquarters, A and B Companies being at Viry Noureuil, and C and D Companies at Tergnier. This day the Battalion was joined by three more officers of the 2/1st Londons, 2/Lieuts. L. F. Wardle, C. B. Francis and C. W. Cumner.

The situation on the 173rd Brigade front during February had been remarkably quiet. The policy adopted had been purely defensive, and our artillery had shown but little activity. The distance separating the British lines from the enemy's and the nature of the terrain had rendered observation a matter of some difficulty; but the enemy's energies appeared to be devoted to strengthening his own defences of La Fère rather than to the preparation of an offensive operation. The general impression gained from the Brigade Intelligence Summary for this month is indeed that the idea of any attack being launched in the La Fère area was rather ridiculous, and that everyone was quite prepared to settle down at Fargniers for life. General Gough, however, as is well known, did not share this comfortable optimism, for almost a month earlier at a conference of his Corps Commanders at Catelet he had made what later proved to be an accurate forecast of the location of the German attack.

The Battalion's work during the three weeks immediately preceding the battle calls for little comment. After two days in Divisional reserve it moved forward to the Battle Zone, in which it relieved the 3rd Londons on the 2nd March, and this position it continued to hold until the offensive was launched, providing daily working parties for the improvement of the defences. The early days of March saw a slight increase of artillery and trench mortar activity on both sides, but the area was still comparatively quiet with but little outward indication of the storm which was shortly to burst over it.

On the 7th March 2/Lieut. D. F. Crawford joined the Battalion.

The skill with which the Germans continued to conceal their intentions was indeed marvellous. For some time past the withdrawal of divisions from the line had taken place, but so widely disseminated had this process been that it had attracted comparatively little notice. The attack divisions had been assembled well in rear of the lines, beyond the reach of our prying aeroplanes, and had there been put through a very thorough course of training, which extended to the smallest detail of what was expected of each division. Finally, about the middle of March this gigantic force had begun to move towards the line, marching by night and closely concealed by day, and by the evening of the 20th the enormous concentration was complete. Von Hutier, commanding the Eighteenth German Army, had now between the Omignon and Vendeuil 11 divisions in line, 8 in close support and 2 in reserve; Von Gayl opposite La Fère had 4 divisions and Von Boehn at St Gobain another 2; making a total of 27 divisions. Opposed to this colossal strength were Butler's 5 and Maxse's 4 weak divisions. Such were the odds on the 21st March 1918.

Before proceeding to the battle itself there is one further point to which we desire to refer, and that is the thick fog which lay over the marshes of the Oise early on the morning of the 21st and the succeeding days. The effect of this fog on what transpired had been variously estimated. The general consensus of opinion of officers and men who took part in the battle is that it was a great disadvantage to the defence. In many ways this was undoubtedly the case. The complete blotting out of all landmarks beyond a few yards' radius rendered any sort of co-operation with adjoining units impossible; the inter-supporting machine-guns between the redoubts were comparatively useless for they could not see when and where to fire. The artillery was also handicapped for it knew not where to lay its barrages to trap the advancing enemy. Many times in the course of the battle, redoubts which thought themselves not yet attacked suddenly realised that in the fog they had been surrounded and cut off. The general result was that the defence degenerated into a series of isolated battles in which companies and platoons made individual stands, unsupported by their comrades and in ignorance of what was occurring on their flanks.

But there is another side to the picture, and the German opinion is equally strong, that but for the fog their success would have been more far-reaching than it actually proved to be. The inevitable loss of direction and touch between attacking columns, the feeling of uncertainty born of drifting forwards without seeing one's surroundings, the strange tricks which fog always plays in the matters of distance and sound—all these could not but affect detrimentally the speed and cohesion of the attack—and speed was of all things the essential for complete German success. Swiftly though the attack came, from the very first day the advances were made far behind schedule, and to this extent the German attack failed. How far it failed through the fog we will not venture to estimate; but that the fog was a contributory factor there can be no doubt.

On the afternoon of the 20th March the order "Prepare for attack" was received from III Corps, and by 3.30 p.m. all companies of the Battalion were ready to man their battle positions.

The scheme of defence has already been alluded to in general terms, and it has been indicated that both the Forward and Battle Zones were divided into a series of defended localities each held by a company. These localities comprised a main keep, supported by two or more subsidiary redoubts, while the space intervening between adjoining localities was covered by the guns of the Brigade Machine-Gun Company.

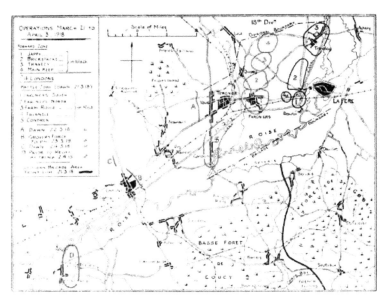

THE RETREAT FROM LA FÈRE, MARCH 1918

Map No. 15 shows the relative positions of the various localities in the scheme of defence, and in the Northern Brigade area, with which alone we are henceforward concerned, the disposition of troops on the night 20th/21st March was as follows:

FORWARD ZONE—2/2nd London Regiment.

Main Keep Locality:	Headquarters and 1 company.
Jappy Locality:	1 company with a standing patrol at Beautor.
Brickstack Locality:	1 company.
Travécy Locality:	1 company.

BATTLE ZONE—2/4th London Regiment.

Headquarters on the Crozat Canal,

Fargniers.

Fargniers South Locality: A Company (Lieut. H. J. M. Williams).

Fargniers North Locality: B Company less 2 platoons (Capt. S. G. Askham).

Farm Rouge Locality: D Company (Capt. C. A. Clarke).

Triangle Locality: C Company (Lieut. G. E. Lester).

The two remaining platoons of B Company were detached as follows:

1 platoon (2/Lieut. D. F. Crawford) at the junction of the St Quentin and Crozat Canals.

1 platoon (Lieut. W. F. Brown) at Condren, where there was also a squadron of the Oxfordshire Hussars.

Quessy Locality: 1 company 1/4th Suffolks (Pioneers).

Brigade Headquarters were at Quessy Château near Crozat Canal, and the 3rd Londons were in Divisional reserve at Viry Noureuil.

It will be seen that the bulk of the defensive force was concentrated—if such a word may be applied to so attenuated a defence—on the right flank, where the line of the Oise marshes, by now practically no obstacle owing to the unusually dry spring, laid open the road to Chauny and Noyon. It was quite evident that should the Germans succeed in breaking through on the St Firmin-Vendeuil front they would almost certainly endeavour to expand the breach behind the British lines and make a south-westerly dash towards Noyon and Compiègne in order to complete the isolation of the British armies from the French. The Oise flank therefore was vitally important.

At 4.20 a.m. on the 21st March the enemy barrage opened with terrific intensity. The messages to man battle positions were already written in Brigade Headquarters, but delay was caused in conveying them to the various units concerned, for during the first few minutes of the bombardment Brigade Signal Headquarters were knocked out by a direct hit, so that this and subsequent messages had to be sent by runner. Lieut.-Col. Dann, in fact, did not receive any orders to move until long after he had, on his own initiative, despatched his companies to their posts.

It is rather difficult to understand why the companies were kept in billets such as cellars under the ruins of Fargniers and Quessy until the last moment, especially as warning of the attack had been received the previous afternoon. Most platoons had several hundred yards, and some as much as a mile and a half, to traverse to their trenches; and under the intense and accurate barrage many casualties were sustained during this forward move. By about 7.30 a.m., however, the companies were all reported in position.

The actual time of the attack is not known, but it probably occurred between 6.30 and 7 a.m., for at 7.10 a.m. a message was received from Lieut.-Col. Richardson (2/2nd Londons) that the enemy was in Jappy Keep, and about the same time the bombardment of the Battle Zone positions became still more intense. It must be borne in mind that fog hung over the whole area like a thick curtain, completely cutting off the Forward Zone from the observation, which it had been reasonably anticipated would be obtained over it. The Battle Zone troops and Brigade Headquarters were thus in the dark as to what was going on in the forward positions.

By 9 a.m. the enemy was reported in possession of Main Keep Locality, which meant a serious incursion into the defences on the vital flank. Steps were at once taken to employ the 3rd Londons (in reserve), one company being directed on Fargniers, while artillery and machine-gun barrages were laid on the Canal crossings at St Firmin and Beautor and on the area west of the captured positions.

Lieut.-Col. Dann now ordered forward patrols from each of the companies to endeavour to keep in touch with the situation, but it seems that if these orders ever reached the companies—they certainly were not received by the left company—the patrols themselves were destroyed by the enemy shell fire, for no information of value was obtained.

All this time no word had been received from the Travécy Locality though attempts were made to communicate from the 2/4th Londons and from the 18th Division on the left, and it is probable that the fog enabled the enemy to surround the garrison before its commander was able to communicate with his Headquarters.

During the morning Lieut.-Col. Richardson asked for counter-attack troops to be sent forward to him in the hope that the enemy in the St Firmin area might be ejected, but this request was refused by Division on the ground that the Battle Zone garrisons must be maintained intact. In consequence, therefore, of the extreme pressure on his front, Lieut.-Col. Richardson was compelled to order a withdrawal of the few remaining details of his shattered battalion on to the Fargniers area occupied by the 2/4th Londons, and by midday the fall of the Forward Zone was complete.

Shortly after midday the fog lifted slightly, and the 2/4th Londons in the Battle Zone became engaged with the enemy, who began to exert pressure on the extreme right flank. At about 2 p.m. the platoon of A Company holding Distillery Post next the Oise Canal was driven in and Lieut.-Col. Dann ordered the company of the 3rd Londons in Fargniers to launch a counter-attack. This effort was only partly successful, and Distillery Post remained in German hands.

About the same time the enemy advanced in large numbers all along the line, especially against the Farm Rouge and Triangle Localities. The former of these had always been regarded as a weak spot in the defences, and two reserve machine-guns were at once turned on to the enemy advancing against it. By 3.45 p.m., after a stubborn resistance against overwhelming numbers, Clarke's weak company was ejected from the Farm Rouge itself, and its grip on the remainder of the Locality much weakened. The assaulting columns continued to press on in the direction of the Quessy Locality, thus isolating the Fargniers position in the corner between the two Canals and completely cutting off Lester, who was still hanging on to his position in the Triangle against impossible odds.

A prompt endeavour to counter this very serious turn of events was taken by Brigade, who sent forward two platoons of the Suffolks to reinforce Clarke and fill the gap between him and Askham. The 3rd Londons also were drawn on again, and a second company was sent forward through Quessy to strengthen the Farm Rouge Locality. Of this company, however, only two platoons ever reached their objective, the others being destroyed by the enemy's fire at the crossing of the Crozat Canal.

At about 6.50 p.m. the Battle Zone, in spite of repeated and heavy enemy attacks, was still intact with the exceptions of the penetrations next the Canal on the extreme right and in the Farm Rouge Locality, and it was decided to lay down a provisional S.O.S. line on the forward edge of the Battle Zone. The enemy, however, was continuing his attacks with great persistence, and the gradual infiltration of his storm troops between our scattered positions was constantly altering the situation. By 7.15 p.m. he had already overrun the new S.O.S. line in the vicinity of the Distillery, and was beginning to close in on Fargniers from the south.

In the 18th Division area on the left the struggle was also raging in the Battle Zone, though one or two posts in the Forward Zone were continuing their glorious yet hopeless struggle. Beyond the 18th Division the 14th had received a severe blow and the Germans had penetrated some miles into the British positions. It appeared by no means improbable that if the enemy's progress in this region were unchecked the left flank of the III Corps would be entirely rolled up. A general withdrawal was therefore inevitable to prevent the line being broken. To conform with these movements it was decided by Division to effect a withdrawal to the line of the Crozat Canal from its junction with the St Quentin Canal as far north as a line running due west between the Farm Rouge and Triangle Localities, which latter was to be held.

Instructions to this end were immediately issued, and Lieut.-Col. Dann was ordered to conduct the withdrawal of the whole of the mixed details now in the Fargniers corner, and all troops in the Battle Zone were placed under his orders. This withdrawal was really a stubborn rearguard action, for the enemy was unrelenting in his efforts to drive in the Farm Rouge gap and reach the Canal. But a stern resistance was offered in which gallant service was rendered by the Suffolks at Quessy, and by midnight Lieut.-Col. Dann was enabled to report his heterogeneous command in position on the west bank of the Canal, with all iron rations, S.A.A., stores and Orderly Room records intact.

The defence of the Triangle Locality must now be referred to as it comprises, owing to the wedge driven into the Farm Rouge Locality early in the day, an isolated battle, and is a magnificent example of stern courage against overwhelming numbers. The casualties suffered from gas shell in this area had been numerous, but apart from the accurate shooting of the Bosche gunners, C Company had been, like the rest of the Battalion, not closely engaged until the Forward Zone was overrun. The lifting of the fog about midday disclosed a large force of the enemy, which is estimated at about a battalion, advancing against Lester's thinly held positions. From this time onwards no orders or messages of any kind reached Lester from Battalion Headquarters or the adjoining companies, and he was left to fight his own battle. The advancing enemy were hotly engaged by rifle and Lewis gun fire, and large numbers were killed. Already D Company were losing their grip on the Farm Rouge, but Lester decided that the only course open to him was to await reinforcements. These never came, and probably, owing to the utter severance of communications, it was never realised how urgent his need was. The only support to this gallant company was one 18-pr. gun firing over open sights from near Quessy. All the afternoon the unequal fight was maintained, though the defenders were much harassed by low-flying German 'planes. With the approach of dusk the mist came down again, surrounding the company with an impenetrable curtain. Again and again Lester sent out runners and patrols to seek connection with the adjoining troops but these never returned. "I still hoped against hope," he writes, "that we should be reinforced, as the Colonel had kept rubbing it in at conferences before the battle that we had to stand fast at all costs." At last it became clear that the flanks were in the air and that the rear of the Company was being encircled, and it was decided to fight back to the

Crozat Canal. On the left the remains of two platoons under Blair managed to get back, but of the others but two men got away, and Lester, Wardle and the remainder of the company, nearly all wounded, were captured.

This splendid fight, maintained till nearly 10 p.m. against hopeless odds, was without doubt of enormous value in holding up the enemy and inflicting severe loss on his picked troops. It also formed a strong buttress to the flank of the 18th Division, without which they would have found the right of their Battle Zone turned; and it gave time for the withdrawal of the 2/4th Londons to the Canal line.

Lieut.-Col. Dann's mixed force on the Canal was of necessity in need of organisation, and the 8th Londons, who had been in reserve at Pierremande, were on their way to relieve the troops who had borne the day's fighting. By 6 a.m. the relief was complete and the 8th Londons were established on the Canal line, while Lieut.-Col. Dann's force, consisting of the remains of the 2/2nd, 3rd and 2/4th Battalions, the Suffolks, and elements of the 503rd Field Company R.E. and of the 182nd Tunnelling Company, who had also been thrown into the fight, were assembled on a line west of Vouel, with Headquarters on the Butte de Vouel. This position was an unfinished work, in parts not more than a foot deep, and extended from the Butte almost due south to the Chauny-Tergnier Road. Brigade Headquarters had withdrawn overnight to Le Bas de Viry.

The Condren position, which had not been attacked on the 21st, remained intact but was reinforced by a company of the Suffolks.

The results of the first day's fighting were tolerably serious. The Forward and Battle Zones had been lost, and thus the greater part of the defences which had been brought to a stage in any way approaching completion were in the enemy's hands. The whole of the available reserves were already inextricably in the fight, and should the attack extend to the Southern Brigade area from Amigny-Rouy to Barisis there would be no means of assisting the defence in that vicinity. Serious losses of personnel had been sustained, and the swiftness and weight of the blow had had their effect, though the morale of the troops were still high. On the other hand the enemy had by no means gained the success which he had anticipated. On the Brigade front of some 5000 yards, held by two weak battalions reinforced by parts of one other battalion, he had employed nearly four divisions, and in spite of these ridiculous odds had only advanced an average of about 5000 yards to find that the defence had successfully withdrawn behind an obstacle of much natural strength. The defence was shaken, but it was not in the least broken, and a break through was the only means of ultimate success to the Germans.

On arrival in the Vouel line in the early hours of the 22nd March, the Battalion, which occupied the north end of the position near the Butte, was reorganised in three companies, with A Company under 2/Lieut. F. G. Williams on the right, B under Capt. Askham in the centre and D under Capt. Clarke on the left. As on the 21st, a dense mist appeared with the early hours, and until it rose, shortly after midday, no infantry movement took place. Under cover of the mist the Battalion was able to do a good deal of work on the Vouel line, and in this they were not much interfered with, as most of the German shells were falling on the road in front.

About 1.15 p.m. the enemy attack opened with great vigour and immense weight on the Canal line and Tergnier. The crossing of the Canal was rendered easier to the enemy by reason of the unfortunate fact that one or two bridges had not been entirely demolished after our withdrawal. All had long before been prepared for demolition, but for some reason the charges did not explode in every case. A certain bewilderment was caused to the defenders at first as the Germans appear to have gained their first footing west of the Canal disguised in British uniforms stolen from the fallen men of the 2/2nd Londons. But as soon as the 8th Londons appreciated what was happening they put up a very stubborn resistance. After getting across the Canal the Bosche seems to have tried to extend north and south along the western bank, and in this he was successful in the northern area. In the south, however, the magnificent fight made by the two companies in Tergnier checked his progress, and time after time his attacks were stopped.

During the afternoon the German 'planes were seeking for the next position held by us, and in spite of the hasty efforts of the Battalion to camouflage its trench, the Vouel line was soon discovered, and ranging on it by the German batteries rapidly ensued. No infantry attack was delivered on the Vouel line, probably on account of the enemy's lack of success at Tergnier.

Late in the afternoon the enemy's pressure on the 8th Londons grew almost intolerable, and little by little he was working his way into Tergnier. It was therefore decided to vacate the position, and after dusk the 8th Londons fell back on to the Vouel line, which they extended to the right from the Viry-Tergnier Road as far as the railway. The two companies in Tergnier were ably extricated by their commander and managed to get clear across the Oise, joining the garrison at Condren, which had not been attacked.

The Vouel line was now the most advanced position, and at 6.30 p.m. the Headquarters of the 3rd, 2/4th and 8th Londons were withdrawn from it to Noureuil. The night passed without any further attempt on the enemy's part to advance, and on our side a good deal of patrolling activity took place. This led to several encounters with small parties of enemy, and resulted in the collection of a quite useful bag of German prisoners as well as a machine-gun and team. Under cover of darkness also touch was regained with the Condren garrison.

Information was received on the evening of the 22nd that French troops were rapidly advancing to our assistance, and that they would be ready to counter-attack the next morning with the object of retaking the Crozat Canal line.

On the 23rd March mist appeared yet once more, considerably hampering our defence and giving the enemy an opportunity of massing for attack. Shortly after 8 a.m. the French attack was launched by two battalions of the 125th French Infantry which passed forward through the Vouel line. The result of the attack is not definitely known as it was impossible to see beyond a radius of about 15 yards. It is certain, however, that it failed to reach Tergnier, and by 11 a.m. the French advance was broken and the troops beginning to drift back into our lines. It should be pointed out in fairness to our Allies that they had been rushed up into the line, incomplete in equipment and transport, and that they were called on to operate without previous reconnaissance over ground which was shrouded in mist and unknown to them. On the extreme left the withdrawal was conducted in some disorder, and it was reported that the 18th Division on our left was also being forced back through Frières Wood. The Vouel line, unfinished and shallow as it was, was already occupied to its fullest capacity, and the French falling back on it caused considerable congestion in the well-dug parts. About the same time the German artillery, which had been plastering the Vouel line fairly steadily all the morning, lifted, and was at once succeeded by an accurate and intense machine-gun barrage. This further tended to create difficulty in the position, for in view of the congestion of the trench it became very hard to get orders along, while work on the gaps between the well dug portions was almost impossible.

Shortly afterwards the mist cleared and the awkwardness of the situation became more apparent. The 18th Division were being pressed back towards Villequier-Aumont, and the left flank was entirely in the air, while the constant pushing of small highly trained bodies of the enemy was enabling them to progress along the Oise marshes on the right. Vouel itself was strongly occupied, and troops were massing for attack. By 12 noon the position was no longer tenable. The enemy was advancing frontally and from both flanks, and Lieut.-Col. Dann ordered a withdrawal on to the Green line. This was a partly dug position which formed a portion of the Rear Zone and was held by troops of the 6th Dismounted Cavalry Brigade and the 18th Entrenching Battalion, on a line east of Noureuil and Viry-Noureuil from the St Quentin Canal to the Vouel-Villequier Road. The withdrawal to the Green line from the Vouel position averaged about 1500 yards, and so hard were the enemy pressing that some platoons had to fight their way back. An attempt was made by the French machine-gunners in the Vouel line to cover the Battalion's withdrawal, but this was not effective and, together with several of our own men, they were captured.

The situation was now critical. The falling back of the 18th Division on the left revealed a gap between the Vouel-Villequier Road and Frières Wood of which the enemy was not slow to take advantage, and there appeared every likelihood that the 173rd Brigade would be cut off from the 18th Division and rolled up against the St Quentin Canal. To meet this threat the left flank of the Green line position, consisting of troops of the Dismounted Brigade and details of the 8th Londons, was thrown back and extended towards Villequier-Aumont in an attempt to gain touch once more with the 18th Division. This line was thin, and under the continued German pressure it suffered severely. During the afternoon the enemy thrust south again and entered Noureuil, thus driving a wedge behind the flank of the Green line troops. A glance at the map will show that a further withdrawal was inevitable if the whole Brigade was not to be rounded up. This began about 6 p.m. and the troops, including all that was left of the fighting ranks of the 2/4th Londons, about 120 all told under Capt. Askham, fell back to a position west of Viry-Noureuil, which village was yielded to the enemy.

During the afternoon, while the fate of the bulk of the Brigade was still in the balance, and it was obviously imperative to check the enemy's advance into Chauny by all available means, the Brigadier ordered Major Grover of the 2/4th Londons, who was at Chauny with battle surplus, to organise all available details for the defence of the town. With remarkable skill and despatch Major Grover collected a heterogeneous force of clerks, cooks, officers' servants, transport drivers—anyone who could hold a rifle—and by dusk reported himself in position on the eastern outskirts of Chauny with a force of 10 officers and 270 other ranks at his command. Of these, 2 officers and 54 other ranks were of the 2/4th Londons. This very brilliant piece of work no doubt did much to save the situation, and "Grover's Force" beyond question deserves to rank high among the various similar "scarecrow armies" which these critical days produced.

During the afternoon Lieut.-Col. Dann was attached for duty to Brigade Headquarters, and the remains of the 2/4th and 8th Londons came under command of Lieut.-Col. Derviche-Jones of the latter Battalion.

The withdrawal from the Green line to the River Helot position was considerably impeded by the French troops who were streaming in a westerly direction, and Brigade therefore endeavoured to ascertain what the intentions of the French Commander were. These were found to be to hold a line from Viry-Noureuil to Villequier-Aumont, and accordingly it was decided that the whole of the 173rd Brigade Group should be withdrawn and reorganised in positions to support the French. This reorganisation was successfully carried out. In view of the rapid and confusing moves which had followed each other in such quick succession, it may be well to state in detail the Brigade positions at dawn on the 24th March:

BRIGADE HEADQUARTERS AT ABBÉCOURT

GROVER'S FORCE—Covering the eastern exits of Chauny from the St Quentin Canal to north of the Chauny—Viry-Noureuil Road.

18TH ENTRENCHING BATTALION—Astride the St Quentin Canal on the right of Grover's Force.

6TH DISMOUNTED CAVALRY BRIGADE—On the left of Grover's Force east of the Chauny—Villequier-Aumont Road.

DETAILS OF THE 2/4TH AND 8TH LONDONS—On the left of Grover's Force west of the Chauny—Villequier-Aumont Road.

The Condren garrison substantially maintained its original positions and was in touch by means of patrols with the 18th Entrenching Battalion, while on the extreme right the 174th Brigade, which had not been attacked, continued to hold the Amigny-Rouy—Barisis front.

On the left of the conglomerate force which now formed the 173rd Brigade Group the line was continued by the 18th and 14th Divisions, with whom French troops were interspersed in the direction of Cugny.

The whole line was strained to breaking-point under the unceasing enemy pressure. Every available man was in the firing line, and the Battalion, which had been now fighting and marching without intermission for three days, was getting worn. But in spite of the enormous odds the Battalion clung on with determination, for it knew that the saving of the situation rested with itself, and attack after attack had failed to give the German masses the break-through which was essential for them.

For the fourth day in succession the Germans were favoured with a thick fog which enshrouded their movements, and under cover of which they were able to prepare a further heavy blow. Early in the morning they attacked and broke through the French outpost line on the River Helot, and about 11 a.m. the lifting of the mist revealed them attacking Grover's Force east of Chauny, and also endeavouring to work round the south of the position next the Canal. This was serious, for a wedge driven in between the Chauny line and the Condren bridgehead, which was also under great pressure from the enemy, might possibly involve the loss of the Oise line, the retention of which was vital for us.

Arrangements were at once made by Brigade for a further withdrawal, and this was rendered the more imperative by the rapid advance made on the left of the Corps front during the day. In this region the enemy were already threatening Guiscard, eight miles north-west of Chauny, and the security of Noyon itself was seriously in doubt.

For several hours Grover's details and the tiny Condren force maintained their fight, but in the afternoon the withdrawal began in accordance with the orders already issued. Under Grover's command the mixed force was skilfully withdrawn, fighting a stubborn rearguard action, to a prepared position about 1000 yards east of Abbécourt, while the detached portion of the 2/4th Londons on Grover's left, now about 60 strong, fell back to Ognes, and marched into Besme across the Oise about midnight. Early in the afternoon Major Grover was wounded and Capt. Askham took over his command. By 4.30 p.m. the Abbécourt position, being no longer tenable, was vacated and the whole of the 173rd Group, including 2/4th and 8th Londons, 503rd Field Company, R.E. and the 6th Dismounted Cavalry Brigade, had crossed the Oise at Manicamp. About the same time the Condren garrison which had held manfully to its positions since the opening of the battle got clear across the river.

Before this withdrawal was completed the whole of the Oise bridges, and also the R.E. Dump at Chauny, were demolished, and it may be remarked that during the four days of fighting not a single gun had been lost except those destroyed by enemy shell fire.

With the withdrawal across the Oise the hardest of the Battalion's fighting in this great battle was finished, though it remained in contact with the enemy with very little rest. The Division now held a river front of over nine miles on the south bank of the Oise from Quierzy to Servais, in addition to the original four miles held by the 174th Brigade in the Forêt de St Gobain. With this enormous front in contact with an enterprising enemy no rest was yet to be expected. The early hours of the 25th March were devoted to sorting out the hopeless tangle of units which the battle had caused, and at 11.30 a.m. Lieut.-Col. Dann became responsible (in conjunction with the 6th Dismounted Cavalry Brigade) for the defence of the river crossings at Quierzy, with a composite force comprising details of four battalions, reorganised in companies as follows:

1 Coy. representing 2/2nd Londons guarding Quierzy bridge.

1 " " 8th Londons on its left.

1 " " 2/4th Londons in support.

This company of the 2/4th Londons was the party of 60 which had reached Besme the previous evening, and was now under 2/Lieut. Griffiths.

The same night (25th/26th March) this composite force was relieved by the 246th French Regiment and withdrew to Besme to refit, Lieut.-Col. Dann taking charge of another composite force of troops of the 175th Brigade. In the meantime the remainder of the 2/4th Londons, which had formed part of Grover's Force and were now under Askham, took up a defensive position under orders of Lieut.-Col. Chart, 18th Entrenching Battalion, east of Manicamp, on the south side of the Canal and the Ailette River. At night this party was also relieved by Lieut.-Col. Dann's force and joined the remainder of the Battalion at Besme.

The 173rd Brigade was now entirely extricated from the line, and a day of reorganisation and collection of scattered details from the various composite forces, which the needs of the moment had created, was of urgent necessity. This respite was obtained on the 26th March when the three original units were reorganised as one battalion, known as the Fusilier Battalion as follows:

No. 1 Coy.—117 other ranks 2/4th Londons under Capt. Askham.

No. 2 Coy.— 88 other ranks 2/4th " " 2/Lieut. Blair.

No. 3 Coy.—179 " " 2/2nd " " Capt. Wright.

No. 4 Coy.—189 " " 3rd " " 2/Lieut. Curtis.

Lieut.-Col. Dann returned from the 175th Brigade to command this newly constituted force. In addition to the Fusilier Battalion, the Brigade included temporarily the 12th Londons under Lieut.-Col. Bayliffe, C.M.G., and the 18th Entrenching Battalion under Lieut.-Col. Chart.

The whole of the III Corps had now been brought south of the Oise, and Noyon fell into the enemy's hands on the 26th. The main weight of the German offensive continued to sweep westward in the direction of

Amiens, but with the details of this part of the fight we are not concerned. The 58th Division, however, was not yet out of the fight, and the enemy made repeated efforts to force a breach in the long river line which it held, but without success. The French troops were now numerous in this area, and though General Butler continued to command his own Corps, the supreme command of the area was taken by the French.

In this battle the Battalion had the extraordinary experience of being driven entirely out of the battle area. It had lost severely and borne several days of the most terrific ordeal that it had yet been called on to face, but with the exception of a deep indentation in its positions at Farm Rouge on the first day there had never been any semblance of a break-through on its front. Frequently hard pressed, often almost surrounded, it had been forced back day after day, stubbornly fighting but never broken.

Constituted as described above the 173rd Brigade took over the Manicamp sector from the 175th on the evening of the 27th March, the 12th Londons occupying the right subsector, with the Fusilier Battalion on the left adjoining Manicamp village. The two 2/4th London Companies were stationed on the Ailette River and in the village. The Brigade remained in these positions strengthening the defences until the night of 2nd/3rd April, when it was relieved by the French, the Fusilier Battalion reaching Blérancourt at midnight. The daylight hours of the 3rd April were occupied in resting and cleaning up, and after dark the Battalion moved to Andignicourt, where it was accommodated in an enormous cave probably large enough to hold a brigade at full strength.

The following afternoon the route was continued and the Battalion reached Amblèny at 8 p.m. Here the Fusilier Battalion broke up, its component companies being once more organised as three battalions under their respective commanders. The 12th Londons returned to their own brigade, being replaced in the 173rd Brigade by the 16th Entrenching Battalion (Lieut.-Col. Nicholls).

The 2/4th Londons were joined on the 3rd April by Major F. G. Tollworthy, 1st Londons, as second in command vice Major Grover wounded.

On the 5th April another evening march was made to Dommiers, and the next day after a very trying march the Battalion reached Villers Cotterets at 8 p.m. Here it entrained with the remainder of the Division for an area further north to which the III Corps had been transferred. The total casualties sustained by the 2/4th Battalion in the second battle of the Somme between 21st March and 3rd April amounted to:

Officers—Lieut. J. Cairns, missing, believed killed; 2/Lieut. F. G. Williams, died of wounds; Major A. Grover, M.C., Capt. C. A. Clarke, M.C., Lieut, H. J. M. Williams, 2/Lieuts. R. W. Chamberlain, C. C. H. Clifford, A. Woodington, E. M. Cuthbertson and C. B. Francis, wounded; Lieut. W. F. Brown, gassed; Lieuts. G. E. Lester, H. W. Durlacher, M.C., 2/Lieuts. D. F. Crawford and L. F. Wardle, captured.

N.C.O.'s and men: 37 killed, 125 wounded and 217 missing.

The total losses of the Division for the same period were 2204, of whom 57 officers and 1606 other ranks were missing.

III. *The Action at Villers-Bretonneux*

In the first portion of this chapter we have endeavoured to give some account of the manner in which the 2/4th Battalion, with the 58th Division and the whole of Butler's III Corps, had been literally pushed aside by the main force of the German onslaught and had been extricated from the fight due southwards through French territory, while the advancing enemy had swept on in a westerly direction towards Amiens.

By the evening of the 28th March, that is to say, a week after the opening of the battle, the Fifth and Third Armies had been forced back from the line of the Somme and over the old Somme battlefields, and had reached the Amiens defence line south of the Somme, while on the north bank the enemy had occupied Albert.

On the 28th March a further attack was delivered on a wide front from north of Arras to Puisieux which resulted in a severe defeat for the Germans; but as only the 1/4th Battalion is concerned in the fighting on this day we propose to defer the account of it to another chapter, and to pursue for the moment the fortunes of the 2/4th Battalion until the final stabilisation of the line in front of Amiens.

The German offensive on the Somme front was now showing signs of weakening, though owing to the enormous losses incurred by our divisions in personnel and material the enemy was still able to make progress. The defences of Amiens in particular were threatened, and Gen. Gough had been entrusted by G.H.Q. with the task of extending and strengthening them. The last days of March saw fierce fighting in this area, and by the 31st of the month the Fifth Army south of the Amiens-Péronne Road had fallen back to the line Villers-Bretonneux-Hangard, both villages inclusive to the British, while on the right the French were holding a small corner of the angle between the Luce and Avre Rivers on the line Hangard-Moreuil

Station. The German attacks finally exhausted themselves by April 5th, after which date there was a short period of trench warfare.

It was to this area, still on the extreme right of the British Armies, that the 58th Division was now directed. From Villers Cotterets, which it left on 6th April, the 2/4th Battalion was railed to Longueau, a suburb of Amiens. The battle line was now quite close to the Amiens-Paris line, a lateral railroad of vital importance to us, and as the Battalion passed Boves the British field guns were in action within a quarter of a mile of the train.

On detrainment the Battalion marched to a reserve position in the Bois de Gentelles, where a long day was devoted to reorganisation. The losses of the latter end of March had not yet been made good by reinforcements, and it was therefore decided to make use of the 16th Entrenching Battalion for this purpose. Accordingly on the 7th April two companies of this unit were transferred to the 2/4th Battalion, making an increase of strength of 4 officers (Capt. B. H. C. Hettler, M.C., and 2/Lieuts. J. W. Bocking, E. V. Grimsdell and W. T. Millar) and 344 other ranks. With this valuable reinforcement it was possible once again to organise four companies as follows:

No. 1	Coy.	under	Capt. G. H. Hetley	
				2/4th London men.
No. 2	"	"	Capt. S. G. Askham	
No. 3	"	"	Capt. B. H. C. Hettler	
				16th Entrenching Battalion men.
No. 4	"	"	2/Lieut. E. V. Grimsdell	

It should be remarked in passing that the Entrenching Battalions had no connection with the Labour Corps. They were trained and combatant troops whose existence as Entrenching Battalions only dated from the Divisional reorganisations of the preceding January, and they represented in effect the troops which had been "left over" after the reorganisation was completed. The bulk of the reinforcement which thus came to the 2/4th Battalion were enlisted in the 6th K.O.Y.L.I., and were undoubtedly some of the finest reinforcements the Battalion ever received: although young they were very keen, and included some most reliable non-commissioned officers.

At 7.45 p.m. on the 7th April the Battalion relieved the 12th Londons in the Reserve system between the village of Gentelles and the Amiens-Roye Road, Nos. 3 and 4 Companies occupying the front line with Nos. 1 and 2 in support to them and Headquarters in the Bois de Gentelles. For ten days the Battalion continued to occupy these positions, constantly employed in working parties on its own defences and on elaborately wiring the lines in conjunction with the R.E.'s. This wire was strengthened to form a considerable obstacle for the Gentelles line, which was the final line of the Amiens defences and was to be held at all costs. During this tour of duty the 2/4th Battalion suffered somewhat from German shell fire, for the British batteries were close behind the Gentelles line.

It was confidently anticipated that the enemy would endeavour once more to break the Amiens defences in this area. The village of Villers-Bretonneux stands on a somewhat prominent hill seven miles east of Amiens, and its possession would have enabled the Germans to play havoc by their artillery with the city itself and our important road and railway communications which radiate from it. Its value to the Germans rendered it a matter of the highest importance to us to defend it stubbornly. In anticipation of an attack, therefore, the battle surplus was sent out of the trenches on the 10th and the work of strengthening the defences pressed on with vigour.

Further reinforcements were received from the Base, numbering in all 127 other ranks. These were mostly young lads under nineteen years of age whose despatch overseas had been rendered necessary by the impossibility of otherwise replacing the deficiencies in the ranks. They were all extremely keen and had received a good groundwork of training at home. But they reached the Battalion at a time when it had just been shaken by one battle and was about to become involved in another, and it can only be deplored that circumstances prevented any opportunity for assimilating them into the Battalion and for giving them some preliminary experience of warfare under quieter conditions. The whole Battalion was indeed rather conglomerate, for of a total of some 650 rifles about 450 were strange to the Battalion and called upon to go into action under a command unknown to them: this important point should be borne in mind in considering the battle which followed.

On the evening of the 18th April the 58th Division took over from the 5th Australian Brigade the front line east of Cachy, the 173rd Brigade occupying the whole sector. This sector extended from the immediate left of Hangard, through the Bois de Hangard to the Villers-Bretonneux-Demuin Road, the 3rd Londons on the right, the 2/2nd in the centre and the 2/4th on the left. The 2/4th Battalion's subsector, in which it relieved the 19th Australian Battalion, about 1500 yards frontage, was held with three companies (Nos. 1, 2 and 4) in the front line and one (No. 3) in support, Headquarters occupying a quarry east of Cachy. The 175th Brigade took over the Blue line while the 174th was in reserve in Cagny.

The Battalion was now straining every nerve to complete the defences. Much work was still to be done. The front line had originally existed as a line of isolated posts, and these were not yet completely connected up nor were they adequately wired. A great deal was to be done in providing efficient fire positions throughout the line in order that if lateral movement should become necessary the defence of the position might not be impaired.

Orders were received that the front line would be held till the last. The support company would be employed for counter-attack purposes in the event of the enemy gaining a footing in our positions; and the success of the defence would clearly depend on the rapidity and skill with which this local reserve was used. The right flank of the Brigade front was further strengthened by the 10th Londons, who were temporarily attached in Brigade reserve.

On the 21st the Battalion suffered a severe loss in the adjutant, Capt. F. W. Walker, D.S.O., who was wounded, his duties being taken by Lieut. S. A. Seys, the assistant adjutant. On the 23rd Capt. Hetley was attached to the 131st French Divisional Headquarters as liaison officer, and his company was handed over temporarily to Capt. W. C. Morton.

The same day information was obtained from Alsatian deserters that the enemy attack would take place at dawn the following morning.

We may restate the distribution of companies in the trenches as follows:

    In Front— No. 2 (Askham) on the right.

No. 1 (Morton) in the centre.

No. 4 (Grimsdell) on the left.

                                                                 In Support —No. 3 (Hettler).

By an extraordinary chance the enemy was yet once more favoured by the weather, for, when his barrage dropped on our lines at 4 a.m. on the 24th April with bitter intensity and great accuracy, the day was dawning on a dense mist which impeded observation beyond a radius of about 50 yards. The bombardment was severe, and in the area of forward battery positions included gas shell.

The attack appears to have developed at widely different hours in different parts of the line: the S.O.S. was received from the 8th Division on the left as early as 5.40 a.m., and from Hangard at 6 a.m., but it was not until 6.20 a.m. that reports indicated that the 173rd Brigade front was generally engaged. On the 2/4th Battalion front all was ready to receive the advancing waves of German infantry, but it must be admitted that some of the stoutest hearts were filled with something approaching dismay when out of the fog, at a distance of 40 to 50 yards, loomed the weird forms of German tanks. So far as can be ascertained about six tanks were directed on the 2/4th Battalion's sector, and it was the only Battalion of the Brigade against which they advanced. The tanks seem to have been uncertain of their bearings in the mist and not too skilfully handled. One at least devoted its energies to describing small circles, firing wildly into the ground where none of our troops were posted.

In spite of this unskilful manœuvring, however, there is no doubt that the sudden appearance of these monsters shook our defence for a moment, and the men fell back a short distance. They remained perfectly under control, and were rapidly rallied by their officers a short distance in rear of the front trench, after which the German infantry, advancing in three waves close behind the tanks, were hotly engaged with rifle and Lewis gun fire, which inflicted heavy loss on them. Askham was hit about twenty minutes after the attack began, and after his departure to the Aid Post charge of affairs in the firing line, so far as control was possible over a wide front in the mist, was assumed by Morton of No. 1 Company. The first news of what was occurring in front was received at Battalion Headquarters from Morton in a message timed 6.30 a.m.: "Tanks have crossed front line trenches, front line has fallen back, have rallied them at Coy. H.Q. line."

Steadily the tanks pressed our line back though our retirement was carried out gradually and at ghastly loss to the German infantry; and finally Morton was able to collect all available men of the 2/4th Battalion in the Cachy Switch.

The support company put up a good fight—Hettler was hit early—and eventually was nearly surrounded; but it cut its way out and managed also to gain the Cachy Switch. The Divisional records time our retirement to the Cachy Switch at 7.40 a.m., but there seems no doubt that the Battalion's resistance was much more prolonged than this would indicate. Certainly Morton was not able to report the organisation of his new position till 10.15 a.m. By this time only about one hundred men of the Battalion with three subalterns, Prince, Sheppard and Ewing, were under Morton's hand, though others rejoined later. The 2/4th Battalion's retirement had involved the risk of leaving the left flank of the 2/2nd Londons on its right in the air, but this Battalion conformed to our movement, though a gap ensued between the two units. This was promptly filled by Brigade, who sent forward a company of the 2/10th Londons. By midday our line was more or less stabilised on a line from the Cachy Switch immediately in front of Cachy village along the Hangard Road. This meant that Hangard Wood was lost, and from the left flank the bad news was also received that Villers-Bretonneux had fallen into the enemy's hands.

Beyond artillery activity no further action of importance occurred on the Battalion's front during the afternoon, which was busily occupied in forming a line of shell hole defences in the new position and in feeling out to the flanks to gain touch with adjoining units.

This was the only occasion on which either Battalion of the regiment was called on to face tanks. There can be no question as to the tremendous moral effect of these machines, though their actual destructiveness—handled as they were—was not great. Under the conditions of mist which prevented any warning of their approach, and the conglomerate composition of the Battalion, a little initial unsteadiness on the part of the less trained elements of the Battalion was almost to be expected in face of such an ordeal. The rapid recovery and steady rearguard fight back to the Cachy line, however, showed that after the first shock the innate discipline of the Londoner asserted itself and the number of enemy dead counted on the field was evidence of the heavy cost to the Germans of their success.

2/Lieut. Ewing should be mentioned. "His behaviour was splendid throughout. During the preliminary bombardment he was constantly up and down his sector encouraging his men, and when the enemy ultimately appeared his fire orders were clear and effective." He was awarded the M.C., as was also Capt. Morton, who displayed throughout the day marked qualities of leadership and coolness. Pte. Petrie, a stretcher-bearer who gained the M.M., exhibited an utter disregard of personal danger in pursuing his work of bringing in and tending wounded.

The heavy casualties sustained this day in "missing" were due to the fact that in retirement the Battalion was forced to leave many men, who might otherwise have been saved, in the enemy's hands. But the R.A.M.C. staff under Lieut. Dunaway worked magnificently under heavy shell fire till the last moment, thereby retrieving many wounded men who must otherwise have been captured.

We have already pointed to the great importance of Villers-Bretonneux in the defence of Amiens, and it is not surprising therefore that its loss was followed by an immediate order from Army Headquarters that it must be recaptured at all costs.

The counter-attack was delivered at 10 p.m. on the 24th April by the 9th Londons, the 54th Brigade and the Australians. Villers-Bretonneux again passed into our hands, while on the 58th Division's front the line was advanced about half-way forward from the Cachy Switch to the original front line.

During the 25th April the 2/4th Battalion was not engaged, though it was all day long subjected to severe artillery fire, which inflicted a good many casualties. On the evening of the 25th the 2/4th Battalion was relieved by troops of the French Moroccan Division, and withdrew on relief to bivouacs in open country east of Boves.

The casualties of the two days' action were:

> 2/Lieut. J. W. Booking, killed; Capts. S. G. Askham, M.C., B. H. C. Hettler, M.C., 2/Lieuts. S. F. G. Mears, P. J. Payne and L. H. Sheppard, wounded; 2/Lieuts. S. C. Geering and C. W. Cumner, missing; and in N.C.O.'s and men 23 killed, 108 wounded and 203 missing.

During the 26th April the Moroccan Division continued the counter-attack, and at the end of the day the line was substantially restored to its position prior to the German attack.

This was the last serious German attempt to reach Amiens. The line had bent perilously, but the offensive in this area had been fought to a standstill. At this point, therefore, we may leave the 2/4th Battalion and deal with the defence of Arras, in which the 1/4th Battalion bore a part.

CHAPTER XXI
THE 1/4TH BATTALION IN THE DEFENCE OF ARRAS, 1918

On the 11th March 1918 the 1/4th Londons took over the Oppy Trenches from the Kensingtons.

There was no room for doubt now that the Germans intended sooner or later to launch a big attack in this area, and the only thing was to ensure that the troops holding the line should be ready whenever the storm might burst. The dispositions now taken up were, therefore, those which had been finally decided on for the scheme of defence, and it was arranged that companies should henceforth always occupy the same positions in order the better to know their ground. These positions will be stated in detail later.

So far as the infantry in the line were concerned the period of suspense was mainly characterised by very hard work on the defences and by particularly active patrolling. Each front line post nightly pushed forward to the enemy wire a listening patrol to give early warning of signs of the enemy's assembly for attack. On the evening of the 12th March 2/Lieut. G. G. Lewis took a patrol into the German trenches near Crucifix Corner, but found them unoccupied. The tour of duty passed quietly, with the exception of a very severe bombardment with mustard gas shells, which began at about 7 p.m. on the 15th March and continued till about 8 a.m. the following morning. At the time this caused little damage, but the heat of the sun later in the day accentuated the effects of the gas, and Lieuts. A. Bath and O. D. Garratt, M.C., 2/Lieuts. G. W. Fisher, E. A. Ratcliffe and 109 other ranks became casualties.

Intelligence reports pointed to the probability of the attack developing on the 12th March; but although nothing occurred, from this date onwards the whole Division daily stood to arms from one hour before dawn till 8.30 a.m., while the Divisional and Corps artillery put a slow barrage on the enemy lines at daybreak. The "stand-to" order was strictly enforced as far back as the transport lines and the Quartermaster.

On the 18th the 1/4th Londons were relieved by the Kensingtons and withdrew in Brigade reserve to Roclincourt, leaving two platoons in support attached to the Kensingtons, and one in front trenches attached to the London Scottish. A rearrangement of the method of holding the line was now ordered by Corps, and the necessary changes which were effected on the night of 21st/22nd March resulted in each division holding its sector with two brigades in line and one in reserve. Each front line brigade had two battalions in trenches and one in support. The effect of this in the 56th Division was to leave the 169th and 168th Brigades in the line, while the 167th was withdrawn to the support area.

The 21st March saw the opening of the great German offensive on the Fifth Army front, but no attack developed opposite the 56th Division. The day was marked by very greatly increased artillery activity on the enemy's part, gas shell being freely used on the Bailleul-Willerval line. This indication of the imminence of active operations caused the cancellation of the relief of the 56th Division by the 62nd. The next day warning was received that the 2nd Canadian Division would take over the line, but this order was also subsequently cancelled.

No definite news of the offensive was received during the 21st March, though it was reported that the enemy had gained the high ground near Wancourt Tower, and was likely by his assault on Monchy to lay the Corps right flank open to attack. Arras was heavily shelled, and all the civilians were cleared out. St Pol also was bombarded by a long-range gun, while low-flying Bosche aeroplanes were over the lines and at night dropped bombs on Thélus.

On the evening of the 24th the 1/4th Londons returned to the front line. Aerial reports of great activity behind the German lines now made it clear that the attack was imminent, and final preparations for the struggle were completed. All spare Lewis guns and magazines were brought up from the transport lines. The men were in splendid fettle, and the high probability that the long weeks of suspense would shortly be over increased their good humour. All were absolutely confident in themselves and each other, and their only anxiety was as to whether they would have the good fortune to be in front trenches to meet the enemy.

At this time Gen. Loch and Lieut.-Col. Marchment made strong representations that the three front line posts ought to be much more lightly held, and that the Company Headquarters in Beatty should be withdrawn to the Marquis line, on the grounds that it was useless to pack men into posts only 100 yards from the enemy, where they were certain to suffer severely from the hostile bombardment and where they had no room to fight. These representations were not received favourably by Corps though the event showed they were well founded. As it was Lieut.-Col. Marchment moved one platoon from Oppy Post, but even with this alteration the Marquis line was too lightly held.

News from the area of battle in the south was still vague, though it was known that the Fifth Army had been forced to give a great deal of ground, and that the Third Army on its left had also retreated, though to a less degree, and to conform to the movements of its neighbour. As the day wore on, however, the enemy's pressure on the Third Army south of the Scarpe increased and by the 27th he had captured Monchy-le-Preux. It became evident that he was aiming at a movement to envelop Arras from the south. A reasonable deduction from this situation was that the blow at Arras would shortly develop also on the north of the Scarpe, by means of an assault on the Vimy Ridge.

In the early hours of the 25th March, shortly after the 1/4th Londons had taken over the line, 2/Lieut. C. H. Board and Coy. Sergt.-Major Matthews of B Company were visiting the sentry groups in Beatty Post when two of the enemy, who had entered the trench by stealth, tried to drag the Coy. Sergt.-Major out of it. A scuffle ensued in which another officer and an N.C.O. joined. The two Germans unfortunately got away after slightly wounding both Board and Matthews.

During the day the artillery on both sides became more active, though no infantry action occurred, and the men were kept busy in constructing trench blocks and improving firesteps. The right flank of the 1/4th Londons' sector had always been regarded as a rather weak spot in the defence, and in view of the expectation that the enemy would assault the Vimy Ridge from the south, it was desirable to provide for the formation by the Battalion of a defensive flank facing south should this area become threatened. To this end work was pushed forward in constructing and improving firesteps in Ouse Alley for its possible use as a "switch line." This precaution, as will be seen, was justified by events.

During the evening a report was received of the examination of a prisoner of the 471st Infantry Regiment, who had been taken near Mill Post on the previous evening. This was to the effect that the attack was to be made on the morning of the 26th, and that the 219th and 23rd Reserve Divisions had been brought forward for the purpose. These troops were accommodated in the Drocourt-Quéant line. They had just arrived from Riga and would attack in conjunction with the 240th and 5th Bavarian Reserve Divisions. They would assemble in the front line system and would advance to a depth of four miles with their right flank on Oppy, then swing round towards Vimy. Three special divisions would capture the Vimy Ridge the next day. The 471st Regiment had already 60 trench mortars in position, and 8 more trench mortar companies were to arrive on the night of the 25th; most of the ammunition was already in the line.

This message, bringing as it did a hope that the wearisome suspense was at last at an end, was received with satisfaction, and instructions to prepare for battle were issued. All night our artillery maintained a heavy fire on the enemy's supposed assembly positions, while No Man's Land was occupied by our listening patrols. At 4 a.m. these came in and the heavy artillery placed a slow barrage on the German front lines. At 4.45 a.m. the Battalion stood to arms, blocks were lowered in the communication trenches and all made ready. No attack developed, and at 7.30 a.m. the order to stand down was received from Brigade, the remainder of the day passing comparatively quietly.

In the evening, in response to urgent appeals from Corps for an identification, all battalions in the line sent patrols to the enemy trenches to try to get prisoners. From the 1/4th Londons two parties went forward at 10.30 p.m. after wire-cutting preparations by the field artillery. 2/Lieut. G. G. Lewis with a platoon of A Company entered the enemy line opposite Oppy Post, but the sentry group was heard running away and no bag was obtained. From C Company 2/Lieut. R. E. Campkin took two men to the German trenches near Crucifix Corner, and had a lively little scrap in the dark with the sentry group. In this case also the Bosche took to their heels, and, in spite of a good set to with fists, managed to get away pursued by Campkin. After remaining two hours in the enemy line both patrols returned bringing some trench notice boards.

The 27th March passed remarkably quietly, nothing of interest occurring beyond the movements of a low-flying Bosche 'plane which appeared to be particularly interested in our trenches. A relief of the German division opposite the Battalion was suspected, but the report was incorrect.

On the night 27th/28th March orders were received that the XIII Corps boundary was to be extended northwards as far as the Souchez River, and that the 56th Division would "side-step" northwards. The side-step was effected by transferring the Kensingtons from the right flank of the 1/4th Londons to the left flank, the Kensingtons taking over two new posts north of the 1/4th Londons from the 8th Canadian Brigade. The gap thus created on the right flank of the Battalion was filled by the 169th Brigade, which extended its left flank. Why this redistribution was effected at the eleventh hour we do not know: obviously it must have been for some very important reason. But whatever the cause, the result was distinctly weakening to the defence. We have already alluded to the well-recognised risk of the 1/4th Londons' right flank being laid open, and now at the last moment the area was occupied by a Battalion entirely strange to the ground. The relief in fact was not completed before the battle opened, for when the Bosche barrage fell on the morning of the 28th March the L.R.B. had not taken over Bailleul East Post, while a company of the 1st Canadian Rifles in the Brown line was still awaiting relief. By the courtesy of the Canadian Brigadier this company was placed under the orders of Brig.-Gen. Loch.

In addition to this eleventh hour change of dispositions a certain difficulty appears to have beset the High Command in reconciling the rôles of the three divisions composing the Corps, and this resulted in a stream of orders each of which altered its predecessor. The Corps order, under which the extension of the 56th Division's line was carried out, laid down that the Bailleul-Willerval line (Red line) was to be the line of resistance, and that the front line system would be regarded as outposts. Later in the evening the front line system was ordered to be held at all costs to conform with the 4th Division on our right; but still later a modification of this was made on the left of the line in order to conform to the defensive line of the 3rd Canadian Division on our left, and the garrison of Arleux Post was ordered, if heavily attacked, to withdraw to the Arleux Loop.

The final dispositions therefore provided five lines of defence, each to be defended at all costs in default of a Divisional order to withdraw. There were:

1. Front line system.
2. Red line (Bailleul-Willerval).
3. Brown line (Farbus-Vimy).
4. Green line (Thélus).
5. La Targette line.

The order of battle of Brigade was as follows:

169TH BRIGADE (RIGHT):

Front line system:	Queen's Westminsters in Towy Post on the right.
	London Rifle Brigade in Mill,
	Bradford and Bird Posts on the left.
Red line:	1/2nd Londons.
Brown line:	1 coy. 1/5th Cheshire Pioneers.
Reserve:	2 coys. 1st Londons (attd. from 167th Brigade).

168TH BRIGADE (LEFT):

Front line system:	1/4th Londons in Beatty, Wood and Oppy Posts on the right.	
	Kensingtons in Tommy and Arleux Posts on the left.	
Red line:	London Scottish.	
Brown line:	2 platoons 1/5th Cheshire Pioneers.	
Green line:	2 coys. 1st Londons, 1½ coys. 1/5th Cheshire Pioneers.	

DIVISIONAL RESERVE:

167th Brigade (less 1st Londons) and 3 field coys. R.E.

The companies of the 1/4th Londons were disposed as follows:

Right:	B Company (Spicer) H.Q. and 2 platoons in Beatty Post. 1 platoon in Marquis and Earl line.
Centre:	C Company (Duthie) 1 platoon in Wood Post. 1 platoon in Marquis line. H.Q. and 1 platoon in South Duke St.
Left:	A Company (H. N. Williams) 1 platoon in Oppy Post. 1 platoon between Oppy Post and Marquis line. H.Q. and 1 platoon in Marquis line.
Advanced Battalion H.Q.:	(Major F. A. Phillips) in South Duke St. (with C Coy.)
Support:	D Company (Cooper) in Bow Trench.
Battalion	(Lieut.-Col. Marchment) in Ouse Alley west of

H.Q.: Bow Trench.

During the night 2/Lieut. R. E. Campkin with two men of C Company again crossed No Man's Land and returned shortly before 3 a.m. on the 28th March reporting that he had seen long lines of men carrying up to the enemy front line what appeared to be large biscuit tins—doubtless the trench mortar ammunition coming in. Evidently this was The Day!

At 3 a.m. on the 28th March the enemy opened an intense high explosive shell fire on Bow Trench, Ouse Alley and Rear Battalion Headquarters, as well as on all the rearward defensive posts. This bombardment, which continued throughout the day, was at first mingled with mustard gas. The forward area was hardly affected by this shelling except for the fact that the wind carried the gas eastward over the front line posts, the garrisons of which had to wear masks for over an hour.

At 5.40 a.m. a terrific trench mortar fire fell on the forward posts doing very severe damage, and causing many casualties. Ouse Alley and the Earl-Marquis line at first escaped this, though later the area of bombardment was extended and they received a full share of it.

A strictly chronological account of an action such as this, in which different parts of the Battalion became involved in the fight at varying hours, is almost an impossibility if the reader is to glean anything but the most confused impression of what occurred. We propose, therefore, to deal first of all with the fight for the front line posts gradually working our narrative westward.

The S.O.S. signal was received in Battalion Headquarters from Oppy Post by wire at 7.15 a.m., and a few moments later flares were sent up from Wood and Beatty. The signal was repeated backwards to Brigade by Battalion Headquarters. "We stood on top," writes Lieut.-Col. Marchment, "to have a look round but could see very little as it was not fully light. We could, however, hear a pleasant noise—very heavy rifle fire!"

Oppy Post on the left had been very badly knocked about by the trench mortaring and the garrison seriously reduced before the enemy came over. A gallant attempt at resistance was put up and rifle and Lewis gun fire were opened as soon as the attacking lines made their appearance. One Lewis gun team was seen from the rear to have climbed on to the parapet, and the gun was being fired from the hip. But it was hopeless from the first. The enemy lines were very close, and by sheer weight of numbers the Post was quickly swamped. Of a garrison of 2 officers and 48 other ranks but 1 officer (2/Lieut. Athey) and 5 other ranks were able to make their way back to the Marquis line which they did by way of Boyne Trench.

On the right Beatty Post had suffered from the trench mortar fire more severely than any, and by the time the Germans appeared its trenches were practically effaced. The attackers appeared in fairly close formation, and in considerable depth, some of the leading wave firing rifle grenades from the hip. Apparently the enemy's trench mortar preparation, severe as it had been, had not dealt effectively with our wire, for the leading wave of attackers was delayed in getting through it, causing those following to bunch up to it. The rapid rifle and Lewis gun fire opened by the garrison of the post was thus able to inflict very severe loss. For about fifteen minutes the garrison stoutly held its own, but at the end of that time it was found that the enemy had already swept over the posts to the right held by the L.R.B., and was working into Marine Trench and Ouse Alley in great numbers. Again sheer weight of numbers made further resistance impossible, and 2/Lieut. G. R. Pitman brought the six surviving men back to the Marquis line over the open, leaving 2 officers (Capt. E. E. Spicer and 2/Lieut. Coombes) and 78 other ranks fallen at their posts.

In the centre a magnificent stand was made by the garrison of Wood Post under Lieut. H. F. Dade and 2/Lieut. H. O. Morris. The night position of the post had been changed a few days before the battle, and the German trench mortar preparation therefore fell harmlessly on the former position. When the trench mortar fire ceased the enemy was seen advancing in an extended line over the open ground left of the Wood and coming through the Wood in groups of about 10 men 50 yards apart. This line was followed by groups of about 30 men some 200 yards in rear. The whole garrison (2 officers, 45 other ranks and 2 Lewis guns) at once opened a heavy fire which undoubtedly caused very severe loss to the enemy. A party of Germans tried to force the block in the trench leading from the new post to the old, but they were effectively disposed of with rifle grenades. For a full hour this gallant garrison held their own, completely checking the enemy in the wood. On the right, however, the enemy had, as already recounted, swept over Beatty Post and was now working his way round Wood Post from the south. Ammunition and bombs were beginning to run short. After a consultation Dade and Morris decided that the position was no longer tenable, and they withdrew their men along Bedford Row and Boyne Trench to the Marquis line. This withdrawal was skilfully executed, the move of the riflemen down Boyne Trench being covered by Lewis guns in Bedford Row. That the garrison held their own to the last is evidenced by the fact that before the post was finally evacuated the Headquarters dugout was in the hands of the enemy, while our own artillery was already shelling the post. The defence of Wood Post cost 25 casualties in other ranks.

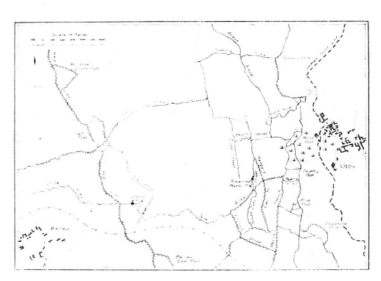

THE DEFENCE OF ARRAS, MARCH 1918

The value of the defence of Wood Post can hardly be overestimated. Apart from the heavy losses which the fire of its garrison undoubtedly inflicted on the enemy, it is certain that its prolonged resistance saved the Marquis line from being overrun in the vicinity of Advanced Battalion Headquarters.

As soon as Williams reported the men back from Oppy Post Lieut.-Col. Marchment had a 6-inch howitzer battery turned on to Oppy Wood.

The forward posts having fallen, the Marquis line became almost immediately engaged, and Capt. H. N. Williams (A Company) displayed great qualities of leadership in his defence of the position. We cannot do better than to relate this phase of the battle in the words of the official account of the action submitted by Lieut.-Col. Marchment:

> The Marquis line easily held up the advancing enemy after the posts had gone. On the right the enemy was strongly established in the Earl line and Viscount Street about fifteen minutes after zero. Major F. A. Phillips at once gave orders to 2/Lieut. O. C. Hudson, whose platoon was in the Marquis line astride Ouse Alley, to form the defensive flank at once. This had been rehearsed previously and consisted not only in manning the block in Ouse Alley to the front, but also in Earl to the right, and manning firesteps facing to the right along Ouse Alley. 2/Lieut. Hudson maintained this position with great gallantry and inflicted heavy casualties on the enemy, whom he caught in enfilade as they broke through over Earl to Viscount Street. The defensive flank was prolonged by Headquarter details who continued

on the firestep in Ouse Alley and held a block near the Aid Post in South Duke Street.

At about 9.30 a.m. a strong party was seen working up Ouse Alley from Viscount Street towards Forward Battalion Headquarters. Major F. A. Phillips at once attacked over the open with about 20 Headquarter details, the men following most gallantly under heavy fire. The enemy were ejected and a block established in Ouse Alley towards Viscount Street. A block was established here and successfully defended with grenades by a party under Sergt. Udall.

In the centre of the Marquis line the attack was not pressed until the Wood Post Garrison had withdrawn. After this the enemy gradually built up a large volume of rifle fire from Oppy Wood, but was prevented from debouching by well-directed rifle and Lewis gun fire from the Marquis line. Rifle grenades were also used on New Cut and Baker Street where the enemy had established himself.

On the left of the Marquis line excellent targets were presented on the left of the Wood, the Lewis gun in the bank (near the junction of Clarence Trench and Kent Road) doing most excellent work.

During the next three hours the enemy twice broke into the line near Boyne, but was thrown out, leaving a good many dead in the trench. Rifle and Lewis gun fire was opened whenever a good target presented itself, and a large number of dead were seen between Wood and Beale Trenches.

Later on the enemy broke in on the left from Clarence Trench. The Lewis gun on the left had finished its ammunition, but reinforced by a few men, the team ejected the enemy with rifle fire and grenades.

Thus, at about 11 a.m., the forward troops were holding the Marquis line beating off attacks to the front and holding a block on the left. On the right, although the enemy pressure was considerable, he was held up splendidly in Earl and South Duke Street and in front and behind in Ouse Alley; the enemy holding Viscount Street on the right and pushing on towards the Red line.

During the whole of this fight information as to the situation came in to Rear Battalion Headquarters rapidly, thanks to a buried cable, and throughout the battle communication was maintained with the troops in front and with Brigade Headquarters and the artillery in rear. Advantage of this was taken when definite news of the fall of the post line was received, and the artillery barrage was dropped to conform to the situation, Earl Trench being shelled with good effect.

We must now turn for a moment to the course of events in the rearward area. The enemy's preparatory bombardment had fallen heavily on Bow Trench, but the garrison (D Company, Cooper) was kept in dugouts, sentries being changed each half-hour, and few casualties were sustained. At 5 a.m. the blocks in Ouse Alley were lowered, and rum and extra S.A.A. issued to the men. On the S.O.S. signal being received the trench was manned; and at the same time Lieut.-Col. Marchment sent the Headquarter Company round to join D Company, retaining with him only a few signallers to work the line, two clerks and a few scouts, in addition to Boutall (Adjutant), Lorden (Works Officer) and Padre Green "to create a calm atmosphere." Lorden was hit here at about 7.45 a.m.

From about 8 a.m. the Headquarters area was quite in the air. The front line system in the adjoining sector on the right (169th Brigade) had gone, with the exception of Towy Post held by the Queen's Westminsters; and the Bosche had worked up the valley on the left and was also for a time in Ouse Alley, and attacking Bailleul East Post in the Red line (held by the London Scottish).

For a time trouble was caused by low-flying enemy aeroplanes, but these went back as soon as our own R.E. 8's appeared. Good contact work was done throughout the day with these machines which called at intervals for flares. Luckily all flares were carried on the men, and they were thus available to show our positions to the aeroplanes. At one time the Battalion code and position call, Q.J.B., was sent to the contact aeroplane by Lucas Lamp worked by Sergt. Hurst, and satisfactorily received.

At about 9 a.m. the enemy was in Viscount Trench, and as stragglers from the L.R.B. reported that he was also working down Ouse Alley, D Company was ordered to despatch one platoon to man Ouse Alley forward of Bow Trench. This was quickly done, and the men, taking up positions on the firesteps facing south-east, were able to engage small parties of the enemy who appeared over the crest in front of Bailleul East Post.

Later in the morning when news was received of the severe odds against which the gallant Marquis line garrison was struggling, the remainder of D Company was ordered to bomb up Ouse Alley to try to join hands with Major Phillips and thus complete the defensive flank. At the same time a carrying party was detailed from Headquarters to carry S.A.A. to the front line should D Company succeed. The place of D Company in Bow Trench was taken by two platoons of the London Scottish placed at Lieut.-Col. Marchment's disposal.

The bombing attack was pushed forward for some 400 yards. Enemy opposition was not very severe and about a dozen were killed. The Germans were, however, continuing to press forward over the open from the right and it seemed likely that D Company would get cut off. A block was therefore made in Ouse Alley which was held by a few men, while another small party manned the firesteps to the right to engage the advancing enemy. The remainder of D Company moved over the open in the valley north of Ouse Alley towards Boyne Dump to carry S.A.A. to the Marquis line, taking full advantage of the ground.

By 11.30 a.m. the situation of the Marquis line troops had become precarious in the extreme. The Germans in Oppy Wood were being reinforced and were developing a considerable volume of fire from that direction. The right and right rear of the position were almost enveloped and an attack was being launched against the left flank. Bombs and ammunition were giving out. It seemed clear that further resistance could only lead to useless loss of life. Influenced by these weighty considerations Major Phillips, after a consultation with his senior officers, decided to try to save the remnants of the garrison by a withdrawal to the Red line. The only available trench for withdrawal, Ouse Alley, was, however, already occupied by the enemy in rear of the position, and the valley from Boyne Dump on the left offered the only loophole of escape from the closing pincers. Lieut.-Col. Marchment writes of this withdrawal:

> The withdrawal was witnessed by myself from my headquarters. I watched it through my glasses. It was carried out in a very steady and orderly way, the men leaving in groups of about a dozen. Although exposed to heavy fire from the front and flanks, they made excellent use of the ground and had few casualties.

The men of D Company, who were meanwhile carrying S.A.A. up to the Marquis line, met the survivors returning and covered their withdrawal.

It is hard to find adequate words in praise of this gallant defence and skilful and well-timed withdrawal. All ranks alike behaved with the greatest spirit under very trying circumstances.

A great loss was suffered in this defence in the capture by the enemy of the Regimental Aid Post. Capt. Maloney, the M.O. was a most popular man in the Battalion, and Sergt. Rossington and the two orderlies, Palmer and Simpson, had all done excellent work. By an irony of fate 2/Lieut. Morris, who had done such good work in the defence of Wood Post earlier in the morning, was hit later, and was having his wounds dressed in the Aid Post when it was captured.

Major F. A. Phillips who, at Forward Headquarters, was in charge of the whole defence of the forward system, did excellent work. He was continually up and down the lines encouraging the men, and was able to keep Rear Battalion Headquarters constantly in touch with the rapid changes in the situation.

The enemy was now in great force in Viscount Street and was beginning to bomb heavily down Ouse Alley, while he showed increasing signs of strength on the ridge to the right of that trench. The party of D Company in Ouse Alley was therefore withdrawn as soon as the survivors of the Marquis line garrison had reached Bow Trench, to avoid the risk of being cut off. Later the enemy appeared in great strength against the block in Ouse Alley forward of Bow Trench. This block was defended by a "slit" cut in the side of Ouse Alley which was covered by a Lewis gun post in Bow Trench and seven of the enemy were killed by Lewis gun fire.

As soon as the Battalion was concentrated in Bow Trench and the Red line, the artillery barrage was dropped to a line about 400 yards in front of Bow Trench, and arrangements were made to increase it to intense should the S.O.S. signal be sent up from Battalion Headquarters.

The enemy skirmishers having been definitely checked the situation now became quieter, and for the next hour there was a distinct lull in the battle.

The Kensingtons on the left had not been attacked but had withdrawn to the Red line to conform to the 1/4th Londons' new position.

In Towy Post, the extreme right of the Divisional front, the Queen's Westminsters had put up a most gallant fight, but the remainder of the 169th Brigade front had rapidly been swamped by weight of enemy numbers, and in this sector the 169th Brigade troops were thrown back to the Red line while the Wood Post garrison was still holding its ground.

The development of this great German attack was a remarkable confirmation of the statement which had been made by the prisoner captured on the 24th March. All the troops mentioned by him were identified in the course of the fighting. On the 1/4th Londons' front two German regiments were identified: the 249th I. Regt. at Oppy Post, and the 10th R.I. Regt. in the shape of a gentleman who broke into Sergt. Plumbley's canteen in Ouse Alley. But having armed himself with a tin of pineapple this luckless marauder fell into the arms of D Company bombing up the trench!

Eleven German divisions took part in this great battle, but they were all checked by the divisions holding the line, the 56th and 4th north of the Scarpe and the 3rd and 15th south of it. That the almost complete failure of the enemy on the 28th March was a severe blow to the German High

Command there can be no doubt, and Ludendorff says, "It was an established fact that the enemy's resistance was beyond our strength."

The regiment has every reason to be proud of its defence this day. For over four hours it retained the front line system under the weight of heavy shell fire and repeated attacks by vastly superior numbers, and, when finally it was forced to give ground to avoid extinction, it withdrew fighting. The casualties were heavy, but considering the enormous service rendered the price paid was not unduly great.

At about 4 p.m. the enemy began to shell the Red line rather heavily, but no infantry attack matured. Shortly afterwards the 1/4th Londons were withdrawn, and by 6 p.m. were under cover of the Railway Embankment north-east of Bailleul, reorganised in two companies (Cooper and Williams), S.A.A. was replenished and arrangements made to man the Brown line and posts south of the Bailleul Road should the enemy break through the Red line. Bow Trench had been handed over to the London Scottish.

The experience of this battle showed the need for holding front line posts lightly, and purely for observation purposes. The uselessness of locking up large garrisons in them—unless they can be effectively concealed as in the case of Wood Post—was clearly demonstrated. The system of trench blocks to which much thought had previously been devoted fully proved its value, while the advantage of rehearsing companies in the rôles they may be expected to play, and especially of acquainting all ranks with the "overland" routes within the area was much in evidence.

The casualties sustained by the 1/4th Londons in this action were:

> Officers: Capt. E. E. Spicer, 2/Lieuts. R. E. Campkin, H. T. Hannay and H. V. Coombes, killed; Capt. A. M. Duthie, D.S.O., and Lieut. H. M. Lorden, wounded; Capt. Maloney, 2/Lieuts. C. W. Denning (attached to 168th L.T.M. Battery), H. O. Morris and C. S. Richards, captured.
>
> N.C.O.'s and men: 15 killed, 43 wounded and 168 missing.

Decorations were awarded to the following:

> Lieut.-Col. A. F. Marchment, M.C., and Major F. A. Phillips, the D.S.O.; Capts. A. M. Duthie, D.S.O., T. B. Cooper, M.M., and H. N. Williams, the M.C.; C.S.M. T. Lock, M.M., the D.C.M.; L.-Corpl. W. J. Hutchin, M.M., Bar to M.M.; Sergts. F. G. Udall, H. V. R. Randall and C. J. Gibbs, Corpls. G.

Hayes and A. Parker, L.-Corpls. S. G. Coates, C. L. Husk and A. J. Deadman, and Ptes. W. A. G. Battershall, P. C. Swinchatt, A. J. Sellars and J. R. Phillips, the M.M.

During the 29th March the 1/4th Londons remained in Brigade support. Much movement was observed in the enemy's lines during the morning, and our artillery was active in anticipation of a renewal of the attack, but as the day wore on it became evident that the enemy was engaged in relieving the attacking divisions. That evening at 7 p.m. the Battalion handed over its trenches to the 87th Canadian Battalion (4th Canadian Division) and marched out to billets at Mont St Eloy, arriving there at 2 a.m. on the 30th March.

CHAPTER XXII
THE 1/4TH AND 2/4TH BATTALIONS DURING THE SUMMER MONTHS OF 1918-- THE RESERVE BATTALION, 1918

In the preceding chapters we have endeavoured to describe the part played by each of the battalions in resisting the mighty German offensive.

As we have seen this gigantic thrust was finally brought to a standstill in front of Amiens at the end of April, while the enemy's hopes in the Arras area had been finally shattered by the magnificent resistance of the 28th March. The German offensive capabilities were, however, by no means exhausted; and in the north the enemy once more taxed the British resources to the uttermost in the Battle of the Lys, which raged from the 7th to the 30th April and bent our lines back to Hazebrouck. With this action, or rather series of actions, we are not directly concerned as the 4th London Regiment had no part in it, and we may therefore turn at once to consider the situation in which the British Armies found themselves when the German attacks were finally spent.

The enormous weight of the German attacks of March and April had involved practically the whole of the British divisions in France, and all were in consequence seriously reduced in numbers and sorely in need of rest and reorganisation. The magnificent efforts which were made at home to replace the lost guns and other material are well known and were of immediate effect; but the task of filling up the gaps in personnel was necessarily a longer one, especially having regard to the waning man-power of the Empire and its commitments in other theatres of war. Moreover, after their arrival in France it was necessary for reinforcements to be thoroughly assimilated into their new units before active work could be expected of them. The serious depletion of force at this time is illustrated by the fact that after temporarily writing off as fighting units no fewer than 8 divisions, and handing over to the French a further 5 at the urgent request of Marshal Foch, there remained but 45—and most of these much reduced in numbers—available for service on the British front.

The enemy's successes had, of course, cost him dear, but it was believed to be by no means beyond the bounds of possibility that he would make yet another effort to achieve a decisive victory, and the position was thus full of anxiety for G.H.Q.

In the meantime the American Army was being poured into France as rapidly as the whole available mercantile marine of the British Empire could bring it across the Atlantic, but here again it was a question of time before these well-trained but inexperienced troops would be sufficiently valuable and numerous to turn the scale against Germany.

The story of the months of May, June and July 1918 is one of preparation, in which the British Armies were being gradually reorganised and used in active defence of the new positions until an equilibrium of strength between the Allies and the enemy was attained, and it was possible once more for the Allies to take the offensive and roll back the tide of invasion in the most remarkable series of victories which the world has ever seen.

We propose, therefore, to deal in this chapter, as briefly as possible, with the operations during this period of reorganisation of each Battalion in turn, until the opening of the Allied offensive in August 1918.

The 1/4th Battalion

Arriving at Mont St Eloy early in the morning of the 31st March 1918 the 1/4th Londons settled down to a few days of so-called rest, days which, for officers at least, are usually quite as hard work as those spent in battle. Companies have to be reorganised and fresh "specialists" trained to their duties, the completion of the men's clothing and equipment, and replenishment of all company stores have to be looked to, in addition to a large amount of clerical work in writing up the official account of the battle and in submitting names for awards, mention in despatches and promotion. The Battalion on this occasion was fortunate in getting the gaps in its ranks rapidly filled. On the 2nd and 3rd April two drafts arrived numbering together 420 fully trained N.C.O.'s and men. Fine drafts which later did gallant service, but which transformed the camp into a mild imitation of the Tower of Babel, for among them could be traced the accents of London, Kent, Surrey, Berkshire, the broader dialects of Yorkshire, Cheshire, Lancashire and Wiltshire, and even the unmistakable tones of Scotland and South Wales. Regulars, Territorials and New Armies were all represented, and the rejuvenated Battalion provided a living example of the unity of the Motherland in a great cause.

This great accession enabled an immediate reconstruction of the four companies to take place, and they were accordingly reformed and the reinforcements absorbed, A Company under Capt. H. N. Williams, M.C., B under Capt. R. S. B. Simmonds, C under Capt. S. J. Barkworth, M.C., M.M., and D under Capt. T. B. Cooper, M.C., M.M.

The troops were largely kept busy in digging new lines of defence round Haut Avesnes, and all were much encouraged by the congratulations received from G.H.Q., Army and Corps on their recent great stand.

Divisional rests, however, have ever proved a snare and a delusion, and those who count on prolonged peace in billets are invariably disappointed. In spite of its so recent gruelling the morale of the Division was high, and on the 6th April it was called upon again to go into the line, this time in the XVII Corps (Fergusson), but still in the First Army, which now extended as far south as Neuville-Vitasse. After spending the night 5th/6th April at Villers au Bois the 1/4th Londons marched on the afternoon of the 6th to Agnez lez Duisans, and proceeded the following afternoon to Ronville Caves. The march through the streets of Arras in the dusk was a great surprise to those who had known this pleasant little city even as recently as the late summer of 1917. The civilians were now all gone, hotels and shops were shut and scarcely a house had escaped the German shell fire. The beautiful Cathedral had met the same ghastly fate as that of Albert, and the Levis and Schramm barracks were but ghosts of their former selves.

In Ronville Caves, a remarkable series of underground chalk quarries, the Battalion found dry and adequate quarters. The caves are of considerable extent, the limits east and west being a crater in old No Man's Land and Levis barracks; but, lighted by electricity and tolerably ventilated, they formed quite healthy billets and, in the wet weather then prevalent, far superior to bivouacs or trenches.

The trenches now to be taken over by the 56th from the 1st Canadian Division lay south of the Arras-Cambrai Road just in front of the village of Tilloy, for as far as this had the German offensive bent our lines back. The front line, Tilloy Trench, ran between Tilloy and the Bois des Bœufs and then southwards towards Neuville-Vitasse, roughly following what had formerly been the east side of the famous German redoubt, The Harp. In rear of the front trench were successively Tilloy Support, View Trench and Tilloy Reserve. Communication trenches were Scottish Avenue, Stokes Lane, Fusilier Lane and Wye Lane, the last named forming the right boundary of the sector. The front and support trenches lay on the forward slope of the hill well under observation from the enemy lines. View Trench was on the reverse slope of the hill, and probably acquired its name in the days when its defenders wore field-grey and looked in the other direction: for us it was well sited with a good field of fire of about 200 yards. Trenches, wire and dugouts were fair. The fact that but a few days earlier this had been a back area was forced on one's attention, for the line ran through ruined Nissen hut camps and horse standings, while in the German front line opposite stood the remains of a Y.M.C.A. hut.

After four days of working parties at Ronville, in which the Battalion was digging a new line, Telegraph Hill Switch, the 1/4th Londons relieved the 8th Middlesex in the line. This tour of duty lasted six days during which the enemy remained inactive on this front, but which saw the outbreak of the Battle of the Lys to which we have already alluded. To those who knew the Neuve Chapelle area it seemed strange to hear of "fighting in Riez Bailleul and Laventie," "the struggle for Estaires," "the fall of Merville." Ruined though some of these places had been in 1916, they had afforded shelter to many hundreds of 1/4th London men, and it was now impossible to refrain from wondering what had become of the villagers who had hitherto clung to their homes, and especially of the little children.

On the last day in the line, the 19th, a raid on a large scale was carried out by one company of the London Scottish on the right, and one platoon of the 1/4th Londons on the left, with the object of advancing the outpost line on the whole sector, and establishing it an average of 500 yards in front of Tilloy Trench. The assaulting platoon was drawn from C Company under 2/Lieut. E. L. Mills, M.C., and afterwards (Mills having been hit) under 2/Lieut. J. L. Backhouse. Zero was at 4.30 a.m., and eight minutes later the 1/4th London platoon rushed their objective after Stokes Mortar preparation. Unfortunately the enemy garrison bolted and no identification was obtained, though they left a machine-gun and many documents and maps in our hands. The London Scottish also reached their objective and touch was gained with them. This advanced line was held all day under German artillery fire, which steadily increased until the Battalion was compelled to call for protective fire from our guns in retaliation.

After 7 p.m. the enemy launched some heavy bombing attacks against the new positions. These were vigorously resisted. A withdrawal to the original line was, however, ordered by Brigade, and by 8 p.m. all the assaulting platoons were back. A good deal of loss was undoubtedly inflicted on the enemy, and the effect of this minor operation on the spirit of the men fully justified its execution. Five N.C.O.'s and men of the Battalion were killed and 24 wounded.

Late that night the Battalion handed over its trenches to the 1/2nd Londons and withdrew in support to Ronville Caves, moving in the evening of the 20th April to Dainville in Divisional reserve.

About this period the 1/4th Londons were unfortunate in losing Major F. A. Phillips, D.S.O., who had been an able second in command for nearly eight months. He was much out of health principally through having swallowed rather too much mustard gas at Oppy, and he did not rejoin the Battalion. His place was taken by Major R. B. Marshall, 8th East Surrey

Regiment, whose battalion had been disbanded in January. Capt. Maloney's duties as Medical Officer had been taken for a few weeks by Capt. J. Ridley, M.C., and subsequently by Capt. E. Woodyeat, a retired naval surgeon, who had served in 1915 and 1916 with the Coldstream Guards.

Casualties in April were light beyond those sustained during the raid of the 19th. Lieut. L. E. Ballance was wounded this month. On the 24th April a draft of officers joined as follows:

> Lieut. J. W. Price, 2/Lieuts. H. W. Attenborrow, C. L. Henstridge, A. Holloway, C. R. Mason, J. D. Miller, A. H. Millstead, W. P. Humphrey and F. S. Wise.
>
> 2/Lieut. R. T. Stevenson (5th Londons); 2/Lieuts. S. Blackhurst, M.C., A. F. Potter, J. A. Voskule, W. Roughton (7th Londons); 2/Lieut. A. M. Bullock (15th Londons).

On the 24th April Major-Gen. Dudgeon fell sick and went to hospital. He had commanded the Division since August 1917 and brought it through two of its most successful actions. A few days later Major-Gen. Hull resumed the command.

On the night 3rd/4th May the Divisional front was extended northwards as far as the Arras-Douai railway, the additional frontage being taken over from the 1st Canadian Division. Thereafter the sector was held with two brigades in line (each with two battalions in trenches and one in support), and one brigade in reserve. Of the reserve brigade two battalions were billeted at Dainville and one at Berneville.

The 1/4th Londons now settled down to their share of the routine of working this sector, and through May and June were in and out of the trenches, in line, in support and in reserve alternately, the tours of duty varying between six and nine days. These summer weeks form on the whole a pleasant memory for all who passed through them. The general situation was indeed grave, and though for G.H.Q. the summer months of 1918 must have been a period of unceasing anxiety, the infantryman in the line saw life from a different angle. The trenches were comfortable, the weather good, the men well fed and clothed. Mornings in the trenches were spent in hard work on the defences, afternoons in resting, evenings under a summer moon divided between digging and wiring. With the added spice of patrolling and raiding, in which a lot of useful work was achieved, and the enemy kept well on the alert, and wishing he was not opposite to the 56th Division, the tours of duty in line passed pleasantly enough with very few casualties. The Battalion was in fine fettle and in good conceit with itself, a wholesome feeling which scored heavily when the time came for the final advance.

The enemy's chief activity was shell fire, and at times this developed to great intensity. On the 27th May in particular, when the 1/4th Londons were in trenches, a very heavy bombardment, high explosive and mustard gas together, burst on the area in the early morning. The Battalion stood to and prepared to receive an attack, but no infantry movement occurred, and it subsequently transpired that the disturbance was to cover an enemy raid on the division on our right. For a time most of the Battalion had made up their minds that they were about to fight. The Londoner is full of superstition, and this day the Battalion was to have boiled rabbit for dinner. Boiled rabbit had figured in the menu on the 28th March!... Throughout the day the enemy artillery carried out hurricane bombardments of various parts of the sector, and it was no surprise to learn later that his offensive against Rheims had broken out.

During the period under review the Battalion paid five visits to the trenches at Tilloy, with one tour of three days in Arras, spent in heavy working parties carrying wire to Telegraph Hill and digging, and six days in support at St Sauveur similarly occupied.

Rests in Divisional reserve were spent at Dainville, in which much good training work was carried out and the routine broken occasionally by excellent sports meetings, shooting matches and concerts. In connection with the concerts we must again refer to the Quartermaster's string band. This excellent orchestra had given its first public performance at St Aubin in January 1918. Receiving every encouragement from the Colonel and the keenest support from the Padre, this band had had an unbroken career of success and given the greatest pleasure to all ranks of the Battalion. At Church Parades when out of the line the band always played the hymns and voluntaries, and many a shattered barn in the villages behind the trenches has re-echoed with the strains of the 1/4th London string band. The keenness and pride of the Quartermaster in his band were as delightful to observe as his remarks when a cornet player was put out of action at Oppy were startling. A portable harmonium was purchased to complete the equipment, and when demobilisation broke the band up early in 1919, this harmonium, decorated with the names of all the villages of France and Belgium in which the orchestra had performed, was presented to the Padre for use in his parish at home.

The general efficiency of the Battalion at this period reached a remarkably high pitch, of which everyone associated with it had reason to be thoroughly proud. It was well equipped, well drilled and disciplined, and a fine fighting unit. This efficiency was not confined to the fighting ranks. At an inspection of the Battalion Transport (Lieut. G. V. Lawrie), the Divisional Commander was so impressed with its turn-out that his remarks were circulated to other units as an example. A fine fighting battalion cannot exist without fine administration, and this was supplied in full measure by the Adjutant (Boutall), and by the rear Headquarters under Mosely, Stanbridge, Faulkner, the Quartermaster, and Lawrie, whose unceasing service to the fighting ranks were of immeasurable value.

Arras Cathedral

Faulkner was a man of peculiarly lovable disposition. "Le gros papa," as he was known to the little children in Dainville, forms in the minds of many French peasants a picture of all that is kind and chivalrous in the British soldier. Mosely writes: "Many is the night when the Huns were dropping bombs on the village"—by no means an infrequent occurrence—"that Faulkner has deliberately set himself to amuse a family of youngsters and keep them screaming with laughter so that their merriment should drown the noise of the explosions."

The following officers joined the Battalion during May, June and July:

> Capt. H. A. T. Hewlett; Lieut. G. E. Stanbridge (recalled from six months' home duty "on exchange"); 2/Lieuts. A. W. Chignell, T. Yoxall and G. H. Sylvester.

In the early days of June the influenza epidemic began to make its ravages, but the Battalion suffered comparatively little. No men were allowed to rejoin in the line from back areas, but were kept at Berneville until the Battalion came out of the trenches. Casualties for May, June and July were very light. 2/Lieuts. W. P. Humphrey and T. H. Mawby were killed, 2/Lieut. A. W. Chignell wounded, and about 12 N.C.O.'s and men killed and 40 wounded.

Early in July Capt. and Adjt. W. J. Boutall, M.C., was appointed to 168th Brigade Headquarters as Assistant Staff Captain, and his duties in the Battalion were assumed by Capt. S. J. Barkworth, M.C., M.M. Boutall had filled the appointment of Adjutant since September 1916 with conspicuous success. His organising ability was high and the standard of his work throughout had been excellent. C Company was taken over about the same time by Capt. H. A. T. Hewlett. 2/Lieut. F. S. Wise was seconded to the Machine-gun Corps.

On the 13th July the 56th Division was relieved in the line by the 1st Canadian Division, and passed into Corps reserve. The 1/4th Londons, who had already been in billets at Dainville for a week, moved to Lattre St Quentin, and during the ensuing fortnight further changes of stations followed each other with rapidity. The Battalion was quartered successively at Grand Rullecourt, Tincques and Marqueffles Farm, the days being occupied with training interspersed with sports and games. While the Battalion was at Tinques the railway station was visited on the night of the 17th July by enemy aircraft, which dropped eight bombs, but caused no loss of personnel.

The last night of July found the Division once more taking over the Tilloy trenches from the Canadians, the 1/4th Londons being at St Sauveur in Brigade support until the 4th August, when they relieved the Kensingtons in the front trenches. On the 8th August, the opening day of the great British advance, the Battalion was relieved by the London Scottish and withdrew to billets in Arras. At this point, therefore, we may leave the 1/4th Battalion until the time comes to deal with its rôle in the great battles of August and September 1918.

The 2/4th Battalion

The experience of the 2/4th Battalion during the summer months was very similar to that of the 1/4th Battalion.

The Battalion spent the whole period in the area of the Amiens defences, where the Germans had penetrated most deeply into our positions. The Amiens defences were now far in rear of the old 1916 line, and the work involved in constructing new defences in what, up to five weeks earlier, had been a line of communication area was immense. Shell hole defences had to be linked into continuous trench lines, provided with support and reserve lines and communication trenches, furnished with dugouts and shelters, and defended with wire entanglements. This formed the greater part of the

Battalion's work when in the line; but it certainly laboured during these months under disadvantages which the 1/4th Battalion did not suffer. The upheaval of the British organisation had been much more widely extended in the Amiens area than it had been in the vicinity of Arras, where the withdrawal of our forces had been comparatively shallow, and for a time "back-of-the-line" organisation was inevitably weak. Billets were few and bad, and for the most part the Battalion bivouacked when out of the line. The same opportunities of resting during periods spent in reserve did not, therefore, occur.

We have also recorded that the casualties suffered by the 1/4th Battalion at Oppy were made good promptly by a veteran draft which was thoroughly absorbed into the unit during the period of waiting for the final advance. The 2/4th Battalion, which had been more knocked about in the great battles of March and April, was reinforced very slowly, and indeed its losses of the early part of the year were never completely replaced. Such reinforcements as it did receive consisted chiefly of immature youths from home—all endowed with magnificent spirit and courage, but by the nature of the case, less valuable soldiers until they had had a good deal of training in the line. The recuperation of the 2/4th Battalion was thus effected under not the most favourable conditions: a consideration which should count in their favour when we come later to consider the victories they helped to gain in August and September.

A few days of rest in the St Riquier area were allowed the 58th Division after relief from the action at Cachy. The 2/4th Londons were billeted at Le Plessiel between the 27th April and the 6th May, and though no large drafts were received, the accessions of strength were sufficient to allow of a four-company organisation being retained. These were organised: A under Capt. F. J. Griffiths, B under Capt. G. H. Hetley, C under Capt. W. C. Morton, M.C., and D under 2/Lieut. E. V. Grimsdell. Ribands were awarded to those who had recently been decorated, by the Divisional Commander, who also inspected the Battalion Transport and commended it most highly on its turn-out.

The III Corps, which comprised the 18th and 47th (London) Divisions, besides the 58th, was now responsible for the Amiens defences on the line west of Albert from the Ancre to Aveluy Wood.

On the 7th May 1918 the 58th Division came from Corps reserve into the line, and from this date until the 8th August, the beginning of the final advance, was continually in action. The 2/4th Battalion's tours of duty were somewhat irregular owing to the constant changes of position which occurred during this period. The first sector for which the Division was responsible was almost due west of Albert, in front of the ruined village of

Bouzincourt. For a fortnight the 2/4th Battalion was in reserve positions, either bivouacked at Molliens au Bois or Warloy or in astonishingly bad billets in Mirvaux, and was given a rôle as counter-attack battalion to be employed as occasion should arise in the event of a renewed enemy offensive. This involved constant readiness and much reconnaissance work by officers. The last ten days of May were spent in trenches, at first in support and afterwards in the front system. Working parties formed the principal item of routine, but a great deal of very valuable patrolling work was carried out. Over the whole Corps front No Man's Land was indeed nightly occupied by our patrols, who were always ready for a scrap with the enemy and endeavouring to pick up an identification. This was partly to train up the young soldiers in the way they should go and partly for the essential purpose of ascertaining the enemy's intentions as to a further attack.

On the last night of May 2/Lieut. George took a fighting patrol across to the enemy front line after heavy trench mortar preparation. It was found that much damage had been done, but though the trench was searched for 200 yards no enemy were met and the patrol withdrew without having suffered loss.

At this period the enemy was comparatively quiet, confining his activity to shell fire in which gas shell figured prominently.

> Lieut. B. Rivers Smith (recalled from six months' duty "on exchange"); 2/Lieuts. H. G. A. Leach and J. W. George (4th Londons); Lieut. H. C. Platts and 2/Lieut. A. L. D. Bold (7th Londons); 2/Lieuts. A. J. N. Sievwright and J. Horsfield (12th Londons); 2/Lieut. A. R. Armfield (20th Londons); 2/Lieuts. H. M. Bradley and W. N. M. Girling (21st Londons). At the end of the month 2/Lieut. Sievwright rejoined his own regiment. Drafts of N.C.O.'s and men totalled 142.

The casualties in May were comparatively light. 2/Lieut. H. M. Bradley and 1 man were killed by the falling in of the dugout they were occupying, and in addition 2 men were killed and 12 wounded.

At the beginning of June the 2/4th Battalion moved back to Contay in Divisional reserve, and resumed its counter-attack duties. Here a severe loss was sustained in Lieut.-Col. W. R. H. Dann, D.S.O., who was appointed to command the 60th Infantry Brigade with the temporary rank of Brigadier-General. Lieut.-Col. Dann had been in continuous command of the 2/4th Londons since November 1916, and during the Battalion's seventeen months of active service he had held the confidence and affection of all ranks. His great skill as a commander, his imperturbable coolness in action, his unfailing care for the welfare of his men, had endeared him to all, and the Battalion said good-bye to him with genuine sorrow. The command was taken temporarily by Major Tollworthy, but on the 8th June Major Grover, D.S.O., M.C., who had been hit at Cachy, rejoined and assumed command with the acting rank of Lieut.-Col.

On the 5th June the Battalion moved to tents and shelters at Mirvaux, where attempts were made to carry out a few days' training. Standing crops, which might on no account be damaged, interfered sadly, and but little was accomplished. The plaint of the Divisional Staff made at the time is rather pathetic: "Training areas have not yet been allotted. As is usually the case the hiring of these is a very lengthy procedure, and is not likely to be completed before the Division leaves the area." Apparently even the full tide of the German offensive had beat in vain against the massive structure of regulations.

The end of May had witnessed the recrudescence of fighting on the French front on the Chemin des Dames. Once again the weight of the enemy's assault had overtaxed our Allies' resources in defence, and by the 4th June the Germans had reached their 1914 line on the Marne at Chateau-Thierry, and were threatening Paris. It was firmly anticipated that this fresh German success would mean another blow against the British front at its junction with the French, and to meet this new menace the XXII Corps was reconstituted under Sir A. J. Godley, in G.H.Q. reserve. To this new formation were posted the 12th, 37th and 58th Divisions, the whole of which were held in readiness to move at two hours' notice. In accordance with this scheme the 173rd Brigade was moved to the Amiens area, the 2/4th Londons being billeted—this time in comfortable quarters—at Guignemicourt on the 10th June.

The German attack between Montdidier and Noyon did in fact develop, and the 37th Division was moved southwards. The 58th Division was, however, not called upon, and, the danger being passed, returned to the line after a week, the 2/4th Battalion moving on the 17th June to Molliens au Bois.

For the remainder of June and the whole of July the 2/4th Battalion remained in forward areas. At first the 173rd Brigade was in line astride the Amiens-Albert Road and the Battalion successively occupied positions in reserve in the La Houssoye line, in support in the Dodo-Hill-Darling system, and in front trenches in the Ethel-Dandy system.

The work on defences and the patrolling activity of the previous month were here continued without abatement, but with very little incident of interest. During the last week of June the weather, which had been uniformly good, was broken by some heavy showers, which at once developed the extraordinary propensity of French mud for turning into glue on the least provocation. This hampered work on the defences but had no effect on the spirit of the Battalion, which with careful training was now developing once more into a well-knit and disciplined fighting unit full of good cheer and confidence.

On the 25th June Capt. F. W. Walker, D.S.O., who had been wounded at Cachy, rejoined and resumed his duties as Adjutant.

The following officers joined in June:

> Lieut. A. R. Muddell (4th Londons); Lieut. G. de G. Barkas, M.C. (to Intelligence Officer) and 2/Lieuts. T. G. Owen and S. T. Morris (1st Londons); 2/Lieut. H. Slater (3rd Londons); Lieut. J. D. Morrison and 2/Lieuts. G. H. Main, R. D. Cotton and K. W. Gauld (14th Londons); 2/Lieut. F. Bidgood (16th Londons); Lieut. C. I. Mansel-Howe (23rd Londons); and Lieut. C. C. Brissenden (A.S.C.).

> Reinforcements of 181 N.C.O.'s and men—mostly young soldiers— were also received.

A few days spent in reserve at Baizieux in the first week of July brought the 2/4th Battalion for the first time into contact with American troops, a battalion of whom were bivouacked here.

The month of July was passed in similar fashion to those which had preceded it. From the 6th to the 18th the Battalion was in the Ethel-Dandy system, astride the Amiens-Albert Road, at first in front trenches and subsequently in support. On the 18th a withdrawal to reserve lines at Baizieux and Laviéville was effected, and here the Battalion remained for nine days. After one day spent in cleaning up in Behencourt the Battalion moved into line again on the 27th July, relieving the 30th Australian Battalion in support trenches around Ribemont, between that village and Buire-sur-Ancre.

Life in the Ribemont sector was comparatively peaceful. As before the men were principally occupied in working parties on the defences and the officers in reconnoitring lines of approach to the front trenches. On the whole the enemy was quiet, though he frequently added insult to injury by dropping on the Battalion gas shells evidently intended for the batteries which were in action just in rear of it. The trenches were comfortable, for all these months of hard work had been to some purpose; and the presence of ruined villages in the near vicinity was the means of adding touches of home life in the shape of a few odd sticks of broken furniture which had formerly graced a cottage home in Buire. An inter-platoon boundary in one of the trenches was marked by what had once been a handsome perambulator, while a little further on a basket-work dressmaker's model stood sentry over a shell hole in ludicrous isolation.

The ravages of the influenza epidemic of June and July were severe, and casualties from this cause far exceeded those inflicted by the enemy. Between the battle at Cachy and the end of July no fewer than 427 other ranks of the Battalion were sent to hospital, though most of these rejoined after a week or two of absence.

On the 19th July the Battalion lost Lieut. S. A. Seys (15th Londons attached), the assistant adjutant, who had served with it since February 1917, and who left for attachment to the staff of the 60th Brigade. An able administrator, Seys, who, though not a 4th London officer, had loyally made the regiment his own during his service with it, left behind him many friends who sincerely regretted his departure.

During July Lieut. A. G. Croll and drafts of 92 other ranks joined the Battalion. 2/Lieuts. Gauld and Cotton rejoined their own regiment. While the Battalion was at Baizieux the medical officer, Lieut. Dunaway, U.S. Army, was presented by the Corps Commander with the Military Cross, awarded him for services in March and April. It is believed that Dunaway was one of the first American officers to receive a British decoration for gallantry in the field.

At the end of July companies were commanded as follows: A by Lieut. C. C. Brissenden, B. by Capt. A. G. Croll, C by Capt. W. H. Parslow and D by Capt. B. Rivers Smith.

All who served in the Albert sector during the summer of 1918 will remember the Albert Road. This was very largely used at night by incoming and outgoing troops who used to join it somewhere in the neighbourhood of Pont Noyelles. The journey up it was an experience which it would indeed be hard to forget. On both sides of the road was ranged battery after battery; it seemed impossible that so many guns could be massed in so small a compass. "A succession of blinding flashes alternated with inky blackness. The road itself was encumbered with ammunition lorries, ration limbers and field ambulances. Thundering detonations from the guns and a continued grating roar from the traffic made the journey a nightmare." So writes Croll. The picture is indeed sufficiently disturbing. But in spite of the noisy horror a Battalion such as the 2/4th Londons, who had made close acquaintance with the seamy side of war in the retreat from La Fère, could not but be heartened by the realisation that already past losses had been made good, and that night by night the roar of the British guns was becoming louder and yet louder, till at last they were ready to roar forth the barrage which was to lead our troops to final victory.

The whole experience of July 1918 indeed, though devoid of exciting incident, was such as to impress the Battalion with the realisation that the time of waiting was nearly at an end, and that the equilibrium, to gain which we had been straining every nerve for three months, was almost attained. Heavy as the German bombardments had been from time to time, our guns with increasing frequency demonstrated their power to silence the enemy artillery. The results achieved by patrolling had shown that in growing measure we were becoming masters of No Man's Land, and encounters with enemy patrols afforded conclusive proof of the individual prowess and courage of our men as well as their superior morale.

Relieved from the trenches at Ribemont by the 1/1st Cambridgeshire Regiment, the 2/4th Londons concentrated at Behencourt on the evening of the 2nd August, and, embussing at once, reached Pernois, in the Domart area, in the early morning of the 3rd. Here it remained till brought back to the line to take part in the great battle of the 8th August.

The Reserve Battalion

In April 1918 the 3rd (Reserve) Battalion moved from Blackdown Camp to Maida Barracks, Aldershot. The reason for this move was primarily to provide troops for use in tactical schemes by students at the Senior Officers' School, then stationed at Oudenarde Barracks.

While carrying out this duty the Battalion was called upon to supply large parties daily for the School where they were commanded by Student Officers. It cannot be said that this duty, which fell largely on the "A IV" platoons, was beneficial to training. The regular course of instruction was interfered with, and a large amount of field work was carried out before the recruits engaged in it were sufficiently advanced to appreciate what they were supposed to be doing. The individual training was thus delayed and its resumption rendered proportionately difficult when at last the attachment to the School ceased. During the period spent at Maida the Expeditionary Company practically ceased to exist, as all N.C.O.'s and men who rejoined from hospital or the Command Depôt were posted temporarily to the 1st (Reserve) Battalion, which remained at Blackdown.

The German offensive of March completely revolutionised the Reserve Battalion. The frightful losses at the front had to be made good immediately at all costs. Training staffs were reduced to a minimum, and every fit officer and N.C.O. as well as every recruit, whose training was advanced enough to lend colourable justification to it, was at once sent overseas. The call for men did not cease here. The General Order forbidding the despatch of "young soldiers" overseas was, under pressure of circumstances, revoked, and volunteers were called for from the "A IV" boys. The response was, as may be expected, magnificent. Under age, under-trained, these gallant boys had but one thought—to join their overseas battalions in the fighting line. At the end of a week the Battalion was almost denuded of recruits under training, while the orderly room and training staffs were on the point of breakdown from almost continuous work and strain.

Among the first to answer the call was Lieut.-Col. Hanbury Sparrow, the Commanding Officer, who rejoined his regiment. His place in command was taken by Lieut.-Col. Sir Hugh Lacon, D.S.O., the Warwickshire Regiment, who retained the appointment till shortly before the Armistice.

So reduced in numbers was the Battalion that it was no longer useful to the Senior Officer's School, and it was accordingly relieved by a stronger battalion and returned to Blackdown early in August, being quartered in Frith Hill Hutments. At the end of August the duties of second in command were assumed by Major H. J. Duncan-Teape, who rejoined from hospital.

Training was resumed on the usual routine at Frith Hill, and at the end of August the emergency order as to despatching "A IV" boys on draft was rescinded. The young soldiers, therefore, reverted to the former scheme of more gradual training. The staff was, however, busily employed with 400 coal-miners, enlisted into the Welsh Regiment, and sent to the 3rd (Reserve) Battalion for training. These miners were excellent material, but their training was not completed until the week following the Armistice, so that they were deprived of the opportunity of seeing active service and were rapidly demobilised. These Welshmen were endowed in large measure with the national gift for part-singing, and were thus enabled to contribute materially to the social life of the Battalion.

During Armistice week a further reduction of Home Cadres involved the amalgamation of the 1st and 3rd (Reserve) Battalions, under the title of 1st (Reserve) Battalion, so that the one reserve unit was made responsible for supply of drafts (few of course were needed) to the whole Fusilier Brigade. The combined unit was commanded by Col. Vickers Dunfee, V.D., until his demobilisation early in December, when command was given to Lieut.-Col. A. Mather (Leinster Regiment).

Shortly after Christmas 1918 demobilisation began to thin the ranks of the Battalion, while further ravages were made by the transfer of most of the "A IV" boys to Young Soldier Battalions, preparatory to their despatch to join the Army of the Rhine. In February 1919 the Battalion moved to

Shoreham-by-Sea, and by the end of the month its disbandment was completed.

CHAPTER XXIII
THE FINAL ADVANCE

I. *The 2/4th Battalion in the Battles of Amiens and Bapaume, 1918*

The middle of 1918 witnessed the veritable low watermark of the Allied fortunes. All the protracted sledgehammer offensives of 1916 and 1917, which had indented the enemy's line at such ghastly cost of life, had within a few short weeks been swept aside as if they had never been, and the advancing tide of the Germans' offensive had carried their eagles forward to the furthest positions they had ever reached in 1914. In Italy the laborious advance of our Allies towards Trieste had been turned, when the coveted goal seemed almost within their grasp, into a defeat which was almost decisive. Roumania had long been utterly overrun, Austria given a new lease of life, and Russia's debacle completed. Scarcely anywhere was there a ray of light on this very gloomy horizon.

We have endeavoured to show that, bad as the situation was, the Allies by no means accepted the crushing blows which had been inflicted on them as decisive, and week by week the position was gradually improving, and the numerical superiority of the enemy was being overcome. In July so great was the British recovery that offensive operations on a small scale were undertaken with a view to local improvement of our positions. Among these the capture of Hamel and Meteren may be mentioned.

The bulk of the fighting, however, was on the French front, where the enemy was endeavouring to enlarge the salient which he had driven down to the Marne. On the east side at Rheims and on the west in the Forêt de Compiègne his pressure was great but weakening. The French powers of resistance were gradually becoming more equal to their task and the German progress correspondingly slower till at last, on the 15th July, the enemy received a definite check. Three days later Marshal Foch had brought forward the reserves which he had jealously conserved through these trying days, and the enemy was in retreat on a front of 27 miles from the Oise to the Marne. Of the French offensive we can say nothing, for our task lies with the British Fourth Army under Rawlinson.

Immediately Marshal Foch had set his own armies in forward motion he ordered the British and American armies to open the offensives they had prepared. The first object of British G.H.Q. was to disengage Amiens, and the vast offensive movement therefore began in Rawlinson's army, which was on the right of the British line from its junction with the French near Moreuil to the north of Albert.

In this part of the great series of victories we have to follow the operations of the 2/4th Battalion, and we shall deal with them in the first instance from the opening of the offensive on August 8th until their final disbandment on September 12th. We shall then proceed to follow the unrolling of the battle northwards and the engagement in it successively of the Third and First Armies, with both of which the 1/4th Battalion fought until the Armistice.

The date fixed for the great attack was 8th August, and on that day Rawlinson's Fourth Army, comprising from left to right the III, Australian and Canadian Corps, would combine with Débeney's First French Army in a supreme effort to relieve Amiens from the menace of the Huns. With the details of the battle beyond the 58th Division's area we are not concerned but we must, in order to understand the rôle which the Division was expected to play, offer some brief description of the terrain and its effect on the Australian advance on the right.

The main advance was to be made on the south bank of the Somme by the Canadians and the Australians, while the III Corps, including the 18th and 58th Divisions in line, operating solely on the north bank of the river, would secure the left flank of the attack as far north as Morlancourt. The establishment of this defensive flank entailed the capture of a very strong naturally defended position, the possession of which was vital to the success of the troops south of the Somme.

The Somme, like the Oise, is a winding canalised river running through a marshy valley. Its south bank, though undulating, has no specially marked hill features, but on the north the adjoining land rises to a considerable height on the spur which traverses the narrow wedge between the Somme and the Ancre. This plateau is furrowed by a number of deep gullies running northward from the river, and the sharp hills between these valleys, falling in places by abrupt chalk cliffs to the Somme, form very commanding features from which it would be possible for a determined enemy to play havoc with any attempt to advance south of the river, for they completely dominate the south bank. The most marked of these spurs is the long saddle immediately east of the village of Chipilly. This feature is almost girdled by the Somme (which makes a narrow sweep round the east, south and west sides of it), and projects almost a mile south of the general line of the river. It thus forms a barrier across the ground for which the Australians would be made responsible.

The capture of the Chipilly Ridge was the task allotted to the 58th Division, while the 18th would complete the defensive flank from the north end of the Ridge at Gressaire Wood to Morlancourt.

The line of advance from the British front trenches was full of obstacles. Immediately in front of the line, and on the river bank was the village of Sailly Laurette, the garrison of which, if not immediately overcome, would be able to enfilade the whole advance as the troops crossed No Man's Land. A mile and a half east of Sailly Laurette lay Malard Wood, covering both slopes of one of the declivitous gullies already alluded to; while halfway between the Malard Wood valley and the final objective on the cliff of Chipilly Ridge, lay a second gully, badly enfiladed from Chipilly village and completely overlooked from the Ridge itself. Heavy going all the way, up hill and down dale, through features eminently suited to machine-gun defence, culminating in a breathless scramble up a steep slope to meet an enemy who would probably defend it to the last; a total advance of about two and a half miles; altogether no light task for a single division.

In view of the obvious difficulty of carrying so strong a position by frontal attack alone it was arranged that the Australians should advance ahead of the 58th Division and occupy the high ground near Méricourt south-east of the Ridge, by the time the 58th was due to deliver its final assault. By this means it was hoped to squeeze the enemy off the Ridge in the direction of Bray without making a fight for it, in order to avoid complete envelopment.

Such was the general idea: and we must now return to the 2/4th Battalion which we left in the preceding chapter at Pernois on the morning of 2nd August, in order to trace how the idea worked out.

The 2nd and 3rd August were spent in resting and cleaning, and on Sunday, the 4th, after company commanders had been admitted to the rumour that large operations were imminent, sudden orders to move were received. At 9.30 p.m. that night the Battalion again embussed to La Houssoye on the Amiens-Albert Road, whence it marched to bivouacs in a wood near Bonnay (two miles north of Corbie, on the Ancre). Fortunately the weather was fine and warm, for the only shelter provided was one bell tent per company.

The 5th August was passed in close cover in the wood in order that our intentions might not be revealed to prying Bosche aeroplanes, and in the afternoon Lieut.-Col. Grover explained the plan of attack to the company commanders. At zero (4.20 a.m.) the 174th Brigade would advance from Assembly line (see Map No. 17) and dig in on the Green line 200 yards east of Malard Wood. The 2/10th Londons (175th Brigade) were especially attached for the capture of Sailly Laurette. The 173rd Brigade would follow close on the 174th in artillery formation, halt in Malard Wood for one hour and adopt attack formation, and then passing through the Green line would take Chipilly Ridge, Red line. The 18th Division would advance on the left of the 58th, the 54th Brigade going as far as the Green line, when the 53rd would leap-frog through it to the Red line. The advance would be made under a creeping field artillery barrage provided by ninety 18-prs. and thirty 4·5 howitzers, while the deep valleys would be dealt with by a heavy howitzer barrage jumping from valley to valley. Twelve tanks were to cover the advance, two of which were allotted to the 2/10th Londons, for Sailly Laurette, the remainder leading the 174th Brigade to Malard Wood, where the 173rd would pick up one per company for the final assault. The 4th Suffolks (Pioneers) would consolidate a position slightly in rear of the final objective.

The order of battle in the 173rd Brigade was: 3rd Londons on the right, 2/4th Londons on the left, leading battalions; 2/2nd Londons, reserve battalion. In the 2/4th Battalion the order of advance was: leading D (Rivers Smith) on the right and C (Parslow) on the left; supporting B (Croll) on the right, A (Brissenden) on the left, with Battalion Headquarters in rear.

Another conference followed on the morning of the 6th, after which company commanders went forward to reconnoitre the point of assembly. On arrival at the 54th Brigade Headquarters it was found, however, that the enemy had just delivered a sharp attack and possessed himself of the very trenches from which we were to "jump-off" the following morning: rather disconcerting and possibly very serious for the whole attack, for the Huns had reached some of the dumps and gun positions prepared for the 8th, and it might be that they would guess our intentions. To guard against any possibility of failure on this score the barrage lines were completely rearranged. Prisoners subsequently captured stated that the British intention to attack had not been discovered, but the extraordinary defence which the Bosche made on 8th, combined with the fact that his field guns were withdrawn east of Gressaire Wood throws some doubt on this.

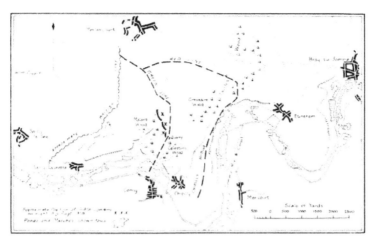

THE BATTLE OF AMIENS, 1918 (2/4TH BATTALION). ACTION AT CHIPILLY RIDGE, AUGUST 8-10, 1918

At all events the company commanders were forced to return without seeing anything of their assembly position or of the ground over which they were to advance, and reported accordingly. The attack, however, could not be postponed as the remainder of the Army and the French also were involved, and final preparations were therefore made for a plunge in the dark.

Battle surplus in charge of Capt. Hetley, who that day returned from hospital, was sent back to Mirvaux, and at 9.30 p.m. the Battalion moved forward to a gully half a mile north-east of Vaux-sur-Somme.

The 18th Division was able to re-establish its position during the 7th, though after such losses that the 36th Brigade (12th Division) had to be put into the attack on the first objective in place of the 54th Brigade. The recovery was too late for reconnaissance, which had therefore to be limited to viewing the approaches to the assembly, and at dusk, laden with all the usual impedimenta of battle, the companies set out on their two and a half mile trudge to the starting-point. The move was made "overland," but alongside a communication trench known as Cootamundra. The advance was not easy; gas masks had to be worn for some distance; intermittent shelling caused delays; tanks now and then drifted through the columns, breaking them up; and as usual shell holes in the dark proved a fruitful source of annoyance; but with all these drawbacks it was a cheerful and optimistic, if blasphemous, Battalion that arrived in the front line well up to time.

Dawn broke at last and the company commanders, eagerly expecting to see the positions which they had never yet viewed, were dismayed to find the sun rising on a dense fog which enshrouded the whole landscape and limited vision to about 20 yards! However, there was nothing for it but to get up and try to keep touch with the assaulting troops. The enemy's barrage came down quickly and heavily, and the companies moved forward rapidly over No Man's Land, though a good many fell. By bad luck most of the Battalion Headquarters, including Lieut.-Col. Grover and Capt. Walker the Adjutant, both severely hit, were knocked out within a few minutes, and this misfortune dogged the Battalion through the day. Moving forward slowly, trusting to a compass bearing to bring them to the north edge of Malard Wood, the companies pushed on, our barrage roaring on far ahead and no troops in sight right or left of them.

Adverse comments have been made on the Division for a serious loss of direction this day. As a matter of fact it was not so serious as has been stated by some writers, but it is true that the 2/4th Battalion at first drifted about 500 yards over its left boundary into the 18th Division territory. This divergence was also followed by the 2/2nd Londons, who encroached on what should properly have been our right company front. This is regrettable, but comprehensible if a close study be made of a contoured map. The gullies which had to be crossed ran obliquely across the line of advance. If anyone cares to try hill climbing in a fog he will realise the extreme difficulty of maintaining a sidelong direction.

Another cause of divergence from the correct direction lay in the numerous small pockets of enemy who had to be mopped up by the companies on route. These small parties offered comparatively little opposition, but they necessitated a cautious advance. Moreover, as they were not all in the exact path of the advancing platoons, it was inevitable to make a deliberate deflection to deal with them, after which the idea of direction in the fog became still more nebulous.

After some time Croll and Parslow, whose companies were in touch, reached a trench lately occupied by the enemy, badly smashed and full of dead Huns. Here a parley was held, and they decided that they were off the line. The advance was resumed in a south-easterly direction, extended order being used owing to the very severe machine-gun fire at this point. Parslow, having received news of the Colonel's casualty, assumed command. During this second advance the enemy's fire began to slacken and the mist showed some signs of lifting. After about 200 yards these companies found one of the tanks which was due to meet them at Malard Wood roaming about disconsolately, having completely lost its bearings, but this was put on the right track and began to follow the companies, though it soon vanished again in the mist: a passing ship!

At about 8.30 the mist began to thin rapidly and B and C Companies reached the hedge at the north end of Malard Wood, where they gained touch with Rivers Smith (D Company), and Parslow pushed out to the right to link up with Brissenden (A Company), who had gained the west edge of the Wood. The 174th Brigade were still in the Wood and had not yet reached the Green line, and the lifting mist disclosed no troops east of it. A company of 8th Royal Berkshires (53rd Brigade) were strung out in a north-easterly direction on the left of the Battalion, while immediately in front was the head of the Malard Wood Gully, about 40 yards wide, and beyond it a cornfield breast high with crops which stretched as far as Gressaire Wood. Sharp bursts of machine-gun fire from Malard Wood and shrapnel bursts from Gressaire Wood took a steady toll of our men and rendered further advance without artillery support impossible. But our artillery had carried its barrage forward to the final objective, believing that the infantry were following it, and was now silent.

At about 9.30 a.m. the Berkshires informed Croll, who had taken charge of the left half of the Battalion, that they were going to attack Gressaire Wood, and asking the 2/4th Battalion to advance with them. Croll immediately sent runners to Parslow and Brissenden in the Wood warning them of this intention; and, swinging half right to conform to the Berkshires, the advance began, but was brought to a standstill on the east edge of the gully by parties of the enemy working forward with machine-guns from Gressaire Wood.

Further advance was out of the question, and leaving three Lewis gun posts east of the gully, Croll withdrew his troops to the hedge previously occupied; there the Battalion began to dig in. After a conference of the few remaining officers it was decided to send 2/Lieut. E. P. Higgs back to Brigade to explain the position and ask for fresh orders and for artillery support to a further advance. Almost immediately after this parley broke up poor Rivers Smith was killed by a piece of shell which hit him in the neck. In the meantime, runners sent out to the right flank returned with the information that the 2/4th and 3rd Battalions were mixed up in Malard Wood, that the 2/2nd had come up and that Lieut.-Col. Miller of the 2/2nd was reorganising the troops.

A gap of 300 yards between the two halves of the Battalion had occurred in the last attempt to get forward, and the position at noon was that Brissenden (Parslow had been hit) was in charge of the right half Battalion on the east edge of Malard Wood, and Croll with the left half lined along the hedge north of the Wood. The Wood was now completely cleared of enemy, but egress from the east edge of it was impossible. Barkas (Intelligence Officer) now came forward from Headquarters to take over command, being cognisant of the position on the right and acquainted with the H.Q. Staffs of the other Battalions. He agreed with Croll that further attempts to push forward were useless without further support. Col. Urquart (L.T.M. Battery) was reported on his way up to take over from Barkas.

While this was happening the barrage had, as already stated, moved forward from the Green line at the scheduled hour on to Chipilly Ridge, but owing to the loss of direction only a few small parties were available to follow it and of these probably none reached the Ridge. The Huns on the Ridge were holding up by machine-gun fire the Australians on the south of the river, and they failed to reach the high ground from which the position was to be outflanked. Unfortunately aerial reports to Divisional Headquarters persisted that the Ridge was in our hands, and this mistake led to serious casualties in the afternoon. The 2/2nd Londons were ordered to advance at 3 p.m., but owing to the false report artillery support was refused them. In these circumstances the attack, though pushed forward by the 2/2nd with great gallantry, was inevitably withered by enemy machine-gun fire from Gressaire Wood.

No further move was attempted that day. At about 4 p.m. Major Sutcliffe of the 2/2nd took over the 2/4th Battalion—the fifth C.O. within twelve hours!—and the positions already occupied were consolidated, Lewis gun posts being pushed forward across the gully. The night positions of the Battalion are shown on the map.

South of the Somme the day had been—except in the area next the river swept from Chipilly Ridge—one of immense success, an advance of about seven miles being made by the Canadians. On the left of the 58th Division the 12th had reached the Green line but had been unable to progress beyond it.

An immediate resumption of the attack to reduce the Chipilly stronghold and so remove the one remaining obstacle to an important advance was obviously necessary, but in view of the restricted success on the previous day a modification of the original intention was essential.

The main object of the attack of the 9th August was to gain the line Bray-sur-Somme—Dernancourt. To ensure that the assault should have sufficient weight to carry it through successfully, and in view of the serious losses of the Division on the previous day, the 133rd American Regiment (Col. Samborn) then in Army reserve some miles in rear was attached for the operation. The main attack on the Divisional front was to be carried out by the 175th Brigade on the left and the Americans on the right; while in conjunction with it the capture of Chipilly and the Ridge was to be entrusted to the 174th and 173rd Brigades.

The distance which the Americans had to advance to reach their starting line necessarily caused a postponement of the operation till late in the afternoon, the earlier hours of the day being employed in side-stepping the 173rd Brigade to face its new objective, and to leave room for the Americans to come into line.

At 6 a.m. Major Sutcliffe issued orders to the Battalion to reorganise and prepare for a further advance, and these orders were followed later, as a result of reports received by aerial reconnaissance, by instructions to push forward fighting patrols to ascertain whether Gressaire Wood were still occupied. The sharp machine-gun fire with which these patrols were met left no room for doubt as to the situation. Brigade received orders for the afternoon attack at 1 p.m., but owing to the lack of telephone communication it was two hours later when Lieut.-Col. Miller, who was in charge of the whole of the advanced troops, sent for Croll. The grim humour of the situation was succinctly summed up in Lieut.-Col. Miller's greeting. "Hullo, Croll, aren't you dead yet?" "No sir!" replied Croll. "Then you damned soon will be!" And orders for the attack were issued: "You will withdraw all patrols and posts at once, move your men under cover of Malard Wood and take up a position as soon as possible in a line of trenches extending for about 400 yards southward from the Quarry. Lieut. Brissenden has similar orders. You will occupy this position and be prepared to advance at 5.30 and capture the original objective, Chipilly Ridge. You will advance in two waves, Brissenden with his half Battalion in the first wave, and you with the remainder of the Battalion in the second wave. The position must be taken at all costs."

This assembly position south of the Quarry was that occupied by the 9th Londons on the previous night, but on arrival it was found to be only a line of shell holes. The 173rd Brigade was to attack with the 3rd Londons on the right, the 2/4th in the centre and the 2/2nd on the left, with the 2/10th attached in reserve. The assembly proceeded as rapidly as possible, though time was short and the barrage could not open until all patrols were in. The Americans, who were rushed up from the rear, had to double nearly a mile to reach their assembly position at Malard Wood, but by a few minutes after zero every unit was moving forward. The side-step of the 2/4th Battalion was carried out under very heavy machine-gun fire from Celestin Wood, the enemy having doubtless seen the movement, and delay was caused by searching for the trench (non-existent) which had been fixed as the start line. Our barrage opened well up to time but the shells fell harmlessly in Chipilly Valley instead of on the Ridge, which again became a hornet's nest of Hun machine-gunners.

Under this heavy fire the Battalion began the advance, much harassed also from Celestin Wood on their right flank. Brissenden was seriously hit early, and Mansel-Howe (B Company) killed. Croll took over the whole remnants of the Battalion and pushed forward, the men behaving with magnificent coolness and advancing by rushes. Every party which rushed forward, however, lost men, and Croll himself was hit in the knee though he bravely struggled on in the endeavour to get his men into some sort of cover. The Americans on the left were not yet up in line, and the fire from the right flank continued. Casualties were now so numerous that it was clear the Battalion could never reach the Ridge in anything approaching assaulting strength, and Croll decided to dig in in the shelter of the Chipilly gully, sending back a runner to Lieut.-Col. Miller with a report of the situation. In this position the Battalion was badly enfiladed from Chipilly village, and to make matters worse groups of Bosche could be seen running down from the crest of the Ridge, evidently in preparation for a counter-attack. This attack, however, was never delivered, for a change of the situation, almost miraculous in its suddenness, occurred. On the right the 2/10th Londons had been fighting stubbornly, and before dark managed to clear Chipilly village and began to work up the south end of the Ridge. Here they were held up by a nest of Bosche machine-gunners firing southwards from the head of Chipilly Valley, but the Americans, advancing on the left with magnificent dash towards Gressaire Wood, mopped up this position. A glance at the map will show the result. Further tenure of the Ridge was impossible for the Bosche, who promptly retreated to avoid being caught by the pincers which were closing on them.

By 11 p.m. the Brigade was firmly established on the Ridge, while the main operation had proved completely successful.

> Officers: Capt. B. Rivers Smith and Lieut. C. I. Mansel-Howe, killed; Lieut.-Col. A. Grover, D.S.O., M.C., Capts. W. H. Parslow, F. W. Walker, D.S.O., and A. G. Croll, Lieuts. G. de G. Barkas, M.C., and C. C. Brissenden, 2/Lieuts. W. N. M. Girling, H. G. A. Leach, J. W. George, A. L. D. Bold, H. Slater, S. T. Morris and J. Horsfield, wounded.
>
> N.C.O.'s and men: 38 killed, 228 wounded and 20 missing, a total of all ranks of 301.

For his excellent work in this action Capt. A. G. Croll was awarded the M.C.

The experience of these two days' fighting had demonstrated clearly that the River Somme was an unsatisfactory boundary between the III and Australian Corps. The hill slopes on each bank formed tactical features so inter-supporting that it was deemed essential to bring both banks into the area of one command; and accordingly on the 10th August the Australian Corps took over with the 3rd Australian Division a sector immediately adjacent to the north bank. This redistribution involved a shortening of the 58th Divisional sector, and the 173rd Brigade, handing over its line to the Australians at about 2 p.m., withdrew to the reserve area, the 2/4th Londons concentrating in bivouacs near Bonnay.

During the 10th an enemy counter-attack set back slightly the positions gained by us the preceding day, but the situation was soon re-established and strong patrols pushed forward by the Division brought them to the line of the outer Amiens defences.

The following day the III Corps was taken over temporarily by Sir A. J. Godley.

This practically brought to a close the first phase of the Fourth Army's great advance, which is officially known as the Battle of Amiens, 1918. Amiens, for so long threatened by a victorious enemy, was now liberated, and, important as was this result of the three days' struggle, other results accruing from the battle were still more vital. The actual loss inflicted on the Huns—upwards of 23,000 prisoners and 400 guns were captured—were in themselves a matter of great moment; but the captures themselves showed that already the Germans were flinging their reserves into the fight. This undoubtedly had the effect of paving the way for the successful French advance which began south of Montdidier on the 10th August. Perhaps the most cheering moral of all was the establishment of the fact that three anxious months of constant strain, following on a retreat of unprecedented rapidity and loss, had left the fighting qualities of our troops unimpaired—perhaps to the surprise of some gloomy folks at home—while evidence was already abundant that the enemy was not standing to it as he had done in former British offensives. His morale was beginning to crack. This is evidenced by actual numbers: 13 British divisions and 3 cavalry divisions had defeated 20 German divisions and secured an advance of 12 miles in 5 days' fighting. To enable us to judge of the enormous effect of this great victory we have the evidence of Ludendorff himself:

> "The Emperor told me that after the failure of the July offensive and after the 8th August, he knew the war could no longer be won."

A good deal of severe criticism has been levelled at the III Corps in general, and at the 58th Division in particular, for the lack of success attained on the first day of battle. It is undoubtedly a fact that the failure to eject the Bosche from Chipilly Ridge on the 8th August caused the infliction of severe loss on our Australian neighbours on the right flank. We do not pose as apologists for the Division or for the 2/4th Londons, and are satisfied that no excuses for them are needed. But we feel justified, in view of what has been said, in pointing to certain circumstances of the battle as contributing towards the restriction of their success. We propose not to argue these circumstances but merely to state them:

1. The enemy attack on the 18th Division on the 6th August not only deprived our company commanders of any opportunity of reconnoitring their ground, but also entirely disposed of the surprise effect gained south of the Somme, for undoubtedly the Bosche expected a counter-attack from us.

2. The mist of 8th August, which made success depend largely on a correct compass march over unseen and shell-torn ground.

3. The fact that no tanks arrived on the Green line to lead the Battalion forward to the second objective, whereby the enemy machine-gun defence was not impeded. We do not wish to pass the blame on to the tanks; their difficulties in reaching the start-line were as acute as our own, and the ground much more difficult for them than it was south of the river.

4. The startling rapidity with which the Battalion command changed during the battle.

These are not excuses for failure. We are prepared to leave to the judgment of impartial critics the decision as to whether the Battalion, and the Division as a whole, did all in its power to perform its duty. That the operations of the Division during these two days' fighting were not altogether unfruitful is evidenced by the fact that their total captures amounted to 1925 prisoners, 68 guns, 190 machine-guns and 36 trench mortars, while the whole area of advance was littered with enemy dead.

A lull in the active operations now occurred while heavy batteries, dumps and all necessary material were advanced in preparation for the next phase of the struggle, which would involve the ejection of the Hun from a strongly defended system of trenches.

After a night's rest the Battalion marched on the 11th August to a wood at Heilly (near Ribemont), where it was joined by the first line transport and the battle surplus, returning on the afternoon of the 13th to Pont Noyelles. Here it was accommodated in billets, the most comfortable quarters since the few days at Guignemicourt.

A few days' rest at Pont Noyelles, now some eleven miles in rear of the battle line, were devoted to reorganisation and to assimilation of several reinforcements of officers, N.C.O.'s and men. On his return from short leave on the 14th August Major Tollworthy assumed temporary command of the Battalion, but a week later Major W. McC. Crosbie, M.C., Royal

Munster Fusiliers, arrived and took over the command. The adjutancy of the Battalion was taken over by Lieut. H. J. King, M.C.

During this period the Battalion was inspected successively by the Brigadier and by the Corps Commander, who saw the troops at training.

The reinforcements received between the 10th and 22nd August were:

> 2/Lieuts. R. E. Glover, L. A. Still, W. J. Till and F. J. Paterson (4th Londons);

and officers of other units attached as follows:

> 2/Lieuts. C. C. W. Goodale, L. A. Palmer and A. W. Tucker (1st Londons);
>
> 2/Lieuts. P. F. Royce, W. C. B. Hall and T. R. A. Maynard (2nd Londons);
>
> 2/Lieuts. J. C. Wood and H. Irvine (3rd Londons);
>
> 2/Lieuts. G. Gilson, H. Lelyveld, J. Slattery, M. F. Giles and H. B. Bartleet (5th Londons);
>
> 2/Lieuts. J. T. Spencer and E. S. McKittrick (8th Londons);
>
> 2/Lieut. W. A. Davies (9th Londons);
>
> and 480 N.C.O.'s and men.

The majority of this large reinforcement consisted of men from the 14th Division, which had suffered very severely in the battles of March 1918. The drafts of young soldiers on which the Battalion had been depending of late, though of excellent material, were obviously not so desirable as fully seasoned soldiers; and the 14th Division men were therefore particularly welcome. With a seasoning of old 2/4th London men and the remnants of the K.O.Y.L.I., who had come from the 16th Entrenching Battalion, they helped to make up once again a really fine Battalion.

On the 21st August the offensive was resumed and though, as we have stated, we propose to continue the record of the 2/4th Battalion's operations in the Fourth Army, it should be borne in mind that henceforth the Army instead of having an inert neighbour on its left flank had an active one in the Third Army, which was now also on the move.

This new great battle (21st August to 1st September), known as the Battle of Bapaume, 1918, extended the area of fighting to the Somme-Scarpe salient.

The increasing enemy resistance at the termination of the Battle of Amiens had drawn G.H.Q. to the decision to break off the battle and transfer their attention to another part of the front; a method which throughout the closing period of the war proved its value. The Germans were kept always in doubt—as the British had been in March 1918—as to whether each fresh offensive was in reality only a feint, in doubt as to where to place their already dwindling reserves. Moreover, the British Armies were now no longer faced by line upon line of almost impregnable trenches as they had been in 1916, and frontal attacks were not the only possibility open to them.

G.H.Q. therefore decided on a vast turning movement. An attack in a south-easterly direction between Albert and Arras would turn the flank of the Somme line of defence about Péronne, and would constitute a distinct forward step towards the further objectives of Cambrai and St Quentin.

The immediate object of the III Corps was to free Albert and to oust the Bosche from the strong defensive system which he had built up round the town during the summer months. On the first day of the III Corps battle, 22nd August, the 58th Division was in Corps reserve, the divisions in line being from right to left, the 47th, 12th and 18th.

The 2/4th Battalion remained at training on the 22nd August, but an early move was made the following morning, when it marched at 4 a.m. to a sheltered valley half a mile south of Méricourt-l'Abbé. In this position it remained all day together with the rest of the Brigade; the 174th Brigade being in the old British line at Morlancourt, at the disposal of the 18th Division. In the centre the 47th Division carried the line forward to the high ground east of the Happy Valley, while on the right the Australians occupied the high ground immediately north of Bray.

The exploitation of this success was ordered by Army H.Q. for the following day, but the situation was altered by a strong German counter-attack, which late in the afternoon drove the 142nd Brigade (47th Division) almost back to their start-line, leaving the Australians at Bray in an awkward salient. That night the 175th Brigade moved from its reserve area near Tailles Wood and took over the line from the 142nd. The following day was occupied in reorganisation, though the advance was continued south of the river, and orders were received for the pressure to be continued on the whole army front on the 24th August.

At 1 a.m. that morning the attack was prosecuted by the 47th Division, in conjunction with the 3rd Australians on the right and the 12th on the left. The 47th Division attack was carried out by the 175th (attached) and 140th Brigades, the battalions of the 173rd Brigade being ordered to support the 175th. For this purpose the 2/4th Battalion was turned out at midnight on the 23rd/24th August and reached a position of assembly in the old Amiens defence line east of Morlancourt at 4 a.m. on the 24th. The attack was entirely successful. The Happy Valley once more passed into our hands, and the 47th Division established itself finally on the farther crest. The Australians occupied Bray, while on the left the 12th Division pressed forward in the direction of Fricourt. The enemy opposition was not severe though between 3 a.m. and 8 a.m. a large amount of high explosive and gas shelling was experienced. The day brought forth further evidence of the increasing demoralisation of the enemy troops, and intelligence reports pointing strongly to the probability that the enemy was fighting a delaying action preparatory to a big retreat, the immediate exploitation of the success was ordered.

This day the 175th Brigade remained in line but came once more under orders of the 58th Division which took over the Divisional sector, the 174th Brigade going into line on the right of the 175th.

During the morning a conference of commanding officers in the 173rd Brigade was held and orders were issued for the further advance. The attack was to be made with two brigades in line, the 175th on the right and the 140th on the left, supported by the 173rd Brigade. This latter was to be led by the 2/2nd and 3rd Londons with the 2/4th Londons in support, the last-named with the rôle of being prepared to support any part of the front and carry it on to the final objective. Owing, however, to the situation remaining obscure on the left flank this operation was postponed till 2.30 a.m. on the 25th, when rapid developments took place.

In accordance with the orders already issued the 2/4th Londons moved from their Assembly position near Tailles Wood, the order of march being A, B, C, D Companies with Headquarters and one section Brigade Machine-Gun Company bringing up the rear, and with 100 yard intervals between companies. In this order it reached a position in the Happy Valley under cover of a dense mist at 4 a.m. on the 25th August. Here it was to stand fast awaiting further orders from the Brigadier.

But in the meantime the Division, evidently still bearing in mind the experience of February 1917, had issued instructions to the effect that should the leading battalions lose touch with the enemy an advanced guard should at once be formed to push forward rapidly and regain contact. This was the contingency which materialised.

At 6.30 a.m. the attacking units reported themselves on their objectives, but in the mist touch with the enemy seemed to be lost, and all units of the 173rd Brigade were ordered to advance. The Brigadier at once issued orders for the formation of the advanced guard, and the 2/4th Battalion, which was more or less definitely located in the Happy Valley and was thus the battalion most easily to be reached in the mist, was selected for this duty.

The advanced guard troops were:

- No. 2 Troop Northumberland Hussars,
- 2/4th Londons,
- 1 Section 86th Brigade R.F.A.,
- 1 Section M.G.C.,

the whole under Major Crosbie.

The line of advance ordered was cross-country as far as Bronfay Farm and thence along the Bray-Maricourt Road. The Battalion was to advance in column of route until ordered to deploy. At 8.30 a.m. the guard was formed and the advance began, A Company under Lieut. V. C. Prince forming the Vanguard with Headquarters, B, C and D Companies following as Main Guard. This was an entirely new role for the 2/4th Battalion, and the sudden development of open warfare conditions, the realisation that the Battalion was in close formation on a road with cavalry operating ahead and the guns following, raised everyone's hopes and expectations to the highest pitch. The move was of course made without artillery support, and until Bronfay Farm was nearly reached very little sign of his existence was vouchsafed by the Bosche, beyond a little desultory shell-fire.

About this time the mist dispersed and the cavalry were checked by severe machine-gun fire from Billon Wood and the high ground to the north of it. The company commanders showed great initiative and dash, and a valuable reconnaissance was made by 2/Lieut. Prince and Cooke, his Sergt.-Major, to ascertain where the bulk of the firing was coming from. Quickly grasping the situation, Prince deployed his company and led it against the south-west edge of the Wood. The rear companies deploying in turn, the whole Battalion became committed to the attack, which, owing to the conditions under which it started, developed a little raggedly as regards the frontages occupied by companies, but still with good discipline and plenty of dash. Hetley (B Company) made for the left or north edge of the Wood along the Maricourt Road, while the gap between him and Prince was promptly taken up by C and D Companies. Observing the action taken by the 2/4th Londons, Brigade promptly pushed forward the 2/2nd Londons to the left flank to deal with the high ground north of Billon Wood, and ordered the 3rd Londons to support the attack.

The enemy shelling had now assumed very severe proportions, and though little resistance was met with by the 2/4th Battalion in Billon Wood, which it cleared without much difficulty, the Bosche gunners were able effectually to prevent it from emerging from the east edge of the Wood. Hetley says about this bombardment, "The shelling of Billon Wood was one of the heaviest I have ever undergone, being quite comparable to Bullecourt or the Salient in 1917." The line in the Wood was rather patchy and Hetley, leaving Grimsdell in charge, returned to Battalion Headquarters where Major Crosbie provided him with a couple of Lewis guns and about twenty-five men. With these he returned, and having got the Battalion into a deep trench, put out observation posts on the east edge of the Wood. The Battalion is credited by Division with having gained a line this day some 200 yards east of the Wood, but it seems doubtful whether this conclusion can be supported.

On the left flank, however, the 2/2nd and 3rd Londons made a good deal of progress up the long spur leading to Maricourt, and at the end of the day had established themselves in a chain of small copses about 500 yards west of the village. Their further progress was here arrested, owing to the fact that the 12th Division on the left was held up before Carnoy, which remained for the time in the enemy's hands.

At midnight the 2/4th Battalion was relieved by the 7th Londons of the 174th Brigade, which side-stepped to the left, and on relief was concentrated at Great Bear Wood north-east of the Happy Valley.

The casualties of the day, due almost entirely to shell-fire, were:

> 2/Lieuts. H. Lelyveld, J. C. Wood, A. Irvine and C. C. W. Goodale, wounded, and in N.C.O.'s and men 15 killed, 166 wounded and 14 missing.

The good work of 2/Lieut. Prince and C.S.M. Cooke has already been referred to. Prince was rewarded with the M.C. Cooke was killed in the Wood, and a few days after his death notification was received that he had been awarded the M.C. for his work on the 8th August. Mention must also be made of Pte. Campion, a battalion runner, who performed invaluable work in locating the scattered parties of the Battalion in the Wood, thereby enabling Hetley to assume proper control of the firing line.

On the 26th August the following congratulatory message was issued by the Brigadier (Brig.-Gen. Charles Corkoran):

> "The Major-General commanding the Division in congratulating you all wishes me to tell you that Sir Douglas Haig, the Army Commander and the Corps Commander have all expressed the highest praise for the way in which the Brigade is fighting. For myself I cannot say how proud I am to be in command of such a brigade as the Fusilier Brigade."

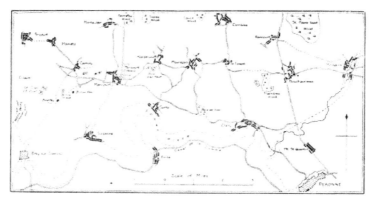

THE BATTLE OF BAPAUME, 1918 (2/4TH BATTALION)

Orders were issued on the night of the 25th/26th August for the prosecution of the attack on the following day, but the 26th proved a day of check. The 3rd Londons, who led the attack, reached Maricourt, but, the flanking brigades being held up, they were unsupported and had to fall back. A threatened German counter-attack south of Maricourt having failed to materialise, the remainder of the day was occupied in consolidation on a line about 500 yards west of the village.

The 2/4th Battalion was moved from Great Bear Wood at 9 a.m. on the 26th in anticipation of a successful attack, and took up a position in considerable depth in the vicinity of Bronfay Farm, where it was occupied in preparations for the battle of the 27th August. This day the Battalion was joined by Lieut. H. P. Lawrence and 2/Lieut. R. Grey, attached from the 10th Londons, and two days later by 2/Lieuts. H. H. Gant (2nd Londons), H. Hearnshaw (7th Londons) and C Brandram (9th Londons).

The objectives of the projected attack of the 27th August were the capture of Maricourt and the establishment of our line in the old British trenches of July 1916 on the eastern fringe of Maricourt Wood, east of the village. Exploitation of the success into the old German trenches as opportunity should allow was also arranged for. The leading battalion of the Brigade was the 3rd Londons, with the 2/4th Londons in close support and the 2/2nd Londons in reserve. Simultaneous attacks were to be made by the 3rd Australians in the direction of Vaux on the right and by the 12th Division towards Maltzhorn Farm on the left.

Early in the morning the 2/4th Battalion was assembled in artillery formation on the line consolidated the previous day, and twenty minutes after zero (4.55 a.m.) it followed the 3rd Londons towards Maricourt. The greater part of the advance was through the village itself and the Battalion soon got rather mixed up with the 3rd Londons in the course of mopping up the numerous dugouts in its ruins. The defence put up by the Germans, at least on the 2/4th Battalion's front, this day showed marked deterioration. It was sporadic and on the whole poor, and with comparatively little difficulty and remarkably small loss to itself, the Battalion gained its final objective east of the Wood, a message from Capt. Hetley to this effect being received in Battalion Headquarters at 7.30 a.m.

The inevitable breaking up of attack formations consequent on passing through a ruined village resulted in a good deal of disorganisation, and on arrival on the objective, which the 2/4th Battalion reached on the extreme left of the Brigade sector, no touch was found with either the 3rd Londons on the right or the 12th Division on the left. Hetley, however, who again assumed control on the spot, soon set this to rights, and leaving C.S.M. Bonser, D.C.M., to reorganise the platoons immediately available, sent C.S.M. Cowland to pick up the 12th Division on the left, while he himself pushed out to the right flank with a patrol. These efforts were entirely successful, and both the neighbouring battalions being found to be well up and the flanks thus secured, Hetley returned and established his headquarters in the railway cutting.

The rapidity of this advance and the completeness of its success leave one breathless after the weary and sanguinary struggles with which this ground had been hardly wrung from the enemy's grip in 1916. Maricourt Wood was full of German dugouts, and evidently these had not been quite completely dealt with during the advance, for later in the morning a couple of German gentlemen, feeling a desire to take the morning air, came quietly strolling down the hill from the Wood to Hetley's headquarters, where his unexpected presence caused them painful surprise.

During the morning C.S.M. Bonser was entrusted with the task of collecting isolated groups of men and with them filling up gaps and forming a support line in case of counter-attack. At this work he proved invaluable. Hetley writes: "He led party after party round dugouts in Maricourt clearing out Bosche, and was later perfectly splendid in organising the men and fetching up reinforcements, that is, rallying isolated parties in the town and Wood, all this under heavy if somewhat wild shell fire." Bonser received a bar to his D.C.M. for this day's work, and later, after the disbandment of the Battalion, when attached to the 2/2nd Londons gained a second bar on September 18th at Epéhy.

On our flanks the day was equally successful, Vaux falling to the Australians, and the high ground at Maltzhorn Farm passing into the 12th Division's hands. No counter-attack was delivered by the Bosche and we were left in undisputed possession of our gains which amounted to some

1700 yards of ground. Orders were issued during the day that the advance should be pressed on to Maurepas Station, but these were subsequently cancelled, as the enemy were found to be holding their old 1916 line in strength with three fresh divisions.

At 8 p.m. Major Crosbie made a reconnaissance of the line and organised the Battalion in two companies; A and B being placed under Capt. Hetley and C and D under 2/Lieut. Grimsdell, the Battalion's right flank resting on the point at which the railway crossed the front trench. Throughout the night the position was heavily shelled, but with very little loss to us.

In spite of the fatigue of the troops Army H.Q. was fixed in its determination to allow the Bosche no breathing space, and at 1 a.m. 28th August orders were received in the line that the attack was to be continued that day. The 3rd Londons were to lead the Brigade again, while the 2/2nd and 2/4th Londons were to remain in reserve in the old British front line. At 4.45 a.m. the attack was launched. The day resolved itself into a series of patrol encounters, in the course of which some very stubborn opposition was met with, notably in the Bois d'en Haut. By the evening the Divisional line had been established another 1000 yards further east, in front of the Bois d'en Haut and in touch on the left with the 12th Division, who had taken Hardecourt after stiff resistance, while the Australians had possessed themselves of Curlu.

That evening the Battalion was relieved, the 175th Brigade taking over the sector, and withdrew to reserve in a valley north of Bray-sur-Somme, a few hundred yards from the site of the old Citadel Camp, a spot well known to the Somme veterans of the 1/4th Battalion.

During the whole of these days in fact the 2/4th Battalion, though a little distance south of the Guillemont heights, had been crossing the tracks of the 1/4th Battalion in the earlier battles of this historic district, but under what extraordinarily different conditions! The painful steps of 1916, which gained perhaps a few hundred yards a week at appalling cost of life, amid the wretchedness of mud and rain, were now victorious strides which had carried our lines forward like an irresistible tide. Since the 2/4th Battalion had moved into the Happy Valley on the 24th August it had advanced some 8000 yards and already half the devastation of the old Somme battlefields was left behind.

The losses of the two days' fighting at Maricourt were, considering the extent of the gains, remarkably light. Lieut A. R. Muddell and 2/Lieuts. E. C. McKittrick and R. Grey were wounded, while Lieut. and Adjt. H. J. King, M.C., and Lieut. H. P. Lawrence were also hit but remained at duty. 114 N.C.O.'s and men became casualties, 9 being killed, 74 wounded and 29 missing.

For their splendid leadership Capt. G. H. Hetley and 2/Lieut. E. V. Grimsdell were rewarded with the M.C.

After the 173rd Brigade came out of the line the 58th Division remained in action and on the 29th August it carried the line forward, against an ever-increasing opposition, to the east of Maurepas. The following day, the 47th Division having taken over from the 12th on our left, the two divisions of Londoners again pressed on shoulder to shoulder. The enemy resistance this day was as stubborn as had been experienced for some time and the advance was eventually checked with the 58th facing the west edge of Marrières Wood, and the 47th extending the line to Priez Farm.

The 29th August was occupied by the 2/4th Battalion in cleaning and resting, and the necessary reorganisation consequent on its losses in the battle were effected. This day Major Crosbie left to take charge of the Battle Surplus Camp and Major F. G. Tollworthy, M.C., once more assumed command of the Battalion. On the 30th August Lieut. A. B. Carpenter (25th Londons) with 29 other ranks joined the Battalion.

The Fourth Army Line was now approaching Péronne, and from Cléry to St Christ the Australian Corps had reached the west bank of the Somme. The stiffening of the enemy resistance which had been so noticeable during the last two days' fighting, and the natural strength of the Somme as an obstacle, made it clear that the enemy was determined to hold out at Péronne as long as possible; and true to its scheme of allowing the Hun no respite, the Army at once made its plans for forcing a bridgehead over the river, with the object of reducing Péronne and the Somme line of defence.

The most favourable point of attack appeared to be the river between Péronne and Cléry, and the capture of the eminence of Mont St Quentin, though likely to be arduous, would give us complete command of Péronne itself and enable us to enfilade the whole of the enemy positions south of the city on the east of the river. The actual capture of Mont St Quentin was entrusted to the Australians in whose path it lay, and the movements of the III Corps to their north formed a part of the scheme for widening the bridgehead once gained. The two days' fighting of the 31st August and the 1st September may therefore be described as the Battle of Mont St Quentin, and our task is now to deal with the part taken in it by the 2/4th Battalion.

The 31st August saw a good deal of heavy fighting by the 175th Brigade, which was still in line, the chief feature of the enemy's resistance being the severity of the shell fire with which his heavy guns plastered the whole Brigade area. Marrières Wood was captured and the line pushed on to a position west of the Péronne-Rancourt Road and overlooking the slope leading down to Bouchavesnes.

At 7 p.m. that night unexpected orders were received by the 173rd Brigade to return to the line and deliver an attack at 5.30 a.m. the following morning. From Bronfay Farm the battalions were conveyed by bus to Hem Wood, whence they marched to assembly in the line, taking it over from the 175th Brigade.

The immediate objective of the attack was the village of Bouchavesnes, after which the line was to be pushed forward to a position overlooking the valley of the Tortille River and the Canal du Nord. The order of battle was: 2/4th Londons on the right, 3rd Londons on the left, with the 2/2nd Londons following in close support. In spite of the short notice for the operation the Battalion was duly assembled without delay on a line 300 yards west of the Péronne-Rancourt Road, and at zero, 5.30 a.m., 1st September, moved forward under a creeping barrage. The advance was made with two companies (A and B, under Capt. F. J. Griffiths and 2/Lieut. C. C. Gibbs) in front and two in support (C and D, under 2/Lieuts. Y. C. Prince, M. C., and G. C. Ewing, M.C.). Each company moved in artillery formation with three platoons in front and one in support.

For once we were favoured with good weather conditions, and though cold the morning was fine with good visibility. On the western outskirts of Bouchavesnes the enemy put up a rather stiff fight, but on being tackled with determination, he once again showed signs of weakening morale, and the remainder of the village was occupied and mopped up with very little opposition.

Although the Bosche infantry showed weakness his artillery work was, as usual, excellent. His counter-barrage came down promptly and heavily, and the bulk of our casualties this day were caused by his shell fire. On several occasions, indeed, during these successful days of August and September the enemy displayed prodigious skill in handling his guns. Field guns remained in action in the copses which are scattered all over this countryside, firing over open sights till the last possible moment; and when these were forced to limber up the fire was promptly taken up by high velocity guns firing at extreme ranges in the rear. On the 1st September, however, the advance was particularly rapid, and several field guns were unable to get away, and fell into our hands. After passing the village the Battalion pressed forward rapidly up the hill to the east of it, collecting a good many machine-gun posts on the way, and by 10.45 a.m. was on its final objective, organised and established on a definite line under the personal control of Major Tollworthy. This line was on the western crest of the Tortille Valley overlooking Moislains, and about 1000 yards short of that village. Some little difficulty was experienced by the divisions on the flanks, but touch was soon gained, the Australians being still on the right and the 47th Division (who captured Rancourt and gained the western edge of St Pierre Vaast Wood) on the left.

No counter-attack developed during the day, and the Bosche seemed to resign himself to the loss of ground. His acquiescence in our success was doubtless partly due to the fact that this day the Australians, after three days' magnificent fighting, captured Mont St Quentin and entered Péronne.

The casualties of the 2/4th Battalion were again extremely light when compared with the importance of the success achieved, but unfortunately they included the loss of two company commanders (Capt. F. J. Griffiths and 2/Lieut. V. C. Prince) killed. Both of these officers had done splendid work and shown themselves capable leaders, and in them the Battalion sustained a serious loss. In addition to these, 2/Lieuts. H. H. Gant and G. Gilson were killed, Lieut. H. P. Lawrence and 2/Lieuts. F. E. Rogers, C. Brandram and R. E. Glover wounded; while 11 N.C.O.'s and men were killed, 49 wounded and 30 missing, making a total list for the day of 99 all ranks.

The captures of the Brigade amounted to 325 prisoners, 40 machine-guns, 8 field guns and one motor ambulance, and once again the prisoners showed that reserves were being flung wholesale into the enemy fighting line. Measured solely by the depth of ground taken, the 1st September was the most successful action ever fought by the 2/4th Battalion, the advance being over 3000 yards, and the achievement was the subject of a congratulatory message from the Brigadier.

The same evening the 58th Division was relieved by the 74th[7] and passed into Corps reserve after a week of hard fighting. The 2/4th Battalion withdrew, after handing over its objectives intact to the 14th Black Watch, to a valley a mile west of Marrières Wood. The Battalion remained in this valley for five days, employed in resting and training, fortunately under weather conditions which were fine and warm except on the 5th September. During this period 2/Lieut. D. A. S. Manning and drafts of 21 other ranks joined the Battalion. 2/Lieut. Bidgood was appointed Intelligence Officer (vice 2/Lieut. Davies, sick).

[7] The 74th Division (Girdwood) was a Yeomanry Division which had been employed in the East. This was its first appearance in the French theatre of war. The 14th Black Watch was formerly the Fife and Forfar Yeomanry.

The days succeeding the relief of the 58th Division were marked by hard fighting, but by the evening of the 4th September the 47th and 74th Divisions had advanced the line east of Moislains and well up the long slope leading to Nurlu. As was to be expected now that the line of the

Somme had been turned the enemy began to fall back towards the next defensive position, the outposts of the Hindenburg line, and on the 5th September the pursuit began in earnest, though it was met at many points with stubborn resistance.

At 7 a.m. on the 7th September the 2/4th Battalion embussed at Hem Wood and were conveyed to St Pierre Farm on the Péronne-Nurlu Road, the whole Division being on its way back to the fighting line. The spectacle of the roads during this forward move was most impressive. Packed with troops, guns and stores of every description moving eastward, it seemed to convey to the troops a greater realisation of the importance of their victories than the actual advances they had made in action.

The Battalion lay in Villa Wood, south-west of Nurlu, during the day, and at 6 p.m. marched to a bivouac area immediately north of Liéramont, where it arrived at 9.30 p.m.

On the 8th September the fine weather of the preceding week gave way to heavy rainstorms, and the Battalion moved into shelters in Liéramont, and in this position it remained resting until a late hour in the evening of the 9th.

During the 8th September troops of the 58th Division endeavoured to advance against the large and strongly defended villages of Epéhy and Peizières, but the position was stubbornly held by the Alpine Corps, and the line became stabilised in trenches on the south and west slopes of the hill on which the villages stand. The following morning determined counter-attacks by the Alpine Corps drove back the Divisional line a short distance.

This stiffening of the defence made it essential for Army H.Q. to be informed as to whether the enemy rearguards were fighting a delaying action, or whether the defence was organised in depth; and to test this an attack by the III Corps was ordered for the 10th September.

The 58th Division was directed on Epéhy-Peizières while the 74th was given Ronssoy Wood as its objective.

The 173rd Brigade was detailed for this attack with the 3rd Londons on the right, the 2/2nd on the left and the 2/4th in close support. The great frontage of the two villages, which topographically are really one, and the high state of their defences made the operation one of great difficulty, and the plan of action was to deal with it in two stages. For the first objective the two leading battalions were to gain the line of the eastern road of the villages, the 3rd Londons in Epéhy and the 2/2nd in Peizières. The 2/4th Londons were to follow the 2/2nd closely in the initial stages and then, turning southwards, were to mop up the area between the inner flanks of the leading battalions and establish themselves in Fishers Keep as a link between the two.

In the second stage the leading battalions were to gain the line of the railway east of the villages where they would join hands, the 2/4th Battalion remaining in the villages. On the left the 21st Division was to push forward immediately after the villages were captured and secure the position by occupying the high ground which dominated them a mile to the north.

This very complicated operation was to be carried out under two creeping barrages, one for each leading battalion, and a machine-gun barrage, while the heavy batteries would engage distant targets.

At 11 p.m., 9th August, the 2/4th Battalion left its position in Liéramont and moved forward to assembly, which, considering the vileness of the weather, the lack of reconnaissance and the extreme darkness, was completed satisfactorily; and at 5.15 a.m. the Battalion advanced to the attack.

The leading battalions met with a good deal of opposition, which on the left flank was centred on Wood Farm. In the 2/4th Battalion A and B Companies, respectively under 2/Lieuts. C. C. Gibbs and G. C. Ewing, M.C., gained their objective at Tottenham Post on the western outskirts of Peizières with comparatively little difficulty. B Company under Capt. Hetley, whose rôle was to penetrate the villages to Fishers Keep, had a much more difficult task. The fighting through ruined streets inevitably led to some disorganisation of platoons, and the villages, moreover, were stiff with Bosche machine-gun posts, which, once the barrage had passed over them, were free to do their worst on the attackers. Severe casualties were sustained, among whom were numbered two platoon commanders, 2/Lieuts. H. B. Bartleet and P. F. Royce, killed. Finding progress impossible among the cunningly concealed Bosche machine-gunners Hetley collected and organised his company on the west edge of the village. A similar fate met D Company (2/Lieut. D. A. S. Manning) which endeavoured to enter Peizières from the west. After gallantly struggling against impossible odds Manning withdrew his men to swell the garrison of Tottenham Post.

The 2/2nd Londons under Capt. Wright made a magnificent attempt to carry out their task, and did in fact reach the railway embankment, but a sharp counter-attack drove them back to the fringe of the village. Unfortunately the flanking movement of the 21st Division on the left failed to materialise, and this doubtless contributed to the failure of the 173rd Brigade. The fact, however, was clearly established that the resistance of the enemy was organised and deliberate, and it became patent that an attack with tank co-operation would be necessary to reduce it. The rifle strength of the three battalions set against these villages on the 10th September was only about 900 in all, and their attack, therefore, lacked the weight essential to success.

In spite of the lack of success, however, the day was not entirely fruitless, for the captures amounted to 80 prisoners, 20 machine-guns and 3 anti-tank guns.

The 2/4th Battalion's losses were: 2/Lieuts. F. Bidgood, P. F. Royce and H. B. Bartleet, killed; 2/Lieut. F. J. Paterson, wounded; 5 N.C.O.'s and men killed, 19 wounded and 3 missing.

During the night following the battle the 2/4th Battalion was relieved by the 12th Londons, and was concentrated in trenches at Guyencourt. Here it remained till 8 p.m. on the 11th September, when it withdrew to shelters in Liéramont.

We may here remark that on the 18th September the 173rd Brigade captured Epéhy and Peizières and thus helped clear the road for the advance to the Hindenburg line.

We have now come to the end of the 2/4th Battalion's story. Owing to the increasing difficulties of maintaining units at fighting strength it had been decided by G.H.Q. to make still further reductions in the number of formations, and to swell the ranks of those remaining with the personnel of those disbanded. This dismal fate befell the 2/4th Londons, and on the 12th September 1918 the whole of its personnel was transferred to the 2/2nd Londons, and the Battalion as a separate entity ceased to exist, after twenty-one months of active service life. Its place in the Brigade was taken by the 2/24th Londons from the 32nd Division.

The last action in which the Battalion fought was admittedly a "feeler," and as such undoubtedly served a useful purpose in the scheme of the Fourth Army's great advance; but perhaps we may be pardoned for regretting that it was not a more successful close to the Battalion's history. It was bad luck. Yet there was a certain degree of poetic justice in the fact that the Battalion had helped fight the Germans back to what had been on 21st March 1918 the British line of resistance, and it can, therefore, justly claim to have redeemed in full its losses in the awful battles of the retreat.

CHAPTER XXIV
THE FINAL ADVANCE

II. *The 1/4th Battalion in the Battle of Bapaume, 1918*

The extension northward of the battle line, which marked the opening of the Battle of Bapaume on the 21st August 1918, involved Byng's Third Army, comprising from right to left the V, IV and VI Corps. As we have indicated in the preceding chapter, the object of the Third Army was to conduct a vast enveloping movement which should turn the flank of the German defence of the Somme line, and throw open the road to Cambrai and St Quentin.

Already the enemy had shown signs of nervousness in the area of the Somme-Scarpe salient and had withdrawn from his most advanced positions at Serre; and it was clear, therefore, that any attack on this front by the British must be prosecuted rapidly to avoid a repetition of the skilful German retreat of February 1917. For an offensive in this area the British troops were far more favourably placed in August 1918 than they had been on the former occasion. They possessed the Bucquoy Ridge, with the consequent advantages of observation which had formerly been denied to them; and the terrain over which the battle would be fought, though certainly devastated and a mass of trenches, did not present the colossal system of inter-supporting fortresses which it had in 1916. The time for a big attack had come, and G.H.Q. decided to strike. The 23rd August saw the Fourth and Third Armies advancing on a front of 33 miles from Lihons to Mercatel.

The suddenness of the German collapse in these latter days of the War is probably unique in the annals of military history. At the beginning of June their star was still in the ascendant. They were occupying ground which they had never previously held during the whole War; their successes of March and April had shaken the Allied defence to its very foundations; and it seemed still doubtful whether they had reached the limit of their capabilities of offence. Yet by the middle of August the whole face of the War had changed. On a wide front the Germans were in retreat; vast masses of material, thousands of prisoners had fallen into our hands; the British morale had been proved stronger than ever, while that of the enemy was giving indications of a serious break.

Whether the High Command anticipated the completeness of this lightning change we cannot say; that the vast bulk of regimental officers and men scarcely contemplated it, is almost certain. Early in July General Hull, in a conversation with Lieut.-Col. Marchment, expressed the opinion that very little would be done in 1918 by way of retrieving the losses suffered during the spring!

The 8th August found the 1/4th Londons at a strength of 42 officers and 892 other ranks withdrawn in Brigade reserve to billets at Arras. Here a quite pleasant week was spent in which the routine of training was varied by a Battalion sports meeting, and a most successful swimming gala—a new feature of recreation—for which purpose the moat at the Citadel formed a splendid bath.

Between the 16th and 18th August the 56th Division was relieved from the Tilloy trenches and passed into Corps reserve, the 1/4th Londons handing over their Brigade reserve billets to the 1/9th Royal Scots and moving to Berneville on the 17th August. For a few days changes of station followed on each others' heels with startling rapidity, and after having been quartered successively at Houvin-Houvigneuil and Magnicourt-sur-Canche, the Battalion reached Grand Rullecourt at 11.30 p.m. on the 20th August.

On the 19th orders had been issued to the Division to take part in an attack with the XVII Corps in the area of the Scarpe, but these were subsequently replaced on the 21st August by a transfer of the Division to Haldane's VI Corps, and orders to join with it in the Third Army attack.

A day of rest at Grand Rullecourt was occupied by the Battalion, in the absence of attack orders, with speculations as to its chances of soon being called upon to fight. Preliminary arrangements were made to march into battle at short notice, and the same evening, the 21st August, the Battalion marched thirteen miles to Berles-au-Bois, arriving at 2 a.m. on the 22nd.

About 10 o'clock that morning Lieut.-Col. Marchment and the company commanders were ordered to Humbercamp to receive battle orders, but after an hour's fruitless waiting the company commanders returned to prepare their companies for action, and the Colonel went to try and get what orders he could at Brigade Headquarters. Here he was informed that the attack would take place in sixteen hours' time—early on the 23rd August! The general idea of the Battalion's rôle was explained to Lieut.-Col. Marchment to be the capture of the village of Boyelles and the Marc system of trenches immediately north of it, the attack to commence at 4.55 a.m. on the 23rd August, two companies in line, one in support and one in reserve. Artillery support would be provided by 6 brigades of field guns firing an unregistered barrage, while 21 tanks would take part in the attack. A section of the Divisional Machine-gun Company would be attached to the

Battalion. With this somewhat sketchy information Lieut.-Col. Marchment hurried back to the Battalion to set it in motion, and by 5 p.m. it was on its way to the first assembly position at Blairville. Here it occupied the old German trenches exactly opposite the first trench sector ever held by the 2/4th Battalion in February 1917.

The line facing Boyelles was at this time occupied by the 59th Division, and the 168th Brigade was detailed to attack through them, with the Guards Division opposite Hamelincourt on its right, and the 52nd Division north of the north branch of the Cojeul River on its left. The Brigade order of battle from right to left was Kensingtons (south of Boyelles); 1/4th Londons (Boyelles); and London Scottish (Boiry-Becquerelle); the 1st Londons being attached in Brigade reserve for the operation.

Leaving the Battalion on the march Lieut.-Col. Marchment hurried on to Blairville by car to see the Brigadier of the brigade in line (59th Division) and was at once faced by another difficulty in finding that the 59th Division had themselves taken over the front trenches only the preceding night! Clearly not much possibility of assistance from them; but they arranged to provide guides to lead our platoons to the positions of final assembly.

The sudden transfer of the 56th Division from the XVII to the VI Corps, and the subsequent difficulty in obtaining orders must have been caused by some reason of great importance: we are not aware what it was. Certainly the effect was not to make things easier. Indeed, when the Divisional attack order was issued by Gen. Hull at 3 p.m. on the 22nd August he had not received the written instructions of VI Corps. But, starting under such inauspicious circumstances, all the more credit is due to the battalions, and in particular to the commanding officers, for the signal successes which were ultimately achieved. Reconnaissance of the ground by officers and N.C.O.'s was obviously out of the question, and Lieut.-Col. Marchment had to content himself with explaining the situation to them while battle stores were issued to the men.

At 10.30 p.m. the Battalion moved off by platoons in charge of the 59th Division guides, who, considering their own scanty acquaintance with the ground, did well, for they brought almost the whole Battalion to its assembly positions in Falcon Trench well on time, though one platoon of A Company and the Headquarter details went sadly astray and did not turn up till long after zero hour. The Padre believes he was taken for a long walk somewhere round Albert! During the march up the enemy was using gas shell freely, and masks had to be worn at times, but little loss was caused.

The Battalion was drawn up as follows:

Right front   —B Company, Capt. R. S. B. Simmonds.

Left front   —D Company, Capt. C. W. Rowlands, M.C.

Support   —C Company, Capt. H. A. T. Hewlett.

Reserve   —A Company, Capt. H. N. Williams, M.C.

The hour or two of darkness before zero was spent in cutting lanes through our wire, and at 4.55 a.m. the barrage opened, intense and well distributed. Lieut.-Col. Marchment describes it as the best and most tremendous he had ever seen. The scene from Headquarters was extraordinary: the intense shrapnel barrage and smoke on the German front line, the medium howitzers firing on Boyelles village beyond, and the heavies cutting up the distant landscape in dense black clouds; and behind it all the sun just rising.

At 5.7 a.m. the companies moved forward. The right company (B) made good use of the railway embankment, and following the line on its south side advanced on a one-platoon frontage to Boyelles Station, while three tanks entered the village. Here the railway was crossed and a good deal of opposition was met with from enemy machine-guns, heavy and light, firing from the eastern half of the village. These were, however, skilfully outflanked and rounded up to the number of 3 heavy and 8 light guns, after which the company pushed forward and caught up the barrage.

Two platoons halted approximately on the Blue line (first objective) on the eastern edge of Boyelles, while two pressed on to Boyelles Trench 500 yards further east. But few enemy were encountered in this advanced position. B Company being now well distributed in depth, the work of consolidation was put in hand. The right flank was not yet in touch with the Kensingtons and was therefore rounded off by pushing two Lewis gun sections and one subsection M.G.C. southwards towards the railway.

D Company on the left met with more stubborn resistance in the Marc system, and the leading platoons were temporarily held up in No Man's Land by enemy firing from the Marc saps. Moreover, the tank allotted to this part of the front failed to reach the Marc front system at all, having apparently lost its way. The support company (C), however, pushed a platoon forward into the sunken road leading northwards from Boyelles, whence it was able to enfilade the Marc trenches, while the right platoon of the London Scottish advancing on our left managed to turn the position similarly from the north. Being practically surrounded the enemy surrendered *en masse*, the bag amounting to 2 officers and 80 other ranks. Little further opposition was encountered, and D company continued the advance to Boyelles Trench, where touch was gained with C Company on the right and the London Scottish on the left. The dugouts in this line were energetically mopped up and many Germans sent marching westward. Two patrols were sent forward towards Boyelles Reserve.

In the meantime the support company mopped up the neighbourhood of the cemetery and the sunken roads in its vicinity, while A Company in reserve occupied the Marc system. This latter proved a very sound move as our start-line was heavily shelled all the morning.

The first news of the attack at Battalion Headquarters was received in the shape of Private Cohen, who appeared wounded but carrying a German light machine-gun—a good omen of success! At about 9 a.m. the lost platoons turned up and their arrival, including as they did the Padre and the Medical Officer, was extremely welcome, for by now the wounded were beginning to filter through, and the small band of five under Lieut.-Col. Marchment were encumbered with some 200 Bosche prisoners—not to speak of their duties of conducting the battle. Communication by wire was rapidly established with brigade and also forward to the companies, a report centre being formed north of Boyelles.

At 9.15 a.m. 56th Division issued orders that the attack would be pressed at 11.30 a.m. into Boyelles Reserve, but owing to temporary dislocation of the signal service these orders did not reach the 1/4th Londons until 11.15 a.m. To start at the scheduled hour was out of the question, but arrangements were made at once for the further advance, which ultimately began at about 5 p.m.

The advance was made by the left front and support companies, the right front company extending to its left to cover the area vacated by them. This second attack met with complete success. The two attacking companies were led by a line of scouts followed by one platoon in extended formation. The remaining platoons followed in artillery formation by sections. Some resistance was offered by light machine-gun teams in Boyelles Reserve, but the widely extended formation saved the attackers from severe loss. The enemy artillery was also active during the advance, but again the formation adopted enabled the rear platoons to pick their way with but few casualties. The whole of the allotted portion of Boyelles Reserve was captured, and patrols pushed forward 500 yards to the east of it. The enemy shell fire now became more intense, but a protective barrage was put down by our guns, and no counter-attack developed. After a while activity on the whole area subsided.

The same evening the 168th Brigade handed over the captured positions to the 167th and passed into Divisional reserve, the 1/4th Londons concentrating north of Hendecourt. By noon on that day the Battalion was back at Blairville.

It is impossible to speak too highly of the men by whom this great success had been gained. The long approach marches in exceptionally hot weather brought the Battalion to the point of battle in an already tired condition; the hurried orders and the total lack of previous reconnaissance created difficulties which were surmounted by the splendid response made by all ranks to the demands imposed on them. The rapid appreciation of the situation by company commanders and the careful dispositions of the commanding officer all contributed in full measure to this important victory, while the skilful use of ground and of suitable formations was the means of securing the gains at a minimum of loss. The excellent work performed by signallers and runners, all of whom had a hard day's work, were of incalculable value to Battalion Headquarters, and enabled Lieut.-Col. Marchment at all times to keep a firm grip of the situation of the moment.

The casualties of the Battalion were extremely light, only 18 being killed, but by ill luck it lost three company commanders, Capts. C. W. Rowlands, M.C., and H. A. T. Hewlett being killed, and Capt. R. S. B. Simmonds, wounded. 2/Lieuts. A. W. Chignell, T. Yoxall and F. S. C. Taylor were wounded. The captures made by the Battalion amounted to 3 officers and 240 other ranks, of the 1st and 2nd Battalions 87th R.I. Regiment, 24 light and 8 heavy machine-guns, 6 light, 1 medium and 1 heavy trench mortar.

After the relief of the 168th Brigade the offensive was continued by the 167th, at first with considerable success, the Division being once again attached to the XVII Corps. An advance in the northern area of the Divisional front of some 2500 yards was made into Summit and Fooley Trenches, but on the south flank the most strenuous efforts of the 56th and Guards Divisions failed to eject the enemy from Croisilles, which was held in great force by machine-gunners. South of the Cojeul River the enemy resistance was increasing, and information was obtained from prisoners to the effect that three fresh German divisions had been brought into the Bullecourt-Hendecourt area. North of the Cojeul, however, the 52nd and Canadian Divisions had registered important successes. The old Wancourt line fell to them on the 26th, and this advance was rapidly followed up by the recapture of Monchy-le-Preux, and a penetration into quite new ground at St Rohart Factory—hardly fought for by the 56th Division in May 1917—and at Boiry Notre Dame. By the evening of the 26th August the 52nd Division had cleared the Hindenburg line from Henin to the Sensée River, and was reported to be east of Fontaine-lez-Croisilles.

Croisilles, however, still held out and the Guards had been pressed back slightly towards St Leger. The result of this fighting was to swing the Corps line round facing roughly south-east astride the Hindenburg line, with a strong pocket of most stubborn Bosche in the ramification of trenches around Croisilles itself, and on both banks of the Sensée River to the north-east.

The 169th Brigade which had now taken over the Divisional front was getting worn by its constant fighting and losses, and reinforcement was needed. After a few hours' rest at Blairville the 1/4th Londons marched at 7.45 a.m. on the 25th August to trenches in front of Boisleux St Marc, moving the following evening to the trenches east of Boiry-Becquerelle, which had been captured by the London Scottish on the 23rd.

A good deal of gas shelling occurred here during the night. A signaller was killed and several men were wounded, among whom the Battalion was unfortunate in losing Sergt. Johnson, the excellent orderly-room clerk, and Corpl. Coates, M.M., of the Scouts.

On the afternoon of the 27th the Battalion moved forward in close support to the 169th Brigade, and occupied Summit Trench immediately north of its junction with Hill, and on the extreme left of the Divisional sector.

It is rather curious to note that in these fights and marches the 1/4th Battalion was in an area which had been traversed by the 2/4th Battalion during the actions of March 1917, while at the same time the 2/4th Battalion in the Fourth Army was bearing its share in recapturing spots familiar to the 1/4th Battalion during the 1916 Somme battles!

The 1/4th Battalion had settled down in Summit Trench to make the best of a very wet evening, when, after dark, orders were received to move at once into the Hindenburg line and to concentrate at River Road, near the banks of the Sensée River for an attack the following morning on Bullecourt. It had been determined, owing to the prolonged resistance of the enemy at Croisilles and the resultant holding back of the right flank, to pursue the operation by an advance towards Bullecourt straight down the Hindenburg line. This would have the effect of completely enveloping and "squeezing-out" the pocket of Germans in the Croisilles-Guardian Trench area.

The concentration of the Battalion was effected successfully, but not altogether without difficulty. A and B Companies moved direct to the point of assembly, while C, D and Headquarters proceeded by way of the Henin-Fontaine Road, and then down the Hindenburg trenches. The whole area was horribly congested. Two brigades of the 56th Division (the 168th and 169th) were moving up for attack, while at the same time a relief was proceeding on the left flank between the 52nd and 57th Divisions. For a time the confusion was rather distressing, and Lieut.-Col. Marchment writes, "It seemed to me that the battalions were forming up to attack north-east, south-east and south-west."

The plan of attack was as follows:—The advance was to be led over the open by the 169th Brigade, the Queen's Westminsters in the van with the line Queen's Lane-Jove Lane, as a first objective, and the trenches south-east of Bullecourt as a final objective.

The 168th Brigade was to follow the 169th in the order 1/4th Londons, Kensingtons and London Scottish, advancing by bounds at a distance of about 1000 yards in rear of the rear battalion of the 169th Brigade. The particular duties of the 168th Brigade were to support the 169th and mop up in rear of their advance, and to protect the right flank should Croisilles remain untaken—a rather difficult and quite unsatisfactory job.

The 1/4th Londons were disposed as follows:—

> D Company (2/Lieut. J. L. Backhouse) on the right—to advance over the area west of the Hindenburg line by way of Sensée Avenue, Nelly Avenue and Queen's Lane.
>
> B Company (2/Lieut. G. G. Lewis) to advance down Burg Support, the old Hindenburg front trench.
>
> A Company (Capt. H. N. Williams, M.C.) and C Company (Capt. J. W. Price), Headquarters and 1 section M.G.C. attached, to advance down Tunnel Trench, the old Hindenburg support trench.

The attack was to be launched at 12.30 p.m. on the 24th August under a creeping barrage.

The fight throughout the day proved a laborious and confused affair. Trouble developed which doubtless originated on the previous evening when the Queen's Westminsters, relieved by the London Scottish in the Summit area, had moved forward to assembly. This gallant regiment had been fighting already for a couple of days and was getting worn—Lieut.-Col. Savill describes his men as "dead beat"—and it had to move up to assembly positions in Burg Support, where it occupied a trench at right angles to the line of its advance. A change of front during an advance had been proved on the Somme in 1916 to be an operation extremely difficult of accomplishment, and so it proved here. True, the attack did not start till 12.30 p.m., but even the hours of morning daylight gave little chance to the Queen's Westminsters to get their bearings. Our map shows the villages of Bullecourt and Hendecourt, but it must be borne in mind that the whole terrain was actually a featureless waste. The ground everywhere was "crumped" to pieces and covered with high grass and rank weeds, while the existence of a village was not suspected till one found oneself stumbling among the heaps of bricks which had formerly been its cottages. As a consequence of all this, two companies of the Queen's Westminsters, followed by a part of the 1/2nd Londons, went hopelessly astray and became entangled in the 57th Division troops near Hendecourt. To add to the confusion the company commander sent back word to 169th Brigade that he was in Bullecourt.

Meanwhile, Lieut.-Col. Savill of the Queen's Westminsters advanced along the Hindenburg line, and having fallen in with the Headquarters of the 1/2nd Londons and the London Rifle Brigade, soon came in touch with strong enemy forces, believing that his companies were ahead of him, and that mopping-up had not been well done. The weak force at his disposal was unable to shift the stubborn Germans opposed to him, and the attack was held up.

The 1/4th Londons moved off from assembly as ordered in rear of the 169th Brigade.

On the right D Company was held up badly at Nelly Avenue where it closed on to a party of the London Rifle Brigade. Several efforts to shift the enemy proved abortive, and it was not until about 7.30 p.m. that, with the help of two Stokes Mortars brought up by the Kensingtons, further progress could be made. By this hour, however, the opposition was overcome, and, with 40 prisoners and 4 light machine-guns to its credit, the company pursued the advance after dark to Queen's Lane.

B Company in Burg Support overtook the Headquarters of the three 169th Brigade battalions, held up as already described, about 200 yards short of the Hump, and a platoon was at once placed at Lieut.-Col. Savill's disposal to help clear the trench. We must remark parenthetically that B Company's fight began almost precisely in the sector of trench which had been first captured by A Company of the 2/4th Battalion on the 15th June 1917: how often, we wonder, has such a coincidence occurred?

The Germans in Burg Support were of a remarkably obstinate variety and progress by bombing was slow. The trench was very full of men, and the congestion was later increased by the arrival from nowhere in particular of a company of the Royal Munster Fusiliers (57th Division), who had quite lost their direction. By 6.30 p.m. the enemy's resistance was overcome by hard fighting, and B Company advanced down Burg Support to the Knuckle, where it established itself in touch with D Company on its right.

A and C Companies on the left, in the Hindenburg Support line, also overtook the 169th Brigade, the remnants of the 1/2nd Londons being held up about Juno Lane. The enemy was in strength in this trench also. At the time it was presumed that by zealous use of his dugouts he had escaped the moppers-up of the leading battalion, but probably, owing to the deflection of the greater part of the 1/2nd Londons, he had not been previously attacked. Progress was slow and the 1/4th London Companies pushed through and engaged the enemy. The resistance at Juno was soon overcome, and the enemy retired leaving us a few prisoners and two light machine-guns. A second check was experienced at the Hump but the enemy was driven back, strenuously debating every inch of ground, till at last by 9.30 p.m. the two 1/4th London Companies reached Jove Lane and the remainder of the Battalion. Attempts were made to gain touch with the 57th Division on the left but without success.

The stubbornness of the enemy resistance in the Hindenburg line this day was remarkable, and we cannot deny a brave enemy an acknowledgment of his valour. Croisilles had been reported vacant by 8 o'clock in the morning but the occupants of the Guardian pocket put up a day-long fight. It was not till late in the evening that the whole area was cleared. Probably the need to the enemy of gradually evacuating this area was the cause of the opposition offered to our advance down the Hindenburg line.

This was a hard day's work for everyone. The 1/4th Londons had bombed their way down about 2000 yards of the Hindenburg line, excellent leadership to the bombing parties being provided by Lieut. V. R. Oldrey and by Capts. H. N. Williams and J. W. Price. The great difficulty throughout the day was for local commanders to get any sort of grip as to what was going on, as so often occurs in trench fighting. The mass of trenches, nearly all stubbornly defended, with which the whole area was pitted, in effect broke up the brigade attack into a series of numerous and more or less isolated scraps in which no one knew much of how his neighbour was faring. And all the time Division believed that the Hindenburg line was clear, and that Bullecourt was in our hands.

The night of the 28th and the morning of the 29th August were occupied in clearing up the situation, and assembling the Brigades on the line Pelican Avenue-Pelican Lane for a continuance of the attack, which was pursued by the 168th Brigade on the right and the 169th on the left.

The 1/4th Londons remained on the 29th August in support with the 1st Londons (attached), the attacking battalions being the Kensingtons on the right and the London Scottish on the left. The Battalion was disposed in Queen's Lane, Burg Support and Borderer Trench. The objective allotted to the Brigade roughly coincided with the Riencourt-Quéant Road, and the whole of the village of Bullecourt, inclusive to the Brigade, was allotted to the London Scottish.

The attack, which was launched at 1 p.m. on the 29th August, met with stubborn resistance, especially on the right where the Kensingtons were held up at Bullecourt Station. After hard fighting the London Scottish managed to capture the village, and by dusk the Divisional line formed a sharp salient, with its horns on Bullecourt Station and the high ground west of the Factory on the Hendecourt Road, and its apex following Tower Reserve and Gordon Reserve Trenches.

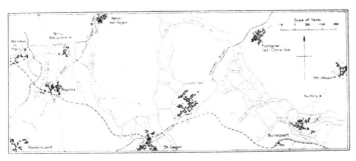

THE BATTLE OF BAPAUME, 1918 (1/4TH BATTALION)

The 1/4th Londons were not called upon as a Battalion, but D Company was sent forward to reinforce the London Scottish, and later to fill a gap in the forward positions between that Battalion and the 169th Brigade on the left.

The enemy resistance this day was extremely stubborn and Tank Reserve was strongly held by the enemy, who resisted effectually the most gallant attempts of the Scottish to emerge from Gordon Reserve.

Late at night the 167th Brigade took over the whole Divisional front, and the 1/4th Londons moved back at 5.30 a.m. to positions in Queen's Lane, Knuckle Avenue, Stray Reserve and Burg Support, where they remained throughout the 30th August. During the withdrawal to these positions the whole area was intensely bombarded with high explosives and gas shell, and it was no surprise to the Battalion to learn that the enemy had delivered a sharp counter-attack in the early morning and driven the 167th Brigade out of Bullecourt back to the Pelican Avenue-Pelican Lane line. The posts north of the village stood firm. This counter-attack was a big affair which affected the divisions right and left, both of them being pushed back a certain distance.

The immediate recapture of Bullecourt was promptly ordered by XVII Corps, and no one in the Battalion was especially delighted to learn that the 1/4th Londons were detailed for the duty.

After a day spent in obtaining such rest as was possible, the Battalion wearily crept off after dark to assembly in Pelican Lane and Borderer Trench in readiness to assault Bullecourt at dawn on the 31st August. The 168th Brigade was drawn up for battle with the London Scottish on the right, the 1/4th Londons in the centre and the 7th Middlesex (167th Brigade attached) on the left, each battalion having a section M.G.C. and a section L.T.M. Battery at its disposal. The Kensingtons were in Brigade reserve.

The morning of the 31st August was dark, and at 5 a.m. the assaulting battalions moved forward under an excellent barrage to which the enemy gave a quick and heavy reply.

On the right, C Company, on a two-platoon front, reached the cross-roads at the extreme western edge of Bullecourt, but was here held up for some time by machine-guns in the village. At the same time D Company, on the left, advancing on the north side of the village penetrated about half-way across it and almost reached the cross-roads on the northern edge, but here they also were checked by machine-gun fire, principally from their right flank.

The support company (B) now entered the village, or rather advanced against the site of the village (for no single building was visible), and began to mop up in the endeavour to form a link between the two leading companies. Progress was slow owing to the overgrown nature of the ground, but by 8.40 a.m. touch was gained between B and C Companies, and together they slowly fought their way forward till C Company was able to join hands with the 7th Middlesex on the Hendecourt Road. In the course of this fighting B Company managed to take 15 prisoners and put 5 machine-guns out of action.

At about 9 a.m. the reserve company (A) was put into the fight to endeavour to fill in the gap across the village between the leading companies.

The right company was still held up on the southern fringe of Bullecourt by two machine-guns mounted in a derelict tank east of the village, and it was not until after noon that, with the aid of two Stokes Mortars, progress was made by bombing up Tower Reserve as far as a point level with the east edge of the village. Here all further advance was definitely checked. Gordon Reserve was strongly held and stubbornly defended, and, moreover, no touch could be gained with the London Scottish on the right.

By 3.30 p.m. the village of Bullecourt was reported clear of the enemy and a line of Lewis gun posts was established on its eastern fringe from Tower Reserve to the Hendecourt Road on the left. During the remainder of the day no material change in the situation occurred. Three several attempts were made by the leading companies to get into Gordon Reserve but the position was too strongly held, and, the trenches leading to it having been flattened out by shell fire, an advance by bombing was impracticable. Shortly after midday aerial reports were received that the enemy was assembling in Tank Avenue and Tank Support. All field guns and heavies at once turned on to this target and the projected counter-attack was promptly broken up. The activity of the enemy in this region continued till late at night, and it was evident that any attempt at further advance would be strenuously disputed.

After nightfall arrangements were made for one company of the Kensingtons to rush Gordon Reserve under cover of Stokes Mortar fire, but the situation remaining somewhat obscure the attempt was abandoned.

Very little progress was made anywhere this day. On the right the London Scottish gained Bullecourt Avenue and the 7th Middlesex on the left captured the factory on the Hendecourt Road. But all along the line the enemy's resistance was stiffening, evidently in view of the near approach of our positions to the junction of the Hindenburg line with the Drocourt-Quéant Switch.

Moreover the country was difficult for the attackers; it had been fought over many times and was utterly broken up, and the assaulting companies were all tired. In the circumstances it was a good day's work, and a day of peculiar satisfaction to the 4th London Regiment, which has a special claim to association with the village of Bullecourt. Here in 1917 the 2/4th Battalion occupied Gordon Reserve in the successful defence of Bullecourt against a heavy German attack after it had first fallen into British hands, and in August 1918 it fell to the lot of the 1/4th Battalion, after the village had been recaptured and again lost, to capture it for ever.

Casualties in officers this day were: Lieut. V. R. Oldrey and 2/Lieut. R. T. Stevenson, killed; 2/Lieuts. W. G. Hook, A. Holloway and A. F. Potter, wounded. 2/Lieut. E. H. Garner was killed on the night 27th/28th August, after having been ten days only with the Battalion. In the ranks the total casualties for the period 23rd to 31st August were 30 killed, 150 wounded and 12 missing. Having regard to the enormous importance of the successes achieved and the depth of the advances, these comparatively light figures are a matter for much congratulation. One shudders to think of what the losses would have been for equal results in the hard slogging of the Somme in 1916 or at Ypres in 1917.

Late at night on the 31st August the 56th Division handed over its positions to the 52nd and withdrew into Corps reserve, the 1/4th Londons reaching the Boyelles Reserve area at Boiry-Becquerelle at 7 a.m. on the 1st September, with a strength of 32 officers and 710 other ranks.

In view of the gallant share which the 1/4th Londons had borne in this splendid series of victories we may perhaps be permitted to quote an extract from an article on the subject of the 56th Division's achievements which appeared in *The Times* of the 16th September 1918: " ... This year it was one of the divisions which beat off the German attack towards Arras on March 28th when the enemy suffered one of the bloodiest defeats of the whole War; so that with this fighting and that at Cambrai to its credit it has probably killed as many Germans as any division in the British Army. Now to this proud record is to be added the splendid advance of which the Commander-in-Chief has told. The 56th Division has proved itself a great fighting division."

The Divisional record in the Battle of Bapaume 1918 may be summarised as advancing through 6 miles of very strongly fortified country in nine days; meeting and defeating three German divisions, and capturing 29 officers, 1047 other ranks, 3 guns, 210 machine-guns and over 50 trench mortars. Of this large booty the share of the 1/4th Londons amounted to 3 officers and 390 other ranks prisoners, 70 machine-guns and 10 trench mortars—a very fair proportion of the whole!

With this action the share of the Battalion in the great envelopment of the Somme line closes.

The following were decorated for services during the period 23rd-31st August:

    2/Lieuts. C. L. Henstridge and A. Holloway, the M.C.

    Pte. E. Clark, the D.C.M.

    Sergt. F. G. Udall, M.M., Bar to M.M.

    Sergts. F. A. Dove, J. T. Norris, F. C. Nickless, Corpls. W. Frost, F. Nash, C. Robbins, Lance-Corpls. J. T. Couchman, J. R. Greenwood, Ptes. G. H. Andrews, G. A. Allen, W. W. Boulstridge, A. C. Barnes, J. Eccles, A. E. Dickerson, G. J. Grant, W. H. Hart, H. H. Mills and W. Ryan, the M.M.

This great battle as a whole resulted in the defeat by 23 British divisions of 35 German divisions, and the capture of 34,000 prisoners and 270 guns. Its importance lay in the ever-increasing signs of the enemy's failing morale; while the captures bore witness to his indiscriminate throwing-in of reserves.

The following day Péronne fell to troops of the Third Army, and two days later the enemy's general retirement from the east bank of the Somme began.

We have already alluded to extensive captures of ground made in the area of the Scarpe at Monchy-le-Preux and other places. These important victories constituted the Battle of the Scarpe, 1918, in which, beginning on the 26th August, the battle front was still further widened and the British First Army also became involved. By the 3rd September the Canadian Corps of the First Army and the XVII Corps of the Third Army had carried the battle line forward through the famous Drocourt-Quéant line, and the enemy had fallen back to the general line of the Canal du Nord from its junction with the Sensée River, east of Lécluse to Péronne.

During this hasty retirement large numbers of prisoners and vast quantities of stores fell into our hands. In the extreme south the French armies also continued to advance, and by the 6th September had regained the line of the Crozat Canal at La Fère.

In the meantime the gradual relinquishment by the enemy of his advanced positions in the Lys salient had begun on the 18th August, and the retirement rapidly becoming general, he had been driven back by the 6th September to the line Givenchy-Neuve Chapelle-Ploegsteert.

CHAPTER XXV
THE FINAL ADVANCE

III. *The 1/4th Battalion in the Battles of Cambrai and The Sambre, 1918*

The changes which the Battalion found at Boiry-Becquerelle in the few days which had elapsed since its last rest there were truly astonishing. The rapidity of the advance had released Boiry from risk of bombardment by all except long range guns, and the necessity for the supply services to keep pace with the fighting troops in their progress eastward had already resulted in a complete metamorphosis of the Boyelles-Boiry area. Already Boyelles Station was a hive of industry, and trains were daily entering it from Arras with supplies. In Boiry-Becquerelle itself, which had been in German hands till the 23rd August, the 1/4th Londons were able to enjoy the luxury of baths and clean clothing on the 2nd September.

The few days' rest obtained here were passed pleasantly amid fine weather in refitting and reorganisation; and the Battalion was fortunately able on the 4th September to commemorate the fourth anniversary of its departure from England. Companies were now commanded as follows: A by Capt. H. N. Williams, M.C.; B by Capt. L. L. Watts, M.M.; C by Capt. C. L. Henstridge, M.C.; and D by Capt. T. B. Cooper, M.C., M.M.

About this time the Battalion Transport, which had been stationed at Boisleux St Marc, was divided into two echelons, of which A was the fighting and B the supply portion. These two echelons were respectively commanded by Lieut. G. V. Lawrie, M.C., and Lieut. G. E. Stanbridge. Although as a rule the two portions moved together, they were each self-contained and ready to operate separately in case of a sudden and rapid advance.

In the meantime the remainder of the XVII Corps was busily chasing the enemy through Quéant, Pronville and down the Arras-Cambrai Road to a point between Villers-lez-Cagnicourt and Buissy. After a warning order to the 56th Division to move forward again into the Corps area of battle, arrangements were suddenly changed—as on numerous other occasions—and on the 5th September the Division was transferred to the XXII Corps (Godley) of the First Army, with orders to relieve the 1st Division in the line.

East of Vis-en-Artois and south of Douai is a stretch of country well watered by numerous streams, and intersected by many ponds and marshes.

At Eterpigny the Cojeul and Sensée Rivers join, and thus augmented the Sensée expands at Etaing into what is practically a chain of lakes. Augmented by the Trinquis River and connected by it to the Scarpe, the Sensée flows eastward past Lécluse, Palluel and Aubigny-au-Bac. At Palluel it receives on its right, or south, bank the equally marshy streams of the Agache and the Hirondelle and is intersected by the northern extremity of the Canal du Nord, which here links up with the Canal de la Sensée. This last-named Canal runs southward from Douai to Arleux and then turning eastward down the river valley joins the Canal de l'Escaut. The whole area thus constitutes a thoroughly complicated system of waterways and marshes which form barriers of very great natural strength to an advance.

The Sensée marshes from Etaing to Palluel had formed the left flank of the Canadian Corps advance in its break through the Drocourt-Quéant line during the Battle of the Scarpe, and now formed a natural defensive flank, facing northwards, to our advanced positions on the Canal du Nord. In this area the 56th Division relieved the 1st Division. On the evening of the 7th September, after a a halt of one night at Vis-en-Artois, the 1/4th Londons took over the positions of the 2nd Royal Sussex on a front from Eterpigny Wood to a point east of Etaing. The line was continued to Lécluse by the Kensingtons and thence by the 169th Brigade.

The Battalion was now in country which hitherto had been in German hands for the whole of the War, and the devastated area was left behind. Villages were still standing and houses furnished. Indeed, the civilians had still been in occupation of them during the battle but had now been moved to the rear by the French Mission. Trenches in the ordinary sense were here non-existent and the front was held by a series of outposts along the line of the Sensée with sentry posts dug in small pits behind the cover of trees and bushes. D, B, and C Companies were in line, with A and Headquarters on the hill above Etaing.

Life in this sector was comparatively uneventful. The defences were improved and a great deal of useful patrolling work carried out in the endeavour to locate fords or other means of crossing the swamps in front. For his excellent reconnaissances and reports Sergt. Heyes, M.M., received commendation.

The previous occupants of the line had evidently been cautious in the use of their transport in forward areas, for rations and stores were dumped each night at a cross-road about 2000 yards in rear of the line; a course involving the nightly labours of some 70 men for carrying duties. The 1/4th Londons altered this and had limbers at night up to the front line without any mishap, thus saving an immense amount of fatigue and trouble to everyone.

After reorganising the outpost line to a strength of two companies the Battalion handed over its positions on the evening of the 12th September to the 1st Londons (167th Brigade), and concentrating at St Rohart Factory on the Arras-Cambrai Road were 'bussed back to Feuchy where they occupied shelters in Battery Valley, an area which a month previously they had held as a front line!

In this area a good deal of useful training with rifle and Lewis gun was put in, and a friendly boxing tournament with the London Scottish one evening afforded a pleasant relaxation. The Battalion was here joined by a large draft of officers, including Lieuts. A. Bath and T. R. Fletcher, and 2/Lieuts. Bradley, R. D. Bushell, J. Coley, P. W. Green and S. P. Ferdinando; and 2/Lieut. S. W. Neville (7th Londons) attached.

Lieut. E. P. M. Mosely's diary for this period affords an excellent illustration of the care taken to maintain the discipline of the Battalion at a high standard by the application of "peace-time" methods whenever the situation allowed:

> ... This sound principle was the means of preventing officers and men from degenerating into the "Ole Bill" type—a type which probably existed nowhere except in caricature. At Feuchy the Battalion was resting. The enemy had been swept back and had left just a desolate landscape, a smashed railway bridge and a collection of shell holes. The accommodation for officers and men consisted of holes in the ground roofed with tarpaulins and cuttings in the embankment which carried what was left of the railway line.
>
> Notwithstanding the entire lack of civilised comforts, at 7.30 in the evenings, standing on the battered arch of the bridge which once carried the line over Spider Corner, a Battalion bugler would sound "Dress for Mess." Officers would then scurry into their holes and half an hour later emerge in slacks, well-groomed, and enter the mess, a white-washed elephant shelter, and partake of a five-course dinner with all customary mess etiquette.

On the 19th September the 168th Brigade returned to the line. The Corps boundaries were being now rearranged and the 56th Division was being side-stepped to its right, a change which was effected by handing over a portion of its left to the 4th Division and extending its right over the front hitherto held by the 3rd Canadian Division. The additional frontage on the right was allotted to the 168th Brigade, which, after the relief, held a sector east of Ecourt St Quentin, with the London Scottish on the right and the 1/4th Londons on the left. The Brigade's left flank was secured by the 167th Brigade, which, facing north-east, held the area from Ecourt St Quentin to Lécluse.

The 1/4th Londons' sector consisted of a line of outposts some 500 yards west of the Canal du Nord, of which both banks were held in force by the Germans, from the Sauchy-Cauchy Road on the right, as far as Mill Copse (inclusive to the enemy), where the line bent back and facing north-east lay astride the Hirondelle River, the village of Ecourt St Quentin being inclusive to us. This line of outposts was held by two companies with Headquarters in a cottage east of Osvillers Lake, while two companies were in support in front of Rumaucourt.

The Battalion was unfortunate on the night of the relief in losing 2/Lieut. A. Cartmell, wounded, while 2/Lieut. S. W. Neville was killed early the following morning.

Like the Etaing area, this sector was marshy and intersected in all directions by dykes and streams. On the opposite bank of the Canal, the right flank around Sauchy-Cauchy was equally swampy; but opposite the centre and left the whole of our area was well under observation from a considerable hill on which stood Oisy-le-Verger—looking like a second Monchy—and the Bois de Quesnoy.

In this sector the artillery on both sides was continually active, though on the enemy's part activity was chiefly confined to counter-battery work. The Battalion was especially active at night in conducting reconnaissances of the ground in front, and some useful information was obtained. Very little was seen of the enemy's infantry, though on two nights he succeeded by stealth in stealing the garrison of one of our advanced posts, his second attempt being rendered successful by the artifice of approaching the post in the guise of deserters.

We must now turn for a moment to the general situation and must briefly consider once more the results achieved by the Battles of Bapaume and of the Scarpe in order to appreciate the further development of the offensive.

In commenting on the achievements of the British Armies in the Battle of Bapaume Sir Douglas Haig in his despatches draws attention to the steady deterioration of the enemy's morale and the increasing lack of organisation in his defence:

> The urgent needs of the moment, the wide extent of front attacked and consequent uncertainty as to where the next blow would fall, and the extent of his losses, had forced the enemy to throw in his reserves piecemeal as they arrived on the battle front. On many occasions in the course of the fighting elements of the same German division had been identified on widely separated parts of the battle front.

> In such circumstances a sudden and successful blow, of weight sufficient to break through the northern hinge of the defences on which he was to fall back, might produce results of great importance.

This anticipation of the Commander-in-Chief was amply fulfilled by the rapid retreat of the enemy towards the Hindenburg line during the first week of September after the close of the Battle of the Scarpe.

After hard fighting at Havrincourt and Epéhy during the third week of September the enemy was definitely within his Hindenburg defences as far north as Havrincourt, north of which he had been pushed beyond them to the line of the Canal du Nord. On the 12th September the Americans drove the enemy out of the St Mihiel salient, and it was decided in discussion between Sir Douglas Haig and Marshal Foch that as soon as possible four vigorous and simultaneous attacks should be launched: by the Americans in the direction of Mézières; by the French in Argonne with the same general objectives; by the British in the direction of Maubeuge; and by Belgian and Allied Forces in Flanders towards Ghent.

> By these attacks, says Sir Douglas Haig, it was expected that the important German forces opposite the French and Americans would be pressed back upon the difficult country of the Ardennes while the British thrust at their main communications.

The long continued blows delivered by the British Armies, although enormously successful, had placed a great strain on the troops, and their losses, though small in proportion to the enemy's and to the results achieved, were in the aggregate considerable. The Hindenburg positions were known to be strongly defended, and an unsuccessful attack on them would have a serious political effect and inevitably revive the declining German morale. An important crisis in the War had been reached and it was essential that the success of the British in this new attack should be decisive. After weighing the various considerations involved Sir Douglas Haig states:

> ... I was convinced that the British attack was the essential part of the general scheme and that the moment was favourable. Accordingly I decided to proceed with the attack....

The battle, which opened on the British front on the 27th September (Battle of Cambrai, 1918), culminated on the 5th October in the capture of all the Hindenburg trenches and of such isolated trench systems as lay in rear of it.

The part of the 56th Division in this great battle was the crossing of the Canal du Nord. This strong natural obstacle was considered to be too stubbornly held to yield to frontal attack on a wide area; and the general plan was therefore for the Canadian Corps to cross it on a narrow front north of Mœuvres and then spreading out fanwise to extend the gains north and south on the east bank.

The 1st Canadian Division, on the left of the Canadian Corps and adjoining the right of the 56th Division, was to cross the Canal south of the Arras-Cambrai Road and carry the line forward to Haynecourt. After this the 56th Division, astride the Canal on a front as far east as Sauchicourt Farm, with the 11th Division on its right, would attack northwards towards Oisy-le-Verger and the Sensée River at Palluel.

The 56th Division attack was entrusted east of the Canal to the 169th Brigade and west of it to the Kensingtons of the 168th Brigade. The London Scottish and 1/4th Londons in line had thus the peculiar experience of the attack actually crossing their front from right to left.

At 5.30 a.m. on the 27th September the crash of the barrage announced the opening of the Canadian Corps attack. The enemy's retaliation was slight and had practically ceased by 6 a.m. The 1/4th Londons' area was occupied by eight brigades of field guns engaged in firing a flank barrage to the main attack until 2.48 p.m., when they were to switch on a creeping barrage for the attack northwards along the Canal. Additional flank protection was furnished by six companies of machine-guns also in our area. In view of this heavy barrage and the possibility of severe retaliation the 1/4th Londons' outpost line was thinned out to two platoons in charge of Lieut. T. R. Fletcher, the remainder of the front companies being withdrawn to the support position.

The Canadian attack went well, but very stiff opposition was encountered in Marquion, so that the 56th Division attack from the Blue line had to be postponed from 2.48 p.m. to 3.28 p.m. Excellent work was done by the 512th and 513th Field Companies, R.E. (56th Division), in bridging the Canal at Marquion.

During the morning the 1/4th Londons' front seemed to be clear, and an officer's patrol under 2/Lieut. O. C. Hudson was sent forward to reconnoitre the enemy positions along the Agache River, which were found to be unoccupied.

At 3.28 p.m. the Kensingtons commenced their attack and progressed without difficulty as far as their first objective, the east and west road through Sauchy-Cauchy. North of this, however, they were met with stubborn resistance from machine-guns in Mill Copse and the marshes east of the Canal. Owing to the restricted avenues of advance through the marsh—there were only two possible routes to Mill Copse—the Kensingtons' attack was checked at about 6.30 p.m. some 500 yards south of the Copse. Excellent information was brought to Headquarters by 2/Lieut. A. M. Bullock as to the situation not only of the Kensingtons but also of the 169th Brigade east of the Canal.

About 5.50 p.m. C and D Companies began to re-establish the almost vacated outpost line, and later in the evening D Company was ordered to endeavour to assist the Kensingtons by pushing through to the Agache River and if possible by working round the Copse. By shortly after 11 p.m. reports were received that D Company had established four posts in touch with the Kensingtons. Mill Copse, however, was still in the enemy hands.

On the right of the Canal the 169th Brigade was also held up by stubborn machine-guns, and it was not till 8 a.m. the following morning that they were fully in possession of their final objective.

In view of the check on both banks the reserve company of the Kensingtons was ordered to clear up the situation as soon as the moon rose, and at 2 a.m. this company advanced astride the Canal as far as Mill Copse, which it found unoccupied. The Kensingtons then organised in depth, having reached their final objective at the surprisingly small cost of nine other ranks wounded.

The prosecution of the advance was ordered for the 28th September, and the 1/4th Londons were detailed to carry the 168th Brigade line forward on the west bank of the Canal towards Palluel, while on the east the 169th Brigade was to advance to the Sensée River.

During the night Battalion Headquarters was persistently shelled from its left rear by guns across the Sensée, with mustard gas.

At 9.30 a.m. D Company, with one platoon of A Company attached, began the advance northward to Palluel in the narrow gut of land between the Canal and the marshes and ponds of the Hirondelle River. Lieut.-Col. Marchment, 2/Lieut. Bullock, Sergts. Randall and Heyes and a few signallers followed in the attack, communication with Headquarters being maintained by a running wire all the way. Very little opposition was met with, and Capt. Cooper, with Lieut. Fletcher and 2/Lieut. Millstead, was soon established on the bridges at Palluel, where touch was gained with C Company and with patrols of the 8th Middlesex (167th Brigade) which occupied the village and advanced beyond it towards Arleux.

The whole 168th Brigade front being now confined to this narrow tongue of land its area was handed over to the 167th Brigade, and the 1/4th Londons withdrew to reserve positions at Rumaucourt. This move was completed by 9.15 p.m. on the 28th September.

This successful operation had been effected at very slight loss, the total casualties of the Division having been only 341 all ranks, while the 1/4th London losses for the whole of September were the happily small total of 30 other ranks in addition to the two officers already mentioned.

During these two days' fighting the 11th Division on the right had also met with considerable success, and on the evening of the 30th September the 168th Brigade was ordered back to the line to take over the positions gained by the left Brigade (the 34th) of the 11th Division. The advanced positions, which extended from the sharp bend in the Sensée Canal south of Brunemont on the left to a point opposite Aubencheul-au-Bac on the right, were occupied by the London Scottish and the Kensingtons.

The 1/4th Londons, who marched from Rumaucourt at 9 p.m. on the 30th September, relieved the 2nd Manchester in the support area, on the high ground south of Oisy-le-Verger and east of Sauchy-Lestrée.

The dispositions in this area were far from good, all the companies being rather mixed up in the railway cutting near the Bois des Puits; and on the following day Lieut.-Col. Marchment effected a redistribution of the Battalion, moving C and D Companies to Cemetery Wood and B Company to Battalion Headquarters near the Aubencheul Road, while A Company remained at the Bois des Puits. For five days the Battalion was busily employed in nightly working parties, digging a line of support posts across the ridge south of Oisy-le-Verger as far east as the old German dump at the cross-roads towards Epinoy. This dump proved to be a rather popular spot for it was found to be amply supplied with large bottles of Seltzer water. Probably a good number of these was taken on unofficial charge of the Battalion.

On the evening of the 5th October the 1/4th Londons took over the right subsection from the London Scottish, on the slope of the hill overlooking Aubencheul and the railway triangle. Hostile activity was slight on the 6th October, and from observation it seemed that the enemy was holding Aubencheul very lightly; in the afternoon orders were received to test the situation with patrols and if possible to penetrate the village and occupy the Canal bank north of it. Considerable fires observed during the morning in Aubigny-au-Bac contributed to the supposition that the vacation by the enemy of Aubencheul, if not already accomplished, was at least imminent.

B Company (Lieut. H. F. Dade) was detailed for the work, and at 7 p.m. No. 7 Platoon, with Lieut. A. M. Bullock, Intelligence Officer, and 4 Headquarters scouts attached, left advanced Battalion Headquarters to try to enter the village and reach the railway bridge over the Canal. The other platoons stood in readiness to move forward if required. By 10.15 p.m. information was received that the platoon was in the village without having met with any of the enemy, and accordingly Nos. 5 and 8 Platoons were at once ordered to move forward to form posts at the railway crossing and the Aubigny-au-Bac Road bridge and to find touch with the 11th Division on the right. These operations were successfully accomplished, though the enemy gave evidence of his occupation of the north end of the bridges.

By 4 a.m. on the 7th October the occupation of the village was complete with two platoons which were in touch with the 2nd Yorkshires (4th Division) on the right, one platoon in the railway cutting south of the village and one still in the old outpost line. No casualties had been sustained.

The following day the 1/4th Londons took over the whole Brigade front, C Company (Capt. C. L. Henstridge, M.C.) on the right, A Company (Capt. L. L. Watts, M.M.) in the centre and D Company (Lieut. T. R. Fletcher) on the left. B Company (Lieut. H. F. Dade) was withdrawn to support. The outposts consisted of a line of sentry posts on the Canal with a line of resistance about 400 yards in rear. A reserve line was occupied on the spurs overlooking the Canal north and east of Oisy-le-Verger. Company Headquarters were located in captured German battery positions, and D Company became the possessors of a complete battery of 8-inch German howitzers which had been taken on the 27th September.

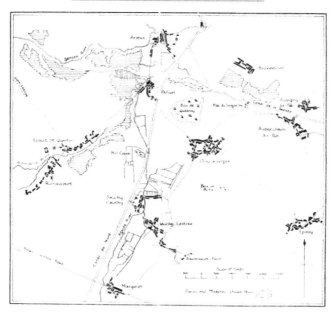

THE BATTLE OF CAMBRAI, 1918. THE CANAL DU NORD

The first phase of the great British offensive may now be said to have been brought to a conclusion. In the nine days' fighting between the 27th September and the 5th October, the First, Third and Fourth Armies had shattered the enemy's last prepared lines of defence. The line of the Canal du Nord had been crossed and left far behind, and the whole of the main Hindenburg defences were in our hands. "The effect of the victory," writes Sir Douglas Haig in his despatches, "on the subsequent course of the campaign was decisive." The threat to the enemy's communications was now direct and instant, for nothing but the natural obstacles of a wooded and well-watered countryside lay between our Armies and Maubeuge.

In this fighting 30 British and 2 American infantry divisions and 1 British cavalry division had met and defeated 39 German divisions at a loss to the enemy of 36,000 prisoners and 380 guns!

The effect of the advance of our Armies on this front now rendered the enemy's positions in the Lys area precarious. Already on the 28th September the Second Army, attacking on a wide front about Ypres, had carried forward our positions in one day a greater distance than had been gained in the whole of the dreary struggles for Passchendaele in 1917. By the 1st October Messines had again been liberated and our troops were approaching Gheluve and Werwicq. On the 2nd October the enemy initiated a general withdrawal on the front from Lens to Armentières.

We have now to follow the course of the second phase of the British advance—the final phase of the War. In this great operation the Fourth and Third Armies and the right of the First Army advanced with their left flank on the Canal from Cambrai to Mons and their right flank covered by our French Allies.

The first stage of this series of battles opened on the 8th October with a vast drive by the Third and Fourth Armies in the direction of Le Cateau. The success of the operation was complete, but we are only concerned with the point that it involved the fall of Cambrai on the 9th October.

This continued advance of the British in the south exposed in increasing measure the flank of the enemy north of the Sensée, and great developments were therefore to be expected shortly in the XXII Corps area. Already the enemy was reported to be withdrawing from his positions in the corner between the Canal de la Sensée and the Canal de l'Escaut, which had been crossed by the Canadians as far north as Ramillies; and to relieve the 11th Division to pursue this movement the 168th Brigade extended its right with the Kensingtons as far as Fressies, which village was to be occupied immediately after the completion of the relief. This was on the 9th October.

The possibility of an early German retirement north of the Sensée also called for great vigilance, and the 1/4th Londons were ordered to probe the situation towards Brunemont and Aubigny-au-Bac, while units of the 167th Brigade were feeling towards Arleux.

The only way to cross the Canal, short of swimming or using a boat, was to use the ruined iron bridges at Aubencheul and Abbaye-du-Verger Farm, and accordingly small patrols, covered by parties on the south bank, began to cross the bridges at about 5 p.m. on the 9th October. Results were soon obtained. At Aubencheul the enemy was alert and the patrol was driven back. At the Farm crossing A Company obtained more success. A post of the enemy about 12 strong was discovered on the Brunemont Road north of the Canal, and these, after firing a few shots, fled, though one of them was captured by Sergt. R. C. Clammer, D.C.M., M.M., after which the patrol returned. The prisoner was from the 103rd I Regiment, and was a destitute wretch, wearing cap, jacket, trousers and boots—and nothing else. Unfortunately, Capt. Watts was killed by a stray bullet while returning to his company headquarters.

The same evening the 1/4th Londons were relieved by the 8th Middlesex (167th Brigade) and withdrew to Brigade support in shelters west of Epinoy. At the same time the Kensingtons and London Scottish effected the extension to the right of the Divisional line above referred to.

Early on the morning of the 11th October the Kensingtons launched a completely successful attack on Fressies and advanced the Brigade line to the Canal at a loss to themselves of only 10 casualties. In the meantime the advance of the VIII Corps north of the Sensée River had driven the enemy from Vitry-en-Artois and was now being directed towards Douai. To assist in this development the 56th Division artillery was ordered to keep under fire the crossings over the northern arm of the Sensée Canal, while the infantry made persistent endeavours to establish themselves beyond the Canal de la Sensée with a view to exerting pressure on the retiring enemy's left flank. On the 12th the 167th Brigade completed the clearance of Arleux which had been initiated by the Canadians, and occupied the Canal triangle south-east of the village. The following day the 169th Brigade occupied Aubigny-au-Bac after a sharp fight, but a vigorous counter-attack later threw them back to the Canal bank. In this fighting magnificent devotion was displayed by the Royal Engineers in bridging the Canal under heavy fire.

By the 16th October the 4th Canadian Division had taken over the Divisional line and the 56th Division withdrew into Army reserve.

The 1/4th Londons were relieved in the Brigade support area by the 1/2nd Londons on the 11th October and passed into Divisional reserve at Rumaucourt, where several days of very welcome rest were obtained.

Both Rumaucourt and Ecourt-St Quentin were still comparatively unharmed and partly furnished. Everywhere were signs of the German occupation. The chief anxiety of the enemy occupants seems to have been fear of British aeroplanes, for every cellar had its capacity plainly written on the door, while large warning bells or "Flieger Alarum" were fixed in all prominent places. In Ecourt-St Quentin were three German field hospitals which afforded unmistakable evidence that the enemy was hard up for bandages, for in place of these he seemed to have used old curtains and paper. An abundant quantity of old civilian clothing was also found here, and rumour has it that the doctor was seen one day sporting an excellent top hat. B Company lived in one of these hospitals and had an excellent time with a grand piano. These good Bosche institutions afforded an opportunity of bathing, of which advantage was taken by the whole Battalion.

During the foregoing spell of active work the Battalion transport had been located near Wancourt. "One day in October," writes Lieut.-Col. Marchment, "a deputation of Company Q.M.-Sergts. appeared at Orders with a request that they might take it in turns to come up with the rations, A and C one night, B and D the next. To this I gladly consented when, looking at the map, I found that they were walking and riding some twenty-six miles a night!"

On the afternoon of the 14th October the Battalion marched to Marquion—till the 27th September in German hands—to entrain for a rest at Arras. The train was due out at 3 p.m., but as things turned out there was no occasion for hurry, since owing to a smash at Boisleux the train did not reach Marquion till 11 p.m. A weary but happy Battalion entrained, confidently expecting to wake up in Arras, but the advent of morning brought no change of scene. The train had not moved an inch! However, in due course the line was cleared and the train gaily rattled over the battlefields of Quéant, Croisilles and Boyelles, and reached Arras by 11.30 a.m. on the 15th. The 1/4th Londons were quartered in comfortable billets in the Rue d'Amiens.

The rest in Arras, with which charming little city the Battalion had been so frequently associated, was probably the most enjoyable that fell to its lot in the whole War. To start with, everyone was in the highest spirits born of the knowledge of their own recent successes in action and of their confidence for the battles to come. Food was good and plentiful. The civilians were returning and shops were beginning to open once again.

Here the Battalion experienced the first visible effects of what the liberation of France meant to the French. Refugees from the liberated villages towards Cambrai were being sent back for safety to Arras, where they were housed in the Schramm Barracks till the French Mission was able to arrange to settle them in other parts of France. Streams of homeless women and children drifted through the streets, clinging to a few treasured objects of their personal belongings, and our men stood at the street corners deeply impressed by such heartrending scenes. Shamefacedly, as if fearful of disclosing the depth of their emotion to their comrades, the men would beg the refugees to be allowed to carry their parcels for them. Three men of one company took complete charge of a distressed family and piloted them to a house where they settled the poor folks, lit a fire for them, bought eggs with their own money, scrounged some bully beef, and then fled to avoid the thanks of their grateful charges.

The average Cockney is not in the habit of wearing his heart on his sleeve. Rather does he conceal his emotion beneath the cloak of "grousing," but scenes of desolation such as these—far more affecting than the sight of a ruined countryside—brought out all the wonderful chivalry which has endeared the simple British soldier to the hearts of the French. "It was only in censoring letters home," writes an officer, "that one realised how deeply touched our men were by the sufferings of the civilians." Of all these saddening sights probably the most dreadful was at the Hôpital St Jean, where little mites of French children were dying of gas poisoning, and old people lying demented by the horrors through which they had passed. To alleviate these sufferings everything possible was done, and our own R.A.M.C. orderlies worked side by side with the French Sisters of Mercy.

One afternoon the Commanding Officer gave permission for the drums to play to the refugees. The performance concluded with the Marseillaise, the glorious strains of which, not heard for four long years, so overcame the audience that in the intensity of their emotion old men, women and children fell upon the drummers and kissed them—much to the embarrassment of those good-natured fellows.

Some excellent training meanwhile was being obtained on the racecourse at Dainville, and several rifle competitions were introduced to add to the keenness of the men. The Battalion was largely reclothed and much done to improve its excellent parade discipline. On the 21st October a Guard of Honour was provided, consisting of 100 all ranks under Capt. H. N. Williams, M.C., for President Poincaré, who was visiting Arras—"the finest Guard the Division ever turned out," as Faulkner described it. The identity of this distinguished visitor remained for a long time shrouded in mystery, and curiosity reached fever-pitch. The Mess decided that the only way to deal with the problem was to have a sweepstake, in which the names of the

Prince of Wales, M. Clemenceau, General Smuts, Marshal Foch and the Lord Nozoo (representing The Field) were included. Captain Williams' return was awaited with breathless anxiety, but, alas, in the dark he had failed to solve the mystery. The Mess paid out on M. Clemenceau—he being apparently the nearest to the distinguished visitor who actually arrived.

During this rest at Arras the Battalion was joined by Capts. H. W. Spiers and D. S. Boorman, M.C. (to command B and C Companies respectively), and by Lieuts. E. G. Dew and H. D. Rees, the latter being appointed Assistant-Adjutant. Regimental Sergt.-Major Jacques, who was returning to England in training for Quartermaster, was replaced by Sergt.-Major Wilson, who had been wounded at Ypres in 1917. The strength of the Battalion was now 38 officers and 721 other ranks.

The latter half of October had seen most rapid and important changes on the British battle front, to which we must refer briefly. The success of the attack towards Le Cateau in the early days of the month had been complete and had driven the enemy back to the line of the Selle River. This enabled G.H.Q. to initiate the second stage of this last phase of the War, which was to force the enemy from the Selle River back to the general line Sambre Canal—western edge of Forêt de Mormal—Valenciennes. The occupation of this line would enable the British Armies to launch their final attack on Maubeuge.

The Battle of the Selle was opened by the Fourth Army on the 17th October, the fight gradually involving the Third and First Armies in succession. By the 20th October the enemy had been driven across the Sambre as far north as Catillon, Le Cateau was occupied, and the Selle River left two miles behind our advanced positions. The main attack developed on the 23rd October, and by the end of the following day the enemy was driven on to the western edge of the Forêt de Mormal, the outskirts of Le Quesnoy had been reached, and the lateral railway connecting Le Quesnoy with Valenciennes had been crossed on a front of about four miles. This latter portion of the success was on the front of the XXII and Canadian Corps of the First Army. The Selle River Battle resulted in the capture of 20,000 prisoners and 475 guns, and in the defeat of 31 German divisions by 25 British and 2 American divisions.

On other parts of the front successes had been equally striking. Laon had fallen to the French on the 13th October. In Belgium, Menin, Thorout and Ostend had been occupied in rapid succession, and by the 20th October the Allied line rested on the Dutch frontier. This advance in the extreme north had the effect of turning the defences of Lille, which was encircled and occupied on the 18th October, after which a steady advance brought our troops to the line of the Scheldt north of Valenciennes to Avelghem.

The critical condition of the Germans is summed up by Sir Douglas Haig in his despatches:—

> By this time the rapid succession of heavy blows dealt by the British forces had had a cumulative effect, both moral and material upon the German Armies.... His reserves of men were exhausted.... The capitulation of Turkey and Bulgaria and the imminent collapse of Austria—consequent upon Allied successes which the desperate position of her own armies in the western front had rendered her powerless to prevent—had made Germany's military situation impossible. If her armies were now to be allowed to withdraw undisturbed to shorter lines the struggle might still be protracted over the winter. The British Armies, however, were now in a position to prevent this by a direct attack upon a vital centre which should anticipate the enemy withdrawal and force an immediate conclusion.

A necessary preliminary to the final attack was the capture of Valenciennes itself, and this was accomplished on the 1st November. The XXII Corps, advancing on a front of six miles to the south of the city, crossed the Rhonelle River, and occupied the high ground overlooking the valley of the Aunelle River, while the Canadians entered Valenciennes and pushed on to the east of it.

On the 31st October the 56th Division rejoined the XXII Corps in the battle area, and the battalions of the 168th Brigade embussed from Arras to Douchy (two miles south of Denain). For a couple of days the 1/4th Londons remained here in very fair billets, receiving a most hearty welcome from the inhabitants, who had been for four years under the heel of the enemy.

At 8 a.m. on the 2nd November the Battalion marched about five miles forward to the staging area at Maing, which it reached at about 11.30 a.m., and that evening advanced again at short notice and relieved the 4th K.O.Y.L.I. (49th Division) in advanced positions facing Saultain, the relief being completed by 2 a.m. on the 3rd November. The advance was led by D Company, which came under heavy shell fire when passing through Famars, and lost 4 men killed and 14 wounded.

The 168th Brigade section which was the left of the Divisional front, the 169th being on the right, was held with the Kensingtons and 1/4th Londons in the line. D Company occupied small sections of trenches in the front line some 500 yards west of the Château de Saultain, while A, B and C Companies were held back in a sunken road south-east of Aulnoy.

Lieut.-Col. Marchment was now in command of the 168th Brigade, General Loch having gone to hospital, and the Battalion was temporarily under Major R. B. Marshall, with Captain T. B. Cooper, M.C., M.M., acting as second in command. Battalion Headquarters opened in Aulnoy.

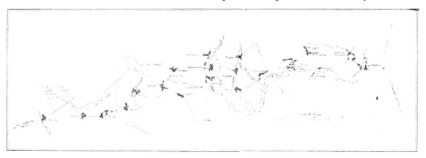

THE BATTLE OF THE SAMBRE, 1918

About the time of the relief it became apparent that the enemy had retired again opposite the Canadians on our left and was about to do so on our own front. At 10.35 a.m. a wire was received in the Battalion stating that the Canadians had entered Estreux, and ordering the Battalion to push strongly supported patrols through Saultain as far as the Ferme du Moulin. D Company moved forward at 11.15 a.m., supported by A Company, and entered Saultain which was found to be unoccupied except for four men of the 109th Infantry Regiment who were taken prisoners. By two o'clock the Ferme du Moulin was occupied with very little opposition and Battalion Headquarters advanced to the Château de Saultain. On the right the Kensingtons had also pressed forward towards the cemetery of Curgies, and touch was obtained with them and with the 4th Canadian Division on the left. This advance—over 2000 yards—was consolidated by the 1/4th Londons, while two squadrons of Australian Light Horse and a company of New Zealand cyclists endeavoured to push forward during the evening to secure the crossings of the River Aunelle. Their attempt, however, was checked about 1000 yards in front of the infantry by enemy machine-gun fire, and in this position the progress for the day was concluded, the Kensingtons occupying with the cavalry and cyclists the advanced line, which extended in a north-westerly direction from the cross-roads at Le Talandier. That night the 1/4th Londons' position was held with D and A Companies in front and B and C Companies in support.

The immediate resumption of the advance being ordered by XXII Corps, arrangements were made by 56th Division with the adjoining divisions to pursue the attack at 6 a.m. the following morning, 4th November, each division operating independently. Orders for this advance did not reach the 1/4th Londons, who were detailed for the attack on the 168th Brigade front, till 1 a.m., and there was thus no more than enough time to assemble the companies close in rear of the line held by the Kensingtons. For reconnaissance there was no time at all. The attack was delivered on a two-company front by B Company on the right and A Company on the left, each moving in square formation of platoons with a screen of scouts and cavalry patrols in front. C and D Companies followed in diamond formation at a distance of about 200 yards. The objective was given as the high ground across the River Aunelle about 500 yards east of Sebourquiaux.

The morning dawned mistily, but in this case the mist was not altogether a disadvantage. The whole of this countryside was a swelling waste of stubble fields with practically no landmarks, but fortunately a line of telegraph poles going due east which was visible through the mist enabled the leading companies to keep their direction well—a great stroke of luck, as the advance lay up hill and down dale over this barren land for some 2000 yards before the crest of the Aunelle Valley was reached, and the objective was for a long time out of sight. The mist thus served to conceal the advance from the enemy till the leading companies breasted the hill overlooking Sebourquiaux itself, and started descending the slope to the village.

The Aunelle River is hereabouts spanned by three bridges, one at Sebourg, one at Sebourquiaux, and one at Le Pissot, north of the latter village. These had already been secured by the cavalry patrols who had, however, been unable to make progress across the river. As the leading companies began to drop down the hill towards the village the mist partly cleared, and the German machine-gunners opened a heavy fire. The leading companies at once dashed down the hill into the cover of the scattered houses and streets which form the outskirts of Sebourquiaux on the west bank of the river; but here they seemed to have fallen into a trap for the enemy at once dropped a barrage of considerable intensity, shells of all calibres falling thick and fast. Forward progress was impossible, and B Company on the right therefore promptly worked round the right flank, crossing the river at Sebourg, and then, turning northward toward Sebourquiaux, cleared the village of the enemy machine-gunners. In the meantime A Company had been heavily machine-gunned from the direction of Rombies, which continued to resist the Canadian attack, and touch with the Canadians was lost.

B Company having cleared the way through the village, A Company was able to cross the river, and together the two companies attempted to force their way up the slope to the east of Sebourquiaux. The machine-gun fire was too intense, and the companies had to fall back to a line on the eastern outskirts of the village, where, joined by C Company (in support), they began to consolidate their position. Touch was obtained with the Queen's Westminsters of the 169th Brigade who had cleared Sebourg on the right, but no connection could be obtained with the Canadians who were still held up before Rombies on the left, and A Company therefore threw a defensive flank astride the Aunelle River facing northwards. The Battalion was now organised on the line which had been gained, all companies having platoons on the forward positions and finding their own supports. All day the village of Sebourquiaux remained under heavy German shell fire, but at about 5.30 p.m. the intensity of the enemy's fire increased and the work of destruction was completed, hardly a house being left standing. A variegated display of Véry lights which accompanied this barrage led to the expectation that the enemy was organising a counter-attack, but no infantry movement on the part of the Germans materialised.

The stiffness of the enemy resistance this day made it abundantly clear that further progress could be made only by means of an organised attack in co-operation with the divisions on either flank, and arrangements for a further advance were promptly made.

That night the 1/4th Londons were relieved by the London Scottish and withdrew in Brigade reserve to the high ground east of Estreux, Headquarters remaining at the Ferme du Moulin. This relief was completed at 3 a.m. on the 5th November, and at 5.30 a.m. the attack was pursued by the London Scottish, with the Kensingtons in support and the 1/4th Londons in reserve. By 6 a.m. the crest east of Sebourquiaux had been gained and the enemy was retiring in the direction of Angre.

On the 169th Brigade front the enemy resistance was not severe, and by 7.30 a.m. the London Rifle Brigade had captured Angreau. The Canadians had also occupied Rombies, but on the ridge between this village and Angre the Germans continued to hold out in great force and to bring very heavy machine-gun fire to bear on the left flank of the 168th Brigade.

At 8 a.m. the 1/4th Londons were ordered forward, and by 11 a.m. the companies, A, B, C and D in line from right to left, were in position in the old German trenches east of Sebourquiaux, with Battalion Headquarters in a farmhouse in the village. In this position the Battalion was practically on the frontier of France and Belgium.

The advance was resumed by the London Scottish under a barrage at 4.15 p.m., and the line was advanced to within about 500 yards of Angre. The enemy machine-gun fire again precluded the possibility of further advance, and eventually a line was consolidated facing north-east in touch with the 169th Brigade on the right and the Canadians on the left.

On the 6th November the attack was pursued by the London Scottish on the right and the Kensingtons on the left, the 1/4th Londons again being in support. Fierce fighting took place, particularly on the left flank where the Kensingtons crossed the Grande Honnelle River, were thrown back, and crossed it again. At the end of the day the leading battalions were in possession of Angre, on the east bank of the Grand Honnelle. The 1/4th Londons moved forward slightly from their positions of the previous day but did not come into action.

The whole of these days were extremely wet, and not a man in the Battalion had a scrap of dry clothing. Trenches were embryonic, and shelters almost entirely lacking—of dugouts there were, of course, none.

Shortly after midnight "Drake" Battalion of the 63rd (Royal Naval) Division relieved the Battalion—the remainder of the Brigade also being relieved—and it withdrew to tolerable billets in Sebourg. The march to Sebourg was only about two miles, but every road was choked with double and even treble lines of transport of all descriptions waiting to follow up the advance. It had been waiting motionless since the previous afternoon and did not get on the move again till 4 a.m. the next morning. In these circumstances the march to Sebourg occupied about four hours—a most unpleasant journey in which desultory shelling by the enemy alternated with heated arguments with despairing transport officers. Dawn, however, found the Battalion enjoying a good breakfast, and drying its clothes, all its troubles forgotten, and every one filled with justifiable satisfaction at the good work that had been done.

This, the last fight of the 1/4th Londons, produced nine prisoners and cost in casualties: 2/Lieut. A. M. Bullock, killed; 2/Lieut. G. H. Sylvester, died of wounds; 2/Lieut. H. W. Taylor, wounded; and in N.C.O.'s and men, 11 killed, 55 wounded and 1 missing.

From now onwards the 56th Division was fighting on a one-brigade front, with the 167th leading, and the 1/4th Londons were engaged in following up the advance by stages so as to be within supporting distance of the leading troops. Nowhere was the enemy's opposition more than trifling, and the advance proceeded rapidly, though under conditions of some discomfort and difficulty. The line of the Division's advance lay almost due east, roughly parallel to the marshes about the Canal de Condé which connects the Canal de l'Escaut with Mons, and the whole countryside is cut up by innumerable small streams discharging northwards into the marsh area. The banks of these streams are everywhere steep, and bridges had been systematically destroyed by the retiring enemy who had also blown craters at almost every road junction. It was an ideal country for a determined enemy to fight a rearguard action, but the Germans' powers of resistance were broken, and beyond the delays caused to the progress of our troops by the wholesale destruction, opposition was negligible. The extreme rapidity of the advance indeed made it almost impossible for the supply services to keep pace, and the damage to the roads prevented lorries from proceeding beyond the Grande Honnelle River till the necessary repairs could be completed. The weather, moreover, had broken, and for three days rain fell incessantly. But these discomforts were slight in comparison with the enormous wave of enthusiasm which passed over all the troops who had the good fortune to take part in this extraordinary victory.

On the 7th November the line of the Bavai-Hensies Road was crossed, and the following day the leading troops had reached the line Petit Moronfait-Rinchon-Ferlibray. The 9th November saw the Mons-Maubeuge Road crossed, and on the 10th the 1st Londons, who were leading, captured Harveng, and after slight opposition pushed forward to Harmignies.

The 1/4th Londons following up the advance moved on the 8th to Autreppe and the following day to Blaugies. The band was now with the Battalion and played on the march. This gave rise to most remarkable patriotic demonstrations on the part of the liberated villagers who everywhere greeted the Battalion with cries of "Vive l'Angleterre!" and showered flowers on the troops, while crowds of children marched beside the band cheering. The plight of these poor people was deplorable. The Germans in their retirement had taken with them practically all food supplies and utensils of every description. Scarcely the bare necessities of life remained. All live stock had also been driven before them by the retreating hordes of the enemy, but when the Battalion reached Blaugies the presence of live stock in the village showed the ever-increasing confusion and speed of the enemy's retirement. At this time the Division was feeding some 16,000 civilians, on an allowance of one iron ration to four people.

On the morning of the 10th November the 1/4th Londons continued their almost triumphal progress to La Dessoue, but there being no accommodation here, found billets in Sars-la-Bruyère, where an overwhelming welcome was accorded them. In this village Sir Horace Smith-Dorrien (II Corps) had had his Headquarters on the 23rd August 1914.

The Brigade Ammunition Column at this time was in charge of Lieut. E. P. M. Mosely, whose diary illustrates the extraordinary spirit of humour which carried the men through this period of hard work and exposure. The Column reached Famars thoroughly tired out one wet night at about midnight, and halted in rear of the advancing troops. The civilians had been evacuated and the men rapidly made themselves comfortable in some of the cottages. One of the transport drivers, according to the immemorial custom of transport drivers, quickly began to forage round, and attired himself in a top hat, white scarf and frock coat, in which remarkable garb he put his head round the door and said: "I've come for the rent!" This, after a hard night's work, shows a spirit which takes a lot of damping.

It was in this advance also that the Column arrived in a battered village late at night, thoroughly worn out and drenched to the skin. The place was muddy, shell torn and desolate, and its exact whereabouts on the map far from certain. The men began to picket their horses and spread tarpaulins over their heaped-up stores, and afterwards disconsolately to search for odd bits of timber in the endeavour to construct some sort of shelter. The O.C. Column produced from a waggon an antique arm-chair, which had somehow attached itself to the Column at an earlier stage of the advance, and in this very much improvised headquarters took up his station in the mud, when suddenly—the post arrived! The Army Postal Service had throughout been so efficient as to become almost a matter of course—but in this effort it surely surpassed itself!

On the night of the 10th November the 56th Division was relieved by the 63rd Division by whom the advance was to be pursued; but early the following morning the news of the Armistice was received and the troops stood fast. The record of this grand culmination of the years of bloodshed is contained in the Battalion Official War Diary as follows:

Sars-la-Bruyère. 11.11.1918.	08.30.	Bde. Memo. B.M. 971 received hostilities would cease at 1100.
		The news had an unexpected effect on the troops: everybody appeared to be too dazed to make any demonstration. Men were much less cheerful than they had been for some days.
	11.00.	Hostilities ceased.
		Transport Personnel and Nucleus rejoined Battn.

The vast Forêt de Mormal had been passed, Mons and Maubeuge had fallen, and the German Army was divided into two parts, one on each side of the natural barrier of the Ardennes.

In his Despatches Sir Douglas Haig sums up the situation on the morning of the 11th November 1918 thus:

> In the fighting since November 1st, our troops had broken the enemy's resistance beyond hope of recovery, and had forced on him a disorderly retreat along the whole front of the British Armies. Thereafter the enemy was capable neither of accepting nor refusing battle.... The strategic plan of the Allies had been realised with a completeness rarely seen in war. When the Armistice was signed by the enemy his defensive powers had already been definitely destroyed. A continuance of hostilities could only have meant disaster to the German Armies and the armed invasion of Germany.

A remarkable incident related by Lieut. Mosely occurred at Sars-la-Bruyère the day following the Armistice.

> The Mess Corporal proceeded to Mons to see if any green vegetables could be procured. Returning from his mission through the streets of Mons he saw a soldier untidily dressed and without puttees, but wearing on his jacket the red circles which were the distinguishing mark of the 1/4th Londons. Said the Corporal, "What are you doing here?" "Looking for my Battalion," replied the man. The Corporal demanded to know why the man had wandered so far from billets and what he meant by being so untidily turned out. To his surprise the soldier informed him that he had come from Germany. A few more words and the Corporal realised that this was one of our own men who had walked out of a German prison when the Armistice was declared. Whipping up the wanderer into the Mess cart, he brought him home, washed him and gave him a big meal. The poor fellow was almost hysterical at being amongst his own once more. He was a man of B Company who had been captured on the 28th March 1918, at Oppy. "We gave him a strong dose of rum," writes Mosely, "and wrapped him in warm blankets. By the next morning he had quite recovered, and was asking for his pay!"

Thus ended the four years' war service of the 1/4th Londons, who at the end of the campaign were within two miles of Malplaquet, where Marlborough's great victory had been won two hundred years earlier. It had the proud distinction of having finished its active service within five miles of Mons, where the first British shot had been fired in August 1914. Of the 1016 officers and men who had left England on the 4th September 1914, only about 30 other ranks remained with the Battalion which had done such glorious service on so many hard-fought fields.

As a tribute to the many unrewarded acts of heroism of which there have been so many examples during the War, a letter, relating to the circumstances attending the death of No. 280872 Pte. S. Greenfield of D Company on the 23rd August 1918, is preserved among the Battalion records. This letter was sent by the Medical Officer, 178th Brigade, R.F.A., who found Greenfield's body, to his relatives, from whom it was received by the Commanding Officer. The following is an extract from this letter, which is dated 24th August 1918:

> ... On searching the battlefield (Boyelles) I discovered the body of your son Private S. Greenfield, No. 280872. He had died fighting, killed outright by a machine-gun. I found him lying on a German machine-gun which I have no doubt he intended to capture. As no more dead were there and no other signs of a fight about the machine-gun nest, I expect he rushed the machine-gunners himself. I may remark the machine-gunners are dead also.

One of the survivors of the original Battalion was Flossie, a small, brown Pomeranian dog. Flossie had served on the railway line in August 1914, had accompanied the Battalion to Malta and been successfully smuggled into France in January 1915. Throughout the War she had journeyed everywhere with the Battalion, and finally came home with the Cadre in 1919. Her principal claim to distinction appears to be that she succeeded in bringing a litter of puppies into a noisy and muddy world in most of the leading towns and villages of Flanders. Throughout she maintained a calm demeanour, and when her maternal cares necessitated transport she rode with her young family in a basket perched on one of the cookers.

On the 15th November a party of the Battalion, under Capt. H. N. Williams, M.C., took part in the triumphal march through Mons, where the troops were received with a tumultuous welcome.

There is little further to be said. The XXII Corps was excluded from the Army of the Rhine and the Battalion remained in the Mons area, training and indulging in educational experiments, while parties visited the battlefields of Mons and Waterloo. Until the ravages of demobilisation reduced the numbers too severely, the evenings were enlightened by some of the Quartermaster's excellent orchestral concerts, and by boxing tournaments in which the Battalion did exceedingly well, Private Miller of the 1/4th Londons becoming XXII Corps Feather-weight Champion.

On the 27th November the Battalion moved to billets in Villers-sire-Nicole, near Maubeuge, and on the 6th March 1919 to Givry and on the

18th March to Cuesmes (both near Mons), in all of which places the routine of training and education was continued. Early in the New Year the arrangements for demobilisation were put into active operation, and rapidly the strength of the Battalion dwindled.

Among the first to leave was the padre, Rev. S. F. Leighton Green, M.C., who had served continuously with the Battalion since December 1916. The padre left on the 13th February 1919, and his departure was felt most keenly by every officer and man in the Battalion. His constant selfless devotion to duty and his kindly personality had made him a true friend to one and all, and the example of his simple life and magnificent courage in action had been a real inspiration to all—and that included the whole Battalion—who had been brought into personal contact with him.

The break-up of the Battalion was the saddest thing which ever happened to it. After so many months and years of good and bad times, and of life in circumstances of such intimacy as can be attained only on active service, the joy of departure for home was severely tempered by the deepest emotion at leaving the comradeship of regimental life, and few said good-bye to the Battalion without genuine sorrow.

By the beginning of May the Battalion was reduced to Cadre strength, about 50 all ranks, Lieut.-Col. Marchment, D.S.O., M.C., remaining in command, with Major T. B. Cooper, M.C., M.M., second in command.

On the 14th May 1919 the Cadre left Cuesmes, entraining at Jemappes for Antwerp. After a few days in the embarkation camp it was played down to the quay by the pipes of the Liverpool Scottish and embarked for Tilbury, where it entrained for Newhaven. On the 21st May the Cadre returned to London by train and was received at London Bridge Station by the Lord Mayor (the Rt. Hon. Sir Horace Marshall, now Lord Marshall of Chipstead, P.C., K.C.V.O., Hon. Colonel of the Regiment), who also took the salute as the Cadre passed the Mansion House *en route* for Headquarters in Hoxton.

The Cadre was received at Headquarters by Lieut.-Col. H. Dade, V.D., Major G. H. M. Vine, T.D., and other officers of the Regiment, and by the Mayor of Shoreditch (Councillor W. Girling), after which its dispersal speedily followed.

Three weeks later the last remnants of the 1/4th Londons were scattered to their homes, and the part played by the Regiment in the Great War was at an end.

APPENDIX I
MALTA

The Dependency of Malta consists of a chain of islands, Gozo, Comino and Malta, stretching from north-west to south-east, about 60 miles from Sicily and about 180 from Africa. Malta itself is about 17½ miles long and 8¼ broad, and, owing to its magnificent natural harbours, it has been the coveted possession of the strongest nations on the sea for the time being, ever since the dawn of maritime trade. These anchorages are nearly all on the east coast of the island, and include—besides the famous harbours of Valetta (the Grand Harbour on the south of the city and the Marsamuscetto Harbour on the north)—the bays of Melleha, St Paul's and Marsa Scirocco.

The population of Malta in 1907 was 206,690, and this phenomenal congestion renders it largely dependent on imported foodstuffs. The area under cultivation is comparatively small, and the fields are composed of terraces by which the soil with enormous labour has been walled up along the contours of the hills to prevent it from being washed away. Viewed from the sea, therefore, the top of one wall appearing above the next produces the barren effect to which reference has been made in Chapter II; but the aspect of the land from the top of the hills in winter and early spring is a beautiful contrast of a profusion of greenness. The principal grain crops are maize, wheat and barley. Vines are also cultivated though the fruit is sold as grapes far more profitably than converted into wine. The chief industry is the production of Maltese lace, which employs some 5000 women and children. The principal resources of the island are derived from the fact of its being an important military station and the Headquarters of the Mediterranean fleet, the prolonged absence of which always produces distress.

The Maltese language is Phœnician in origin, the popular idea that it is composed largely of Arabic being erroneous. Until recent years the language of the courts was Italian, in spite of the fact that this language is unknown to 86 per cent, of the population.

Malta has had a most chequered history from the earliest times when the Mediterranean was the centre of all civilisation and commerce. The Phœnicians occupied the islands at a very early date, being followed in the 6th century B.C. by the Carthaginians, and later by the Romans, who regarded the Maltese not as conquered enemies but as allies. On the final division of the Roman Dominions in A.D. 395, Malta was assigned to the

Empire of Constantinople, and during the next 500 years suffered three Arab invasions, though these left little mark upon the people either by language or by inter-marriage. In 1090 the Counts of Normandy captured the island and finally expelled the Arabs, retaining possession until 1265, when it passed into the hands of the Aragonese, Kings of Sicily.

It was in 1530 that the most interesting period of Maltese history commenced, for in that year the islands were granted by the Emperor Charles V to the Knights of St John, who had been expelled from Rhodes by the Turks; and some thirty years later the Knights of the Order and the Christian Maltese combined under de Valette, the Grand Master, whose name survives in the town of Valetta, in resisting the last effort of the Mohammedan power to gain the ascendancy in the Mediterranean. The Siege of Malta, which was most gallantly resisted by the Knights, proved successful, and they remained, although *de jure* owing allegiance to Sicily, *de facto* masters of Malta, until they were finally expelled in 1798 by the French under Napoleon, who used the island as a base for his disastrous expedition to Egypt in that year.

The staunch allegiance of the Maltese to the Church of Rome soon brought them into conflict with the French, whose plundering of the churches provoked a revolution in which the Maltese invoked the aid of Nelson. The Treaty of Amiens, 1802, provided for the return of the island to the Knights of Malta, but the Maltese, realising that this would entail a revival of French influence, protested vigorously, with the result that in 1814 the Treaty of Paris finally secured Malta to the British Empire. Since this date the story of Malta has on the whole been one of advancement in every direction.

The chief towns of the island are Valetta, the seat of government, and Citta Vecchia (otherwise known as Notabile or Medina), the ancient capital and stronghold; other places of importance being Musta, Birchircara and Attard—all of which will be well remembered by all ranks of the Regiment.

The head of the Government and Commander-in-Chief and Governor-General was in 1914 General Sir Leslie Rundle, G.C.B., G.C.M.G., G.C.V.O., D.S.O.

The garrison consisted of three battalions of British Infantry, two companies of Fortress Engineers, together with detachments of Royal Garrison Artillery, Royal Army Medical Corps, Royal Army Service Corps, and in addition two battalions of Malta Militia (Infantry), and the Malta Artillery.

APPENDIX II
HONOURS AND DECORATIONS

NOTE.—This Honours List has been compiled from official sources, and is believed to be accurate, but, owing to the manner in which honours were announced in the *London Gazette*, its completeness cannot be guaranteed.

DISTINGUISHED SERVICE ORDER

Capt. W. G. Clark	*London Gazette*	3. 7.15
2/Lieut. W. II. Webster	"	12. 3.17
2/Lieut. (A/Capt.) G. E. A. Leake	"	26. 7.17
2/Lieut. F. W. Walker.	"	19.11.17
Lieut. (A/Capt.) A. M. Duthie	"	4. 2.18
Lieut. (A/Capt.) C. J. Graham, M.C.	"	11. 1.19

MOST EXCELLENT ORDER OF THE BRITISH EMPIRE (MILITARY DIVISION)

Companion—

Lieut.-Col. (Hon. Col.) Vickers Dunfee, V.D.	*London Gazette*	3. 6.19

Officers—

Major L. T. Burnett	"	"
Hon. Lieut. and Q.M. W. J. Gragg.	"	"
Major S. Elliott	"	"

Major W. Moore	"	"
Major (A/Lieut.-Col.) H. P. L. Cart de Lafontaine	"	1. 1.20

MILITARY CROSS

2/Lieut. A. R. Moore.	*London Gazette*	23. 6.15
2/Lieut. J. R. Pyper.	"	14. 1.16
2/Lieut. (Temp. Lieut.) G. L. Goodes	"	3. 6.16
2/Lieut. S. J. Barkworth, M.M.	"	14.11.16
2/Lieut. E. McD. McCormick	"	"
Rev. R. Palmer (C.F.)	"	"
Lieut. (A/Capt.) W. J. Boutall	"	1. 1.17
2/Lieut. O. D. Garratt.	"	4. 6.17
2/Lieut. D. S. Boorman	"	25. 8.17
2/Lieut. (A/Capt.) S. Davis.	"	27.10.17
Lieut. (Temp. Capt.) C. J. Graham	"	1. 1.18
2/Lieut. E. L. Mills	"	4. 2.18
2/Lieut. (A/Capt.) C. A. Clarke	"	23. 4.18
Lieut. (A/Capt.) T. B. Cooper, M.M.	"	22. 6.18
Lieut. (A/Capt.) A. M.	"	"

Duthie, D.S.O.		
Lieut. (A/Capt.) S. G. Askham	"	26. 7.18
Lieut. H. S. Daw	"	"
2/Lieut. W. Rosen	"	"
2/Lieut. G. C. Ewing	"	16. 9.18
Lieut. (A/Capt.) A. G. Croll	"	7.11.18
Rev. S. F. Leighton Green (C. F.).	"	11. 1.19
2/Lieut. C. L. Henstridge	"	"
Lieut. (A/Capt.) G. H. Hetley	"	"
2/Lieut. A. Holloway.	"	"
2/Lieut. V. C. Prince.	"	"
2/Lieut. A. H. Millstead	"	2. 4.19

BAR TO MILITARY CROSS

2/Lieut. (Temp. Capt.) G. L. Goodes, M.C.	*London Gazette*	14.11.16
Lieut. (A/Capt.) C. J. Graham, M.C.	"	26. 7.18
Lieut. (A/Capt.) J. R. Pyper, M.C.	"	8. 3.19
Lieut. (A/Capt.) T. B. Cooper, M.C., M.M.	"	2. 4.19

DISTINGUISHED CONDUCT MEDAL

2170	L/Cpl. G. L. Colomb	London Gazette	5. 8.15
217	L/Sergt. A. C. Ehren	"	"
1153	Cpl. W. J. Knowles	"	14. 1.16
487	C.S.M. E. H. Risley	"	"
1054	C.S.M. R. Davis	"	22. 9.16
4354	Pte. J. O'Brien	"	14.11.16
3351	Pte. H. S. Payne	"	"
2163	Sergt. T. Clark	"	1. 1.17
281267	Sergt. E. P. G. Brand	"	25. 8.17
281477	Pte. F. Anthony	"	19.11.17
282450	L/Cpl. F. Austin	"	"
282051	Pte. W. H. Bolton	"	"
295070	Pte. H. C. Bull	"	"
282496	Pte. J. Taylor	"	"

282444	Sergt. B. A. Watson	"	"
281972	L/Cpl. E. S. Brown.	"	4. 3.18
280032	Sergt. G. Norris	"	"
282706	Pte. C. H. W. Roberts	"	"
280937	L/Cpl. T. H. Sankey	"	"
7261	R.S.M. J. O'Brien	"	17. 4.18
283138	Cpl. B. Vaughan	"	3. 6.18
281613	Cpl. C. E. Freeman	"	26. 6.18
280019	C.S.M. T. Lock, M.M.	"	3. 9.18
281718	Cpl. A. Martin	"	"
280079	Sergt. H. W. Moss	"	"
282171	L/Cpl. (A/Sergt.) H. F. Watson	"	30.10.18
280605	Sergt. R. C. Clammer	"	1. 1.19

MILITARY MEDAL

2144	Cpl. C. T. Coates	*London Gazette*	1. 9.16
3261	Pte. H. E. Hyde	"	"
3130	L/Cpl. H. Whitehead	"	"
1174	Cpl. J. Castle	"	11.11.16
1899	Pte. C. F. Collins	"	"
2161	Pte. A. E. Colvin	"	"
2202	C.Q.M.-Sgt. R. Forbes	"	"
1854	Sergt. H. C. Gearle	"	"
4786	Sergt. R. Hebberd	"	"
2827	Pte. F. Hedger	"	"
2272	Sergt. C. James	"	"
1893	Pte. W. Lawrence	"	"
280019	Sergt. T. Lock	"	"

534	Sergt. H. H. Merrell	"	"
3586	L/Cpl. A. J. Moger	"	"
2216	L/Cpl. A. Sergeant	"	"
3579	L/Cpl. L. R. Webb	"	"
3662	Pte. W. Buckingham	"	9.12.16
3113	Sergt. R. R. L. Hyde	"	21.12.16
2105	Sergt. H. J. Cott	"	19. 2.17
280102	Sergt. A. E. Gardiner	"	17. 4.17
280308	Sergt. W. A. King	"	11. 5.17
281020	Pte. C. H. Thomas	"	"
281204	Cpl. G. L. Rossington	"	1. 6.17
283725	Pte. J. G. Turner	"	18. 6.17
283371	Pte. J. Grierson	"	18. 7.17
281242	Cpl. A. W. Lintott	"	"

282189	Sergt. H. S. Monk	"	"
282490	Pte. P. J. Olinski	"	"
282493	Pte. A. J. Selby	"	"
282152	Pte. C. W. Spence.	"	"
282344	L/Cpl. F. C. Spencer	"	"
283708	Pte. A. Thurkettle.	"	"
283836	L/Cpl. G. Coates	"	21. 8.17
280930	Pte. W. Pratt	"	18.10.17
283691	Pte. A. Robinson	"	"
283530	Pte. C. S. Ruel	"	"
280894	L/Cpl. H. G. Smith	"	"
281270	Pte. A. G. Trayler	"	"
283660	Cpl. W. H. V. Wilkins	"	"
282537	Pte. J. P. Brooke	"	12.12.17

283818	Cpl. W. A. Cooper	"	"
283025	Pte. J. W. Ling	"	12.12.17
295261	Pte. A. Westcott	"	"
295248	Sergt. H. O. Wilderspin	"	"
295152	Sergt. F. W. Yandle	"	"
281390	L/Cpl. E. J. Bewsey	"	17.12.17
282246	Pte. J. T. Ball	"	4. 2.18
283082	Pte. A. Cohen	"	23. 2.18
280301	Cpl. J. W. Johnson	"	"
283148	Pte. F. G. Senyard	"	"
280728	Pte. G. Tyrell	"	"
280714	Cpl. H. W. Wallder	"	"
280465	Sergt. F. Arklay	"	13. 3.18
283813	Pte. B. M. J. Barnett	"	"

298008	Cpl. T. J. Court	"	"
282021	Pte. H. Evans	"	"
280154	Sergt. G. J. Grant	"	"
280472	Sergt. A. E. Haynes	"	"
281734	L/Cpl. T. Hodgkins	"	"
282737	Pte. W. J. Hutchin	"	"
295177	Pte. J. Pritchard	"	"
283652	Pte. R. Southern	"	"
295223	Pte. J. Wickens	"	"
283808	Pte. W. A. Willmott	"	"
280389	Pte. W. A. G. Battershall	"	12. 6.18
282916	Cpl. A. G. Beale	"	"
280840	Pte. S. G. Coates	"	"
283154	L/Cpl. A. J.	"	"

	Deadman		
281965	Sergt. C. J. Gibbs	"	"
280967	Cpl. G. Heyes	"	"
283623	L/Cpl. C. L. Husk	"	"
283643	Cpl. A. J. Parker	"	"
295122	Pte. J. R. Phillips	"	"
281174	Sergt. H. V. Randall	"	"
283193	Pte. P. C. Swinchatt	"	"
280292	Sergt. F. G. Udall	"	"
295096	Pte. R. H. Bryan	"	27. 6.18
281472	Sergt. J. A. Kingston	"	"
281130	L/Cpl. R. H. Pryor	"	"
282607	Pte. F. A. Stewart	"	"
281319	Pte. A. J. Zeeck	"	"

283184	L/Cpl. F. F. Salter	"	16. 7.18
283323	Pte. T. J. Sanders	"	"
283570	Pte. J. W. Abbott	"	6. 8.18
280922	Cpl. D. E. Davis	"	"
282263	L/Cpl. G. Humphrey	"	29. 8.18
295508	Pte. J. Nisbett	"	"
280695	Sergt. T. Peters	"	"
295475	Pte. M. Lemon	"	11.12.18
298089	Pte. A. S. Adams	"	24. 1.19
282029	Pte. A. C. Barnes	"	"
282323	Pte J. Eccles	"	24. 1.19
280534	Cpl. W. Frost	"	"
283617	Pte. J. R. Greenwood	"	"
281822	L/Cpl. W. H. Hart	"	"

282198	Cpl. S. T. E. Norton	"	"
283803	Pte. W. W. Boulstridge	"	11. 2.19
283288	Sergt. F. A. Dove	"	"
281741	Cpl. F. Nash	"	"
282915	Sergt. F. C. Nickless	"	"
295615	Sergt. J. T. Norris	"	"
281043	Sergt. W. C. Bird	"	14. 5.19
280605	Sergt. R. C. Clammer, D.C.M.	"	"
280212	L/Cpl. P. McGregor	"	"
280617	Sergt. (A/C.S.M.) W. Honig	"	23. 7.19

BAR TO MILITARY MEDAL

283530	Pte. C. S. Ruel, M.M..	*London Gazette*	13. 3.18
282737	L/Cpl. W. J. Hutchin, M.M.	"	12. 6.18

280292	Sergt. F. G. Udall, M.M.	"	24. 1.19
280489 2272	C.S.M. C. James, M.M.	"	20. 8.19

MERITORIOUS SERVICE MEDAL

280846	Pte. J. W. Atkins	*London Gazette*	17. 9.17
280665	Pte. H. Bunker	"	2.11.17
280505	Sergt. W. Bean	"	17. 6.18
282237	Sergt. G. F. V. Bunyan	"	"
280914	L/Sergt. S. A. Edwards	"	"
280471	Cpl. L. C. Hawkins	"	"
280435	Sergt. H. Hurst	"	"
280555	R.Q.M.-Sergt. L. T. Davies	"	18. 1.19
280128	C.S.M. A. D. McLaren	"	"
281464	C.Q.M.-Sergt. P. C. Peters	"	"
280646	L/Cpl. H.	"	3. 6.19

		T. Giles		
280420		Sergt. G. A. Richardson	"	"

MENTION IN DESPATCHES

2/Lieut. A. R. Moore.			*London Gazette*	22. 6.15
Major (Temp. Lieut.-Col.) L. T. Burnett			"	1. 1.16
Capt. (A/Major) W. G. Clark, D.S.O.			"	"
2/Lieut. (A/Capt.) J. R. Pyper			"	14. 1.16
Lieut.-Col. (Hon. Col.) Vickers Dunfee, V.D.			"	13. 7.16
	280154 1151	Sergt. G. J. Grant	"	4. 1.17
	4798	R.S.M. M. Harris	"	"
2/Lieut. H. Jones			"	"
	280128	C.Q.M.-Sergt. A. D. McLaren	"	"
	280171	Pte. H. V. Neal	"	4. 1.17
	280505	Sergt. W. Bean	"	25. 5.17
	280307	R.Q.M.-Sergt. W. Henley	"	"

Lieut. (A/Capt.) L. G. Rix			"	"
2/Lieut. W. H. Webster			"	"
Lieut. (A/Capt.) C. A. Clarke			"	24.12.17
Lieut. (A/Capt.) T. B. Cooper, M.M.			"	"
Hon. Lieut. and Q.M. W. J. Cragg			"	"
Capt. (A/Major) W. A. Nunneley			"	"
2/Lieut. R. E. Stavert			"	"
	280639	Sergt. A. Taylor	"	"
2/Lieut. F. W. Walker, D.S.O.			"	"
Major V. H. Seyd			"	16. 1.18
Lieut. (A/Capt.) S. J. Barkworth, M.C., M.M.			"	25. 5.18
Lieut. C. W. Denning, M.M.			"	"
Lieut. (A/Capt.) A. M. Duthie, D.S.O.			"	"
	281174	Sergt. H. V. Randall	"	"
	283264	Pte. G. E. Wright	"	20.12.18
Lieut. L. R. Chapman			"	30.12.18

Lieut. H. W. Dennis	"	"
Lieut. (A/Capt.) C. J. Graham, M.C.	"	"
Major (A/Lieut.-Col.) H. P. L. Cart de Lafontaine	"	10. 7.19

The names of the following were brought to the notice of the Secretary of State for War for services rendered in connection with the War (not gazetted):—

Lieut.-Col. (Hon. Col.) Vickers Dunfee, V.D.	24.12.17
280126 Cpl. W. Noquet	9. 8.18
Major L. T. Burnett	13. 8.18
281197 Cpl. E. Brown	13. 8.18 15. 3.19
Lieut. (A/Capt.) F. A. Coffin	13. 8.18

FOREIGN DECORATIONS

Médaille Militaire (*France*)—

280336	Sergt. D. Fulford	*London Gazette*	24. 2.16

Croix de Guerre (*Belgium*)—

280802	C.S.M. F. W. Amos	"	12. 7.18
281426	Sergt. A. V. Loveless	"	"
282692	Sergt. J. R. Tibbott	"	"

| 280713 | Pte. C. W. Budgen | " | " |
| 295089 | Cpl. W. Govan | " | " |

The following decorations were awarded to Officers, non-Commissioned Officers, and Men of other regiments for services rendered while attached to and serving with the 4th London Regiment:—

DISTINGUISHED SERVICE ORDER

Major (Temp. Lieut.-Col.) W. R. H. Dann (Bedfordshire Regiment)	*London Gazette*	18. 7.17
Major F. A. Phillips (Montgomery Yeomanry)	"	22. 6.18
Major A. Grover, M.C. (Bedfordshire Regiment)	"	26. 7.18
Major (A/Lieut.-Col.) A. F. Marchment, M.C. (1st London Regiment)	"	26. 7.18

BAR TO DISTINGUISHED SERVICE ORDER

Major (A/Lieut.-Col.) W. R. H. Dann, D.S.O., (Bedfordshire Regiment)	*London Gazette*	26. 7.18

MILITARY CROSS

2/Lieut. H. E. Jackman (21st London Regiment)	*London Gazette*	26. 9.17
Lieut. E. H. R. Altounyan (R.A.M.C.)	"	1. 1.18
2/Lieut. C. W. Rowlands (1st	"	4. 2.18

London Regiment)

Capt. (A/Major) A. Grover (Bedfordshire Regiment)		"	18. 3.18
Lieut. G. V. Lawrie (6th Scottish Rifles)		"	3. 6.18
Lieut. (A/Capt.) H. N. Williams (4th Royal Welsh Fusiliers)		"	22. 6.18
Lieut. (A/Captain) W. C. Morton (1st London Regiment)		"	16. 9.18
G/95036	C.S.M. T. Cooke, D.C.M., M.M. (K.O.Y.L.I.)	"	7.11.18
Lieut. C. E. Dunaway (Medical Officer, U.S. Army)		"	—.—.18
Lieut. (A/Capt.) E. V. Grimsdell (K.O.Y.L.I.)		"	11. 1.19
Lieut. (A/Capt.) H. F. Dade (3rd London Regiment)		"	2. 4.19

DISTINGUISHED CONDUCT MEDAL

G/95066	C.S.M. A. Bonser	*London Gazette*	22.10.17
G/95036	C.S.M. T. Cooke, M.M.	"	"
781426	L/Cpl. F.	"	3. 9.18

- 450 -

	Goatcher		
G/76294	Pte. E. Clark	"	5.12.18

BAR TO DISTINGUISHED CONDUCT MEDAL

G/95066	C.S.M. A. Bonser, D.C.M.	*London Gazette*	5.12.18

SECOND BAR TO DISTINGUISHED CONDUCT MEDAL

G/95066	C.S.M. A. Bonser, D.C.M.	*London Gazette*	18. 2.19

MILITARY MEDAL

G/68176	Pte. J. F. Blair	*London Gazette*	27. 6.18
202684	Pte. A. E. Churchyard	"	"
225485	Sergt. C. A. Cowland	"	"
251439	Pte. W. A. Pasterful	"	"
G/76227	L/Cpl. F. Harding	"	6. 8.18
G/68259	Pte. L. Petrie	"	29. 8.18
G/76275	Pte. G. A. Allen	"	24. 1.19
G/80610	Pte. G. H.	"	"

	Andrews		
252254	L/Cpl. J. T. Couchman	"	"
G/95108	Sergt. J. Fanshaw	"	"
225682	Pte. J. T. Freshwater	"	"
228610	Pte J. C. Goree	"	"
G/75396	L/Cpl. G. J. Grant	"	"
G/95115	Pte. E. Stott	"	"
G/84057	Sergt. R. L. Addison	"	11. 2.19
G/95177	L/Cpl. W. Bradley	"	"
251265	Pte. A. E. Dickerson	"	"
G/76243	Pte. H. H. Mills	"	"
250439	Cpl. C. Robbins	"	"
G/80608	Pte. W. Ryan	"	"
G/71053	Pte. J. Anderson	"	13. 3.19
233640	Cpl. G. F.	"	"

	Coleman		
204593	Pte. A. E. Pullen	"	"
G/90091	Pte. J. Upperton	"	"
253803	Pte. T. H. A. Brown	"	14. 5.19
G/68177	Pte. W. Bunce	"	"
G/95143	Pte. H. Atkinson	"	"

Mention in Despatches

Capt. and Adjt. G. B. Scott (Leinster Regiment)		*London Gazette*	1. 1.16
Lieut. G. V. Lawric (6th Scottish Rifles)		"	18.12.17
Major (A/Lieut.-Col.) A. F. Marchment, D.S.O., M.C. (1st London Regiment)		"	30.12.18
204527	Sergt. S. W. Childs	"	"

APPENDIX III
THE RECONSTRUCTION OF THE 4TH LONDON REGIMENT IN 1920

After the return to England of the Cadres early in 1919, the Territorial Force remained in abeyance for the remainder of the year, and beyond the formation of an Old Comrades' Association, under the Presidency of Lieut.-Col. Harry Dade, V.D., nothing could be done in the 4th Londons to maintain *esprit de corps* at the high standard which it had reached during the War.

When orders were issued early in 1920 for the reconstruction of the auxiliary forces under the title of the Territorial Army, the effect of eight months' inactivity became painfully apparent, and the 4th London Regiment, which was revived in February 1920, experienced, in common with most other units, great difficulty in recruiting, owing to the rapidly cooling enthusiasm of the greater number of its former members. By great good fortune a large number of old officers returned to the Colours, and command was given to Lieut.-Col. L. T. Burnett, O.B.E., T.D., while Major H. J. Duncan-Teape, T.D., was appointed Second in Command, and Captain W. A. Trasenster, M.C., The Royal Fusiliers, Adjutant. The Company Commanders and Headquarters Officers were:—

Major R. N. Arthur	D Company.
Major W. Moore, O.B.E.	A Company.
Major H. P. L. Cart de Lafontaine, O.B.E.	C Company.
Major S. Elliott, O.B.E.	B Company.
Captain F. C. Grimwade	Assistant Adjutant.
Lieut. H. B. A. Balls	Lewis Gun Officer.
2/Lieut. E. P. Higgs	Signalling Officer.
Lieut. C. F. Warren	Transport Officer.

Lieut. E. S. Tomsett   Quartermaster.

A capable Permanent Staff was supplied from the Royal Fusiliers, Regtl. Sergt.-Major W. Hunt becoming the senior Warrant Officer, while ex-Regtl. Sergt.-Major M. Harris enlisted, and was appointed Regtl. Q.M.-Sergt.

The following old Warrant Officers and N.C.O.'s enlisted, and were posted as stated:—

Coy. Sergt.-Major W. H. Edwards	to A Company.
Coy. Q.M.-Sergt. J. C. Hibberd	
Regtl. Q.M.-Sergt. W. Henley	
Coy. Sergt.-Major G. L. Matthews	to B Company.
Coy. Q.M.-Sergt. B. A. Watson, D.C.M.	
Coy. Sergt.-Major A. Mennie	to C Company.
Coy. Q.M.-Sergt. E. J. T. Nash	
Coy. Sergt.-Major J. Lewis	to D Company.
Coy. Q.M.-Sergt. F. McLaren	

With this excellent stiffening the Battalion soon began to make progress, and rapidly took—and held—the lead in numbers in the 1st London Brigade.

The first Annual Training was held at Shoreham-by-Sea, the time being devoted principally to musketry and recreational training. For the first time in the Battalion's history, the winter following was marked by the continuance without a break of the drill season; and throughout the winter of 1920-21 attendances at the weekly drills at Headquarters reached an unusually high percentage of the strength. The Battalion appeared to be well on its feet, and making steady progress towards efficiency, when, in April 1921, the Coal Strike completely dashed all hopes of a successful summer training season. The Territorial Army was temporarily in abeyance, and for three months its headquarters were handed over to the Defence Force, to which was entrusted the maintenance of peaceful conditions throughout the country.

A Defence Force Unit was raised at the 4th Londons' Headquarters, and joined by some of the members of the Battalion, command of it being taken by Major R. N. Arthur, with the acting rank of Lieut.-Col. The disbandment of the Defence Force was fortunately effected in time to enable the Annual Training to be held at Shorncliffe in August, but the serious delay already caused to the individual training of the men rendered it less valuable than had been hoped; and a far too great proportion of the training hours had to be spent on the range, in the Musketry Practices, which should have been completed early in the year.

During the spring of 1921 the Battalion suffered a severe loss in the death, after a prolonged and painful illness, of the Quartermaster, Lieut. E. S. Tomsett, to whose invaluable services reference has been made in the preceding pages. After Lieut. Tomsett's death, Regtl. Q.M.-Sergt. M. Harris was gazetted Lieut. and Quartermaster.

The beginnings of the 4th London Regiment in the revived Territorial Army have been small, but every step has been made secure by careful organisation, and by applying the experience of Territorial soldiering in peace and war; and there is every reason to suppose that the laurels gained by the Regiment in the Campaigns in which it has taken part will remain untarnished, and that its glorious traditions will be jealously guarded as long as the Regiment remains in existence.

www.ingramcontent.com/pod-product-compliance
Ingram Content Group UK Ltd.
Pitfield, Milton Keynes, MK11 3LW, UK
UKHW030603180225
455202UK00005B/331